KNOWING

AND THE

TRINITY

"This book begins simply enough, but soon we discover that it opens our eyes to refreshing new ways of viewing God, the Bible, ourselves, and the world from multiple perspectives, all grounded ultimately in the mysterious triune nature of God. Poythress has given us in this book the valuable fruit of a lifetime of reflection on the teachings of the whole of Scripture."

—**Wayne Grudem**, Research Professor of Theology and Biblical Studies, Phoenix Seminary

"In this fascinating and highly accessible book, Dr. Poythress puts his perspectival method to work in a wide-ranging exploration of Trinitarian theology. Underlying his discussion is the conviction that while this is a mystery surpassing our capacities, God has revealed himself in creation and grace, his triune fingerprints evident wherever we turn. Any discussion of the doctrine of God should take Poythress's important contribution into serious consideration. I know of nothing else quite like it."

—**Robert Letham**, Professor of Systematic and Historical Theology, Union School of Theology (formerly Wales Evangelical School of Theology)

"In recent decades, many evangelical scholars, students, and laypeople have found triperspectivalism extraordinarily helpful, but they have also found it confusing. Vern Poythress has given us what amounts to a primer on this subject. His explanations are brief and clear. He securely anchors his outlooks in the Scriptures and in orthodox Trinitarian theology. The illustrations and glossary make Poythress's discussions accessible to a wide range of readers. Study questions encourage both theoretical and practical reflection. This book is a window into ways of thinking about and living the Christian faith that will greatly benefit us all."

—**Richard L. Pratt Jr.**, President, Third Millennium Ministries

"Poythress has done it again. *Knowing and the Trinity: How Perspectives in Human Knowledge Imitate the Trinity* is a fresh discussion on how a robust understanding of God's triune being deepens, challenges, and expands our notions of human knowledge and theological method.

Poythress dispels myths of perspectivalism (especially the all-too-common objection of relativism) and persuasively argues for the deeply related and organic nature of God's revelation. My hope is that Poythress's example will produce much biblically faithful theological creativity."

—**Joseph E. Torres**, Editor, John M. Frame's *Apologetics: A Justification of Christian Belief*

"For many years now, we have seen the fruitful use of multiperspectivalism or triperspectivalism in the Reformed theology of John Frame and Vern Poythress. Poythress now opens up for us a window onto the rich tapestry of the triad of perspectives in *Knowing and the Trinity*. He grounds the use of perspectives in the being of the triune God of Scripture and demonstrates their theoretical and practical value. These perspectives do not undermine the absolute truth of God and his Word but expose us to the ever-increasing depth that we discover in God's Word and world. Poythress shows us that triadic perspectives are analogues of God's triune being as Father, Son, and Holy Spirit, are revealed in the flow of salvation history, are experienced in our space and time, and culminate in the glory of the new heaven and the new earth. Here we have unpacked for us the rationale behind triperspectivalism, and the author demonstrates its theological wealth. I heartily recommend this new book."

—**Jeffrey C. Waddington**, Stated Supply, Knox Orthodox Presbyterian Church, Lansdowne, Pennsylvania

KNOWING AND THE TRINITY

How Perspectives in Human Knowledge Imitate the Trinity

VERN S. POYTHRESS

P&R PUBLISHING
P.O. BOX 817 • PHILLIPSBURG • NEW JERSEY 08865-0817

Italics within Scripture quotations indicate emphasis added.

Printed in the United States of America

ISBN: 978–1-62995–319–9 (pbk)
ISBN: 978–1-62995–320–5 (ePub)
ISBN: 978–1-62995–321–2 (Mobi)

Library of Congress Cataloging-in-Publication Data

Names: Poythress, Vern S., author.
Title: Knowing and the Trinity : how perspectives in human knowledge imitate the Trinity / Vern S. Poythress.
Description: Phillipsburg : P&R Publishing, 2018. | Includes bibliographical references and index.
Identifiers: LCCN 2017042806| ISBN 9781629953199 (pbk.) | ISBN 9781629953205 (epub) | ISBN 9781629953212 (mobi)
Subjects: LCSH: Trinity. | Knowledge, Theory of (Religion) | Philosophical theology.
Classification: LCC BT111.3 .P695 2018 | DDC 231/.044--dc23
LC record available at https://lccn.loc.gov/2017042806

To John Frame,
who taught me about perspectives

Contents

Illustrations

Figures

Tables

Foreword

AUGUSTINE WAS WISE when he wrote in his landmark work *De Trinitate*: "In no other subject is error more dangerous, or inquiry more laborious, or the discovery of truth more profitable."[1] To write a book that contributes to our understanding of and love for God the Trinity is surely a crowning achievement for any theologian. It is therefore a privilege to serve as the doorman to welcome readers into the remarkable world of reflections that Dr. Vern Poythress provides for us in this substantial work.

I suspect that if we were to ask, "How long did it take you to write *Knowing and the Trinity*?," it would be appropriate for Professor Poythress to answer (with his engaging and modest smile), "My whole life." Yet while the exposition he gives here of the Trinity may be the capstone of his work thus far, there is also a sense in which it has been the foundation stone of everything else he has written. For just as the beginning of the Christian life is marked by baptism into the name of the Father, the Son, and the Holy Spirit and then the whole of the Christian life is lived in the light of this reality, the same may be said of Vern Poythress's many contributions to our understanding of the gospel.

Every book, no matter what the subject, is in some sense an expression of the author's autobiography. Even a work such as Alexander Cruden's *Concordance* finds its place in the story of its compiler's life. Similarly, readers familiar with Dr. Poythress will be able to detect various streams of preparation in his life as they converge in *Knowing and the Trinity*. Appropriately, perhaps, three of them stand out.

Here we meet the mind of a mathematician. Valedictorian of the class of 1966 at California Institute of Technology, Vern Poythress soon earned a Ph.D. in mathematics from Harvard. It is perhaps not surprising, then, that he has long been fascinated by the mystery of the

1. Augustine, *De Trinitate*, 1.3.5.

Three-in-One God, or that the young professor of mathematics soon transitioned to theological studies and a lifetime in theological education in which he has both explored and taught the principle that the Trinity is the mystery in which all other mysteries ultimately make sense.

I once teased another mathematician friend who was professor of number theory in one of the ancient British universities: "Are you paid to sit in a darkened room all day to do nothing but think about numbers?" He gave the adept riposte, "Not at all. I am doing the same thing you do—studying theology—only without words!" In this, of course, he was simply echoing Johannes Kepler's *bon mot* about "thinking God's thoughts after him."[2] Vern Poythress stands in this great tradition. *Knowing and the Trinity* expresses a mind trained to move with careful logic in the process of reaching its conclusions and with admirable patience in taking the reader step by step through his reasoning processes.

Here we also meet the mind of the theologian and professor of New Testament interpretation at Westminster Seminary in Philadelphia who has also devoted himself, among much else, to the study of linguistics, epistemology, and hermeneutics. All of this—involving some fifty years of preparation—comes to expression in these fascinating chapters and contributes to their distinctiveness.

At the same time, readers will notice a third stream running into and through these pages. The great Dutch theologian Herman Bavinck once noted: "It is absolutely necessary that the person who cultivates any branch of knowledge first of all, and most of all, study to be modest and humble. This applies especially to the theologian. He should not think of himself more highly than he ought to think."[3] In that same spirit, *Knowing and the Trinity* is suffused with a humble desire to submit all the preformed and inherited thoughts we bring to the study of theology to the scrutiny of the revelation that God himself gives of himself. No theologian's mind is a *tabula rasa*. But all our preconceptions must be laid in tribute before God's own self-revelation, to be cleansed, expanded, and, when necessary, corrected. Deeply embedded in these pages is the principle that the study of theology is always an exercise in cognitive repentance. Here, too, the

2. "Johannes Kepler," *New World Encyclopedia*, http://www.newworldencyclopedia.org/entry/Johannes_Kepler (accessed February 13, 2018).

3. Danny Wyatt, "Reformed Meditations," http://reformedmeditations.blogspot.com/2010/?m=0 (accessed February 13, 2018).

first of Martin Luther's Ninety-five Theses applies: "When our Lord Jesus Christ said 'repent' he meant that the whole of the Christian life should be repentance."[4] In keeping with this, the student of theology who brings thoroughly orthodox concepts and language to the exploration of the Trinity discovers that progress in understanding always involves a renewal of the mind in the light of divine revelation.

It is in this spirit that Dr. Poythress undertakes the task of helping us to see the sheer wonder of God as we reflect on his self-testimony. Recognizing that we do this "with all the saints" (Eph. 3:18), he shows appropriate reverence for the great theological tradition, its concepts, and its vocabulary. In addition, he shares the love for God's person that was present in the work of the early fathers. (Students who lack patience with them surely think too little of how deeply offended they themselves would be if someone they knew and loved were carelessly described!)

Knowing and the Trinity makes no attempt to *solve* the mystery of the Trinity (as though God's triune being were a problem to himself!), nor to *dissolve* that mystery (which so endangers the pride of man's desire for autonomous reasoning, making himself the measure of all things). Rather, as has been true of every theologian who passes Bavinck's test, Vern Poythress allows the mystery to shine in all its glory so that in its light we see light, believing with John Robinson (the Pilgrim fathers' pastor) that "the Lord hath more truth and light to break forth from his holy Word."[5] He thus takes his place in a long line of theologians going back through John Owen (with his great experiential-theological contribution *On Communion with God the Father, Son, and Holy Ghost*) to John Calvin (with his insistence on the autotheistic nature of the Son), and behind them to Anselm (who wrote on the procession of the Holy Spirit), to the Cappadocian fathers and Augustine and then to Tertullian (to whom we owe the very term *trinitas*).

We ourselves are always pilgrim theologians. Our theology is a *theologia viatorum* until the knowledge of faith is consummated in the *visio Dei*. Perhaps even then it may continue to deepen, just as holy seraphim ever enunciate their *Trisagion* without coming to an end of either their comprehension or their adoration. Until that day, the theologian's task

4. "Ninety-five Theses," *Wikipedia*, https://en.wikipedia.org/wiki/Ninety-five_Theses (accessed February 13, 2018).

5. David H. Bauslin, "Freedom of Teaching," *The Lutheran Quarterly* 39 (April 1909): 200.

is to lead us to the limits of divine revelation, recognize the presence of the perimeter fence, and then, as Dr. Poythress does from time to time in these pages, invite us to bow in adoring wonder before the greatness of the incomprehensible triune God, who has made himself so fully known to us.

Who can speak of God? We must. Yet, Job-like, we then place our hands over our mouths and bow down in worship. At the same time, in this, the greatest of all pursuits, we recognize with Thomas à Kempis, "What profit will it be to you if you can argue profoundly about the Trinity if you are empty of humility and thus have become displeasing to the Trinity?"[6] But we also want to be able to say with Jeremiah, "Let him who boasts boast in this, that he understands and knows me, that I am the LORD" (Jer. 9:24).

In *Knowing and the Trinity*, Vern Poythress helps us to do precisely this. So now, having completed my doorman's task, I bid you to explore and enjoy!

Sinclair B. Ferguson
Chancellor's Professor of Systematic Theology
Reformed Theological Seminary

6. Thomas à Kempis, trans. and ed. William C. Creasy, *The Imitation of Christ by Thomas a Kempis: A New Reading of the 1441 Latin Autograph Manuscript*, 2nd ed. (Mercer University Press, 2015), 3.

Introduction: Reflections of the Trinity

MY FRIEND JOHN FRAME and I have been using and discussing perspectives for over forty years.[1] I would now like to write about where they come from.[2] They are a gift from God. But in what way? They reflect God's Trinitarian nature.

What is the Trinity? The Bible teaches that God is one God in three persons—God the Father, God the Son, and God the Holy Spirit. (We will review the biblical teaching on the Trinity in chapter 6.) God the Creator is distinct from everything that he created. No created thing has exactly the same kind of unity, the unity of being three in one.

So it might seem strange to say that there are reflections of the Trinity in the created world. But God did *make* the world. So his character is reflected in it (Ps. 19:1; Rom. 1:19–20). In fact, his Trinitarian nature is reflected in God's actions toward us and his relation to us, as we will see.[3]

1. Short introductions include John M. Frame, "A Primer on Perspectivalism," 2008, http://www.frame-poythress.org/a-primer-on-perspectivalism/, republished in *John Frame's Selected Shorter Writings, Volume 1* (Phillipsburg, NJ: P&R Publishing, 2014), 1–18; Vern S. Poythress, "Multiperspectivalism and the Reformed Faith," in *Speaking the Truth in Love: The Theology of John M. Frame*, ed. John J. Hughes (Phillipsburg, NJ: P&R Publishing, 2009), 173–200, http://frame-poythress.org/multiperspectivalism-and-the-reformed-faith/. More elaborately, Vern S. Poythress, *Symphonic Theology: The Validity of Multiple Perspectives in Theology* (Grand Rapids: Zondervan, 1987; repr., Phillipsburg, NJ: P&R Publishing, 2001); John M. Frame, *Theology in Three Dimensions: A Guide to Triperspectivalism and Its Significance* (Phillipsburg, NJ: P&R Publishing, 2017). For more historical information, see John M. Frame, "Backgrounds to My Thought," in *Speaking the Truth in Love: The Theology of John M. Frame*, ed. John J. Hughes (Phillipsburg, NJ: P&R Publishing, 2009), 9–30. See also Timothy E. Miller, *The Triune God of Unity in Diversity: An Analysis of Perspectivalism, the Trinitarian Theological Method of John Frame and Vern Poythress* (Phillipsburg, NJ: P&R Publishing, 2017).

2. I am grateful to Timothy E. Miller for helping me to see the value of writing on this subject (Miller, *The Triune God*).

3. See Fred Sanders, *The Deep Things of God: How the Trinity Changes Everything* (Wheaton,

A Reflection of the Trinity in Salvation

Let us begin with an example, by considering how God saves us. God the Father has planned our salvation from all eternity: "He [God the Father] chose us in him [Christ] before the foundation of the world" (Eph. 1:4). "He predestined us for adoption to himself as sons through Jesus Christ" (v. 5). God's planning took place "in him," that is, in Christ. Then in the fullness of time, Christ came to earth and accomplished our salvation in his death and resurrection (Rom. 4:25; Gal. 4:4). The Father and the Son then sent the Holy Spirit in order to apply Christ's accomplishment to the church and to each individual in it (John 15:26; Acts 2:33; Eph. 1:13–14). All three persons of the Trinity are involved. The entire program of God is one unified program, in which each person of the Trinity participates in a distinct way, but each person of the Trinity is present with the others in every work.

God is always the Trinitarian God—even before he created the world. In addition, within the world he reflects who he is in the way in which he accomplishes salvation. Everyone who is saved by God relies on what each person of the Trinity has done and is doing.

A Reflection of the Trinity in Adoption

One aspect of salvation is that God undertakes to adopt us as his sons through Jesus Christ. When he adopts us, we become part of his family of children, with whom he establishes a fatherly relation of intimacy. This intimacy is a precious aspect of being saved.

God's act of adoption involves the work of all three persons of the Trinity. God the Father is the one who adopts us, so that we become his sons. God the Son became incarnate and identified with us, so that we might be forgiven and receive the status of sons through his unique sonship: "God sent forth his *Son* . . . to redeem those who were under the law, so that we might receive *adoption as sons*" (Gal. 4:4–5). Then God the Holy Spirit comes to dwell in us and testify that we are God's sons by crying with us, "Abba! Father!" (Rom. 8:15; Gal. 4:6).

In sum, God's Trinitarian character is reflected in the way he works to adopt us as sons. When we who are Christian believers relate to God

---

IL: Crossway, 2010). Sanders's book stimulated this introductory chapter.

as our Father, we are relying on God's Trinitarian character, which is at work in our adoption.

A Reflection of the Trinity in God's Speech

Let us consider another example: the example of God's speech. Long ago, God spoke orally to Abraham, Isaac, and prophets such as Isaiah and Jeremiah. He also commissioned some of his servants to write his words down for subsequent generations, and we have his word in permanent form in the Bible. The climactic communication from God comes in his Son: "Long ago, at many times and in many ways, God spoke to our fathers by the prophets, but in these last days he has spoken to us by *his Son*" (Heb. 1:1–2). This climactic communication is also reflected in a subordinate way in all of God's speech to us, because Christ is the Mediator for God's speech. God the Son and God the Holy Spirit are present with God the Father when he speaks.

We can see how this speech took place in a focused way when Jesus was on earth. He says, "I have given them [the disciples] the words that you [the Father] gave me" (John 17:8). He also promises that the Holy Spirit will speak what he hears from the Father and the Son:

> When the Spirit of truth comes, he will guide you into all the truth, for he will not speak on his own authority, but whatever he *hears* he will speak, and he will declare to you the things that are to come. He will glorify me, for he will take *what is mine* and declare it to you. All that the Father has is mine; therefore I said that he will take what is mine and declare it to you. (John 16:13–15)

The word of God comes from the Father to the Son, and through the Holy Spirit it comes to be received and believed by the disciples. What took place while Jesus was on earth illustrates in climactic form a broader pattern. The second person of the Trinity is "the Word," according to John 1:1. Particular words from God offer us an expression of this eternal Word. All of God's speech takes place in the words of the Son. And the Holy Spirit is always present to bring those words to their destination. Thus, God's Trinitarian character is reflected when he speaks. When we listen to God speaking, as we read the Bible or hear a sermon based on it, we rely on the Trinitarian character of God, according to which all three persons are present and at work when God speaks.[4]

A Reflection of the Trinity in God's Presence

God's Trinitarian character is also expressed in the way in which he makes himself present to us. One of the names given to Jesus is *Immanuel,* which means "God with us" (Matt. 1:23). The name implies not only that Jesus has come to be with us, but that in him God the Father is with us. This presence finds its fulfillment when Jesus sends the Holy Spirit:

> And I will ask the Father, and he will give you another Helper, to be *with you* forever, even the Spirit of truth. (John 14:16–17a)

> If the Spirit of him who raised Jesus from the dead *dwells in you,* he who raised Christ Jesus from the dead will also give life to your mortal bodies through his Spirit who *dwells in you.* (Rom. 8:11)

Thus, when we are saved and we experience the intimate presence of God with us, we rely on the Trinitarian character of God.

A Reflection of the Trinity in Prayer

Christians who are praying to God rely on God's Trinitarian character. We pray to God the Father (Matt. 6:9), and Jesus the Son intercedes for us (Heb. 7:25). The Holy Spirit who dwells within us "intercedes for us with groanings too deep for words" (Rom. 8:26). God's Trinitarian character is reflected in the way in which God meets with us as we pray.

Reflections of God in Perspectives

In sum, God's Trinitarian character is displayed in the ways in which he establishes a personal relation to us—in salvation, in adoption, in verbal communication to us, in his presence with us, and in our prayers. So it is fitting to ask whether God's character is reflected in still other ways. One of these ways might be in giving us *perspectives.*

As we think about perspectives, we can grow in appreciating wonder

4. Ibid., chap. 6.

of who God is. We can grow in praising him and standing in awe of him. That is the goal. Such praise is exemplified in many passages of the Bible:

> Praise the LORD!
> Praise God in his sanctuary;
>   praise him in his mighty heavens!
> Praise him for his mighty deeds;
>   praise him according to his excellent greatness! (Ps. 150:1–2)

> Worthy are you, our Lord and God,
>   to receive glory and honor and power,
> for you created all things,
>   and by your will they existed and were created. (Rev. 4:11)

God has given us many works in creation, providence, and redemption for which we can lift our voices in praise. The gift of perspectives can be included in the list.

Key Terms

adoption[5]
application of redemption
God's speech (God's word)
perspective
prayer
presence (of God)
salvation
Trinity

Study Questions

1. In what ways do we see God's Trinitarian character reflected in his works? Consider aspects of redemption in particular.
2. Why is the Trinity important?
3. How can the biblical teaching about the Trinity be briefly summarized?

5. Key terms in **bold** are defined in the glossary at the end of this volume.

4. How should we respond to the revelation of God in his Trinitarian character?

For Further Reading

Frame, John M. "Backgrounds to My Thought." In *Speaking the Truth in Love: The Theology of John M. Frame*, ed. John J. Hughes, 9–30. Phillipsburg, NJ: P&R Publishing, 2009. A survey of the backgrounds that influenced the thought of John Frame, including the backgrounds for his use of perspectives.

———. "A Primer on Perspectivalism." 2008. http://www.frame-poythress.org/a-primer-on-perspectivalism/. Republished in *John Frame's Selected Shorter Writings, Volume 1*. Phillipsburg, NJ: P&R Publishing, 2014. A brief summary of the meaning and use of perspectives, such as those that occur in the works of John M. Frame and Vern S. Poythress.

———. *Theology in Three Dimensions: A Guide to Triperspectivalism and Its Significance*. Phillipsburg, NJ: P&R Publishing, 2017. An expanded explanation of triperspectivalism, with a discussion of its implications.

Poythress, Vern S. "Multiperspectivalism and the Reformed Faith." In *Speaking the Truth in Love: The Theology of John M. Frame*, ed. John J. Hughes, 173–200. Phillipsburg, NJ: P&R Publishing, 2009. http://frame-poythress.org/multiperspectivalism-and-the-reformed-faith/. A brief summary of the use of perspectives and the history of their development, together with a discussion of how their use is related to the Reformed faith, which is held by John Frame and Vern Poythress.

———. *Symphonic Theology: The Validity of Multiple Perspectives in Theology*. Grand Rapids: Zondervan, 1987. Reprint, Phillipsburg, NJ: P&R Publishing, 2001. On the use of perspectives in studying the Bible and theology.

Sanders, Fred. *The Deep Things of God: How the Trinity Changes Everything*. Wheaton, IL: Crossway, 2010. An exploration of how the Trinity is discussed and presupposed in the piety and practice as well as the theology of evangelicals.

PART 1

WHAT ARE PERSPECTIVES?

WE EXPLAIN PERSPECTIVES and then consider three kinds: spatial perspectives, personal perspectives, and thematic perspectives. A spatial perspective is a view of a visible scene from a particular vantage point in space. A personal perspective is the view that an individual person has concerning the world or some subject. A thematic perspective is a temporary thematic starting point for exploring a subject matter, with the hope of discovering more and growing in truth.

1

The Mystery of Perspectives

WHAT IS A *PERSPECTIVE*? We will address that question in the next few chapters. In one sense, the idea of using a perspective is fairly simple. You observe a physical object from a new angle. If you do, you may notice something that you did not notice before. The same principle applies to studying a particular subject matter, such as politics or music or the family. You can sometimes learn things by asking new kinds of questions about a subject, or looking at it using a new theme.

The Mystery of God

It would be simple if we could just leave it at that. But mysteries open up if we ask why human beings can use multiple perspectives, and why they are useful. Ultimately, the chain of *why* questions goes back to God. He created us. He made us with these capabilities. This pathway leads to still wider questions: who is God, and why did he create us the way he did?

According to the Bible, God is *Trinitarian*. He is one God in three persons. What significance might the Trinity have for understanding *perspectives*? Over the years, John Frame and I have employed groups of three perspectives. Is the number *three* significant? Is it related to the Trinity?

A Triad of Perspectives

Let us take an example. John Frame explains God's lordship by using three perspectives or ways of looking at lordship: *authority*, *control*, and *presence*.[1] Let us consider these three, one at a time. First, God exercises

1. John M. Frame, *The Doctrine of the Knowledge of God* (Phillipsburg, NJ: Presbyterian and

authority over us, and we are responsible to him to live in accordance with his instruction and his righteousness. Second, as Lord over all, God *controls* the world and all human agents within it. Third, God is *present* all over the world, and every human being lives in his presence. All three of these truths about God are practical. As human beings, we should respond to God by acknowledging his authority, by experiencing and submitting to his control, and by enjoying his presence.

So we have three terms: *authority, control,* and *presence.* Why three rather than two or four? We may note that these three all function together to expound one coherent body of truth about God's lordship. There is only *one* Lord; at the same time, there are these three perspectives for appreciating his lordship. It is one in three. Is that just an accident?

John Frame and I have from time to time pointed out relationships between a triad of perspectives and the three persons in God. Frame observes that God the Father claims *authority* over all. God through his Son *controls* the world. Through Jesus the Son we experience the power of God, saving us from our sins. And God is *present* everywhere especially through the Holy Spirit, who comes to dwell in those who believe in Christ the Savior.[2]

So what is the relationship between the Trinitarian character of God and the triad of perspectives on lordship? Does the triad somehow *derive* from the Trinity? If so, how? And would the same be true for other triads? How could more than one triad derive in the same way from the same source?[3]

The Importance of the Trinity

People who have interacted with John Frame and me over the years have sometimes wondered about these questions. I propose, then, to

---

Reformed, 1987), 15–18; John M. Frame, *The Doctrine of God* (Phillipsburg, NJ: P&R Publishing, 2002).

2. Frame, *Doctrine of God,* 727; John M. Frame, "A Primer on Perspectivalism," 2008, http://www.frame-poythress.org/a-primer-on-perspectivalism/, republished in John Frame's *Selected Shorter Writings, Volume 1* (Phillipsburg, NJ: P&R Publishing, 2014), 1–18.

3. It is interesting that Saint Augustine explores analogies in creation that he finds dimly reflecting the Trinitarian character of God (Augustine, "On the Holy Trinity," in *Nicene and Post-Nicene Fathers,* 1st ser., ed. Philip Schaff [London: T&T Clark, 1980], 17–228). At the same time, Augustine indicates that none of these analogies or illustrations fully captures the nature of God; all of them have limitations. The same holds for the analogies that we explore.

tackle the questions head-on. Let us look at perspectives and explore their relation to the Trinity.[4] This process is potentially valuable, because we can grow in knowing God. We can grow in knowing the Trinity. God made us with the purpose that we would know him. So knowing him is of vital importance for us as creatures. It is also of vital importance for our salvation. We need God to rescue us from sin and rebellion. One aspect of that rescue process is that we come to know him (John 17:3). We come to know him as the Trinitarian God.

The Challenge of the Trinity

But before we plunge into our task, we need a few explanations. To reflect directly on the nature of perspectives is a deep challenge. Why? We find ourselves asking about God. God is the central mystery of the Christian faith. We adore him without completely understanding him.

To be sure, God does give us understanding. God reveals himself in the world that he has made, according to Romans 1:18–23:

> For the wrath of God is revealed from heaven against all ungodliness and unrighteousness of men, who by their unrighteousness suppress the truth. For what can be known about God is plain to them, because God has shown it to them. For his invisible attributes, namely, his eternal power and divine nature, have been clearly perceived, ever since the creation of the world, in *the things that have been made*. So they are without excuse. For although they knew God, they did not honor him as God or give thanks to him, but they became futile in their thinking, and their foolish hearts were darkened. Claiming to be wise, they became fools, and exchanged the glory of the immortal God for images resembling mortal man and birds and animals and creeping things.

God's revelation through the creation is called *general revelation*. It leaves human beings "without excuse" (Rom. 1:20). But it does not lead human beings to spiritual health, because they "suppress the truth" (v. 18). Sin has corrupted human beings in every aspect of their lives. The corruption extends to the mind as well. Our reason is not normal,

4. Timothy E. Miller's book has already undertaken a similar exploration (Miller, *The Triune God of Unity in Diversity: An Analysis of Perspectivalism, the Trinitarian Theological Method of John Frame and Vern Poythress* [Phillipsburg, NJ: P&R Publishing, 2017]).

but fallen and corrupted by sin. One effect is that we suppress the truth. We need the *special revelation* of the Bible to enlighten us. We also need Christ's work of salvation, accomplished in his crucifixion and resurrection from the dead, in order to reconcile us to God. And we need the Holy Spirit to come and apply the work of Christ to our hearts and lives. We need God in the work of all three persons of the Trinity.

We should acknowledge that there are two kinds of people in the world today. There are those who remain in their fallen and sinful condition, with corrupted minds. And then there are those who have been saved by Christ and reconciled to God. They have been renewed in the mind through the work of the Spirit of Christ in them. Yet as long as they are in this life, their renewal is partial: they fall into sins, including sins due to corruption in the mind. This book is imperfect and fallible, partly because of the remaining effects of sin.

When God gives us new spiritual birth through the Holy Spirit, we are changed people. We begin to know God in the way that we should, through Christ, who shows us who God is (John 3:3, 5; 14:9; 17:3). We know God, I say. We know him truly and genuinely and personally. But we do not *become* God. God is infinite. God's knowledge is infinite. And his knowledge of *himself* is infinite. God in his Trinitarian character is infinite. God is unique, so that nothing that God made is completely like him.

God is not mysterious to himself, but he is mysterious to us, because our knowledge is always less than his and always derivative from his. Therefore, the Trinity is mysterious to us. We can talk about and appreciate what God tells us about the Trinity through the Bible, but we never *master* God or *master* what he says.

So we cannot do what some people might like to do, that is, to explain the Trinity. No human being can "explain" God so as to sweep away the mystery. For the same reason, we cannot "explain" the relationship of the Trinity to one of the triads of perspectives.

So what might we do? Not much, in comparison with the infinity of God. Nothing at all, unless Christ empowers us: "apart from me [Christ] you can do *nothing*" (John 15:5). As God helps us, we are going to try to look at perspectives and their relation to the Trinity. But we must remember that all our discussion is taking only a few steps in pointing to God in his unfathomable infinity. We must recognize the limitations in human knowledge—limitations made worse by the corruptions from sin.

Throughout our discussion, I will be incorporating John Frame's ideas. John Frame and I have influenced each other over the course of years, so that sometimes it is not feasible to sort out every distinct influence.[5] Both of us are comfortable using some of the same perspectives, and we use them in similar ways.[6] John Frame's works further illustrate the topic of perspectives. In this book, I am attempting to venture at times beyond what the two of us have already said, and to make explicit some ways in which perspectives have their foundation in the Trinity.

Starting Points

This book attempts to be self-contained, so that people can read this book without having to read everything that John Frame and I have written over the years. Obviously, people can learn more about perspectives by observing how John Frame and I have used them in practice. That helps to fill in a lot of detailed texture concerning what we mean and how someone else could do the same thing. But here I am going to try to include fresh explanations, to avoid the problem of constantly referring to other sources.

At the same time, it is not feasible in this book to cover again the whole scope of biblical teaching—the whole of systematic theology. If you are not a follower of Christ, you need to start with finding out who God is, and who Christ is, by reading the Bible—particularly the four Gospels, Matthew, Mark, Luke, and John. There are many additional resources to help you.[7] If you are a follower of Christ, I assume

5. John M. Frame, "Backgrounds to My Thought," in *Speaking the Truth in Love: The Theology of John M. Frame*, ed. John J. Hughes (Phillipsburg, NJ: P&R Publishing, 2009), 23; Vern S. Poythress, "Multiperspectivalism and the Reformed Faith," in *Speaking the Truth in Love: The Theology of John M. Frame*, ed. John J. Hughes (Phillipsburg, NJ: P&R Publishing, 2009), 182.

6. Timothy E. Miller found a source in which I said (in 1988), "I am in complete agreement with Frame" on perspectivalism (Miller, *The Triune God*, 30, quoting Vern S. Poythress, "God's Lordship in Interpretation," *Westminster Theological Journal* 50, 1 [Spring 1988]: 29n4). In his analysis of perspectivalism, Miller then announces that "we will freely quote from Poythress as well as Frame in defining perspectivalism." I think that his strategy is basically warranted, because Frame and I are indeed very close. But Miller also illumines some subtle "methodological differences" between Frame and me, at least with respect to emphasis and manner of speaking (Miller, *The Triune God*, 30).

7. Timothy Keller, *The Reason for God: Belief in an Age of Skepticism* (New York: Dutton,

that you know about the way of salvation through Christ. I will also assume that you know that the Bible is the Word of God and has a central role in instructing us in knowing God. You know also that God is the Trinitarian God, one God in three persons. We will start from there.

Knowing Truth

Given the possibilities for misunderstanding, it is important also to say something about truth. Some strands of postmodernist thought use the word *perspective* with a skeptical twist. They may say that everyone has his "perspective"; everyone has what he regards as "truth for him." But, according to these postmodernists, no one really knows. Allegedly, each of us is trapped within the limits of his context.

By contrast, when John Frame and I use the word *perspective,* it does not have this postmodernist twist. We radically disagree with postmodern skepticism and the way that it relativizes truth. We believe in absolute truth—the truth of God. As Frame says, perspectivalism "presupposes absolutism."[8]

God is the absolute standard for all truth. And he makes truth known to human beings through general and special revelation. Christ says that he is "the truth" (John 14:6). In our discussion of perspectives, we assume this framework of understanding. Rightly understood and rightly used, perspectives give us access to truth rather than keeping us away from truth.

Let us consider a simple comparison. A perspective is like a window in my living room, looking out on a garden. The garden represents the truth. In using a perspective, I actually encounter, see, and appreciate truth. I look *through the perspective* at the truth. I really do see the truth—I see the garden. For postmodernist skepticism, on the other hand, a "perspective" is like a rectangular screen that has a picture of a garden on it. The skeptic thinks there is no way to tell what he is really looking at. Is the picture a picture of the garden behind the screen, seen through a more or less transparent screen? Or is the garden seen through a distorting medium, which has altered its colors and shapes? Or is the picture projected onto the screen by a hidden light source? Or is the

2008); J. I. Packer, *Knowing God* (Downers Grove, IL: InterVarsity Press, 1993).

8. Frame, "A Primer on Perspectivalism."

picture produced by the screen itself, like a flat-panel TV screen? Or is the picture projected by the mind of the viewer, as in a dream?

The fundamental difference between the skeptic and me is that I believe in and know the God described in Scripture. I understand that God has produced the garden and me and the window and their relations to one another, in such a way that all aspects work together to give me the blessing of his presence and the presence of truth that originated from him. I can go to another window and see the same garden. Through a window, I can access truths about the garden and know things about the garden.

Dependent Ideas

We need also to be aware that some of our knowledge is solid, but other ideas are tentative. Our knowledge of God through Christ is solid: "This is eternal life, that they [disciples] know you the only true God, and Jesus Christ whom you have sent" (John 17:3). We know that God is who he is, and that he is Trinitarian, because he has clearly taught us in the Bible.

But not everything that we try to derive from the Bible is equally clear or equally solid. The Bible does not *explicitly* talk about perspectives. We can try to make inferences from what the Bible says or implies indirectly. But when we do it, the results remain dependent on the clearer teachings of the Bible.

Key Terms

authority[9]
control
general revelation
knowledge of God
lordship
new birth
perspective
postmodern skepticism
presence
special revelation

9. Key terms in **bold** are defined in the glossary at the end of this volume.

Study Questions

1. What relation does John Frame think exists between the persons of the Trinity and the triad for lordship, consisting in authority, control, and presence?
2. What are the limitations in our knowledge of God? How does our knowledge of God relate to God's knowledge of himself?
3. In what sense do non-Christians know God?
4. How do we differentiate between what we know with confidence and what is less certain? Why is this distinction significant for the church and for a Christian believer's relations to other people?

For Further Reading

Frame, John M. *The Doctrine of the Knowledge of God*. Phillipsburg, NJ: Presbyterian and Reformed, 1987. Pp. 15–18. An explanation of the triad of perspectives on lordship: authority, control, and presence.

———. "A Primer on Perspectivalism." 2008. http://www.frame-poythress.org/a-primer-on-perspectivalism/. Republished in *John Frame's Selected Shorter Writings, Volume 1*. Phillipsburg, NJ: P&R Publishing, 2014. Here is contained a brief explanation of the triad of perspectives on lordship: authority, control, and presence.

2

Spatial Perspectives

EVENTUALLY, WE ARE going to relate perspectives to the nature of the Trinity. But we will not start with a discussion about the Trinity itself. We will get there gradually. It is easier if we start with ordinary observations. Rather than moving directly to a discussion of perspectives in theology, let us start more simply with the question, "What is a *perspective*?" Simply put, a *perspective* is *a view from somewhere*. But the word *perspective* applies to more than one *kind* of "view" and more than one kind of "somewhere." So in this and the following two chapters, we consider three kinds of perspectives. We will mostly illustrate these kinds of perspectives from ordinary life. We will apply our insights to theology later on, beginning in part 3 of this book.

Understanding a Perspective

As the first of three kinds of perspectives, we consider *spatial perspectives*. A spatial perspective is a view of a visible scene from a particular position.

Let us consider an example. Let us suppose that Carol has a chair in front of her. She can move around and look at the chair from several locations. Each time she relocates, she obtains a new spatial *perspective* on the chair. She can look at it from directly above it. She can look at it from directly in front of it. She can look at it from either side. She can look at it from a position that is both above it and in front of it, or from above and behind it, or halfway between being in front and being to the left side of it. Small changes in her position tend to produce only small changes in what she sees. But the major shifts, such as a shift from being above to being in front, may result in major changes in what parts of the chair she sees, and what exact shapes the parts present to her eyes.

Principles about Spatial Perspectives

We experience these kinds of changes all the time, and we get so used to them that we stop paying attention. But when we pay attention once more, we can see several notable features about our experience.

1. It is the same chair. Of course, we can focus on our changes in experience as we move around the chair. We could talk about "chair experiences" or "chair views" that are distinguishable in their sensory input. But often we are more focally aware of the sameness of the chair as we change positions.

2. Each perspective gives us a distinct chair-experience in the visible details. When we reflect, we easily become aware of several perspectives. We can distinguish them by both the location of the viewer and the detailed texture of what the viewer sees from his location.

3. What stands out about the chair, and what is most easily noticeable, depends on our spatial perspective. Moreover, some details are easier to notice from some perspectives than others. Perhaps we notice a place on one side where there is a scratch. Or we notice a crack in one of the legs of the chair, or a knot in the wood on one side of the back of the chair.

4. What we see depends on the environment as well as the chair. What we see in detail depends on the light that is falling on the chair. We understand that it is the same chair no matter what lighting it currently enjoys.

5. Given time, we can integrate information obtained from a variety of perspectives. Our total knowledge of the chair is then present in our minds or our memories even though we are currently looking at the chair from only one location.

6. We can infer or remember what the chair looked like from perspectives other than the current one. We can picture from the current perspective the effects of the other perspectives.

7. Much about the chair may be tentatively inferred by using only one perspective. Perhaps one of the legs is hidden from us by the seat of the chair. But we instinctively infer that it probably looks like the legs that are visible to us. Those legs are visible only on the side that is closest to us. But we infer that each leg has a back side as well. Suppose that the chair Carol is looking at has round legs, more or less the shape of a cylinder. From the rounded character of the visible part of the legs, she infers that the back side of each leg is round as well.

Perspectives on a Diamond

Consider next the spatial perspectives on a well-cut diamond. We can see through a diamond. By looking carefully, we can see the facet of the diamond at which we are looking, and see *through* the facet into the whole of the diamond and its other facets. We may be able to see every facet of the diamond refracted or reflected in some way through one facet.

If we could see everything in the diamond through one facet, in theory we would not need any other spatial perspective in order to know everything about how the diamond looks from every other perspective. But of course, it would take a lot of work to infer the other perspectives. Points 3 and 7 above, which we developed using the chair, would have to be modified for a diamond because the backward-facing facets of the diamond that would be concealed in an opaque object are indirectly accessible through one forward-facing facet. But much about the use of perspectives is similar, whether applied to a chair or to a diamond. The relative accessibility or prominence of some feature changes as we change our spatial perspective.

In addition, some perspectives are not so useful. If we are too far away from the chair, or are in a different room, or have our backs turned toward the chair, we cannot learn much about the chair with that spatial perspective. Sometimes it may take a search to find a perspective that is more revealing.

Praising God for Perspectives

Even when we consider perspectives in ordinary ways, we are examining God's world and the way in which he has created us. When we look at how God made us, we find that we have capabilities to understand and use perspectives. God in his marvelous wisdom has given us our capabilities and the ways in which we interact with the world. God has made a marvelous world. We are marvelous creatures. And these marvels reflect the final marvel of God himself, who is supremely marvelous. All the marvels within this world should stimulate our praise for God, who made the world and us and who governs it according to his marvelous wisdom.

Key Terms

inference
seeing through
spatial perspective[1]
total knowledge
view

Study Questions

1. What is a spatial perspective?
2. How might spatial perspectives differ from perspectives of other kinds?
3. How do distinct spatial perspectives differ from and also cohere with one another?
4. What do we learn about knowledge by considering spatial perspectives?
5. How does memory enter into the appreciation of multiple perspectives?

For Further Reading

Poythress, Vern S. "An Information-Based Semiotic Analysis of Theories concerning Theories." *Semiotica* 2013, 193 (February 2013): 83–99, esp. § 4. http://frame-poythress.org/an-information-based-semiotic-analysis-of-theories-concerning-theories/. This may be challenging reading, but section 4 contains a perspectival examination of how we treat space.

———. "Semiotic Analysis of the Observer in Relativity, Quantum Mechanics, and a Possible Theory of Everything." *Semiotica* 2015, 205 (2015): 149–67, esp. §§ 4–5. http://frame-poythress.org/semiotic-analysis-of-the-observer/. More advanced reading about space.

1. The key term in **bold** is defined in the glossary at the end of this volume.

3

Personal Perspectives

NEXT, LET US consider *personal perspectives.* A personal perspective[1] is the viewpoint that a particular person has concerning the world or whatever topic is being discussed. Here is where differences among persons become visible.

Differences among Persons

Differences may be major or minor. Sue's favorite color is red, while Carol's favorite color is green. So Sue and Carol have different personal perspectives on color preference. Differences may include differences in knowledge. Sue thinks that the chair she is sitting on is a perfectly good chair. Carol, from her angle, can see that one of the legs looks like it might break. Sue and Carol have differing personal perspectives about the structural perfection of the chair.

Sue has an engineering background, so that if she knew about the weak leg, she might still be able to infer that the chair is held up pretty well by reinforcing cross-links. Carol does not have such a background, and is not accustomed to thinking about the details of what goes into making chairs sturdy or unstable. So Sue and Carol have differing personal perspectives on how to analyze the sturdiness of the chair.

Differences in personal perspective may include differences in moral and religious views. Consider a moral issue. Sue thinks that sexual union outside marriage (fornication) is wrong, while Carol thinks that it is morally neutral, as long as there is mutual consent. It is up to each person to do whatever he or she is most comfortable with. So they have

1. Timothy E. Miller uses the same terminology (*The Triune God of Unity in Diversity: An Analysis of Perspectivalism, the Trinitarian Theological Method of John Frame and Vern Poythress* [Phillipsburg, NJ: P&R Publishing, 2017], 33–34).

differing personal perspectives about the morality of fornication. They also differ in their religious views. Sue thinks that God exists, while Carol thinks that nature is all that there is.

We can see that the idea of a personal perspective is in some ways analogous to the idea of a spatial perspective. Sue and Carol differ in their spatial locations, so that Carol notices the weak leg on Sue's chair, but Sue does not. The difference in spatial location is analogous in some ways to other kinds of differences between Sue and Carol. In our own thinking, we can travel from being aware of a difference in spatial perspective to being aware of a difference in *knowledge*. For instance, we see that Carol's spatial perspective also affects her knowledge. Her location gives her a key bit of knowledge about the chair that Sue does not have.

By analogy, we can also travel from thinking about spatial perspectives to thinking about other sources of differences in knowledge and commitments. Sue and Carol differ in knowledge about engineering, not because of a mere temporary difference in spatial location, but because Sue spent time in a location where an engineering program was being offered. But it was not merely a matter of time and spatial location. Sue picked up some extra knowledge while she was at a particular location. What makes Sue differ is not space in itself, but "environment" in a broader sense, an environment of learning and growth in knowledge. And in the end, the environment includes Sue's own mind and memory, which supply her with a kind of "mental location" differing from Carol's.

Answering Postmodern Skepticism

The differences between Sue's and Carol's personal perspectives offer one main starting point for postmodern skeptics. An extreme skeptic might claim that Sue's and Carol's personal perspectives are equally valid. Both people have an equal personal "right" to their views, and all we can do is to try to respect each person's viewpoint as "valid." But most postmodern skeptics would not go quite that far when it comes to the weak leg in Sue's chair. Sue does not think it is weak. But she is capable of finding out. All Carol has to do is to point it out. Sue can position herself roughly where Carol was and look in the direction that Carol was looking. There is a lesson from this. Personal perspectives are not airtight prisons, allowing no interaction between persons. Sue can learn from Carol.

We can also observe that there actually is a truth about the chair. The chair leg is in fact weak. Carol is right and Sue is wrong. Whether or not either of them knows the situation adequately, God knows. His knowledge is the ultimate standard for truth.

What about Sue's preference for red? That case, too, is one in which Sue and Carol can learn from each other. But the learning takes a different form. Carol can find out what Sue's preference is. And Carol can learn to take it into account if she is about to buy a present for Sue. Such differences in preference do not bother most of us, because we understand the differences for what they are. They are part of the fascination of how God created each of us to be a distinct person, different from everyone else.

The more painful difficulties come with differences in moral and religious views. Postmodernist skeptics may "give up" on these differences, and consider them to be only differences in preference, like the difference between preferring red or green. These skeptics give up partly because it does not seem to them that there is any way of settling moral and religious differences. On this subject they themselves have a viewpoint, a personal perspective, namely, that moral differences are merely subjective personal preferences.

But their personal perspective has left God out of the account. God does exist; he is who he is, regardless of what various religions may say. And moral standards do exist, based on God's character and on his instruction to human beings in the Bible. The standards exist, regardless of what people may prefer in their own minds and regardless of what they may *say* about moral standards. Moreover, God has made human beings so that they have a moral sensitivity and a sense of right and wrong, though this sense gets twisted because of sin. Everyone does know right from wrong, but also twists and conceals the truth in order to get a selfish advantage (see Rom. 1:32).

Learning from One Another

The example with the weak chair leg gives us a hint about the possibility for learning. Each of us is finite. Each of us has finite experience in the past. Each of us has finite learning in the past. For example, Sue learned engineering. Perhaps Carol learned French literature. No one human person knows the full extent of human knowledge. So we have books and educational institutions and Internet resources, and situations in which Sue can learn from Carol, and Carol from Sue.

God has to be brought into the picture as well. God is personal. Human beings can have personal relations with God as well as with other human beings. God speaks to us through his Word, in the Bible.[2] We can learn from him. And because of our propensity to sin, we had *better* learn from him, or we will make *ourselves* the final object of our allegiance. Each of us makes himself into a little god. It takes God to unravel all the tangles that sin has made in our notions of morality and our notions of religion.

At a fundamental level, there are two kinds of human beings—those whom God has saved and reconciled to himself through Christ, and those who are not saved. The two kinds of people have two different orientations in their hearts. Those who are saved have had their hearts renewed, and this renewal gives them a new perspective on God and on the whole world (2 Cor. 5:16–17). But within this life, the renewal is not yet complete.

It is difficult to straighten out our knowledge not only because of individual sin, but because of the sins of other people. We cannot thoroughly trust another human being to tell us the truth all the time, because human beings are sinful. Sometimes they deliberately lie. Sometimes they tell us lies or half-truths that they themselves believe.

To put it in another way, sin has corporate effects. Whole cultures can go astray and encourage one another in some particular sin. Ancient Greek culture had some admirable aspects, but it also had human slavery. And this slavery was an accepted fact of life even among "enlightened" philosophers of the Greeks. They could not see beyond the propaganda of their culture. The same, of course, holds for us. Christian believers have the Bible to enable them to criticize surrounding cultural assumptions, but sometimes—too often—they fall victim nevertheless.

Much more could be said about the value of personal interaction

2. I do not wish to ignore the difficulty that human beings face because of the conflicting claims of multiple religions. It would take us far afield to thoroughly defend the truth of the Bible and the counterfeit character of claims from other religions. The presuppositional apologetics of Cornelius Van Til is relevant (Cornelius Van Til, *The Defense of the Faith*, ed. K. Scott Oliphint, 4th ed. [Phillipsburg, NJ: P&R Publishing, 2008]; see also John M. Frame, *Apologetics: A Justification of Christian Belief*, 2nd ed. [Phillipsburg, NJ: P&R Publishing, 2015]).

and distinct personal perspectives in learning. But we should pass on. Our purpose is not so much to understand every aspect of learning, but to reflect on the nature of the perspectives that contribute to learning.

Principles about Personal Perspectives

The principles that we might draw up for personal perspectives are similar to what we observed in the previous chapter for spatial perspectives. If we are dealing with Sue's and Carol's personal perspectives on a chair, one of the main differences may be generated by the difference in spatial location between Sue and Carol. That kind of difference involves two distinct people, rather than two successive spatial locations for a single individual. But in many ways, the differences between Sue's and Carol's spatial perspectives are akin to the differences between Sue's spatial perspective now and her perspective two minutes later when she positions herself where Carol once was. This kind of difference is comparatively easy to understand.

A more complex difference arises from the fact that Sue has learned engineering and Carol has not. The two persons bring to bear a different stock of knowledge and different skills in observation. In mainstream modern cultures heavily influenced by science, many people assume that science is a neutral common possession of educated people, so that it can enable us to decide confidently about the actual state of the chair. Morality and religion, on the other hand, are left to subjective preferences. But this common perception is itself influenced by corporate personal perspectives belonging to culture.

We cannot get into a full discussion here of all the cultural influences and the role of science. But science is done by people, and people have various biases, so that it may not always be simple to decide what is true in matters of science. Conversely, morality and religion have a final standard in God, so that issues that arise receive a definitive answer from God, rather than being merely matters of subjective preference. In science, morality, and religion alike, personal perspectives make a difference. Sometimes the differences are subtle, but sometimes they are monumental.

For the sake of simplicity, let us take a case in which there clearly is a dispute—namely, over the moral assessment of fornication. What do we say about Sue's and Carol's personal perspectives on fornication?

We can observe the same principles at work as we noticed concerning spatial perspectives. To illustrate the similarity, I will carry over much of the same wording used in the principles listed for spatial perspectives. But we need to introduce some modifications because of the problems with half-truths and sinful distortions of the truth that get entangled with personal perspectives.

1. It is the same fornication. That is, fornication is the same reality no matter who is looking at it. Relativists may, of course, deny that sameness. But when we bring God into the picture, we have good reasons for disputing the relativist version of fornication. The relativist version, which claims that the moral evaluation of fornication is *merely* a matter of personal preference, is itself part of a personal perspective. It is a personal perspective that contains a false view of fornication, and behind that a false view of God.

2. Each personal perspective gives us a distinct viewpoint on fornication. When we talk with Sue or Carol about fornication, we may become aware of two perspectives. We can distinguish them both by the moral and religious background of the person and by the detailed texture of how the person evaluates fornication.

3. In interpreting fornication, what stands out, and what is most easily noticeable, depends on one's personal perspective. Some details are easier to notice from some perspectives than others. Sue, who is against fornication, may find herself becoming impatient as she listens to arguments that she has already heard before, arguments appealing to each person's right to self-fulfillment in whatever sexual experience suits the person. Carol, who thinks fornication is OK in principle, may not want to think about whether human sexuality has deeper significance beyond the moments of pleasure-seeking. What is its meaning if it has been designed by God?

4. What we see depends on the "environment" as well as the issue. We are influenced by heart attitudes and by culture. Sue sees the issue of fornication in terms of God's purposes for human sexuality, and in particular his prohibition of fornication. Carol thinks of fornication in terms of human freedom—the freedom of the individual to do what most pleases him or her.

5. Given time, we can integrate information obtained from a variety of perspectives. Our total knowledge of fornication is then present in

our minds or our memories even though we are currently looking at fornication from only one perspective. But with personal perspectives, we deal with cases having two incompatible perspectives. Sue and Carol cannot both be right.

Can their disagreement be harmonized by bringing in a *third* personal perspective from Barbara? Influenced by postmodern relativism, Barbara from her personal perspective says that what is "true" for Sue need not be "true" for Carol. Though superficially this relativistic perspective may sound friendly and "tolerant," it is actually intolerant of any contrary claim. Both Sue and Carol disagree with Barbara, because Sue thinks that fornication is wrong for *everyone* (and therefore that Carol is mistaken), while Carol thinks that in principle fornication is OK for everyone (and therefore that Sue is mistaken).

In addition, Barbara is in danger of disagreeing even with herself. Would she admit that her personal perspective about relativizing truth is "true" for her but not for Sue? If so, she has no leverage to use to change Sue's mind. She has admitted that Sue's position is just as valid as her own. If not, she is intolerantly privileging her own personal perspective, contrary to her alleged love of tolerance.

Moreover, God provides the ultimate standard for moral judgments. This means that moral truth is real, just as real as the law of gravity. We can illustrate with an extreme example. Suppose that Carol and Sue are standing on the observation deck of a tall building. Carol thinks that the law of gravity is subjective, and that each person is free to keep it or not. Sue thinks that the law of gravity is universally true. The truth in this case makes a difference. It would be disastrous for Carol to throw herself off the observation deck to show that gravity is merely subjective. Likewise, it would be disastrous for Barbara to advise Carol and Sue that each person's view of gravity is true for her. In a similar way, it is disastrous in the presence of God to ignore moral truth.

This situation with several distinct and mutually exclusive moral positions is different from what we can casually observe about spatial perspectives. Persons can be mistaken, and their mistakes and biases can at times be deep. The mistakes are not always obvious or innocent. Some mistakes arise from moral corruption, moral darkness in the heart, by which we flee from God. There is no easy or obvious remedy to these corruptions. The good news about salvation through Jesus Christ is the only remedy. He said, "I am the way, and the truth, and the life. No one comes to the Father except through me" (John 14:6).

But there is one sense in which we can "integrate" incompatible personal viewpoints, namely, by understanding each viewpoint and noting the incompatibilities (as well as any points of partial agreement). We can still learn from others. We can understand someone else's point of view, and yet still not agree with it. But the degree to which we can learn is limited by human corruption.

6. We can infer or remember what fornication looked like from perspectives other than the one that we hold.

7. Much about fornication may be tentatively inferred by using only one personal perspective. But the inferences can radically go astray if our heart is corrupt.

Key Terms

human corruption
learning
morality
moral standards
personal perspective[3]
personal preferences
postmodern relativism
religion
science
sin
tolerance

Study Questions

1. What is a personal perspective?
2. What is the difference between a personal perspective and a spatial perspective? How are the two similar?
3. In general, how may two people's views about the same subject differ and yet have some overlap?
4. What can we learn about human communication from being aware of personal perspectives?

3. Key terms in **bold** are defined in the glossary at the end of this volume.

5. When two people differ in their views and contradict each other, can they both be right?
6. How would you respond to someone who claims that what you say is "true for you" but not for him?
7. Discuss in what sense it is "tolerant" or "intolerant" to affirm that everyone's point of view is true for him. Does lack of agreement imply "hate"?

For Further Reading

Carson, D. A. *The Intolerance of Tolerance*. Reprint, Grand Rapids: Eerdmans, 2013. A critical exploration of the dangerous confusion in appeals to "tolerance."

Poythress, Vern S. *Symphonic Theology: The Validity of Multiple Perspectives in Theology*. Grand Rapids: Zondervan, 1987. Reprint, Phillipsburg, NJ: P&R Publishing, 2001. Pp. 9–11. Illustrations of personal perspectives.

4

Thematic Perspectives

THE THIRD KIND of perspective to consider is a *thematic perspective.*[1] A thematic perspective is a temporary thematic starting point for exploring some subject matter, with the hope of discovering more and growing in the truth. For example, we can examine the subject matter of the family from the perspective of economics or the perspective of love or the perspective of movements of the family members. Each of these perspectives has a key theme: economics or love or movement, respectively.

Prophet, King, and Priest

It is easiest to understand the idea of a thematic perspective by considering a particular biblical example. We consider a triad of perspectives: prophet, king, and priest.[2] But how do these function as *perspectives*?

Prophets, kings, and priests are people who hold three prominent kinds of offices in the Old Testament. We will start with offices, not perspectives. (See fig. 4.1.) The offices are significant, not only because of what prophets, kings, and priests do within the bounds of the Old Testament, but because the three offices all point forward to Christ. Hebrews 1:1–3 sets forth in a single passage how Christ fulfills all three offices:

> Long ago, at many times and in many ways, God spoke to our fathers by the *prophets*, but in these last days he has spoken to us by his Son, whom he appointed the heir of all things, through whom also he created the world. He is the radiance of the glory of God and the exact

1. Timothy E. Miller calls this "a *focal perspective*" (*The Triune God of Unity in Diversity: An Analysis of Perspectivalism, the Trinitarian Theological Method of John Frame and Vern Poythress* [Phillipsburg, NJ: P&R Publishing, 2017], 34–36 [italics original]).

2. We will comment on the order of the list in chapter 15 and Appendix I.

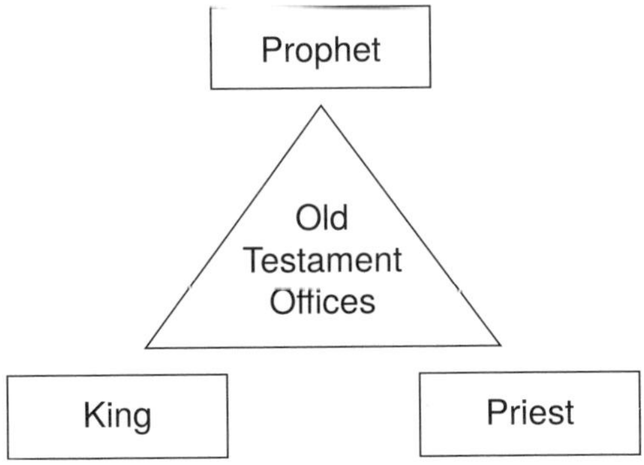

Fig. 4.1. Old Testament Offices: Prophet, King, and Priest

> imprint of his nature, and he *upholds* the universe by the word of his power. After making *purification* for sins, he sat down at the right hand of the Majesty on high.

Hebrews 1:1 speaks explicitly about the Old Testament prophets. Verse 2 compares them to "his Son," through whom God "has spoken to us" climactically and finally. That is, Christ is the final Prophet. Verse 3 indicates his kingly authority, by saying that he "upholds the universe by the word of his power," and by using the expression "sat down at the right hand of the Majesty on high," which indicates his position of kingly authority. Verse 3 also speaks about his priestly work, by talking about "making purification for sins." Thus, Christ fulfills all three Old Testament offices. (See fig. 4.2.) These principles are confirmed elsewhere in the New Testament. For example, in Acts 3:22–26, Peter claims that Jesus is the final Prophet prophesied by Moses. Matthew 1:1–17 and 2:2 indicate that Jesus is the messianic King in the line of David. Hebrews 7–10 indicates that Jesus is the final Priest, superior to the priests in the line of Aaron found in the Old Testament.

Jesus' fulfillment of Old Testament offices has been noted in confessional statements, such as the Heidelberg Catechism:

> Question 31. Why is he called *Christ*, that is, *Anointed*?
>
> Answer. Because he is ordained of God the Father, and anointed with the Holy Ghost, to be our chief Prophet and Teacher, who fully reveals

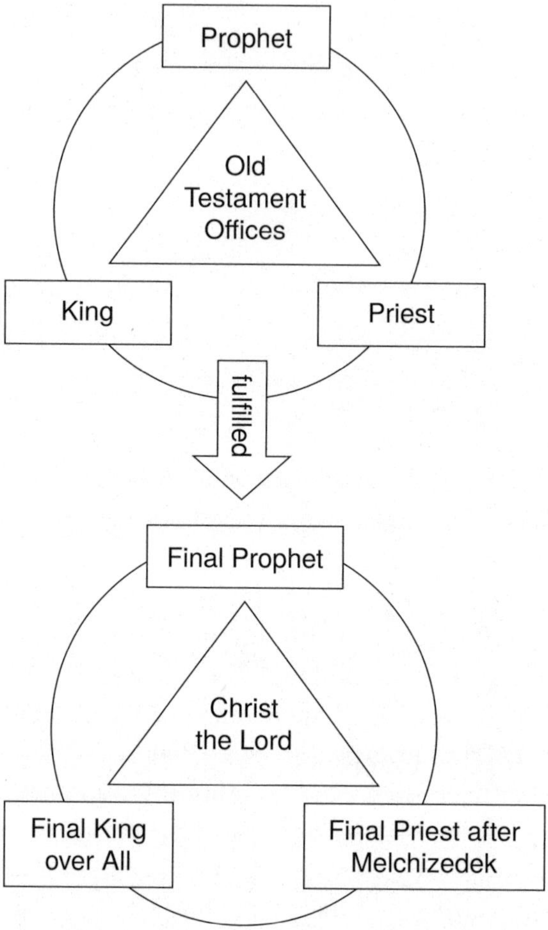

Fig. 4.2. Christ's Fulfilling the Three Old Testament Offices

> to us the secret counsel and will of God concerning our redemption; and our only High Priest, who by the one sacrifice of his body has redeemed us, and ever liveth to make intercession for us with the Father; and our eternal King, who governs us by his Word and Spirit, and defends and preserves us in the redemption obtained for us.[3]

3. *Heidelberg Catechism*, English translation from Philip Schaff, *The Creeds of Christendom with a History and Critical Notes* (repr., Grand Rapids: Baker, 1966), 3:317–18 (italics original). It is available online at http://reformed.org/documents/index.html?mainframe=http://reformed.org/documents/heidelberg.html. See also Westminster Confession of Faith 8.1; Westminster Larger Catechism questions 42–45.

In the Old Testament, the three offices were for the most part held by distinct persons. In the New Testament, the offices come together in one person, the person of Christ. But it is still possible to distinguish different *functions* that Christ performs. As a Prophet, he *speaks* on behalf of God. As a King, he *rules* with the righteousness of God. As a Priest, he *offers sacrifice, makes atonement* to God, and *intercedes* for his people.

So Christ works in three distinct ways, namely, in the offices of prophet, king, and priest. At the same time, he is one person. The New Testament and later confessions recognize a unity in all his redemptive work and proclaim that he is the one *Mediator* between God and man:

> For there is one God, and there is one *mediator* between God and men, the man Christ Jesus, who gave himself as a ransom for all. (1 Tim. 2:5–6)

> Therefore he is the *mediator* of a new covenant. (Heb. 9:15)

The three offices come together in a complementary way, as Hebrews 1:1–3 recognizes when it puts them together in the person of Christ. We have three distinct offices, but one person exercising all three offices.

At this point, we are close to the idea of perspectives. The perspectives would be three perspectives on one Christ and on one work of Christ. But we are not quite there. We have to see that a broader principle is represented by each of the three Old Testament offices and by each of the three aspects of Christ's work, in which he fulfills the offices.

First of all, we can think again about the work of Christ. During his earthly life, he was a teacher. This teaching is an exercise of his *prophetic* office. He also worked miracles, which displayed his *kingly power*. In his crucifixion and death, he was both the *priest* and the sacrifice atoning for sins. So on an elementary level, we can distinguish the three offices.

Transition to Three Interlocking Themes

But Jesus' life shows deeper meaning. For example, he often accomplished his miracles by *speaking*. So these miracles also illustrate his prophetic speech. Conversely, his prophetic speech taught about the kingdom of God, and his speech was filled with authority and kingly power. So his prophetic speech turns out to display his kingship.

He pronounced forgiveness of sins to the paralytic (Matt. 9:1–7). Forgiveness from God comes through sacrifice, so this prophetic pronouncement also displays his work as Priest. His pronouncement of forgiveness anticipates his work of sacrifice on the cross. His work on the cross includes verbal communication that he gave on the cross. But more broadly, the cross itself *communicates* the nature of salvation, especially as it is later expounded by the apostles. So the cross serves prophetic as well as priestly purposes. And through the cross, Jesus triumphs over the satanic powers:

> This [the legal accusation] he set aside, nailing it to the cross. He disarmed the *rulers and authorities* and put them to open shame, by triumphing over them in him. (Col. 2:14–15)

By triumphing over evil powers, Jesus shows his *kingly* or ruling authority in the very context of his death.

We conclude, then, that we can expand our conception of the offices of prophet, king, and priest. We can distinguish these offices when we confine ourselves to the most obvious observations. But when we probe more deeply, we can also see that all of Jesus' actions belong together: he is the *one Mediator*. In an extended sense, a metaphorical sense, all of Jesus' life *speaks* about his work of reconciliation. All of it is *prophetic*. All his life shows an exercise of kingly power because he *is* the King, both as God and as Messiah. All his life exhibits his work in forgiveness and reconciliation to God—all of it is priestly, in an extended sense.

Themes as Perspectives

When we view all of Jesus' life as prophetic, we are using the theme of prophet as a *perspective* on all of Jesus' life. In doing so, we have temporarily expanded the scope of what we consider *prophetic*. But we still have a distinct *theme*, namely, the theme of prophetic speech, broadly understood. If we are careful, we are not introducing any confusion here. We can still tell that there is a difference in texture between a narrow focus and a broad one. We use a narrow focus when we consider the Old Testament office of prophet. We broaden the focus when we use the idea of prophet as a window or lens for looking at everything in Jesus' life. (See fig. 4.3.)

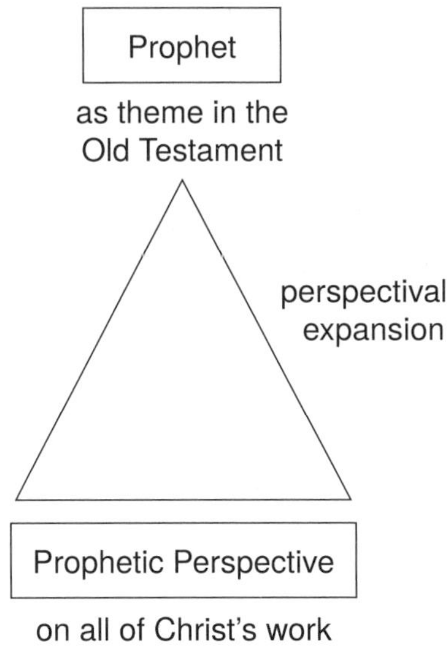

Fig. 4.3. From the Theme of Prophet to the Prophetic Perspective

The Old Testament prophets remain what they always were. And yet we also understand more deeply why God raised up prophets. He wanted us—those of us who live in the "last days" mentioned in Hebrews 1:2—to appreciate a relationship of analogy between the narrow office and the broader principle of God's *speaking* through everything in the life of Christ.

We can make similar observations about king and priest. On the one hand, we have the Old Testament office of king. On the other hand, we have everything that comes into view when we expand the idea of kingship to include every exercise of divine power among human beings through Christ. (See fig. 4.4.) And so it is also with priest. (See fig. 4.5.)

Let us now return to the *prophetic perspective*. We can further expand this perspective by using it not only to look at the whole of Christ's work on earth, but also to look at the preparation for that work in the Old Testament. For the office of prophet, the broader principle for both the Old Testament and the New is that of speaking. God speaks to himself in the communication among the persons of the Trinity. When he created man, he undertook to speak to human beings, from Genesis 1:28–30 onward. The Bible shows that he spoke in verbal communication to individuals such as Noah, Abraham, Isaac, Jacob, and Moses.

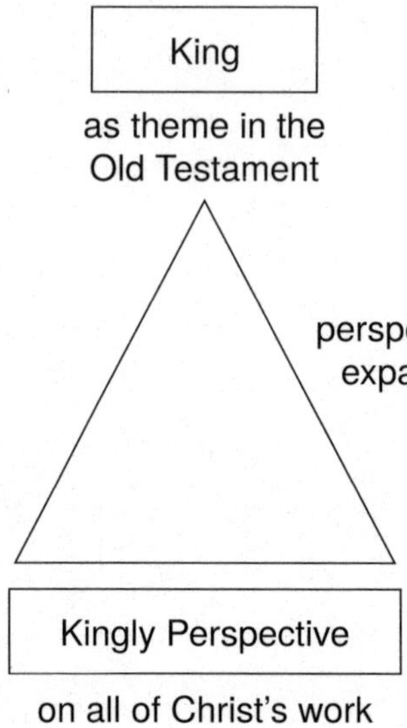

Fig. 4.4. From the Theme of Kingship to the Kingly Perspective

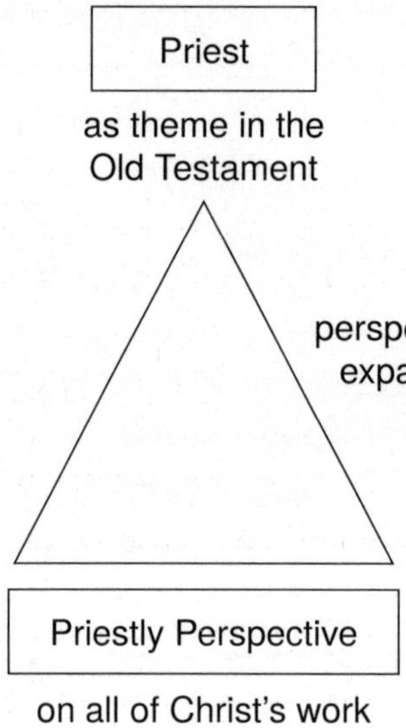

Fig. 4.5. From the Theme of Priest to the Priestly Perspective

But in a broader sense, his miracles and his providential works "speak" about who he is:

> The heavens *declare* the glory of God,
> and the sky above *proclaims* his handiwork.
> Day to day pours out *speech*,
> and night to night *reveals knowledge*. (Ps. 19:1–2)

So we can use a prophetic perspective on all the works of God, and see all his works as "speaking" about him.

From the fall onward, human beings are guilty sinners. They would be destroyed by the holiness of God's speech to them if it were not for the intervention of a mediator. Therefore, all the way through the Old Testament the mediation of Christ is being presupposed, even though Christ has not yet come to earth and accomplished his work. Mysteriously, God reckons the benefits of Christ's work backward into the Old Testament. Animal sacrifices and prophetic promises minister these benefits to the people. Otherwise, no one could be saved! So God's *speech* to sinful people presupposes priestly sacrifice and mediation to overcome guilt and death. It also presupposes kingly power at work, because God's word has power to bring about what he says. So now, having started with the prophetic perspective, focusing on speech, we see that God is exerting kingly power and giving priestly forgiveness for sin.

Next, let us employ the *kingly* perspective. Consider God's kingly rule throughout history. God rules all things:

> The LORD has established his *throne* in the heavens,
> and his kingdom *rules* over *all*. (Ps. 103:19)

So the kingly perspective is a perspective on all of God's work. It is all a work in which he is *ruling*.

But starting with the kingly perspective, we can also note the presence of a prophetic perspective. God rules by *speaking*, as Hebrews 1:3 reminds us: "he upholds the universe by the *word* of his power." His rule includes gifts graciously given to people who do not deserve them. So his rule presupposes grace, obtained through priestly mediation. In fact, Christ the Son of the Father is present in speaking and ruling all through the Old Testament, even before his incarnation. The incarnation is a wonderful and unique event, once in history. But its benefits, together with the benefits of the life and death and resurrection of Christ, must already be mysteriously in operation through the course of Old Testament history, in order that people may not be immediately destroyed because of their sins.

In fact, then, the speaking and ruling and priestly mediation from God take place together throughout the Old Testament. Priestly mediation is mediation of the *presence* of God; it provides *communion* with God. God's presence comes in both blessing and curse. The curse is the inevitable outcome of the fall of man into sin. Blessing comes, in spite of human guilt, because Christ bore guilt and sin on the cross.

Speaking and ruling and the presence of God go together. Each implies the other two. Each one—speaking, ruling, and being present—characterizes all of God's interaction with human beings, and indeed with creation as a whole. Each is a *perspective* on a whole. Each is also a *perspective* on the other two. But we can still distinguish the three themes, namely, prophetic speech, kingly rule, and priestly presence in communion. They are like three "windows" on God's actions toward us.

Each perspective functions like a window through which we not only see the whole of God's interaction with creation, but also see the other two perspectives with deepened understanding. For example, it helps to understand that all of God's speech displays kingly authority and priestly presence. All of God's rule over us displays the wisdom of his speech and the blessing (and sometimes curse) of his presence. (See fig. 4.6.)

Thematic Perspectives in General

The triad of prophet, king, and priest is a triad of Old Testament offices. And from there, when we expand our conception, we obtain three thematic *perspectives,* namely, the prophetic, kingly, and priestly perspectives. They are *thematic* perspectives because they start from a specific theme—say the theme of prophet. They are *perspectives* because they function like a window to look out on the whole landscape—in this case, the "landscape" of God's work throughout history. They are useful because we can grow in understanding things about prophecy and kingship and priesthood as we appreciate how these specific offices fit

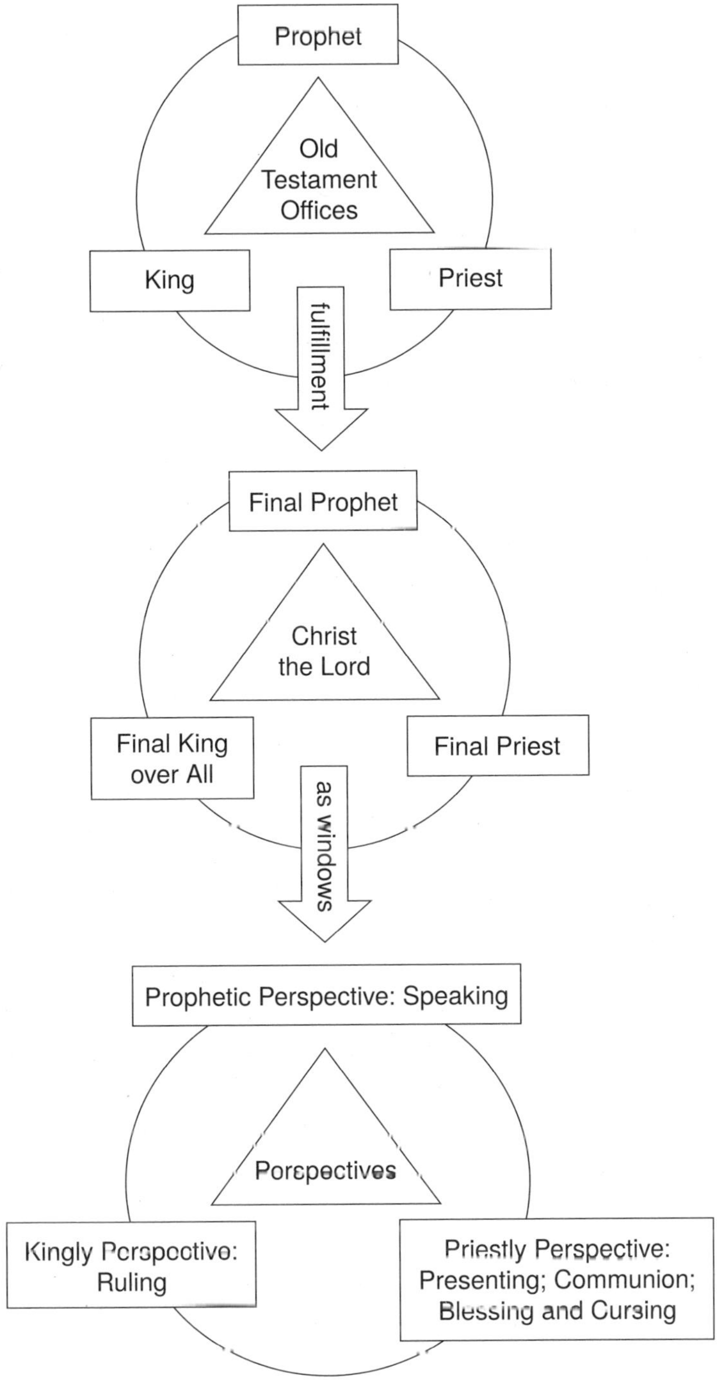

Fig. 4.6. Offices Expanded to Perspectives on Christ's Work

into God's overall plan. And we see more about the significance of each one when we use the other two perspectivally in our process of growth.

The same is true with respect to other themes. We can pick a theme in the Bible, whether large or small. It could be the theme of God's goodness (a large, extended theme) or the theme of olive oil (a small theme). And then we can ask ourselves how that theme can be expanded into a perspective, a window through which we attempt to notice relationships within the unified plan of God.[4] Of course, our own understanding is always fallible. But as we keep returning to Scripture and asking more questions, we can grow in understanding.

What happens when we start with the theme of God's goodness? God's goodness is displayed directly or indirectly on every page of Scripture. And human goodness and kindness should reflect God's goodness. So God's goodness becomes a perspective on all the Bible.

Olive oil is a small theme, and therefore less promising. But we may observe that in connection with the ceremony of anointing, oil is sometimes used as a symbol for the Holy Spirit (Isa. 61:1). The Holy Spirit is given to Jesus in his ministry, empowering him (Luke 4:18). We can use the power of the Holy Spirit as a perspective on all of God's work. So oil *as a symbol* can become a perspective on the whole of God's work.

The same is true in principle even when we take a theme that we pick up from general revelation rather than special revelation. We must recognize that general revelation needs special revelation—not to mention the inward work of the Holy Spirit—to be properly understood. But God rules the whole world. So his purposes are everywhere expressed, even though there is always mystery in our human understanding.

We should be admiring God for his wisdom and praising him for the many ways in which he has revealed himself in the world and the ways that he gives us to grow in knowing him.

Principles for Thematic Perspectives

We can summarize what we have found about thematic perspectives using the list we have drawn up in the preceding two chapters, but modifying the wording to describe thematic perspectives. For simplicity,

4. Vern S. Poythress, *Symphonic Theology: The Validity of Multiple Perspectives in Theology* (Grand Rapids: Zondervan, 1987; repr., Phillipsburg, NJ: P&R Publishing, 2001).

we consider what happens when we use the prophetic, kingly, and priestly perspectives to analyze the healing of the paralytic, described in Matthew 9:1–7.

1. It is the same healing. That is, Jesus' healing of the paralytic is the same reality no matter who is looking at it.

2. Each thematic perspective gives us a distinct viewpoint on the healing of the paralytic. A prophetic perspective may focus on Jesus' words, while a kingly perspective focuses on the power he exhibited in the miracle of healing.

3. What stands out about the healing, and what is most easily noticeable, depends on one's thematic perspective. Some details are easier to notice from some perspectives than others. From the priestly perspective, it is easier to notice the key significance of Jesus' forgiving sins, because forgiving sins is one of the functions of the priestly office.[5]

4. What we see depends on the environment as well as the story. In this case, the key environment is the larger theme—prophet or king or priest.

5. Given time, we can integrate information obtained from a variety of perspectives. Our total knowledge of the incident of healing the paralytic is then present in our minds or our memories even though we are currently looking at the incident from only one perspective.

6. We can infer or remember what the healing incident looked like from perspectives other than the one that we are currently using. We can picture other perspectives through the one that we are using.

7. Much about the healing incident may be tentatively inferred by using only one thematic perspective. But the inferences can radically go astray if our heart is corrupt. Every insight must ultimately be tested by comparing it with the whole of the Bible.

Key Terms

expansion of a theme
king[6]
kingly office
kingly perspective

5. Technically, during the Old Testament period, forgiveness came not directly from the priest but from God. But priests through their actions mediated forgiveness to the people.

6. Key terms in **bold** are defined in the glossary at the end of this volume.

office
priest
priestly office
priestly perspective
prophet
prophetic office
prophetic perspective
thematic perspective

Study Questions

1. What is a thematic perspective?
2. How does a thematic perspective differ from a spatial perspective or a personal perspective? How are they similar?
3. What are the three key Old Testament offices to which God appoints people in order to express his covenantal relation to them? What is distinctive about each of the three offices?
4. What is the difference between an office and using the office as a perspective?
5. What is the value of expanding a theme into a perspective?
6. How may we grow in honoring and praising God by using perspectives?

For Further Reading

Poythress, Vern S. *Reading the Word of God in the Presence of God: A Handbook for Biblical Interpretation*. Wheaton, IL: Crossway, 2016. Chapter 23 on "Typology" discusses prophet, king, and priest.

———. *The Shadow of Christ in the Law of Moses*. Reprint, Phillipsburg, NJ: P&R Publishing, 1995. The first part has discussion of how prophets, kings, and priests point forward to Christ.

———. *Symphonic Theology: The Validity of Multiple Perspectives in Theology*. Grand Rapids: Zondervan, 1987. Reprint, Phillipsburg, NJ: P&R Publishing, 2001. Chapter 3 discusses theological themes and how they can be used as perspectives.

5

Commonalities in Perspectives

WE HAVE NOW completed our brief tour through three kinds of perspectives: spatial perspectives, personal perspectives, and thematic perspectives. Certain patterns seem to recur.

Shared Patterns

What patterns are similar with all three kinds of perspectives?

1. Stable, shared knowledge. When we use several perspectives to look at the same subject matter, the subject matter remains the same. There is unity in the thing that we are examining.

2. Distinctions of perspectives. The multiple perspectives that we may consider are indeed distinguishable. The distinction in our experience does not disappear even if we have the same overall knowledge of the subject using the distinct perspectives.

3. Distinctions in what is prominent. What is most obvious or most in focus or most easily noticeable varies with our perspective.

4. Presence of other perspectives. Each perspective gives us a view not only of the subject but indirectly of other perspectives.

5. Reinforcement. Two or more perspectives can reinforce one another, and we may grow in knowledge by using more than one. Each perspective may grow to "include" everything that is seen in other perspectives.

Possible Relations to the Trinity

These shared features of perspectives have certain tantalizing similarities to features that we find in our human knowledge of the Trinity. We can highlight the similarities by describing our knowledge of the Trinity in analogous ways.

1. There is only one God whom we have come to know.

2. We can distinguish the persons of the Trinity.

3. What stands out about God varies subtly, depending on which person of the Trinity serves as our starting point for thought. Moreover, we can discern an order among the persons of the Trinity: the Father, the Son, and the Holy Spirit are usually presented in that order.

4. Knowledge about one person of the Trinity cannot be separated from knowledge of the other two. For example, in knowing Christ, we know the Father, whom he reveals (Matt. 11:27; John 14:9). We also know the Spirit, whom Christ promises to send as "another Helper" (John 14:16). It is through the Holy Spirit's work in our hearts that we come to have saving knowledge about Christ (1 Cor. 2:10–16).

5. Knowledge gained about one person of the Trinity enhances and deepens our knowledge of the other two persons.

These features concerning our human *knowledge* of the Trinity seem to reflect features that belong to God himself, as the Trinitarian God. We can list five features about God:

1. There is only one God.

2. The persons of the Trinity are distinct.

3. Each person of the Trinity knows the other two persons. Each person is a starting point in his own knowledge. There

is, moreover, an order among the persons of the Trinity: the Father, the Son, and the Holy Spirit.

4. Each person of the Trinity is fully present to the other persons.

5. Each person of the Trinity indwells the other persons.

What is the significance of these similarities? Does the Trinity have anything to do with perspectives, or are these similarities merely accidental? Before trying to answer these questions, we should first review the doctrine of the Trinity, as taught in Scripture and summarized in the classic creeds.[1]

Key Terms

deepening knowledge
human knowledge of God
personal perspective[2]
person of the Trinity
spatial perspective
thematic perspective

Study Questions

1. What are the three kinds of perspectives?
2. What features are common to all three kinds of perspectives?
3. What analogies exist between perspectives and our knowledge of the Trinity and the Trinity itself?

For Further Reading

The Nicene-Constantinopolitan Creed. Accessed November 19, 2014. http://www.antiochian.org/674. A classical creedal summary of Trinitarian doctrine.

1. See esp. the Nicene-Constantinopolitan Creed (Philip Schaff, *The Creeds of Christendom with a History and Critical Notes* [repr., Grand Rapids: Baker, 1966], 2:57–59), online at http://www.antiochian.org/674, and other places.

2. Key terms in **bold** are defined in the glossary at the end of this volume.

PART 2

THE TRINITY

WE CONSIDER THE basic aspects of biblical teaching about the Trinity.

6

Basic Biblical Teaching about the Trinity

WE NOW REVIEW the basic biblical teaching about the Trinity. Whole books have been written on the subject.[1] There is much to be said. In the end, the doctrine of the Trinity is based on the teaching of the whole Bible. In addition, the doctrine of the Trinity is *presupposed* as a background framework when the Bible discusses how God saves us, how he adopts us, how he speaks to us, and how he makes his presence known among us and in us (see Introduction). Many texts speak directly or indirectly about it. And these texts fit into a larger context of biblical teaching. Here we include only a summary of a few key texts and their implications. After the summary, we want to spend our time thinking about *implications* based on the Trinitarian character of God, rather than focusing mainly on confirming the doctrine of the Trinity.

The Unity of God

Our first point is that there is one God. Both the Old Testament and the New Testament testify that there is only one true God.

1. John M. Frame, *The Doctrine of God* (Phillipsburg, NJ: P&R Publishing, 2002), 619–735; Robert Letham, *The Holy Trinity: In Scripture, History, Theology, and Worship* (Phillipsburg, NJ: P&R Publishing, 2004); Peter Toon, *Our Triune God: A Biblical Portrayal of the Trinity* (Wheaton, IL: Victor, 1996). John Owen takes an approach similar to mine, but musters many more verses (John Owen, *A Brief Declaration and Vindication of the Doctrine of the Trinity* [1669], in *The Works of John Owen*, ed. William H. Goold [repr., Edinburgh/Carlisle, PA: Banner of Truth, 1965], 2:365–454). Owen also has another, longer work, in which he discusses the saints' communion with the persons of the Trinity: *Of Communion with God the Father, Son, and Holy Ghost* [1657], in *The Works of John Owen*, ed. William H. Goold (repr., Edinburgh/Carlisle, PA: Banner of Truth, 1965), 2:1–274; the same work is available in modernized language: John Owen,

> To you it was shown, that you might know that the LORD is God; there is *no other* besides him. (Deut. 4:35; see also v. 39)

> Hear, O Israel: The LORD our God, the LORD is *one*. (Deut. 6:4; see Mark 12:29)

> Therefore, as to the eating of food offered to idols, we know that "an idol has no real existence," and that "there is no God but *one*." For although there may be so-called gods in heaven or on earth—as indeed there are many "gods" and many "lords"—yet for us there is *one* God, the Father, from whom are all things and for whom we exist, and one Lord, Jesus Christ, through whom are all things and through whom we exist. (1 Cor. 8:4–6)

> You believe that God is *one*; you do well. Even the demons believe—and shudder! (James 2:19)

The Deity of God the Father

Our next point is that God the Father is the true God.

> There is one *God, the Father*, from whom are all things and for whom we exist. (1 Cor. 8:6)

This truth is seldom challenged, because the word *God* regularly designates God the Father or refers preeminently to him. "God our Father" and "God the Father" are regular titles for the first person of the Trinity:

> Grace to you and peace from *God our Father* and the Lord Jesus Christ. (Rom. 1:7; 1 Cor. 1:3; 2 Cor. 1:2; Gal. 1:3; Eph. 1:2)

> Then comes the end, when he delivers the kingdom to *God the Father* after destroying every rule and every authority and power. (1 Cor. 15:24)

Communion with the Triune God, ed. Kelly M. Kapic and Justin Taylor (Wheaton, IL: Crossway, 2007).

The Father is also called "the God and Father of our Lord Jesus Christ" (Rom. 15:6; 2 Cor. 1:3) or simply "God":

> The grace of the Lord Jesus Christ and the love of *God* and the fellowship of the Holy Spirit be with you all. (2 Cor. 13:14)

The Deity of Christ the Son

Next, Christ the Son, the Word of God, is God.

> In the beginning was the Word, and the Word was with God, and the Word *was God*. (John 1:1)

> Thomas answered him [Jesus], "My Lord and *my God*!" (John 20:28)

Christ was the Mediator in the creation of the world:

> All things were *made through him* [the Word], and without him was not any thing made that was made. (John 1:3)

> There is . . . one Lord, Jesus Christ, *through whom are all things* and through whom we exist. (1 Cor. 8:6)

> For *by him all things were created*, in heaven and on earth, visible and invisible, whether thrones or dominions or rulers or authorities—all things were created through him and for him. And he is before all things, and in him all things hold together. (Col. 1:16–17)

In addition, the New Testament applies to Christ some Old Testament verses that use the tetragrammaton (*Lord, YHWH*), the most sacred name for God in the Old Testament:

> And it shall come to pass that everyone who calls on the name of *the Lord* [YHWH] shall be saved. (Joel 2:32)

> For "everyone who calls on the name of *the Lord* will be saved." (Rom. 10:13; note that an earlier verse, Romans 10:9, has identified Jesus as "Lord")

Jesus also proclaims his deity in John 8:58:

> Jesus said to them, "Truly, truly, I say to you, before Abraham was, *I am*."

The expression "I am" implies that he existed before his incarnation—and "before Abraham was." The expression is still more striking because it is present tense instead of the past tense "I was" that might have been expected. His existence is eternal and transcends time. Furthermore, the expression "I am" echoes the special name that God gives himself in Exodus 3:13–14:

> Then Moses said to God, "If I come to the people of Israel and say to them, 'The God of your fathers has sent me to you,' and they ask me, 'What is his name?' what shall I say to them?" God said to Moses, "I AM WHO I AM." And he said, "Say this to the people of Israel, 'I AM has sent me to you.'"

Jesus identifies himself as the same God who is "I AM" in what he says to Israel.

The Deity of the Holy Spirit

The Holy Spirit is God. This truth is evident from the fact that lying to the Holy Spirit is the same as lying to God:

> But Peter said, "Ananias, why has Satan filled your heart to lie *to the Holy Spirit* and to keep back for yourself part of the proceeds of the land? While it remained unsold, did it not remain your own? And after it was sold, was it not at your disposal? Why is it that you have contrived this deed in your heart? You have not lied to men but *to God*." (Acts 5:3–4)

The Old Testament is what *God* says and also what the *Holy Spirit* says:

> *He* [God] says, "Let all God's angels worship him." (Heb. 1:6)

> The *Holy Spirit* spoke beforehand by the mouth of David. (Acts 1:16)

Hebrews 1:6 quotes from Deuteronomy 32:43. The wording "he says" in Hebrews 1:6 implies that Deuteronomy, as part of the Old Testament, is what God says. Acts 1:16 indicates that the Old Testament is what the *Holy Spirit* says. The underlying assumption is that the Holy Spirit is God.

Similarly, the Holy Spirit is mentioned in parallel with God as the source of David's inspired words:

> The oracle of David, the son of Jesse[:]
>
> . . . .
>
> "The *Spirit* of the LORD speaks by me;
> *his* word is on my tongue.
> The *God* of Israel has spoken;
> the *Rock* of Israel has said to me . . . ." (2 Sam. 23:1–3)

The Distinct Person of the Son

Next, we consider Scripture verses that indicate that the three persons of the Trinity are distinct from one another.

The Son is a person distinct from the Father. We see the distinction from the statement in John 1:1 that "the Word was *with* God." We see it also from the fact that the Father *sent* the Son into the world: "God *sent forth* his Son" (Gal. 4:4). The one sending and the one sent are necessarily distinct. The conversation that Jesus has with God the Father in John 17 also reveals a distinction between the person of the Son and the person of the Father.

In this context, the word *person* needs special attention. What does it mean? God is God. He is the Creator, and no creature can compare with him ("O LORD, who is *like you*?," Ps. 35:10). So a human person is not a person in quite the same sense as a divine person. No analogy with created things can capture the uniqueness of who God is. Yet it is clear from Scripture that both the Father and the Son love and speak and hear and know, which are activities characteristic of persons. They love and speak and hear in relation to each other. Even here, there remains the distinction between the Creator and the creature. God's love is the love of the infinite Creator. It is analogous to human love; human love imitates divine love. God is the original pattern or archetype for love.

Human beings love *on the level of the creature*; they have love in a derivative form.

The Distinct Person of the Holy Spirit

The Holy Spirit is a person distinct from the Father and distinct from the Son. This distinctness is shown by the fact that he is *sent* by the Father and by the Son:

> But the Helper, the Holy Spirit, whom the Father will *send* in my name. . . . (John 14:26)

> But when the Helper comes, whom I [Jesus] will *send* to you from the Father, the Spirit of truth, who *proceeds from the Father*, he will bear witness about me. (John 15:26)

Jesus also distinguishes the Holy Spirit by calling him "another Helper":

> And I will ask the Father, and he will give you *another Helper*, to be with you forever, even the Spirit of truth, whom the world cannot receive, because it neither sees him nor knows him. You know him, for he dwells with you and will be in you. (John 14:16–17)

The Holy Spirit is a person, not merely a force, because he can be lied to:

> "Ananias, why has Satan filled your heart to *lie to the Holy Spirit* . . . ?" (Acts 5:3)

Other passages indicate that the Holy Spirit hears, speaks, intercedes, and can be grieved (John 16:13; Rom. 8:26–27; Eph. 4:30). These descriptions all imply that the Holy Spirit is a person.

Moreover, by calling the Holy Spirit "another Helper" (John 14:16), Jesus indicates that the Spirit has characteristics like Jesus himself, who is the first Helper while he is on earth. This similarity between the Holy Spirit and Jesus implies that the Holy Spirit is a person in the same way that Jesus is a person.

The Distinction of All Three Persons

The distinction of all three persons comes to expression in the fact that Jesus sends the Holy Spirit "from the Father":

> But when the Helper comes, whom I [Jesus] will *send* to you *from the Father,* the Spirit of truth, who *proceeds from the Father,* he will bear witness about me. (John 15:26)

The distinction is also depicted vividly when Jesus is baptized by John the Baptist:

> And when *Jesus* was baptized, immediately he went up from the water, and behold, the heavens were opened to him, and he saw the *Spirit of God* descending like a dove and coming to rest on him; and behold, a *voice* from heaven said, "This is my beloved Son, with whom I am well pleased." (Matt. 3:16–17)

Jesus is the Son of God. The voice from heaven is the voice of the Father, as is evident from the fact that it says, "This is *my* beloved Son." The Holy Spirit is present, "descending like a dove." All three persons are clearly in the scene, and each person can be distinguished from the other two.

The expression "another Helper" in John 14:16 distinguishes the Holy Spirit from Jesus. The description in Romans 8:26–27 of the Holy Spirit's interceding with God distinguishes the Holy Spirit from God the Father, before whom he intercedes.

Putting Together the Picture

In summary, we know from the Scripture that there is only one God. This God is three persons. Each of the persons is fully God—not a part of God, not merely a creature, not merely a subordinate, finite, god-like being. In addition, each person is distinct from the other two. (See fig. 6.1.)

These truths have an impact on salvation and on worship. Only God has the power and wisdom necessary to save us. If, on the contrary, salvation were being worked out by persons who were less than God, it would undermine the very nature of salvation. Or if several gods were

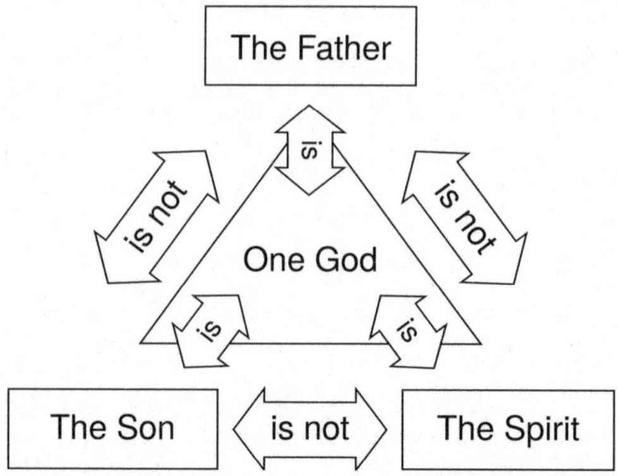

Fig. 6.1. Three Persons in One God[2]

working on it, it would undermine the full unity of salvation. Similarly, the doctrine of God has an impact on *worship*. God himself prohibits worshiping anything except God (Ex. 20:3–6). If the Son or the Spirit were not fully God, it would disallow our worship. Or if we were to worship three gods, we would no longer have unified worship. Thus, it is important not only that the doctrine of the Trinity be true, but that we *know* it to be true, for the sake of our confidence in salvation and the integrity of true worship.

But how can the doctrine of the Trinity be true? How can there be three distinct persons and only one God? It is a mystery. As we have already said, God is not like any creature. There is no perfect analogy within the created order that would enable us to unravel the mystery. This mystery and profundity about God should stimulate us to adore him.

When people have attempted to unravel the mystery, they have ended in heretical teachings. Some of them affirm the unity of God, but deny the distinction of persons. Or they affirm the distinction of persons, but make Jesus and the Spirit into subordinate, limited "gods." They try still other options. But none of the alternative, heretical theories does justice to the full testimony of Scripture.

2. A diagram similar to this one can be found in a number of places, such as J. Hampton Keathley III, "The Trinity (Triunity) of God," May 18, 2004, https://bible.org/article/trinity-triunity-god; Justin Taylor, "Trinity 101," Desiring God, October 12, 2007, http://www.desiringgod.org/articles/trinity-101. It appears in Cotton Faustina manuscript B. VII, fol. 42v,

Key Terms

deity[3]
heresy
person
Trinity

Study Questions

1. What is the biblical teaching on the Trinity?
2. What verses show the full deity of the Son? of the Spirit?
3. What verses show the reality of the distinctions between the Father, the Son, and the Spirit?
4. Why are people tempted to deny the doctrine of the Trinity?

For Further Reading

Frame, John M. *The Doctrine of God.* Phillipsburg, NJ: P&R Publishing, 2002. Pp. 619–35. An exposition of the biblical teaching on the Trinity.

Letham, Robert. *The Holy Trinity: In Scripture, History, Theology, and Worship.* Phillipsburg, NJ: P&R Publishing, 2004. An exposition of the Trinity, in relation to biblical teaching and church history. The first three chapters deal with the biblical foundations for the doctrine.

from about A.D. 1210, British Library, https://en.wikipedia.org/wiki/File:PetrusPictaviensis_CottonFaustinaBVII-folio42v_ScutumFidei_early13thc.jpg.

3. Key terms in **bold** are defined in the glossary at the end of this volume.

7

Coinherence

IT IS IMPOSSIBLE for us to understand comprehensively how the three persons of the Trinity are one God. Scripture gives us an additional aspect of mystery by speaking about the fact that the persons of the Trinity dwell "in" one another.

Indwelling in the Bible

Passages about indwelling come up particularly in the Gospel of John:

> Do you not believe that I [Jesus] am *in* the Father and the Father is *in* me? The words that I say to you I do not speak on my own authority, but the Father who *dwells in* me does his works. Believe me that I am *in* the Father and the Father is *in* me, or else believe on account of the works themselves. (John 14:10–11)

> That they may all be one, just as you, Father, are *in* me [Jesus], and I *in* you, that they also may be *in* us, so that the world may believe that you have sent me. (John 17:21)

John 17:21 also talks about believers' being in the Father and the Son (the phrase "in us"). We who are human do not become divine ourselves, but the fellowship that we have with the Father and the Son is analogous to that exalted and perfect fellowship that the Father and the Son have with each other.

What about the Holy Spirit? Christ promises to send the Holy Spirit as the means through whom the Father and the Son dwell in believers:

> You know him [the Spirit of truth], for he dwells with you and will be *in* you. (John 14:17)

A few verses later, Jesus talks about believers' participating in an indwelling involving the Father and the Son:

> In that day you will know that I am *in* my Father, and you *in* me, and I *in* you. (John 14:20)

> If anyone loves me, he will keep my word, and my Father will love him, and we will come to him and *make our home with* him. (John 14:23)

In addition, Romans 8 indicates that if the Spirit is dwelling in you, Christ is dwelling in you:

> You, however, are not in the flesh but in the Spirit, if in fact the Spirit of God *dwells in* you. Anyone who does not have the Spirit of Christ does not belong to him. But if Christ is *in* you, although the body is dead because of sin, the Spirit is life because of righteousness. If the Spirit of him who raised Jesus from the dead *dwells in* you, he who raised Christ Jesus from the dead will also give life to your mortal bodies through his Spirit who *dwells in* you. (Rom. 8:9–11)

First Corinthians 2:11 implies that the Spirit is *in* God, by analogy with a human spirit's being in a human person:

> For who knows a person's thoughts except the spirit of that person, which is *in* him? So also no one comprehends the thoughts of God except *the Spirit of God*.

We may conclude that each person of the Trinity is *in* each of the other two persons. (See fig. 7.1.)

Indwelling in Theological Explanation

Theologians have several equivalent terms for describing this indwelling among the persons of the Trinity: *circumincessio*, *circumcessio*, *circumcession* (an English transliteration of the Latin), *perichoresis* (from

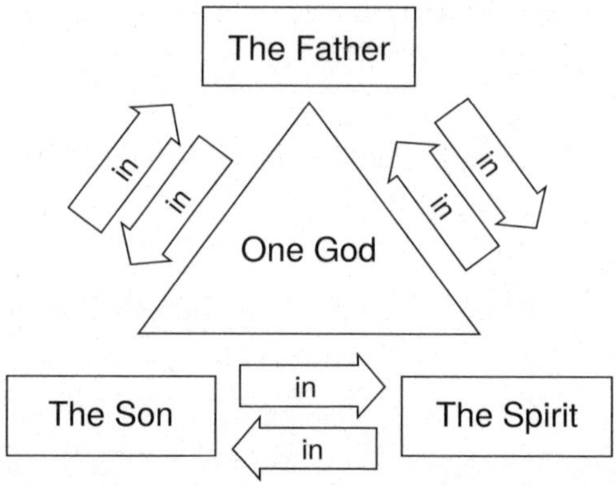

Fig. 7.1. Coinherence in Indwelling

Greek), and *coinherence*. In this book, I will use the last of these terms, *coinherence*. The terms arose not only to summarize the biblical language that directly speaks of indwelling of persons of the Trinity, but to affirm the harmonious involvement of all persons of the Trinity in the works of God—creation, providence, redemption, and consummation. The work of one person involves the presence and work of the other two. We can see one illustration of this mutual involvement in the baptism of Jesus. At Jesus' baptism (Matt. 3:13–17), all three persons of the Trinity are present and involved. But in this case their actions are distinguishable: the Father speaks from heaven; the Son is baptized and receives the Spirit; and the Spirit descends like a dove. Together the three persons participate harmoniously in the inauguration of Jesus' public ministry.

Likewise, all three persons of the Trinity are involved in the work of salvation, the work of adoption, God's speech to us, God's presence with us, and prayer (see Introduction). The idea of coinherence is a practical one because it underlines the unity of God's work in salvation, adoption, speech, and so on. So the language that directly speaks about being "in" or "dwelling in" a person is only one way of articulating the mystery of harmony among the persons. The whole of Scripture testifies to this harmony in various ways.

Coinherence in Knowledge

For brevity, we can choose three main ways to explore the harmony. The first way is to choose indwelling as our focus; this we have already done. The second is to use knowledge as our focus. Each person of the Trinity *knows* the other persons:

> All things have been handed over to me by my Father, and no one *knows* the Son except the Father, and no one *knows* the Father except the Son and anyone to whom the Son chooses to reveal him. (Matt. 11:27)

Similarly, the Holy Spirit *knows* the things of God:

> For the Spirit *searches* everything, even the depths of God. For who *knows* a person's thoughts except the spirit of that person, which is in him? So also no one *comprehends* the thoughts of God except the Spirit of God. (1 Cor. 2:10–11)

This knowledge is complete and exhaustive, unlike the limited knowledge that human beings have of one another. (See fig. 7.2.)

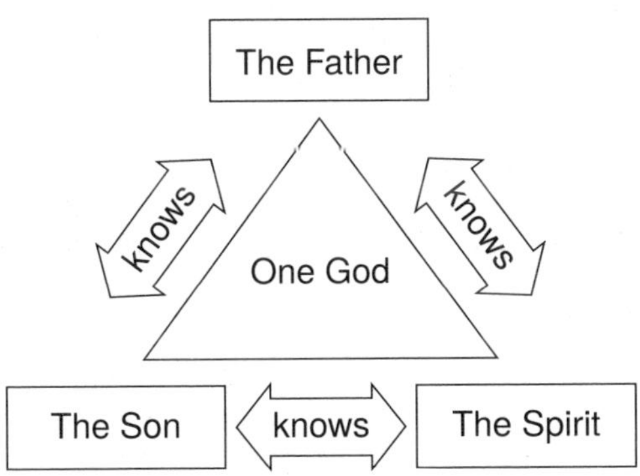

Fig. 7.2. Coinherence in Knowledge

It is noteworthy that these discussions of exhaustive knowledge take place in contexts that also draw implications for our human knowledge. Matthew 11:27 talks about the knowledge of the Father that is given to "anyone to whom the Son chooses to reveal him." This human knowledge is real and reliable precisely because of the Son, who mediates the knowledge when he reveals the Father. The fullness and exhaustive character of the Son's knowledge of the Father offer the ultimate guarantee that the knowledge that we receive from the Son is real and solid. Similarly, the knowledge by the Holy Spirit, mentioned in 1 Corinthians 2:10–11, forms the basis for knowledge that we receive from him:

> These things God has *revealed to us* through the Spirit. (v. 10)

> Now we have received not the spirit of the world, but the Spirit who is from God, that *we might understand* the things freely given us by God. (v. 12)

We receive real knowledge from the Son and from the Spirit. But we remain finite. Our knowledge is genuine and at the same time not exhaustive. In the language of classical theology, we *know* God truly, but we do not *comprehend* God; that is, we do not know him exhaustively. We do not know him with the thoroughness that the Son knows the Father and the Father knows the Son.

Parallel implications hold in the case of indwelling. In John 17, which discusses the mutual indwelling of the Father and the Son, one of the implications is that we who believe in the Son come to enjoy a mutual indwelling: "that they also may be in us" (v. 21); and "I in them" (v. 23). This mutual indwelling is real, but not on the same level and not with the same divine exhaustiveness that belongs to the mutual indwelling of the Father and the Son in the Trinity. It is real and solid because it derives from the ultimate indwelling that belongs to the persons of the Trinity.

Coinherence in Exercising Power

A third way of considering coinherence is to focus on God's exercise of power. The creation of the world comes about through the work of the Father, the Son, and the Holy Spirit. All three persons are intimately involved. We can see this implication from John 1:1–2 and Genesis 1:1–2. John 1:1–2 speaks of the involvement of the Father and the Son, that is, the Word. First Corinthians 8:6 confirms the involvement of both persons. Genesis 1:2 mentions the Spirit as "hovering over the face of the waters," implying that he is present in the work of creation. Psalm 104:30 says, "When you send forth your *Spirit*, they are created," referring to the next generation of animals. In theological terms, this creation of the next generation of animals is *providence*, but Psalm 104:30 describes it as analogous to the original creation in Genesis 1. So we conclude by analogy that the Spirit was also being "sent forth" in God's acts of creation in Genesis 1.[1]

Similar joint working of the persons of the Trinity takes place in providence, redemption, and consummation. In general, each person of the Trinity works *with* the working of the other persons in the works of God.[2]

All three ways of considering coinherence can be seen in the light of the basic reality: there is only one God. Each of the persons is God. The "sharing" or coinherence is as profound as could be, because God is one.

Implications from One Way of Description to Another

On this matter of the Trinity and on the matter of coinherence, it is wise for us to start with biblical teaching in its detailed textures. Some people would like to logically deduce various things about God, starting with just a single proposition or a single truth about God. But since we are not God, we cannot be confident that we know enough just from one short formulation of truth or one single verse of the Bible. It is important for us to be guided by the full teaching of Scripture. The larger body of biblical teaching helps to guide our understanding of any one verse.[3]

Once we have gathered a good deal from biblical teaching, we may explore cautiously and temperately whether we can see some ways in which the various aspects of biblical teaching reinforce one another. For example, can we see a way in which we could start with the truth about coinherent indwelling of persons, and move from there to see how it makes sense that the persons would know one another completely?

We say that it might "make sense" to us. We are not the ones who

1. The distinctions between persons of the Trinity and the full doctrine of the Trinity were not fully revealed in the Old Testament. God reveals himself *progressively* through periods of Old Testament history. But when we look back at Genesis 1:2 from the standpoint of the fuller revelation about the Trinity in the New Testament, we can see that Genesis 1:2 anticipates the knowledge we now have about the Holy Spirit.

2. John Owen, *Communion with the Triune God*, ed. Kelly M. Kapic and Justin Taylor (Wheaton, IL: Crossway, 2007), 105–6.

3. See also chapters 10 and 29 below, and the more thorough discussion of the nature of logic in Vern S. Poythress, *Logic: A God-Centered Approach to the Foundation of Western Thought* (Wheaton, IL: Crossway, 2013).

determine who God is or how the persons of the Trinity relate to one another. God, not humanity, is the all-controlling determiner. But when we receive from God knowledge about himself, we can still trace some connections. We can see how one truth reinforces another or one truth leads naturally to another. If we describe the process as "deducing" one truth from another, we run the risk of suggesting that one truth can be used in isolation, or that it can be used to "control" who God is. So we will use other terms. One truth *leads* naturally to another and one truth *reinforces* another. The reinforcement takes place within a human context, where we acknowledge that our grasp of truth is limited and derivative from God. We are continually guided by and informed by the full revelation of God in the whole of Scripture.

Within this context, does it make sense to travel from coinherence in indwelling to coinherence in exhaustive knowledge? Does one lead naturally to the other? Does one truth reinforce the other? Yes. A precedent for this kind of reasoning seems to be present in 1 Corinthians 2:10–11:

> For the Spirit searches everything, even the depths of God. For who knows a person's thoughts except the spirit of that person, which is in him? So also no one comprehends the thoughts of God except the Spirit of God.

The text uses an analogy between the spirit of a human being and the Spirit of God. For a human being, the spirit of the person "is in him." By being in him, the spirit "knows a person's thoughts." The expression "so also" that begins the last sentence in 1 Corinthians 2:11 indicates that there is an analogy between a human person and God. The analogy would then lead to the conclusion that because the Spirit of God is *in* God, the Spirit "comprehends the thoughts of God." That is to say, indwelling in the fullness of the Trinity (being "in God") reinforces fullness of knowledge. What is true of the Spirit is also true of the other persons of the Trinity. In sum, coinherence in indwelling leads us naturally to coinherence in knowledge. We see the connection between the two kinds of coinherence, not from one verse alone (1 Cor. 2:11), treated as if it were isolated, but from this verse when understood in harmony with the rest of the Bible.

We can also reason in the reverse direction, from knowledge to indwelling. Consider the word *except* in 1 Corinthians 2:11a: "*except* the spirit of that person." The key word *except* shows that *only* what dwells in a person can know his thoughts thoroughly. So knowing the thoughts implies dwelling in the person. The second half of verse 11 applies the principle to the Holy Spirit. Only someone dwelling in God can know the depths of God. That is, if someone knows the depths of God, he can have that knowledge only because he is dwelling in God. Hence, with respect to God, having knowledge leads to indwelling. So coinherence in knowledge leads to coinherence in indwelling.

Similarly, it seems natural to say that the presence of each person *in* the other persons means participation in the works of each person. So we infer that the works of God involve all three persons. Coinherence in indwelling leads to coinherence in power.

If the works of God are works that coherently involve all three persons, the three persons must be present to one another for the sake of coherence in the work. So mutual involvement of the persons in the work of God—coinherence in power—leads to coinherence in indwelling.

Now let us try to reason from coinherence in power to coinherence in knowledge. The three persons work together harmoniously in the works of God. If knowledge is a necessary prerequisite for the wise work of God, mutual involvement of the persons of the Trinity in the work of God reinforces the idea that there is mutual involvement in knowledge. That is to say, coinherence in power leads to coinherence in knowledge.

Now we consider how to move from coinherence in knowledge to coinherence in power. It does not seem to be quite as simple. If we consider knowledge on a human level, sharing knowledge does not always lead to cooperation in specific works. But we can move from one to the other if we put in an intermediate step. One way of doing it is through coinherence in indwelling. We argued earlier that coinherence in knowledge leads to coinherence in indwelling. And coinherence in indwelling leads to coinherence in power. So by using these two truths together, we see that coinherence in knowledge leads to coinherence in power.

Another way of arriving at the same conclusion is to use love as an intermediate step. In the case of God, knowledge among the persons of the Trinity implies love. To know God as he ought to be known is also to love him. And the same is true of the distinct persons of the Trinity. So coinherence in knowledge leads to coinherence in love, in which the persons of the Trinity all love one another with perfect and infinite love. Love implies desire to cooperate, and so coinherence in love leads to mutual participation in the work of God, that is, coinherence in power.

Coinherence and Deity

All these kinds of coinherence are consistent with the fact that each person is fully God. If the Son is fully God, he has the omnipresence of God. He therefore is present to the other persons by indwelling. If the Son is fully God, he has the fullness of knowledge of God. He therefore knows the other persons completely. If the Son is fully God, he has the omnipotence of God. And God's omnipotence involves not only his ability to control, but actual involvement in control. So the Son is involved in all the works of God, in harmony with the other persons of the Trinity. The same reasoning holds for each person of the Trinity. Deity leads to coinherence in all three aspects—coinherence in indwelling, coinherence in knowledge, and coinherence in power.

Conversely, coinherence reinforces deity. Only God knows God fully. Since the Son uniquely knows the Father, according to Matthew 11:27, he has knowledge in divine fullness, showing that he is himself divine. The comprehensive knowledge that the Holy Spirit has, according to 1 Corinthians 2:10–11, leads to the conclusion that the Spirit has knowledge in divine fullness, and therefore he is himself divine.

Perspectives on Coinherence

Altogether, the Bible offers three perspectives on Trinitarian coinherence: coinherence in indwelling, coinherence in knowledge, and coinherence in power. These three perspectives articulate one reality: the reality of coinherence. They can rightly be called *perspectives* because they represent examples of thematic perspectives (chap. 4). Each starts with a distinct theme: indwelling, knowledge, or power. Each uses this starting theme to look at the same reality of coinherence. Moreover, each perspective *includes* the other two. When we reflect on one, we see that it involves the other two. It presupposes the other two as truths already in the background, so to speak. And it reinforces the other two.

We can summarize some of the relations among these three

perspectives with several points, analogous to what we have seen with earlier instances of perspectives:

1. There is only one reality of coinherence because there is only one God.

2. The three perspectives on coinherence are distinct because each one starts with a distinct theme.

3. What stands out about coinherence varies subtly, depending on which perspective serves as our starting point for reflection.

4. Each perspective on coinherence is fully present to the other two perspectives, so that it implies the others.

5. Each perspective indwells the others. It is already there in the idea of coinherence, and we can perceive it by using one starting perspective on coinherence.

As in chapter 5, we can observe that these features look similar to the features belonging to the persons of the Trinity. Is this similarity merely an accident? If not, how do we explain it? We will have to travel further before considering these questions directly. (See Appendix J.)

For the moment, we may stop to stand in awe of the mystery of God in the mystery of the Trinity. There is a wonderful harmony about coinherence. We can appreciate this harmony, but we do not know it comprehensively. Only God knows himself comprehensively.

Key Terms

coinherence[4]
coinherence in indwelling
coinherence in knowledge
coinherence in power
exhaustive knowledge
indwelling

4. Key terms in **bold** are defined in the glossary at the end of this volume.

Study Questions

1. What is the doctrine of coinherence?
2. Which verses indicate that the persons of the Trinity indwell one another?
3. Besides the language of "dwelling" and being "in" a person, what other kinds of expressions indicate the close relation of the persons of the Trinity to one another?
4. How can different expressions of coinherence be seen as perspectives?
5. In what ways is the doctrine of coinherence a practical doctrine? (Hint: see John 15:7; 17:21–23.)

For Further Reading

Frame, John M. *The Doctrine of God*. Phillipsburg, NJ: P&R Publishing, 2002. Pp. 693–94. On coinherence.

8

Analogies for Relations in the Trinity

WE SURVEYED IN chapter 6 some of the biblical passages that teach the Trinitarian character of God. The Bible also contains passages that give more specific pictures of the relations among the persons of the Trinity. As usual, these pictures give us real knowledge, but not exhaustive knowledge. God uses analogies that compare him to significant things and processes that belong to the created world. All of Scripture is relevant for helping us to understand the relations among the persons of the Trinity. For simplicity, we focus on three main analogies in the Bible that involve all three persons of the Trinity: an analogy with communication, an analogy with a family, and an analogy with images or reflections. Let us consider these, one at a time.

The Analogy with Communication

One analogy used in the Bible is the analogy with communication. The Son is called "The Word of God":

> He is clothed in a robe dipped in blood, and the name by which he is called is *The Word of God*. (Rev. 19:13)

> In the beginning was *the Word*, and the Word was with God, and the Word was God. (John 1:1)

Both verses designate the second person of the Trinity as "the Word." This designation implies that there is someone who speaks this Word. By implication, the speaker is God the Father.

The verses compare God's speech with the speech of human beings. The comparison involves an analogy. God's speech is analogous to human speech. Human beings are made "in the image of God" (Gen. 1:27), so it should not be surprising that this analogy using speech or communication is valid and has an important function in God's instruction to us.

Is the Holy Spirit involved? He is not directly mentioned either in John 1:1 or in Revelation 19:13. But he clearly has a place in the larger context of the Gospel of John and the book of Revelation. In both books, the statement that Jesus is the Word of God does not stand in isolation, but has relationships to many places where Jesus is the witness and proclaimer of the truth of God. He does this proclamation in the power of the Holy Spirit. The Spirit is the power that brings the proclamation to its destination.

For example, in John 3 Jesus says:

> Unless one is born of water and *the Spirit,* he cannot enter the kingdom of God. That which is born of the flesh is flesh, and that which is born of the Spirit is spirit. (John 3:5–6)

Jesus indicates that Nicodemus does not yet understand the things of the Spirit (John 3:10). It is the Spirit that gives new birth, and in new birth he provides new understanding of the things of God, including the meaning of Jesus' work of redemption. This giving of new birth and new understanding is the way in which the Spirit works in power to bring Jesus' verbal proclamation to bear on those who will be saved. In addition, the Spirit sent by Jesus guides the disciples into the truth (16:13). The Spirit "will teach you all things and bring to your remembrance all that I have said to you" (14:26). The Spirit takes the message from Jesus and applies it to the hearts of the disciples, enabling them to remember and to understand.

A similar work of the Holy Spirit occurs in the book of Revelation. In Revelation 2–3 we find the repeated refrain, "He who has an ear, let him hear what the *Spirit* says to the churches" (2:7, 11, 17, 29; 3:6, 13, 22). The messages to the seven churches are messages from Christ. They are identified as such by an introductory expression, "The words of him who holds the seven stars in his right hand" (2:1), or an analogous expression (2:8, 12, 18; 3:1, 7, 14). The Spirit brings the words of Christ to bear on the recipients. In fact, we know from Romans 8:15 and Galatians 4:6

that the Spirit stands *with* believers in teaching them to respond to the gospel with the cry, "Abba! Father!" Believers confess their adoption as sons because the Spirit empowers them and enlightens them.

The Spirit speaks to us, but only because he has heard and understood the things of God:

> These things God has revealed to us *through the Spirit*. For the Spirit *searches* everything, even the depths of God. For who knows a person's thoughts except the spirit of that person, which is in him? So also no one comprehends the thoughts of God except the Spirit of God. Now we have received not the spirit of the world, but the Spirit who is from God, that we might *understand* the things freely given us by God. (1 Cor. 2:10–12)

The Spirit has heard what belongs to the Father and the Son:

> When the Spirit of truth comes, he will guide you into all the truth, for he will not speak on his own authority, but whatever he *hears* he will speak, and he will declare to you the things that are to come. He will glorify me, for he will *take* what is mine and declare it to you. All that the Father has is mine; therefore I said that he will take what is mine and declare it to you. (John 16:13–15)

In divine communication, the Spirit is the recipient of the word of God. God the Father speaks through the Word, and the Spirit speaks what he has first heard and received from the Father and the Son.

We also find passages where the Holy Spirit is compared to the *breath* of God bringing the word of God to fruition. In Ezekiel 37:1–14, God gives Ezekiel a vision of a valley of dry bones. The bones represent "the whole house of Israel" (v. 11). He tells Ezekiel to "prophesy to the *breath*; prophesy, son of man" (v. 9). Then breath comes into the bones and makes them live (v. 10). In verse 14, the life-giving breath is identified as "my Spirit." The word for "Spirit" and "breath" is the same Hebrew word, *ruach*. Thus, the name *Spirit* for the Holy Spirit has a close tie to this analogy with communication from God. The Holy Spirit participates in divine communication in a way analogous to human breath in human communication. (See fig. 8.1.)

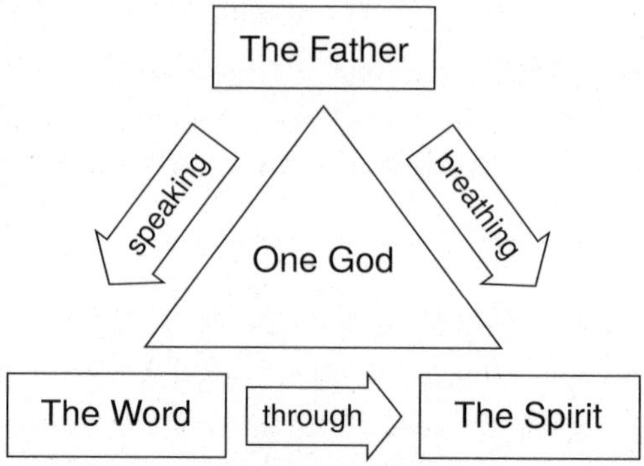

Fig. 8.1. The Analogy with Communication

Figure 8.1 should be seen as a summary of some of the main ways that the Bible represents the origin of God's speech. But since the persons of the Trinity indwell one another, the various aspects of divine communication are not isolated from one another. As we saw earlier, in John 1:1 God the Father speaks the Word. But later on in John, the Father speaks to the Son (12:49), and the Son speaks to the Father (17:1–26). The Father and the Son speak to the Spirit (16:13–15). The Spirit speaks to the Father (Rom. 8:15, 26–27). Jesus *breathes* on the disciples to impart the Holy Spirit (John 20:22). The richness in personal relations among persons of the Trinity cannot be captured by any simple diagram. Figure 8.1 represents a summary of *some* of the fundamental relations. These relations are also reflected in particular acts of communication among persons of the Trinity.

So figure 8.1 must not be understood as *excluding* other instances of communication. Each person communicates with words and breathlike power to each of the other persons, and to us as well. (See fig. 8.2.) Each person speaks to the other persons in the Trinity. Each person speaks to us when we receive the Word of God in Scripture. And we speak to each person when we pray, since we address God and each person in the Trinity is God.

Focus on Persons in Their Distinctiveness

We should still note something special about the key verses John 1:1 and Revelation 19:13 with which we started. Both verses identify the Son as "the Word" of God. This identification shows that the Son has

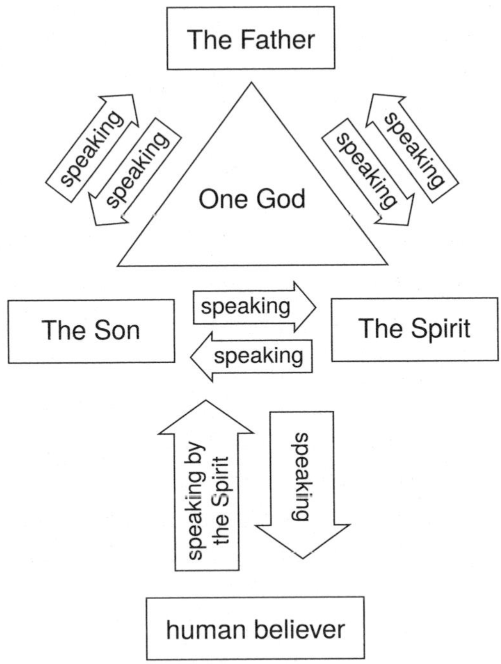

Fig. 8.2. Rich Communication in the Persons of the Trinity

a unique function in relation to the Father. He is "the Word" that the Father speaks. Similarly, the verses comparing the Spirit to the breath of God show a unique function of the Spirit. These unique functions show a differentiation in the ways that the three persons participate in divine communication. By differentiating distinct functions, verses such as John 1:1 go beyond what we observe in figure 8.2, where the functions of the persons are not directly differentiated. As figure 8.2 reminds us, it is indeed true that the Father, the Son, and the Spirit speak. These truths apply to all three persons. But they do not reveal by themselves what *distinguishes* one person from another, that is, what feature holds true for one person and *not* for the other two persons, at least not in the same way.

In our discussion we are interested in the distinctiveness of the persons, and not merely in what they share. So in our subsequent discussion we will customarily use the analogy with communication as an analogy that reveals the distinctiveness of persons. That is, we will use the analogy to think about the Father as the speaker and the Son as the Word;

we will not use it to stress the principle, true though it is, that all three persons can speak to one another and to human beings.

The analogy with breath is not far from the analogy in which the Holy Spirit receives the message from the Father and the Son. In human communication, breath is the medium and the power that brings human speech to its destination in the hearer. In Ezekiel, the breath also has the power to bring people to new spiritual life. The Holy Spirit receives the message from God in order to bring life, the life of new birth in the Spirit.

This analogy with communication has a practical bearing on Christian living. Christians receive God's Word and hear God speaking when they read the Bible, which is the Word of God. This practical experience involves all three persons of the Trinity. God the Father is the preeminent speaker. God the Son, our Lord Jesus Christ, is above all present in the content of the message. God the Holy Spirit dwells in us to enable us to understand what the Father says (1 Cor. 2:14–15). This experience of receiving the Word of God reflects the original communication among the persons of the Trinity.

The Analogy with a Family

A second analogy used in the Bible is the analogy with a family. The Gospel of John often designates the first person of the Trinity as "the Father," and the second person of the Trinity as "the Son." This language indicates that the relation of the Father to the Son is analogous to the relation between a human father and a human son.

It is analogous, but obviously not identical. Human fathers become fathers by a biological process of procreation. God is God and does not have a body and does not biologically procreate. Human sons come into existence at a certain point in time. The divine Son always existed (John 1:1). These are some of the obvious differences.

But there are also similarities, or else the analogy between divine fatherhood and human fatherhood would not be appropriate. Good human fathers love their sons. God the Father loves his Son: "The Father loves the Son and has given all things into his hand" (John 3:35; cf. 5:20). Human fathers speak to their sons; the divine Father speaks to his Son: "For I have given them [the disciples] the *words* that you gave me" (John 17:8). Human fathers send their sons to do certain tasks; the heavenly Father "sent forth his Son" (Gal. 4:4).

Does the Holy Spirit participate in this analogy with a family? He does. One key passage is found in John 3:34–35:

> For he [the Son] whom God has sent utters the words of God, for he gives *the Spirit* without measure. The Father loves the Son and has given all things into his hand.

To whom does God give the Spirit in verse 34? To human beings? No, that idea, though true, does not fit the immediate context. The giving in verse 34 is closely related to the giving in verse 35: God "has given all things into his hand." The Father gives the Spirit to the Son. This interpretation is confirmed by the final expression in verse 34, "without measure." We who believe in Christ do receive the Holy Spirit from Christ, but we receive the Spirit only in a measure. Christ is unique in having the Spirit "without measure." What we receive is "measured" by the finality of what Christ possesses (Eph. 4:7).

John 3:35 indicates that this giving is an expression of the family love between the Father and the Son. So the Holy Spirit expresses family love.

In sum, within the Trinity, the Father is the initiator in love. The Son is the recipient of love. And the Holy Spirit given by the Father is the expression of the Father's love. These relations in love within the Trinity are analogous to loving relations within a human family. We can call this analogy for the Trinity the *analogy with a family* or the *love analogy*. It is both. (See fig. 8.3.)

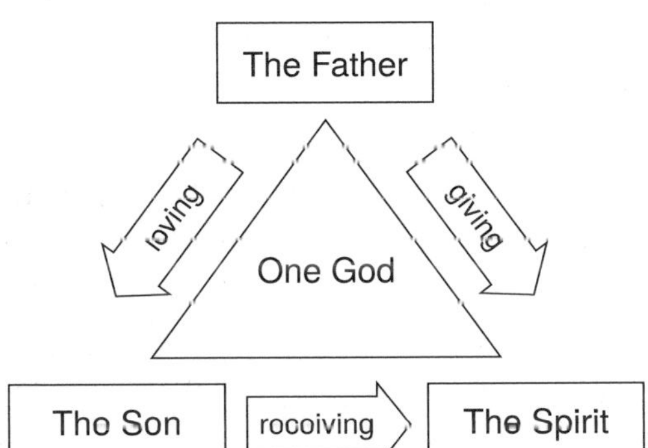

Fig. 8.3. The Analogy with a Family or Love Analogy

We can observe here a similarity to what we saw in the analogy with communication. Figure 8.3 summarizes one of the main ways that the Bible talks about relations among the persons of the Trinity. But it does not exclude other relations that involve loving and giving. Each person of the Trinity loves each of the other two persons, and gives as an expression of love. The love that we receive from God as human beings is an expression of the original love within God. (See fig. 8.4.)

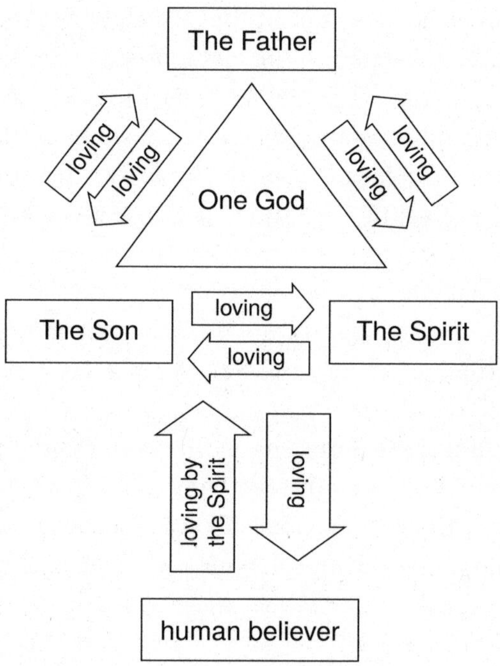

Fig. 8.4. Rich Relations Expressing Love

Love characterizes all three persons of the Trinity. But we can still see something special about verses that use the distinct terms *Father* and *Son* and the verses in John 3:34–35 that give a distinct function to the Holy Spirit as an expression of love. The Father and the Son are not interchangeable. The Father is the Father, and the Son is the Son. They exist in a special relation to each other, in the fellowship of the Holy Spirit. These truths show us a differentiation in the relations and functions of the persons. In this respect, they make a deep contribution; it is different from just observing that all three persons of the Trinity exercise love.

What is true of all three persons does not reveal what *distinguishes* one person from another, that is, what feature holds true for one person and *not* for the other two persons. We are interested in the distinctiveness of the persons, and not merely in what they share. So in our subsequent discussion, we will customarily use the analogy with a family as an analogy that reveals the distinctiveness of persons. That is, we will use the analogy to think about the Father as the Father and the giver of love, and the Son as the Son and the recipient of the Father's love. We will not use the analogy with a family to stress the principle, true though it is, that all three persons in the Trinity love one another and can give love to human beings.

The analogy with a family has a practical bearing on Christian living. It shows us the ultimate foundation for our *adoption*. The original family relation is the relation between the Father and the Son, a relation that exists eternally. Through Christ the Son, the Father adopts us as sons (Gal. 4:4–5). Our adoption is based in this way on the Trinitarian character of God. As adopted sons, we experience God's fatherly love toward us, through the Holy Spirit: "God's love has been poured into our hearts through the Holy Spirit who has been given to us" (Rom. 5:5).

The Analogy with Reflections

A third analogy is the analogy in which an image reflects an original. According to the Bible, Christ is the image of God the Father:

> The light of the gospel of the glory of Christ, who is the *image* of God. (2 Cor. 4:4)

> He is the *image* of the invisible God, the firstborn of all creation. (Col. 1:15)

> He is the *radiance* of the glory of God and the *exact imprint* of his nature. (Heb. 1:3)

These verses use the word *image* and the closely related expression *exact imprint*. In our own discussion, we will mostly use the words *reflect* and *reflection*, which represent broader conceptions. We choose the broader language because we want to talk about instances of reflection within the created order, as well as the original, uncreated, eternal relation between the Son of God and the Father.

One of the backgrounds in the Old Testament for this language about reflections is the occurrence of *theophanies*, that is, specially appointed appearances of God.[1] A number of these theophanies involve a human form, anticipating the incarnation of Christ. For example, we can see similarities between the description of Christ in his glory in Revelation 1:12–16 and the description of the central manlike figure in Ezekiel 1:26–28 and Daniel 7:9 and the "man" in Daniel 10:5–6. Christ in his incarnation is the permanent visible appearing of God. He reflects the character of God the Father. His permanent appearing is the climax corresponding to the temporary, preliminary appearances in the Old Testament.

So the dialogue with Philip makes sense:

> Philip said to him, "Lord, show us the Father, and it is enough for us." Jesus said to him, "Have I been with you so long, and you still do not know me, Philip? Whoever has *seen* me has *seen* the Father. How can you say, 'Show us the Father'? Do you not believe that I am in the Father and the Father is in me? The words that I say to you I do not speak on my own authority, but the Father who dwells in me does his works." (John 14:8–10)

Does the Holy Spirit participate in theophany and in the process of reflecting God? Theophanies in the Old Testament reflect God by displaying the *glory* of God (Ex. 16:10; 24:16–17; 33:22; 40:34–35; Lev. 9:23; Num. 14:10; etc.). A number of texts associate the Holy Spirit closely with the glory of God:[2]

> If you are insulted for the name of Christ, you are blessed, because the *Spirit* of *glory* and of God rests upon you. (1 Peter 4:14)

1. For a fuller discussion of the ideas of image and theophany, see Vern S. Poythress, *Theophany: A Biblical Theology of God's Appearing* (Wheaton, IL: Crossway, 2018).

2. See further Meredith M. Kline, "The Holy Spirit as Covenant Witness" (Th.M. thesis, Westminster Theological Seminary, 1972); Meredith G. Kline, *Images of the Spirit* (Grand Rapids: Baker, 1980).

Then he remembered the days of old,
    of Moses and his people.
Where is he who brought them up out of the sea
    with the shepherds of his flock?
Where is he who put in the midst of them
    his Holy Spirit,
who caused his glorious arm [Hebrew: arm of his *glory*]
    to go at the right hand of Moses,
who divided the waters before them
    to make for himself an everlasting name . . . ? (Isa. 63:11–12)

The text in Isaiah 63:11 mentions that God "put in the midst of them his Holy Spirit." The reference is probably to the cloud of glory that was in the midst of Israel during the people's wilderness wandering. The cloud of glory covered the tabernacle after it was consecrated (Ex. 40:34–38), and filled Solomon's temple after it was completed (1 Kings 8:10–11). The cloud represented God's presence with his people, and so foreshadowed the coming of the Holy Spirit on the day of Pentecost (Acts 2:2–4).

In Old Testament theophanies, we can see a movement outward. The movement has God himself as its origin. God manifests himself in a theophany, which may include a human shape, as in Ezekiel 1:26. The outward side of theophany shows the glory of God to the human recipient, as in Ezekiel 1:28: "Such was the appearance of the likeness of the *glory* of the LORD." These three stages in movement have connections with the three persons of the Trinity: (1) God the Father is at the origin. (2) God the Son is closely connected with the human appearance, which anticipates the Son's incarnation. (3) God the Holy Spirit is connected with the glory that characterizes the outward display to a human recipient. This pattern has a fulfillment in the New Testament. God the Father sends the Son, who becomes incarnate and displays the Father in visible form (John 14:9). When we are illumined by the Holy Spirit, we see the glory of the Son. The Holy Spirit brings this glory to bear on us (2 Cor. 3:18; 4:6; 1 Peter 4:14). The Son is the image of the Father; the Holy Spirit applies the glory of this image through his presence.

Putting all this information together, we can say that Jesus is the image of the Father and displays the glory of God, in connection with the presence of the Holy Spirit, who displays that glory to us. (See fig. 8.5.)

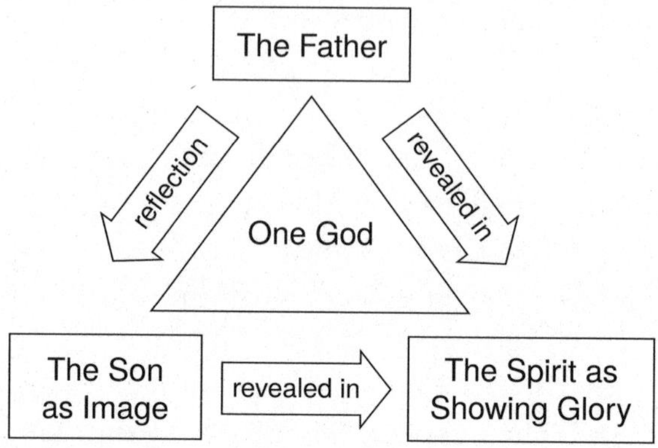

Fig. 8.5. The Analogy with Reflections

When we focus on the Son as image and the Spirit as the manifestation of glory, we do not mean to *exclude* other relations. The glory of God is the glory of the Father, and of the Son, and of the Holy Spirit. Because of the indwelling of persons (coinherence), we cannot confine the glory to the Holy Spirit. Likewise, since the Holy Spirit is God, in a broad sense he displays and reflects both the Father and the Son. When God comes to us, he reveals his glory to us. And when we are transformed into the image of Christ, we ourselves reflect his glory. (See fig. 8.6.)

The special verses that identify Christ as the image of God indicate a differentiation in function among the persons of the Trinity. So they show us something in addition to the general principle that each person in the Trinity displays the glory of God and shows us the character of God.

The analogy with reflections has practical implications. It is closely related to the theme of God's presence. Christ the Son, in his incarnation, is "God with us" (Matt. 1:23). He is God, and by being God he makes God present to human beings. He is the fulfillment of the Old Testament theophanies that were temporary manifestations of God's presence. The theophanies reflected God's character. Christ, who is the image of God and who is God, is the supreme reflection of God—God,

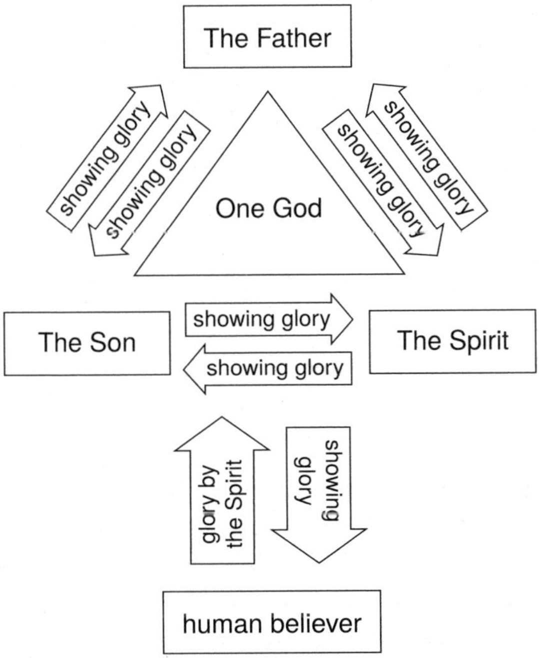

Fig. 8.6. Rich Display of Glory

who has come down to us. The character of Christ is worked in us as the Holy Spirit transforms us into the image of Christ (2 Cor. 3:18).

The Special Character of the Three Analogies

Altogether, we have now considered three analogies for the Trinity: the analogy with communication, the analogy with a family, and the analogy with reflections. In each of the three cases, the analogy at its heart reveals distinct functions for distinct persons of the Trinity. For example, in the analogy with communication, the Father is the speaker and the Son is the speech, that is, the Word. These two—speaker and speech—are not interchangeable. The speaker and the speech are distinct and irreversible.

The Bible uses many analogies in teaching about God. God is the King over all; he is a rock and a fortress and a deliverer (Ps. 18:2). God's compassion to his people is like a father's compassion to his children (103:13). But only a few of these analogies give us insight into *distinctions* between different persons of the Trinity. The three that we have discussed—the analogy with communication, the analogy with a family, and the analogy with reflections—are the main ones.

Analogies in Biblical Context

All these analogies need to be interpreted within the larger context of biblical revelation. All three analogies occur within a larger and richer context of biblical teaching. They are not self-standing, self-contained analogies that exist in isolation. We must not treat them as if they were, nor should we neglect the larger context as though it were merely "secondary" to these primary affirmations.

Consider the analogy with communication. The analogy with communication is clear in two texts that designate the second person of the Trinity as "the Word" or "the Word of God" (John 1:1; Rev. 19:13). These texts fit into a larger context in the Gospel of John and in Revelation where Jesus is the revealer and witness. Hebrews 1:2 has something similar when it says that God "has spoken to us by his Son." But the detailed textures in Hebrews 1:1–2 make a connection between the Son and the prophets who pointed forward to him. Hebrews does not directly identify him as "the Word."

The Holy Spirit is not explicitly mentioned in either of the two key texts (John 1:1; Rev. 19:13). We can coherently add the Holy Spirit to the picture of communication based on *other* texts. But the addition of the Spirit represents a step toward a *synthesis* of several texts. Such a synthesis is justified, but it inevitably leaves things out as well as highlighting others. We should respect the fact that the Bible has a certain restraint in its discussions of the Holy Spirit. The Holy Spirit glorifies the Father and the Son, rather than himself, so much of the teaching in the New Testament focuses more on the Father and the Son than on the Spirit as such. Our analogy with communication makes *explicit* the way in which the Spirit participates. That represents a difference in comparison to the two main starting texts in the Bible (John 1:1; Rev. 19:13).

Similar observations hold for the other two analogies. Two texts directly identify the second person of the Trinity as the image of God (2 Cor. 4:4; Col. 1:15), and Hebrews 1:3 has the closely related expression "the exact imprint of his nature." Philippians 2:6 talks about Christ's being "in the form of God," a related expression. But none of these passages mentions the Holy Spirit directly. We have to synthesize the import of several passages to see how the Holy Spirit is implicitly present in the idea of reflecting God's character.

In the analogy with a family, the Holy Spirit is mentioned in John 3:34 as the gift of the Father's love. But other texts that use aspects related to the analogy with a family have their own textures. There are many of these texts. Any summary will not capture everything.

Robert Letham observes the richness:

> Overall, the Bible paints a complex picture of the relations of the Spirit to the Father and to the Son. . . . The Holy Spirit hears the Father, receives from the Father, takes from the Son and makes it known to the church, proceeds from the Father, is sent by the Father in the name of the Son, is sent by the Son from the Father, rests on the Son, speaks of the Son, and glorifies the Son. The relation between the Spirit and the Son is not one-directional, but mutual and reciprocal.[3]

Key Terms

adoption[4]
analogy
analogy with a family
analogy with communication
analogy with reflections
breath
communication
family
father
hearing
image
incarnation
love
original
reflection
son
theophany

3. Robert Letham, *The Holy Trinity: In Scripture, History, Theology, and Worship* (Phillipsburg, NJ: P&R Publishing, 2004), 204.

4. Key terms in **bold** are defined in the glossary at the end of this volume.

Study Questions

1. How are the relations among the persons of the Trinity illustrated by human speech? What principal texts affirm this analogy?
2. How are the relations among the persons of the Trinity illustrated by a human family? What principal texts affirm this analogy?
3. How are the relations among the persons of the Trinity illustrated by a pattern and its image or reflection? Which principal texts affirm this analogy?
4. How do all the persons of the Trinity actively communicate? love? show glory?

For Further Reading

Köstenberger, Andreas J., and Scott R. Swain. *Father, Son, and Spirit: The Trinity and John's Gospel.* Nottingham, England: Apollos; Downers Grove, IL: InterVarsity Press, 2008. Includes a discussion of Trinitarian analogies used in the Gospel of John.

Owen, John. *Communion with the Triune God.* Edited by Kelly M. Kapic and Justin Taylor. Wheaton, IL: Crossway, 2007. An older work expounding the distinct communion that a Christian has with each of the three persons of the Trinity.

Poythress, Vern S. *Theophany: A Biblical Theology of God's Appearing.* Wheaton, IL: Crossway, 2018. Chaps. 16–17. A discussion of the relation of Christ, the image of God, to theophanies.

9

Comparing Analogies for the Trinity

WE MAY NOW compare the three main analogies for personal relations in the Trinity, and see how they reinforce one another.

The Principle of Limited Knowledge and the Importance of Biblical Context

As usual, we must exercise care. We have to respect that our knowledge of the Trinity is derivative and limited. At the same time, God has given us knowledge through the many specific passages in the Bible. And when he saves us, he gives us actual personal experience of fellowship with him. We experience salvation, adoption, verbal communication, personal intimacy, and prayer. All these experiences take place because God comes to us in harmony with his Trinitarian nature. Based on what God tells us in the Bible, and illustrated by our experience, we can see that there are appropriate, suitable relationships between the three distinct analogies. We can make sense of how one analogy reinforces others. We explore these reinforcements not by pretending to master God through would-be autonomous reasoning, but by admiring and adoring the mystery of God's character (as we said at the end of chapter 7).

So in gratitude to God, who has revealed himself, we may explore how one analogy may lead to the others and reinforce the others.

From the Analogy with a Family to the Analogy with Reflections, and Back

We begin with the analogy with a family. On a human level, a son is like his father. Adam "fathered a son in his own *likeness*, after his *image*, and named him Seth" (Gen. 5:3). Included in sonship is the idea that the son is an image of his father. When we apply this insight to God, we see that the analogy with a family leads to the idea of reflection. In analogy with the fact that a human son reflects his human father, on the divine level the Son reflects his Father. Thus, the analogy with a family reinforces the analogy with reflections.

Now suppose that we start with the analogy with reflections. The second person of the Trinity is the image of the first. Since the first is a person, it makes sense that the second is also a person, reflecting the personhood of the first. God has within himself the original relation of one person's reflecting another, because the Son reflects the Father. The instances of reflection that take place among human beings are reflections of that original. In particular, the relation between Adam the father and Seth the son is a reflection of the original divine relation of reflection between the Father and the Son. If so, the *divine* relation of reflection is the origin for the human relation of father and son. The original pattern for human fathers and sons is in God; it does not merely have an ultimate origin in human beings. Thus, God the Father and God the Son are the original or *archetypal* Father and Son. The Father and the Son have an eternal relation that God helped us to understand by creating human fathers and sons. Adam and Seth are derivative father and son. The derivative pattern is called an *ectype*. Thus, we have traveled from the analogy with reflections to the analogy with a family.

From the Analogy with Communication to the Analogy with Reflections, and Back

Next, let us start with the analogy with communication. The Father is the speaker and the Son is his Word. Since God is truthful, the Word of God actually expresses the very character and mind of the Father. That is, in his *expression* of the original, the Word is the image of the Father and reflects the Father. So the analogy with communication leads naturally to the analogy with reflections. Now consider the Holy Spirit. With respect to the analogy with communication, the Holy Spirit carries the divine communication to its destiny. Does this work of the Holy Spirit correspond to a similar work in the context of theophany, that is, the context of God's reflecting his character? In theophany, the Spirit represented by the cloud of glory carries to its destiny the presence of God manifested in the Son. So the work of the Spirit in communication reinforces his work in theophany.

Can we move in the opposite direction, from the analogy with reflections to the analogy with communication? The analogy with reflections is illustrated in theophanies. Theophanies *tell* us about God through visual display. Verbal communication is another form of telling about God. In theophany, an appearance of a human shape foreshadows how the Son tells us about the Father. Similarly, in the context of verbal communication the Son as the Word expresses the character of the Father. So the analogy with reflections in theophany reinforces the analogy with communication.

From the Analogy with Communication to the Analogy with a Family, and Back

Can we move from the analogy with communication to the analogy with a family? Since God is love, his love will be expressed through his speech. God's speech is full of his love. This presence of love is true of the eternal Word. Since God is love, the *relation* between God and the Word will also be full of love. So we are led to see that there is a loving relation between God the Father and his Word. This rich personal relation implies an analogy between God and the human father-son relationship. So we may move from communication to the analogy with a family.

Or we may start with the analogy with a family. Can we move from there to the analogy with communication? The Father loves the Son. Love includes within its scope the expression of love, and expression of the meaning of love. So it is natural for it to find expression also in the verbal sphere. The Father in loving the Son *communicates* his love to the Son. The Son himself is then the expression of the meaning of the Father's love, and so it is natural to see the Son as the expression of the Father or as the Word of God.

Interlocking Perspectives

The three analogies offer three thematic *perspectives* on the relations among the persons of the Trinity. The starting themes are (1) communication, leading to the communication perspective; (2) the family, leading to the family perspective; and (3) reflection, leading to the reflection perspective. These three are naturally in harmony because there is only one God, who is in harmony with himself. His revelation of himself uses these analogies to express the inner harmony of who he is. (See fig. 9.1.)

We also experience harmony when God comes to save us. He

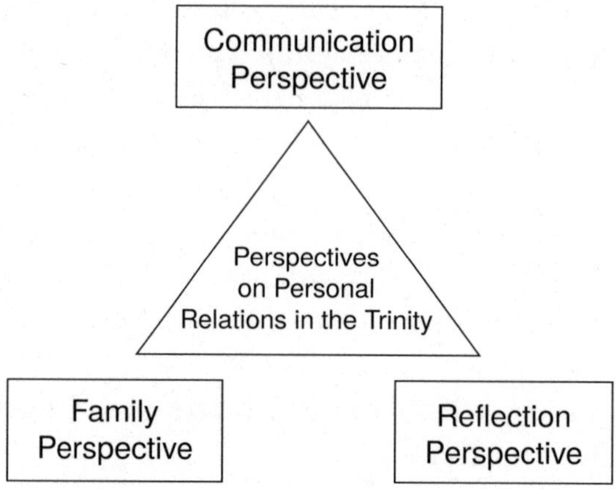

Fig. 9.1. Perspectives on Relations in the Trinity

communicates to us verbally in the gospel, based on the analogy with communication. He gives his love to us and adopts us, based on the analogy with a family. He comes to be present with us and in us, based on the analogy with reflections. All these three kinds of action cohere because God's work with us is consistent and harmonious.

We may summarize these three perspectives or analogies with points similar to what we have seen in earlier chapters:

1. There is only one reality of personal relations in the Trinity because there is only one God.

2. The three perspectives on personal relations in the Trinity are distinct because each one starts with a distinct theme (communication, family love, or reflection).

3. What stands out about relations in the Trinity varies subtly, depending on which perspective serves as our starting point for reflection.

4. Each perspective on relations is fully present to the other two perspectives, so that it implicitly includes the others.

5. Each perspective indwells the others. It is already there in the idea of relations in the Trinity, and we can perceive it by using one starting perspective on relations.

We have here a wonderful harmony among the three main analogies or perspectives for Trinitarian relations. As usual, this pattern of perspectives has similarities to the pattern that we see in the relations among persons of the Trinity. Once again it raises the question whether the pattern *derives* from the Trinity.

A Fourth Analogy: The Analogy of Carrying Out the Work of God

Theologians have explored another analogy for Trinitarian action, namely, an analogy based on the working out of the history of redemption. God the Father is the planner of redemption and of all of history. God the Son is the executor. And God the Holy Spirit is the sanctifier and consummator.[1] It has been suggested that 1 Peter 1:2 is relevant:

> according to the *foreknowledge* of God the Father, in the *sanctification* of the Spirit, for obedience to Jesus Christ and for *sprinkling* with his blood.

The foreknowledge of God the Father is closely related to his activity in planning redemption. Jesus Christ executes the plan by accomplishing redemption in his life, death, and resurrection. This accomplishment of redemption is alluded to in the phrase "sprinkling with his blood." And the Holy Spirit is mentioned as the sanctifier.

There does seem to be a movement involving distinct functions for the persons of the Trinity. The New Testament repeatedly uses language about the Father's *sending* the Son. This language suggests that the Father is the planner and the Son is the executor. Other passages indicate the intimate involvement of the Holy Spirit in the application of Christ's accomplished redemption to believers and to the church. Christ *sends* the Spirit to his disciples so that they receive redemption and its benefits (John 15:26).

Moreover, the consummation of all things in the new heaven and the new earth includes the consummate presence of the glory of God in Christ (Rev. 21:23; 22:5). The glory of God, displayed in the consummation, is closely linked to the Holy Spirit, as is the theme of the

1. John M. Frame, *The Doctrine of God* (Phillipsburg, NJ: P&R Publishing, 2002), 694.

presence of God. So we can say that the Holy Spirit is associated with the work of consummation. More broadly, in sanctification the Holy Spirit applies the work accomplished by the Son.

This distribution of functions for the three persons of the Trinity needs qualification. As we indicated earlier, all the works of God in creation, providence, redemption, and consummation involve all three persons of the Trinity. Planning, execution, sanctification, and consummation involve all three persons, not just one. We can easily see this involvement in the consummation, because Revelation 21:23 says that the "glory of God" (that is, the glory of God the Father) gives the city light and that "its lamp is the Lamb" (God the Son). God the Father and God the Son clearly have significant participation in the meaning of the consummation and the display of the glory of God. The same holds for Revelation 22:1, in which the throne is "the throne of God and of the Lamb" and "the river of the water of life" may symbolize the Holy Spirit's proceeding from the Father and the Son, in harmony with the identification of the Spirit as "living water" in John 7:37–39.

We may still affirm an association of God the Father with planning, God the Son with executing, and God the Spirit with application, sanctification, and consummation. But we should say that this association is a matter of prominence of one person of the Trinity with respect to a particular activity. We do *not* imply that the other persons do not participate in the activity. If we wish, we can call this analogy the *action analogy*, and summarize it in a diagram (fig. 9.2).

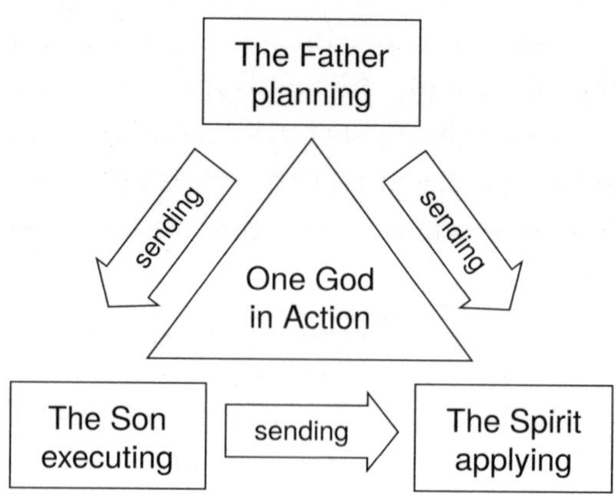

Fig. 9.2. The Action Analogy for the Trinity

Since the activities of planning, executing, and applying are all actions of one God, it is also true that all three persons are mysteriously involved in all three phases of activity. (See fig. 9.3.)

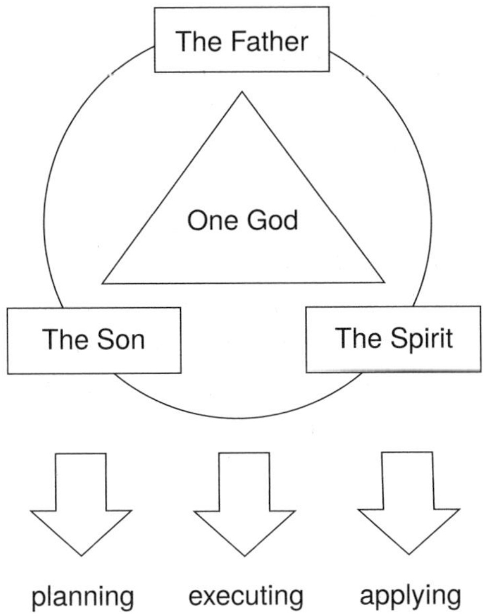

Fig. 9.3. Rich Divine Activity

We can provide another kind of summary of God's work, coming from John Owen. Owen reflected extensively on the distinct functions of the Father, the Son, and the Holy Spirit in our communion with God. He provides this summary of the distinctions in communion with each person:

> The Father does it [gives communion] by the way of *original authority*; the Son by the way of communicating from a *purchased treasury*; the Holy Spirit by the way of *immediate efficacy*.[2]

This way of explaining it makes clear the fact that we are not dealing with three distinct works, separated in time from one another, but rather one

2. John Owen, *Communion with the Triune God*, ed. Kelly M. Kapic and Justin Taylor (Wheaton, IL: Crossway, 2007), 104 (italics original).

work of giving communion. In this work, the Father, the Son, and the Holy Spirit participate in distinct ways.[3] And as Owen goes on to say in the same book, our response in communion includes a distinct relation to each of the three persons.

How should we classify this fourth analogy, the action analogy? I have chosen *not* to consider this fourth analogy as completely like the first three. For one thing, as an analogy it does not mainly focus on the *relations* among persons of the Trinity. Rather, it focuses on God's activity in carrying out his purposes in history. In God's work in history, a unique function belongs to one person, and then another unique function belongs to the second person, and another to the third. Second, this analogy is somewhat vaguer than the rest, because it does not become so clearly visible in any one passage (though Romans 8:11 and 1 Peter 1:2 come close). Rather, it becomes visible primarily through synthesizing the contents of many texts.[4]

This analogy has practical implications. When we are saved, all three persons of the Trinity are involved in powerful action. This action includes planning, execution, and application.

A third reason for considering this analogy to be of a different kind has to do with what kind of divine activity it explains. It explains divine activity *in the world*, activity in history working out God's plan in time.

3. Note also Owen's important qualification to all his reflections:

> First, when I assign any thing as *peculiar* wherein we distinctly hold communion with any person, I do not exclude the other persons from communion with the soul in the very same thing. Only this, I say, *principally*, in such a way, and by the way of eminency....
>
> Second, there is a concurrence of the *actings* and operations of the whole Deity in that *dispensation*, wherein each person concurs to the work of our salvation, unto every *act* of our communion with each singular person. (Ibid., 105–6 [italics original])

4. Even in the immediate context of Owen's summary statement, given above, he provides several supporting texts. For the Father's agency: John 5:21; 14:26; 15:26; James 1:18. For the Son's: Isa. 53:10–11; Matt. 28:18; John 1:16; 5:25–27; Phil. 2:8–11; Col. 1:19. For the Holy Spirit's: Rom. 8:11.

The last verse, Romans 8:11, does contain a reference to the distinct agencies of all three persons of the Trinity: "If the *Spirit* of *him* who raised *Jesus* from the dead dwells in you, *he* who raised *Christ Jesus* from the dead will also give life to your mortal bodies through his *Spirit* who dwells in you." Owen comments:

> Here is the Father's authoritative quickening ("He raised Christ from the dead, and he shall quicken you"), and the Son's mediatory quickening (for it is done in "the death of Christ"), and the Spirit's immediate efficacy ("He shall do it by the Spirit that dwells in you"). (Ibid., 104)

The three main analogies that we already explored in chapter 8 do have illustrations in history, but they also describe eternal relations between persons of the Trinity. For example, the Son is eternally the Word in relation to God the Father. His function as the Word is before the creation of the world. "In the *beginning* was the Word" (John 1:1). In addition, the Father eternally loves the Son. The Son is eternally the "exact imprint" of his nature (Heb. 1:3). By contrast, execution and application are activities that take place in time. The planning of God is eternal, but we see the planning through execution and application. God's acts in time do show something about who God is, and about the persons of the Trinity, but they show it *through* the interaction of God with the created world. That way of reflecting the Trinity is not on the same level as the analogy with communication, the analogy with a family, and the analogy with reflections.

Relationship between the Action Analogy and the Analogy with a Family

Finally, the action analogy is close to being a kind of reexpression of the analogy with a family or of the analogy with communication when either of these is applied to God's work in history. Let us first consider the analogy with a family. The passages in John that mention the Father's love for the Son and the giving of the Holy Spirit have a close relationship to the accomplishment of redemption. Let us consider this tie between love and redemptive accomplishment.

In the key verse in John 3:34, the giving of the Spirit by the Father has a particular purpose. The Spirit is active in the work of Christ, as Christ accomplishes the work for which the Father sent him. The gift of the Holy Spirit does not result in immediate rest for Christ, but rather activity. We can see this activity in the first part of John 3:34: "he whom God has sent *utters* the words of God." This description points to the rest of the Gospel of John, and indeed to all of Jesus' ministry, because Jesus speaks to us. He speaks "the words of God," and he does this speaking in the power of the Holy Spirit. His speech leads to the response of believing in him and having life: "Whoever believes in the Son has eternal life" (3:36).

Other passages confirm this picture. In Luke, Jesus indicates that he has received the Holy Spirit for the purpose of accomplishing God's redemptive work:

> The *Spirit* of the Lord is upon me,
> because he has anointed me
> to proclaim good news to the poor.
> He has sent me to proclaim liberty to the captives
> and recovering of sight to the blind,
> to set at liberty those who are oppressed,
> to proclaim the year of the Lord's favor. (Luke 4:18–19, quoting
> Isa. 61:1–2)

A similar participation by the Holy Spirit is seen at Pentecost:

> Being therefore exalted at the right hand of God, and having *received* from the Father the promise of *the Holy Spirit,* he [Christ] has *poured out this* that you yourselves are seeing and hearing. (Acts 2:33)

In John 5:20–21, the family love between the Father and the Son is the basis for the Son's miraculous work:

> For the Father *loves* the Son and shows him all that he himself is doing. And greater *works* than these will he show him, so that you may marvel. For as the Father raises the dead and gives them life, so also the Son *gives life* to whom he will.

In sum, the loving relation between the Father and the Son leads to the accomplishment of redemption.

We can reexpress the same truths in another way. We have mentioned the expressions in the Bible that speak of the Father's "sending" the Son. This sending is an aspect of the analogy with a family, typically occurring in wider contexts that contain the terms "Father" and "Son" (see John 5:23; 10:36). The terminology of "sending" leads directly to the picture of the Father as the planner and the Son as the executor. We have also seen that, within the analogy with a family, the Holy Spirit is a gift to the Son. The gift is given to carry out the purposes of the Father and the Son, and this idea of carrying out divine purposes leads to considering the tasks of application, sanctification, and consummation.[5]

5. John Owen speaks of "immediate efficacy" in the Holy Spirit's communion with us (ibid.).

The Holy Spirit also carries out God's purposes in creation: the Spirit of God is present in God's acts of creation, according to Genesis 1:2 and Psalm 104:30.

God expresses his love in action in the world. All his actions are loving actions. The planning, accomplishment, and application of redemption are acts of love. So it is convenient to view the action analogy, the analogy of carrying out the work of God, as the result of the analogy with a family being applied to God's work in history. (See fig. 9.4.)

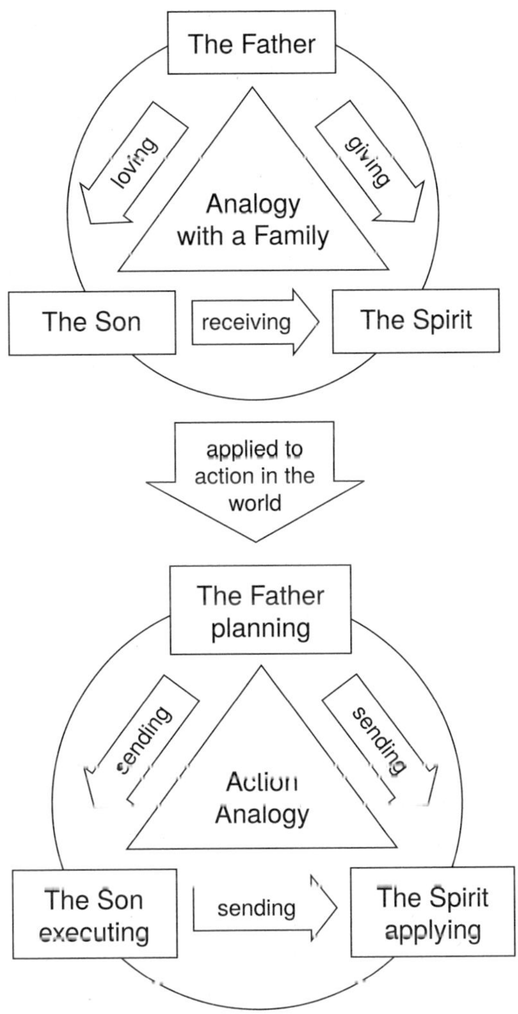

Fig. 9.4. Combining the Action Analogy and the Analogy with a Family

Relationship between the Action Analogy and the Analogy with Communication

We can also take our point of departure from the analogy with communication and move toward the action analogy. The analogy with communication applies to the eternal relation between God and his Word, as we have observed. But it is also the source for the pattern of action when God speaks to govern the world. God the Father plans what he says. God the Son embodies the expression of the Father by being his Word, which leads to words of command that execute the plan of the Father in time. God the Holy Spirit is present like the breath of God to apply the word and bring it to its destination. So the analogy with communication reinforces the action analogy. The eternal reality of God's eternal speech is reflected in his speech in time, which accompanies his acts in time. (See fig. 9.5.)

Key Terms

action
action analogy[6]
application
archetype
consummation
ectype
execution
planning
reinforcement
sanctification

Study Questions

1. How does the analogy with a family reinforce the analogy with reflections, and vice versa?
2. How does the analogy with communication reinforce the analogy with reflections, and vice versa?
3. How does the analogy with communication reinforce the analogy with a family, and vice versa?
4. What is the relation between the three main analogies: the

6. Key terms in **bold** are defined in the glossary at the end of this volume.

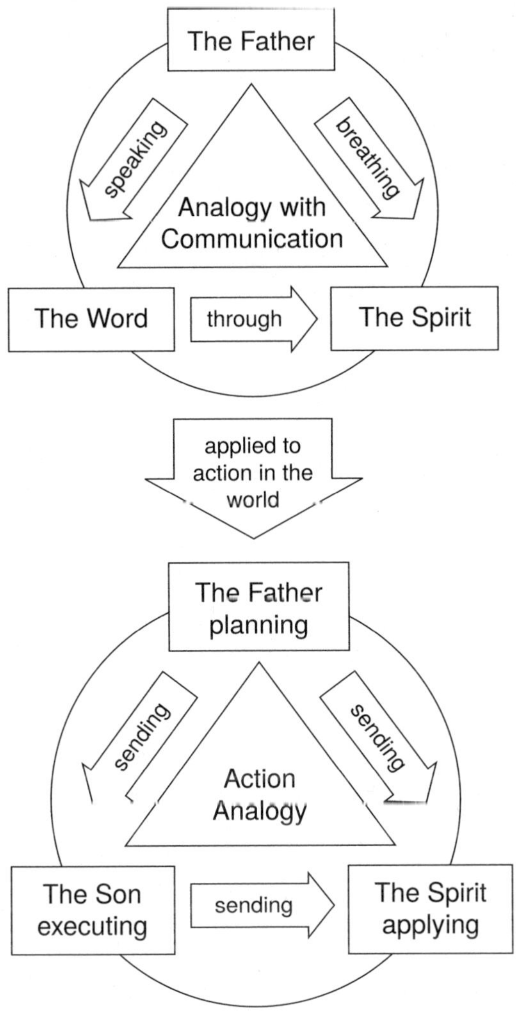

Fig. 9.5. Combining the Action Analogy and the Analogy with Communication

analogy with communication, the analogy with a family, and the analogy with reflections?

5. How does each person of the Trinity participate in a distinctive way in divine work, as illustrated by God's actions in redemption?
6. Discuss whether God's execution of his plan is the work of the Son alone, or of the Son in fellowship with the Father and the Spirit.

7. What relation does the action analogy have to the analogy with a family? to the analogy with communication?

For Further Reading

Owen, John. *Communion with the Triune God.* Edited by Kelly M. Kapic and Justin Taylor. Wheaton, IL: Crossway, 2007. An older work expounding the distinct communion that a Christian has with each of the three persons of the Trinity.

10

Knowledge of the Trinity

WE SHOULD NOW consider how we know all these things about God. In particular, how can we know about the Trinity, since the Trinitarian character of God is mysterious and not like anything within the created world?

The basic answer is that we can know about God only if God reveals himself. And God *has* revealed himself. According to Romans 1:18–23, he reveals himself in the things he has made:

> For the wrath of God is revealed from heaven against all ungodliness and unrighteousness of men, who by their unrighteousness suppress the truth. For what can be known about God is plain to them, because God has shown it to them. For his invisible attributes, namely, his eternal power and divine nature, have been clearly perceived, ever since the creation of the world, *in the things that have been made*. So they are without excuse. For although they knew God, they did not honor him as God or give thanks to him, but they became futile in their thinking, and their foolish hearts were darkened. Claiming to be wise, they became fools, and exchanged the glory of the immortal God for images resembling mortal man and birds and animals and creeping things.

As we indicated earlier, this display of God's character through created things is called *general revelation*.

God also reveals himself through *special revelation*, found in Scripture. Scripture is the very Word of God. And it gives us more than what is found in general revelation. In particular, it reveals the way of salvation in Christ. Through Christ's salvation working in us, our minds are transformed and we come to know God more and more deeply (Rom.

12:1–2). We receive God's salvation, adoption, verbal communication, and presence.

In sum, we need to bear in mind several principles in considering human knowledge of God:

1. All people know God.

2. But knowledge of God through creation is suppressed and does not lead to salvation.

3. Through the work of the Holy Spirit, believers in Christ come to know God in a saving way.

4. The knowledge given by the Holy Spirit through the Bible is true and valid.

5. Since God is infinite, human beings do not know God exhaustively or comprehensively. Only God knows himself comprehensively.

Frame's Square of Transcendence and Immanence

These principles about our knowledge can be conveniently summarized in a diagram invented by John M. Frame that has come to be known as *Frame's square of transcendence and immanence.*[1] (See fig. 10.1.) The left-hand side of the square represents the Christian understanding of God's transcendence and immanence, while the right-hand side of the square represents the non-Christian understanding (which is a distortion of the truth).

The Christian view of transcendence (corner 1 of the square) says that God is the Creator and Sustainer of the world, and has authority and power over it. The Christian view of immanence (corner 2) says that God is present in the world. The non-Christian view of transcendence (corner 3) says that God is far away, inaccessible, and irrelevant. The non-Christian view of immanence (corner 4) says that God is identical with the world.

1. John M. Frame, *The Doctrine of the Knowledge of God* (Phillipsburg, NJ: Presbyterian and Reformed, 1987), 14.

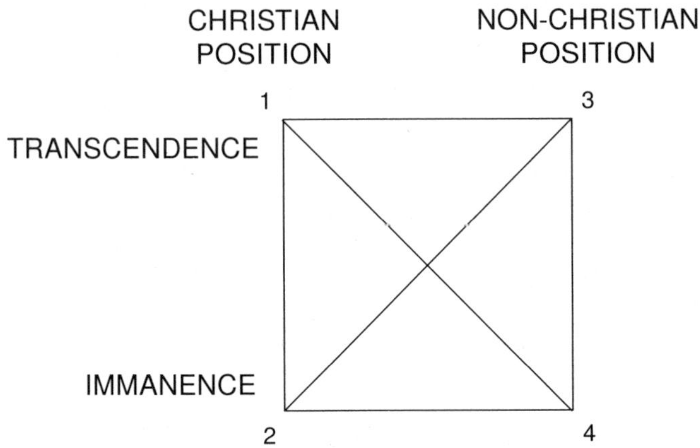

Fig. 10.1. Frame's Square of Transcendence and Immanence

God's transcendence and immanence have implications for knowledge. According to God's transcendence, God is the standard for all knowledge, including knowledge of God himself (corner 1 of the square). God knows himself completely. According to God's immanence, God makes himself truly known to human beings (corner 2). Precisely because God knows himself completely and controls all things according to his knowledge, he is fully able to reveal himself to us. Transcendence provides the basis for immanence; the two go together in harmony. This is the position taught in the Bible, and accordingly it is the Christian position. (People who call themselves Christians may sometimes be inconsistent or confused, but they *should* accept the position taught in the Bible.)

Now let us contrast this position with the non-Christian position. In a sense, there are many different non-Christian positions, corresponding to the many different kinds of idolatry, which arise when people exchange the true God for idolatrous substitutes. The substitutes can be physical idols in the form of statues, such as those in ancient Greece and the ancient Near East. Or they can be conceptual substitutes, such as the idea that nature is god (*pantheism*). Or people can worship money or pleasure, when they give their ultimate allegiance to money or pleasure. Though at a superficial level there are many forms of idolatry, the common pattern is summarized in Frame's square.

The non-Christian view of transcendence says that God is

unknowable (corner 3 of Frame's square). Since non-Christians suppress the knowledge of God, we could also say that they think that what is ultimate is unknowable. The people who serve money or pleasure implicitly hold this view. Money or pleasure receives their allegiance because they have given up on seeking anything more ultimate.

The non-Christian view of immanence says that human knowledge or an individual's knowledge can effectively serve as the ultimate standard for knowledge (corner 4 of Frame's square). There is a kind of kinship between non-Christian transcendence and non-Christian immanence. If God is unknown (transcendence), nothing is left except human viewpoints (immanence). Yet there is also deep tension in this view, because the absence of an ultimate standard really implies that there is no standard, rather than implying that human knowledge is the standard. The standard for knowledge is both infinitely inaccessible (transcendence) and perfectly accessible (immanence). This kind of tension is to be expected. Non-Christians live in God's world and cannot actually escape God. So their position can never work.

The diagonal lines in Frame's square represent contradictions. The non-Christian view of transcendence (corner 3) says that God is unknowable, while the Christian view of immanence (corner 2) says that he is not only knowable but known. The non-Christian view of immanence (corner 4) says that human knowledge is the standard, while the Christian view of transcendence (corner 1) says that God's knowledge is the standard.

The horizontal lines in Frame's square represent similarity in wording. The Christian view of transcendence (corner 1) can *sound like* the non-Christian view of transcendence (corner 3). Both use the word *transcendence*. Both might say that God is "exalted." The two sides have "formal similarity." But they *mean* different things. The non-Christian view makes itself plausible only by borrowing some language from the Christian side and distorting it.

The similarity means that we have to be careful. If we have believed in Christ for salvation, we are fundamentally saved, while others are lost. But we are not completely freed from sin, including sins of the *mind*. We can unconsciously slide over into forms of non-Christian thinking. The square is therefore useful not only in distinguishing Christian thinking from non-Christian thinking, but also in reminding those of us who are

Christians of the need to think consistently in a Christian manner. That is not as easy as it may seem, because sin can subtly creep in.

We may conveniently summarize the principles for *knowledge* by filling out Frame's square as it applies to knowledge. (See fig. 10.2.)

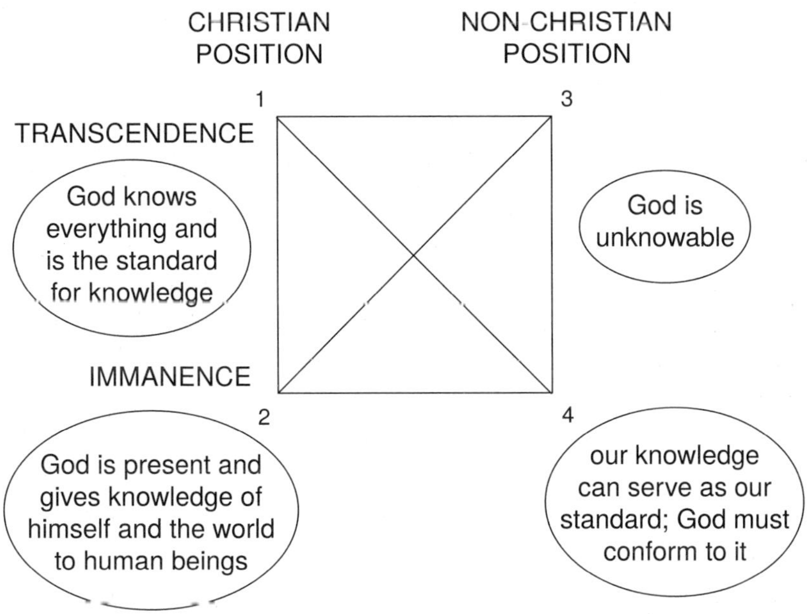

Fig. 10.2. Frame's Square for Knowledge

This diagram is a *summary* that synthesizes much teaching in the Bible. It is useful as a summary, but in the end, that is all it is. The Bible itself has much more detail and much richer textures in its teaching about the knowledge of God. The summary is meant to remind us of this full-orbed biblical teaching, rather than to stand on its own, as if it were a complete, self-enclosed statement.

Mystery in the Trinity

Because of the nature of our knowledge, we should not be surprised that we find mystery in the doctrine of the Trinity. There is mystery for us because we are creatures. We are not the standard of knowledge (we deny non-Christian immanence, corner 4). God knows himself completely, and there is no mystery for him (corner 1). Heretical teachers have gotten into trouble when they have ignored this situation. They may say that the Trinity is "irrational," and therefore that it cannot be what the Bible really teaches. Or they may say that the Bible contradicts itself and cannot be trusted. But in this move they fall into a non-Christian view of immanence, under which they make themselves their own standard for what God can and cannot be like.

Knowing God as He Really Is

The principles for knowing God are also relevant in another way. On the basis of Scripture, we can be confident that God, by speaking to us in the Bible, tells us who he really is. We can know who he really is. The Trinity as described in the Bible is what God really is. In expressing this confidence, we reexpress the Christian view of immanence.

This principle is important in dealing with God's eternal existence. We know from the Bible that God always exists. He existed even without the created world, while the created world came into being by God's activity: "In the beginning, God created the heavens and the earth" (Gen. 1:1). God did not have to create the world, but he did. Biblical teaching includes a fundamental distinction between God and the world. In opposition to the false teachings of pantheism and panentheism, the Bible makes it clear that the world is not God and is not a part of God. To worship any created thing or the world as a whole is idolatry (Rom. 1:18–23). Nothing within the world duplicates God. There is mystery for us about God's eternal existence, because we as human beings have experiences in time. We find that we cannot fully conceptualize what it would mean for God to exist independent of the universe in which we live.

What about the Trinitarian character of God? God is always the Trinitarian God. He did not "become" Trinitarian only by creating the world. This eternality of the Trinity is clear from John 1:1: "In the beginning was the Word, and the Word was with God, and the Word was God." John is here speaking about what God is like even apart from the acts of creation that are mentioned later in verse 3. The Word was God, and at the same time the Word was distinct from God the Father "in the beginning."

At this point, theologians distinguish between the *ontological Trinity* and the *economic Trinity*. The *ontological Trinity* (also called the *immanent Trinity*) is the Trinitarian character of God, apart from his work of creation. It concerns what God *is*. The *economic Trinity* is the Trinitarian character of God expressed in activity toward the world—creation, providence, redemption, and consummation. It concerns what God *does*. The word *economic* here has a special technical meaning. Etymologically, it comes from the Greek word *oikonomia,* which means "household management." The term *economic* is applied to God because God "manages" all the created order and "manages" the whole design and accomplishment of salvation.

The Bible focuses a great deal on what God does, because that is what we need to know. We need to know that he created the world and that he providentially controls it. We need to know how he accomplished salvation in Christ, and how we can receive this salvation and participate in it. We need to understand how he is working in us through the power of the Holy Spirit. All these things concern the *activities* of God—his "economic" management. Through these activities and what he says about them, we also know God. We know him *through* what he says and what he does.

The same is true for the Trinitarian character of God. We understand the Trinitarian character of God by what he says and does in connection with his "economic" management. For example, we know that the Father *sent* the Son into the world; we know that the Son became incarnate. We know that the Son was exalted to the right hand of God, and poured out the Holy Spirit (Acts 2:33). In these events, the persons of the Trinity are interacting with the created order and with us, creatures within that order. We have seen how the Trinitarian character of God is displayed in God's work of salvation, planned by the Father, executed by the Son, and applied by the Holy Spirit. Our adoption as sons, God's speech to us, and God's presence with us also express his Trinitarian character.

So do we know God *as he really is*—the ontological Trinity? The answer is yes. The Bible stresses that we *know* God. We know God, not a substitute. To worship a substitute instead of the true God is idolatry, as Romans 1:23 indicates. We know God *through* what he says and does. We could put it this way: that through God's *economic* activity, we know God *ontologically*. That is the only way that it could happen, because God must reveal himself (economic) for us to know him (ontological).

God's economic activity includes his work in history, his communication to us in the Bible, and the work of the Holy Spirit *in* us, illumining our hearts.

It is easy here to fall into a non-Christian view of transcendence, and to undercut the genuine character of human knowledge of God. It may sound humble to say that we know only created manifestations of God, not God himself. But that is not right. We know *God*, precisely through the created manifestations that are mentioned in Romans 1:20, "the things that have been made." We know God even more deeply when he teaches us through the Holy Spirit's illumination of Scripture. Scripture comes through created media—human writers, and stone or papyrus or parchment on which the biblical books are written. It is proclaimed by human preachers. Through these means, God addresses us with divine power, and makes himself known with divine efficacy. He succeeds. We know him.

This means that we also know the ontological Trinity. We know the ontological Trinity through the economic Trinity. God reveals himself in harmony with who he is. So the revelation of the Trinity in economic terms is in harmony with the ontological Trinity. If we deny this, we fall into a form of non-Christian transcendence, in which we imply that the ontological Trinity becomes unknowable. If God were unknowable, it would destroy genuine worship. An unknowable God could not be worshiped properly, because the actual object of worship would be some God-substitute; it would be merely our best (but false) idea of who God is.

Dealing with Biblical Texts

We have actually been presupposing these truths in the earlier chapters of this book. Most of the biblical passages that we have examined describe God in connection with his works of redemption. That is, they focus on economic activity of God. The passage in John 1:1 is an exception. It talks about what was "in the beginning," that is, even apart from God's acts of creating the world.

But even here, this passage is preparing the way for understanding that Jesus in his person and in his proclamation communicates who God the Father is. He communicates to *us* as ones who are in this world, and he communicates for the sake of *redemption*. So even the verse John 1:1, which gives us a direct description of aspects of the ontological Trinity, is not really focused exclusively on the ontological Trinity. It is preparing us for the economic Trinity. God acts redemptively in the events described in the rest of the Gospel of John. And the Gospel of John is itself the Word of God, written to those of us who are in the world.

John 1:1 confirms the close relation between the ontological Trinity and the economic Trinity. John 1:1 tells us who God is—ontologically. God the Father is eternally the speaker, and God the Son is eternally the Word. Precisely because he is who he is, in his Trinitarian character, God reveals himself to us through Jesus the Word. Jesus in his ministry of proclamation on earth faithfully reveals God: "Whoever has seen me has seen the Father" (John 14:9). We have seen the Father. We know God, *through* the economic Trinity. Jesus also says, "And this is eternal life, that they know you the only true God, and Jesus Christ whom you have sent" (17:3). To have eternal life, we must "know you the only true God." If we know only a finite, created substitute, we are sunk. We have missed eternal life. We may put it another way: if we know *only* the economic work of God, in a way that is alleged to be independent of who God really is, we are sunk, because we have missed knowing the true God that Jesus the Son knows. But for Christians, the key assumption (the *if*) is false. God does make himself known to us through his economic activity.

John 1:1 also alludes to the account of creation in Genesis 1. Because the Word is eternally the Word, God creates the world by speaking words, such as "Let there be light" (Gen. 1:3). The work of God in creation reflects who God always is. And the specific words of command in Genesis 1 reflect the eternal Word who is God and who is always with God (John 1:1). In other words, the economic Trinity expresses the ontological Trinity.

Thus, with respect to both creation and redemption, the economic Trinity expresses the reality of the ontological Trinity. Consequently, in discussing Scripture in the preceding chapters, we have presupposed that the passages show us the true Trinitarian character of God. In considering the passages, we start with the activities of the Trinity (economic Trinity). We infer the nature of the Trinity, including the relations among the persons of the Trinity (ontological Trinity). When faithfully done, this procedure respects the derivative character of our knowledge, and the fact that we must base our knowledge on what God tells us in Scripture. At the same time, we respect the reality of the knowledge that God has given. We know God. And we know the persons of the Trinity in their relations to one another. These relations existed even before the world began. The acts of God in time are naturally expressive of and in harmony with the pretemporal personal relations in the Trinity.

It is also true, of course, that not every feature we see in the world should be naively projected back onto God. God ordained that there should be horses. But God is not a horse. God ordained a world in which human beings grow in knowledge over time. But God himself does not grow in knowledge. When we respect everything that the Bible teaches about the distinction between God the Creator and the created world that he has made, we have guidelines for seeing in what respects God's actions in the world reflect who he is, and in what respects God is different from the creatures he has made.

Meaningful Descriptions

The principles about knowing God also have implications for our assessment of the *meaning* of biblical passages about God. Consider John 1:1 again. We describe God the Father as speaking the Word. But does he speak in exactly the *same* way that we experience human beings speaking to one another? No. We speak in time. Our speeches are spread out. And we do not completely think out all the implications of what we say. God speaks eternally. And his knowledge of his speech is complete.

So do we know completely what we *mean* when we say that God speaks? No. God is God. His speaking is unique. His speaking is *analogous* to ours, but is not on the same level. There is mystery here, as always. If we thought we could understand divine speaking completely, we would be making our understanding the standard for divine speech. We would be using the non-Christian view of immanence.

But we must also avoid the non-Christian view of transcendence. We should avoid saying that God is unknowable or that the Bible verse John 1:1 is unknowable. We *do* understand that God speaks. When the Bible uses the expression *the Word,* the expression is meaningful. It tells us something (by the principle of Christian immanence, corner 2 in Frame's square). It is not just a blank, as it would be if we made up a new nonsense syllable: "In the beginning was the Bloor." The use of the expression *the Word* shows us that the second person of the Trinity in his relation to the Father presents us with an analogy with other instances of communication that we know.

We avoid two extremes. In the one extreme, an expression used for God has no relation to anything else. This extreme is *equivocism*. It equivocates on meaning—in this case, the meaning of *Word*. Complete equivocation makes knowledge impossible. It is non-Christian transcendence in operation.

The other extreme considers an expression used for God, and forces it to mean exactly the same thing in every respect as it would if it were used any other way. This extreme is *univocism*. It emphasizes *single* meaning (*uni-*, "one," plus *voc-*, "voice"). This view misrepresents the truth because it dishonors the unique character of who God is. This extreme represents non-Christian immanence. In non-Christian immanence, God must "submit" to *our* idea of meaning.

Among all these forms of speaking, which is the *original* speech? We may further appreciate the nature of God's communication in the Bible if we reflect on the question of what is original, and what is derivative, when we use analogies to describe God. God speaks, and human beings speak. The relation between the two is neither univocism (non-Christian immanence) nor equivocism (non-Christian transcendence). It is a relation of analogy. In this analogy, which is the original?

Clearly, God is the original. God made man in his image (Gen. 1:27). That is why we can speak. Before God created human beings, he was already a speaker, as we can see from Genesis 1:3 and the other verses in Genesis 1 where God issues commands to bring forth creation. We may use the term *archetype* for the original and the term *ectype* for the copy. So God's speech is the archetype, while man's ability to speak is the ectype. In God's speech, there is an even more ultimate archetype, namely, the eternal Word. The eternal Word existed even before God began to create. The eternal Word is therefore the *archetype* in relation to the instances of *ectypal* specific speeches, such as "Let there be light" (Gen. 1:3).

It is important that we reckon with God's being the original. That is one way in which we affirm the Christian view of transcendence. God is the standard for meaning. Meanings within creation, such as the meaning of human speech to other humans, are not self-sufficient. Only God is self-sufficient. Meanings within creation have God as their ultimate standard. God has specified these meanings, beginning with who he is as God.

It is *also* important that we affirm that meanings in human speech do retain a relation to the original. If in our own mind we try to cut off or deny all relations with God's meanings, we leave ourselves with a situation of equivocism in any attempt to talk about God. We have no way of talking about God unless God supplies it by giving us meanings that in fact are analogically related to who God is.

In consequence, we make two related affirmations. First, God *really* does speak, and in this speech the eternal Word *really* is the Word. He is the original Word, and without him there is no communication at all, either in God or in us. Second, we do not understand our own language with perfect mastery. Our own language is entangled in the mystery of God's language, to which it is inextricably related. Because God is the standard, and not us, God alone is the perfect Master. Because God reveals himself, we do have meanings. We can communicate. We can communicate even about God, because the meanings that he gives us are already—before we begin to speak—analogically rooted in God as the origin of meanings.[2]

Father and Son

The same principle applies when we use the words *Father* and *Son* to describe the persons of the Trinity. The word *Father* shows an analogy between God the Father and human fathers. The word *Son* shows an analogy between God the Son and human sons. If we treat the analogy like an identity, it is *univocism*. We fall into non-Christian immanence, and we pretend that we can bring God down to our level and capture perfectly the nature of God the Father. On the other hand, if we treat the analogy as though God's fatherhood were *completely different* from human fatherhood in every respect, we have *equivocism*. We fall into non-Christian transcendence, according to which God is unknowable. As a result, *Father*, when used to describe God, means nothing at all.

2. Vern S. Poythress, *In the Beginning Was the Word: Language—A God-Centered Approach* (Wheaton, IL: Crossway, 2009).

Value for Worship

These observations are valuable as we endeavor to worship and praise God as he deserves. For true worship and praise, we must know the God we worship and worship him according to who he is. Otherwise, we fall into idolatry; we worship a substitute of our own devising. At the same time, worshiping God means acknowledging his supreme greatness. We stand in awe of him, and so we confess that we do not know him completely. His infinite superiority to us is one motivation for true worship.

Key Terms

archetype[3]
comprehensive knowledge
contradiction
economic
economic Trinity
ectype
equivocism
father
Frame's square of transcendence and immanence
general revelation
immanence
immanent Trinity
knowledge of God
meaning
non-Christian immanence
non-Christian transcendence
ontological
ontological Trinity
revelation
self-sufficiency
son
special revelation
tension (in non-Christian understanding)
transcendence

3. Key terms in **bold** are defined in the glossary at the end of this volume.

univocism
worship

Study Questions

1. What does it mean to know God?
2. Do non-Christians know God? If so, how?
3. What is the difference between Christian and non-Christian knowledge of God?
4. What is the difference between Christian knowledge of God and God's knowledge of himself?
5. How can we be confident that we know God truly?
6. What is equivocism, and why is it a problem?
7. What is univocism, and why is it a problem?
8. What is the relation between the ontological Trinity and the economic Trinity?
9. What kinds of non-Christian views of knowledge can interfere with our understanding of what it means to know the Trinity?

For Further Reading

Frame, John M. *The Doctrine of God*. Phillipsburg, NJ: P&R Publishing, 2002. Pp. 706–7. On the ontological Trinity and the economic Trinity.

———. *The Doctrine of the Knowledge of God*. Phillipsburg, NJ: Presbyterian and Reformed, 1987. Esp. pp. 14–18. A wide-ranging exposition of the biblical teaching on the knowledge of God, including in its early pages Frame's square of transcendence and immanence.

Letham, Robert. *The Holy Trinity: In Scripture, History, Theology, and Worship*. Phillipsburg, NJ: P&R Publishing, 2004. Pp. 261, 291–98. On the ontological Trinity and the economic Trinity.

Poythress, Vern S. *In the Beginning Was the Word: Language—A God-Centered Approach*. Wheaton, IL: Crossway, 2009. A Christian view of language and analogy.

———. *Theophany: A Biblical Theology of God's Appearing*. Wheaton, IL: Crossway, 2018. Chap. 12. A summary of the knowledge of God.

PART 3

PERSPECTIVES FROM THE TRINITY

NOW WE CONSIDER some triads of perspectives that originate from the Trinity.

11

Perspectives on Reflections

LET US NOW consider more closely the analogy with *reflections* for the Trinity. From this analogy we can obtain some perspectives.

Three Perspectives on Reflections, Related to Fatherhood

According to the analogy with reflections, the Son is the image of the Father (2 Cor. 4:4; Col. 1:15; Heb. 1:3). He reflects the Father. This Trinitarian relation of reflection is analogous to the case in which Adam fathered Seth "in his own likeness, after his *image*" (Gen. 5:3).

So let us begin by thinking about Adam's fathering Seth. We can choose to look at the relation of Adam and Seth from any of three complementary thematic perspectives.

First, we can look at it from the standpoint of Adam as the original. We start with Adam, and we consider how Seth is like him and how Adam brought Seth into being by a process of procreation. Let us call the perspective that starts with Adam as the original the *originary* perspective.

Second, we can look at the relation from the standpoint of Seth as the image. We start with Seth, and we consider how Adam is like him and how Seth came to be. Let us call this way of looking at the relation the *manifestational* perspective, because Seth as an image of Adam "manifests" things about Adam, who was the original after which the reflection was patterned.

Third, we can look at the relation between Adam and Seth *as* a relation, in which many similarities hold between Adam and Seth. We notice all the ways in which things about Adam and things about Seth agree with each other and connect to each other. Let us call this way of looking at the relation the *connectional* perspective.[1] (See fig. 11.1.)

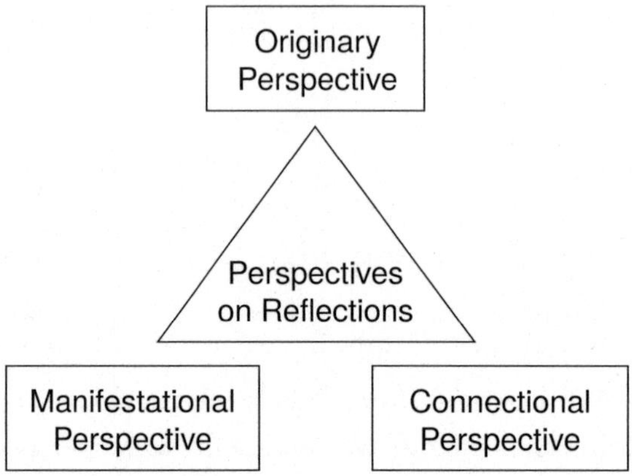

Fig. 11.1. Three Perspectives on Reflections

Each of the three perspectives leads to the other two and includes the other two. For example, if we start with the originary perspective, we begin with Adam as original. But the original leads to the copy, to Seth. In a sense, Adam was "original" even before he had a son. That is, he existed at the origin of the human race. (God is the absolute original, who exists even before the creation of the world, and independently of creation.) But the word *original* often designates someone or something that not only is first in time, but functions as the origin *for something else.* In that sense, for an original to be an original implies the existence of a copy, from which we can then look at the original and the process leading to the copy. So the copy is included in the complete picture. Thus, the originary perspective implicitly includes the manifestational perspective.

The situation of being an original also implies the existence of a relation between the original and what has been produced as a copy. So the connectional perspective is implicitly included in the originary perspective. Similarly, the existence of a copy implies the original and a relation between the original and the copy.

Finally, the connection between original and copy arises by the same

1. Vern S. Poythress, *God-Centered Biblical Interpretation* (Phillipsburg, NJ: P&R Publishing, 1999), 36–42. In this earlier book, I call the third perspective the *concurrent perspective.* I have decided to rename it the *connectional perspective* because the latter term is more clearly descriptive.

process that produces the copy. The connection originates in the original and exists only because both original and copy exist. The connectional perspective presupposes the originary perspective and the manifestational perspective. The original is an original in relation to the copy only because there is a connection between the two. So the originary perspective presupposes the existence of the connectional perspective.

As usual, we can see some general principles about the relations between the three perspectives:

1. There is only one reality of Seth's being in the image of Adam because there is only one God who brought it about.
2. The three perspectives on reflections are distinct because each one starts with a distinct thematic focus.
3. What stands out about reflections varies subtly, depending on which perspective serves as our starting point for thought.
4. Each perspective on reflections is fully present to the other two perspectives, so that it implicitly includes the others.
5. Each perspective indwells the others. It is already there in the idea of reflection, and we can perceive it by using one starting perspective on reflections.

The three perspectives on reflections are themselves a reflection of the Trinity in several features. The five principles mentioned above with respect to the perspectives on reflections also hold for the persons of the Trinity:

1. There is only one reality of God.
2. The three persons in God are distinct.
3. What stands out about God varies subtly, depending on which person serves as our starting point for thought.
4. Each person in the Trinity is fully present to the other two.

5. Each person indwells the others. He is already there, indwelling each other person, and we can perceive this by using any one of the three persons as the starting point.

Thus, each of the five points represents one aspect of the analogy between the Trinity and the three perspectives on reflections. If we like, we can condense these five points into three:

a. (corresponding to 1) The three perspectives all focus on the same subject matter, which is analogous to the fact that in the Trinity the three persons are one God. The unity of the three perspectives reflects the unity of God.

b. (corresponding to 2) There are three perspectives, each of which is a reflection of a distinct person of the Trinity. (Also, because each perspective is distinct, what stands out would naturally vary, as in 3.)

c. (corresponding to 4 and 5) The *relations* among the persons of the Trinity, in coinherence, are reflected in the *relations* among the three perspectives.

As a further subpoint under point c, we may also mention an analogy with respect to the *dynamics* of relationship:

6. The *dynamics* of the relations are also in harmony. As the Son is the image eternally *generated* from the pattern of the Father, so the manifestational perspective is a reflection *generated* from the originary perspective. How so? The manifestational perspective imitates the originary perspective, in the fact that it starts from one pole within a relation of reflection, and moves out to the other pole. This imitation is itself a form of reflection. But the manifestational perspective moves in the reverse direction: it starts with the reflection generated from the original.[2]

2. If we wish, we can confirm that the relation between any two of the six listed principles is itself perspectival. Points a, b, and c correspond, respectively, to the classificational perspective, the instantiational perspective, and the associational perspective, defined later in chapter 26. The

The three perspectives on reflections can be applied not only to analyze the relation of reflection between Adam and Seth, but to analyze *any* relation of reflection, including the archetypal relation between God the Father and God the Son, as we will see.

Three Perspectives on Reflections in Theophany

Let us first apply the three perspectives on reflections to the instances when God appears to human beings in theophany. In these instances, God himself is the original. His visible manifestation—let us say in human form as in Ezekiel 1:26–28—is a kind of reflection of God. Ezekiel 1:28 speaks of "the appearance of the *likeness* of the glory of the LORD."

God brings about the manifestation. He is the original in relation to the manifestation. We can speak of an *originary* perspective when we are looking at the theophany from the standpoint of its origin in God. Or we may start with the specific manifestation. The point of the manifestation is that it is a manifestation *of God*. When we start with the manifestation, we are using a *manifestational* perspective. From there, we travel in our thinking and find that this manifestation is a manifestation of God, who is the original.

The glory that appears in the manifestation is the glory of the manifestation and the glory of God that it manifests. The theme of glory connects the original and the manifestation. The same is true for other attributes of God. For example, the righteousness of God is revealed when God appears as Judge, such as in Daniel 7:9–10. The righteousness belongs both to God and to the manifestation of God. We might say that the glory and the righteousness in the original (God) and his manifestation (his reflection) are *connected*. The *connectional* perspective starts with the common features belonging to the original and the manifestation. These common features give meaning to the claim that the first subject (God himself) has a reflection in the second (the visible manifestation).

---

points a–c arise when one applies the classificational, instantiational, and associational perspectives to the issue of unity and diversity in a triad of perspectives.

Within point c, the subpoints 4, 5, and 6 correspond, respectively, to the particle view, the field view, and the wave view (defined in Appendix D) when these views are applied to coinherence.

Principle 3, concerning what stands out, is an instance of applying the perspective of prominence (from Appendix F) to the diversity of perspectives (point b).

In all these instances with visible manifestations of God, we must take care to affirm the distinction between the Creator and the creature. God the Creator is distinct from his creatures, including the creaturely phenomena involved in his visible manifestation. At the same time, the visible manifestation does actually reveal the true God.

For any instance of theophany, several principles hold for the perspectives on theophany:

1. Only one reality of God appears in the theophany.

2. The three perspectives on reflections—the originary, the manifestational, and the connectional—are distinct, because each one starts with a distinct thematic focus.

3. What stands out about the theophany varies subtly, depending on which perspective serves as our starting point for thought.

4. Each perspective on reflections is fully present to the other two perspectives, so that it implicitly includes the others.

5. Each perspective indwells the others. It is already there in the idea of reflection, and we can perceive it by using one starting perspective on reflections.

As we saw before, these five points reflect the analogous principles that hold for the persons of the Trinity.

The Work of the Holy Spirit in Theophany

We should note a difference between the work of the Spirit in theophany and the connectional perspective. The Holy Spirit functions to bring God's presence to human beings. The connectional perspective reaches back to focus on the connection between God and his manifestation.

Let us be more specific. In an earlier chapter (chap. 8), we observed that the Bible associates the Holy Spirit with the cloud of glory in Old Testament theophanies. The cloud functions as a kind of outward side to theophanies such as the one in Ezekiel 1. The glory of theophany touches and influences the person or persons who see the vision. In some sense, what they "take away" from the experience is a reception of the glory of God. This outward expression and impact of theophany are akin to the special work of the Holy Spirit in the New Testament. The Spirit *applies* the work of Christ and expresses most directly and intimately the presence of God *to* those who believe, and *in* believers (by the fact that he dwells in them).

On the other hand, when we use the connectional perspective, we focus on the connection between the original and the manifestation. We might think of the connectional perspective as a way of standing between the original and the manifestation.

Nevertheless, the two approaches to theophany are related. The Spirit brings the glory of God to its human reception. But what is received is communion with the presence of God in his manifestation, and the glory revealed is indeed the glory of both the manifestation and God himself, who reflects himself in his manifestation. So it is appropriate to see the connectional perspective as especially related to the Holy Spirit. Moreover, the Holy Spirit establishes and maintains a connection between theophanies and their human recipients. The connectional perspective can be used to focus on the connection not only between the original and its manifestation, but between the manifestation and its absorption in a human recipient.

In addition, the Holy Spirit is associated in the Bible with the presence of God and the dwelling of God with us and in us. The presence of God functions to connect us to God. The dwelling of God with us establishes an intimate connection with God. So more than one theme helps to affirm a close association of the Holy Spirit with communion, the connection between God and man. By analogy, we may infer that the Holy Spirit functions also to mediate communion among the persons of the Trinity. The Holy Spirit's work reflects who he always is as a particular person of the Trinity.

Theophanies Foreshadowing Christ

The Old Testament theophanies in their temporary character foreshadow the permanent "theophany" of God in Christ (John 1:14). So the analogy between the Old Testament appearances and Christ as the image of God is a genuine analogy. It is an analogy, but not an identity. The incarnation is unique. The Old Testament theophanies were temporary; the incarnation is permanent. The Old Testament theophanies used visual and aural media such as a cloud, fire, and thunder; the incarnation involves the existence of the full human nature of Christ, with a complete human body. His human nature is permanently united to his divine nature.

This analogy between Christ and Old Testament theophanies encourages us to apply to Christ the triad of perspectives that we just used with theophanies. God the Father is the original and Christ is the image. Christ is the *reflection* of God the Father, to use our key category of reflection. There is a relation of reflection between the Father and the Son. If we look at this relation from the starting point of God the Father, we have an *originary* perspective on reflection. God the Father is the original pattern or archetype. The Son is the manifestation of this archetype. The Son is the image of the Father because the Father reflects his own character in the Son. If we start with the Son as the image, we may say that we know the Father through the Son, who is the image of the Father. We are using the *manifestational* perspective, with the Son as our starting point for contemplating the nature of God the Father and for knowing God the Father.

In the case of God, we must observe that these descriptions apply to the Father and the Son *eternally*. The Son is always the Son and always the image of the Father, even before the creation of the world. Christ became incarnate at a particular point in time, and then in his incarnation and his earthly existence he reflects the character of God the Father. But the Son did not begin to exist only at the moment of incarnation. He always exists, and he is always the image of the Father, even before he begins to reflect the Father in his incarnate state (Heb. 1:3).

Second Corinthians 4:4 associates Christ the image with the *glory* of God. It says that unbelievers are blinded "to keep them from seeing the light of the gospel of the *glory* of Christ, who is the image of God." Against the background of the Old Testament, this reference to "glory" alludes to the glory of God as it appears in Old Testament theophanies. We have already seen that the Holy Spirit is closely related to the theme of glory (1 Peter 4:14). In theophanies, the glory of God is present in two *connected* aspects: (1) God as the original and (2) the theophanic appearance of God as the manifestation. This connection reflects the work of the Holy Spirit. In God himself, the Holy Spirit is present in God the Father and in Christ the Son. The Holy Spirit also brings the glory of Christ to us as recipients. *We* become connected to his glory.

Christ in his incarnation manifested the glory of God. This manifestation took place in time. But as usual, it is in harmony with who God always is. The pattern of reflection in theophany and in Christ represents to human beings what God actually is. Now, as we have seen, the pattern in theophany includes the threefold structure of perspectives, namely, the originary, manifestational, and connectional perspectives. This threefold pattern is in harmony with who God is. So we expect to find an analogous threefold pattern when we consider God himself in his own being.

And we do indeed find such a threefold pattern, as we saw above. Christ is the image of God the Father. This relation was true even before the creation of the world (Col. 1:15; Heb. 1:3). It is in fact one aspect of the necessary foundation for God's acts of creation.

Once again, the same principles for perspectives hold true:

1. There is only one reality of God.

2. The three perspectives on reflections—the originary, the manifestational, and the connectional—are distinct, because each one starts with a distinct thematic focus.

3. What stands out about God varies subtly, depending on which perspective serves as our starting point for thought.

4. Each perspective on reflections is fully present to the other two perspectives, so that it implicitly includes the others.

5. Each perspective indwells the others. It is already there in the idea of reflection, and we can perceive it by using one starting perspective on reflections.

The relation between the incarnation and Old Testament theophanies is complex. The Old Testament theophanies come earlier in the history of revelation. God meets with his people in temporary theophanies, and these temporary manifestations foreshadow and anticipate the incarnation. But they are only shadows in comparison to the fullness of God's coming in the incarnation. They anticipate the incarnation, and we can see that from the standpoint of human knowledge, the earlier records of theophanies help us to make sense of the incarnation when it comes.

Conversely, when the incarnation takes place, it helps us to make sense of the earlier theophanies. God brought about the earlier appearances as a kind of foreshadowing of the incarnation, because he had already planned the incarnation. In this way, the theophanies are reflections backward in time of the incarnation, and are subordinate to it in character, according to the plan of God. So even though theophanies come earlier in time, they come "later" from the point of view of the logic of God's plan, according to which they are subordinate reflections of the incarnation that is still to come.

In sum, there are analogical relations between (1) reflection in God himself, (2) reflection in God in the incarnation of Christ, and (3) God's manifesting himself in theophany. The second is a kind of reflection of the first, and the third a reflection of the first and the second. We can summarize these analogical relations in a diagram. (See fig. 11.2.)

All these instances embody the pattern of three perspectives on reflections, namely, the originary, manifestational, and connectional perspectives. The perspectives themselves reflect the Trinitarian character of God. (See fig. 11.3.)

Reflections of Reflections

Since the three perspectives on reflections reflect God, they function as a kind of reflection of the Trinity. The pattern of reflection within the created world reflects God, who has within himself the archetypal instance of reflection. The archetypal reflection is in the Son, who is the image of the Father.

This kind of repetition of reflections is what we saw already with Adam. Adam fathered Seth as a son in his image. This instance of reflection imitated and reflected the archetypal reflection between God the Father and his Son. We can also have reflections of reflections. Adam is a reflection of the Son, who is the image of the Father. Seth had a son in his likeness, namely, Enosh (Gen. 5:6), who was a reflection of Seth, the

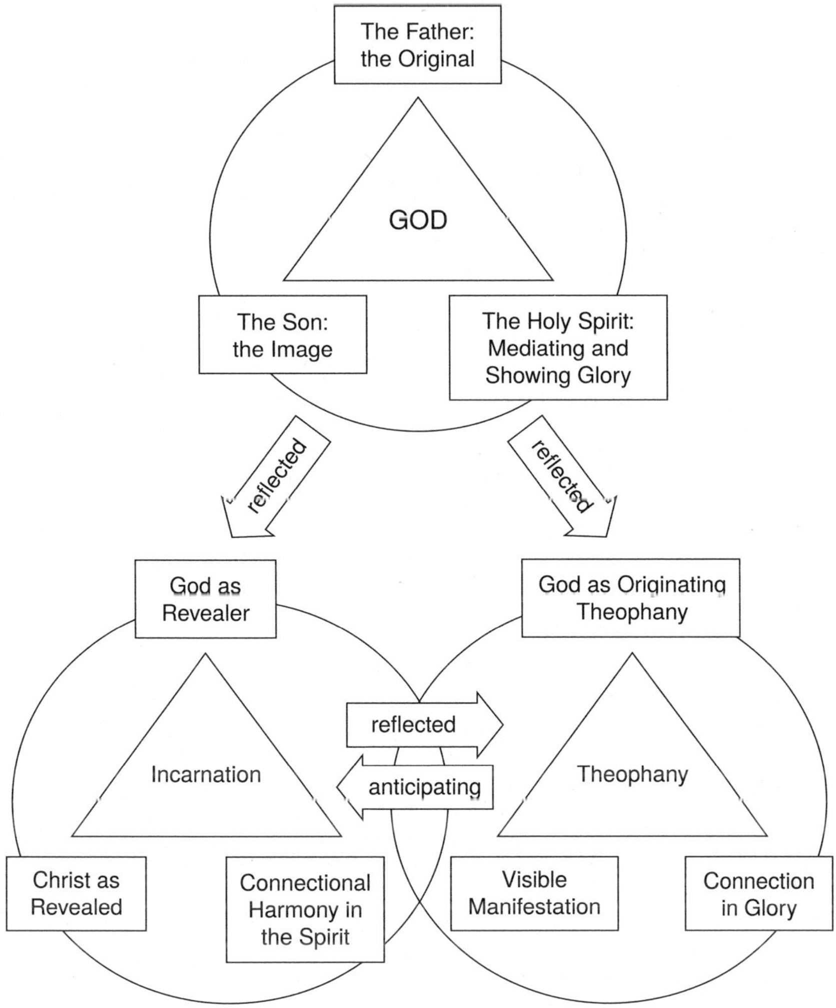

Fig. 11.2. Patterns of Reflection in God and His Manifestation

reflection of Adam, the image of God. We can also have reflections of the *process* of reflection. The process of Adam's fathering a son reflects the creation of man in the image of God. And this process of creation reflects the eternal begetting of the Son from the Father.

The glory in a theophany, we have said, is a feature belonging to God the original and to the specific visible manifestation. The visible manifestation displays God. But glory is also *itself* a kind of manifestation of one aspect of the visible reflection of God. It is then a reflection of a

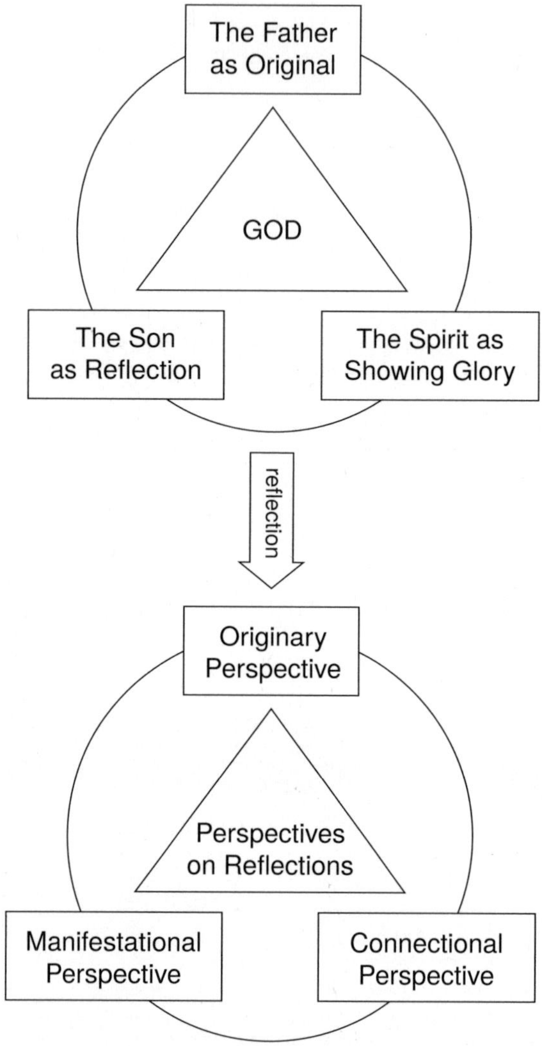

Fig. 11.3. From the Trinity to Perspectives on Reflections

reflection. The same is true concerning the work of the Holy Spirit. The Holy Spirit "manifests" Christ in us by dwelling in us (Rom. 8:9–10). The Spirit as "another Helper" (John 14:16) helps us in a way that manifests or reflects Christ the helper and his help for us. The help of the one is the help of the other.

Since God himself is the original, in relation to us as creatures, we can apply the pattern of reflection in understanding God's relation to us. God is the original. God's manifestation in Christ is the central manifestation. God's manifestation in Old Testament theophanies reflects the climactic manifestation in the incarnation. The Holy Spirit reflects the manifestation of Christ in our hearts, as we receive the gospel and the Holy Spirit teaches us. Then our reception through the Holy Spirit results in a reflection in the form of understanding and knowing God in our own minds. Included in this understanding is an ability to understand the process of reflection, using originary, manifestational, and connectional perspectives. These three perspectives within our minds constitute a mental reflection of God, who is the original. (See figs. 11.4, 11.5.)

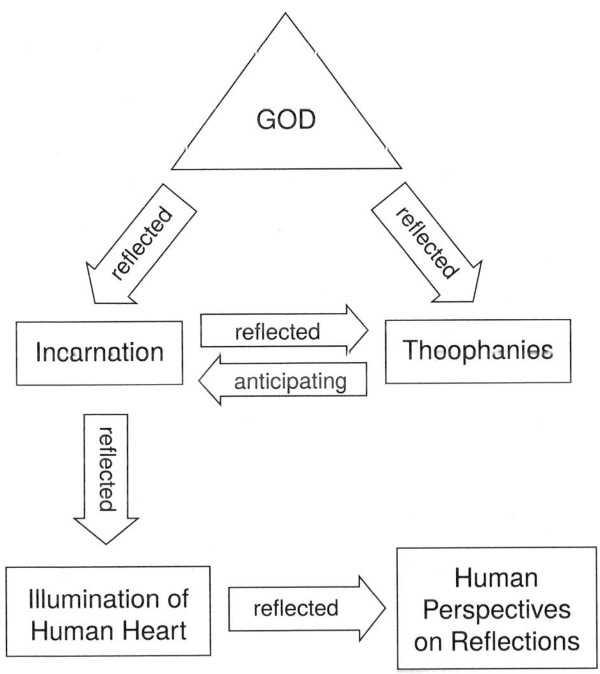

Fig. 11.4. The Reproduction of Reflections

Having received the Holy Spirit, we in turn begin to manifest the glory of God in our words and actions: "You are the light of the world" (Matt. 5:14; cf. Eph. 5:8). This means that, through the Spirit, we become a proximate source of light, which is then manifested in the world. (See figs. 11.6, 11.7.)

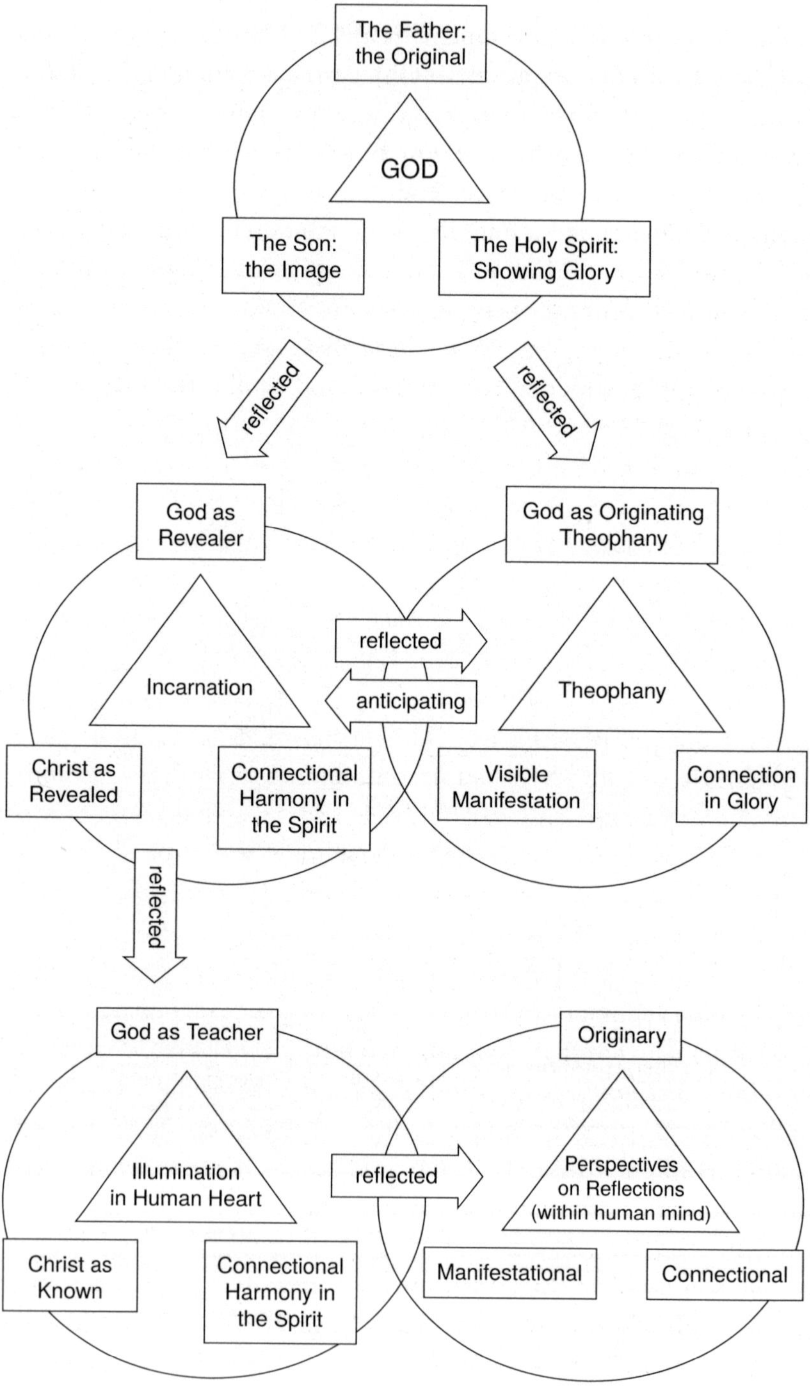

Fig. 11.5. Repeated Reflections in Divine Manifestations

God → Incarnation → Illumination of Christians → Light Shining *from* Christians

Fig. 11.6. Reflection Extending to Christians

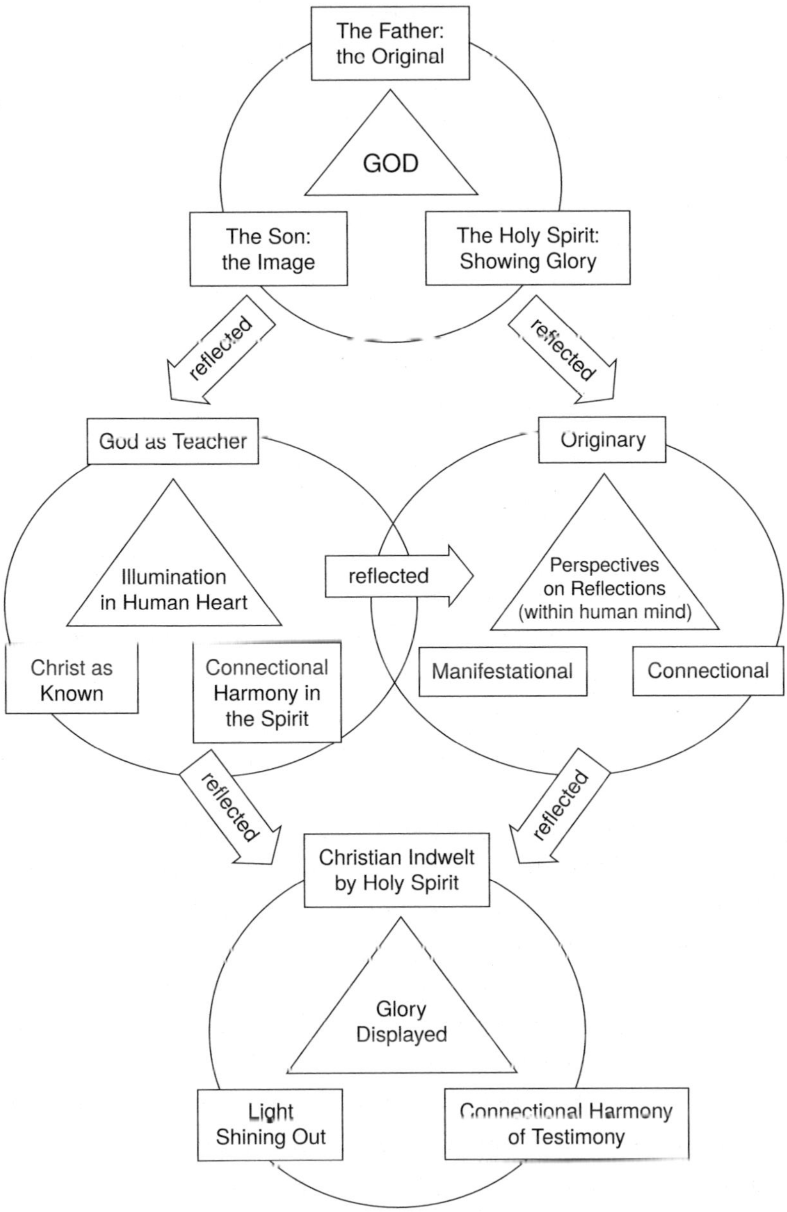

Fig. 11.7. Christians' Manifesting the Light of God

The Reality of Perspectives from the Trinity

We conclude that there is a genuine, organic relationship between the relationship of reflection in God himself and the three perspectives on reflections. We obtain these perspectives precisely by thinking about how God shows himself to us. The three perspectives that we use in our minds are a reflection within us of the divine personal relations within the Trinity. They are a reflection by means of theophany, which is a visible reflection of the invisible God.

Reflections of Coinherence

If the perspectives on reflections themselves reflect God, it is natural that they reflect the coinherence of the persons, such as we have discussed in chapter 7. That is, the coinherence among the persons of the Trinity is reflected in a kind of derivative coinherence among the perspectives. (See fig. 11.8.)

Coinherence in the Person of the Trinity	→	Coinherence among Three Perspectives

Fig. 11.8. Reflected Coinherence

On this point of "derivative coinherence" we must maintain appropriate reserve and caution. God is unique. Accordingly, the coinherence among the persons of the Trinity is unique. Using the word *coinherence* for anything *other* than the persons of the Trinity runs the risk of obscuring the uniqueness of the persons in God. We should acknowledge this danger. We should vigorously affirm and appreciate the *uniqueness* in the coinherence in the persons of the Trinity. (See fig. 11.9.)

While we acknowledge this uniqueness, we choose nevertheless to use the word *coinherence* more broadly, in order to make a complementary point. God in his uniqueness displays his character in the things that he has made. This display includes theophanies, as particularly intense displays of his character. So we should not be shocked if he also displays within creation reflections of his coinherence. We ourselves as human beings are made in the image of God, yet we are not God. So the perspectives that we use in our minds can reflect God without being strictly identical with the coinherence of the Trinity.

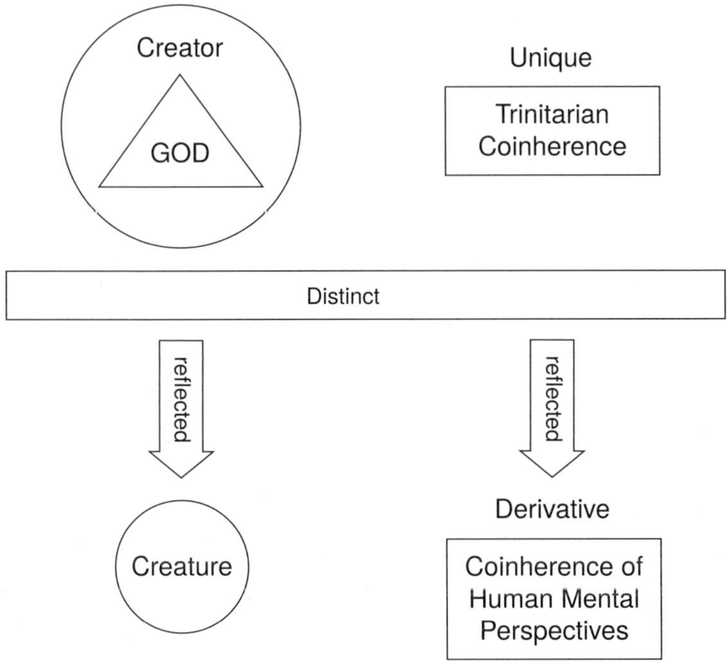

Fig. 11.9. Unique Coinherence

As usual, we must endeavor to preserve a Christian view of human knowledge of God. When we are taught by God through his Word in the Spirit, we have genuine knowledge of God, and this includes genuine knowledge of coinherence. Our reflection of coinherence in our minds has a genuine relation to the divine original, though it is also distinguishable from the divine original because we are creatures and not God.

In fact, the Bible uses the language of indwelling not only with respect to the persons of the Trinity, but with respect to God's dwelling in us and our dwelling in God. We have already seen this kind of language coming up in John 17:

> I do not ask for these only, but also for those who will believe in me through their word, that they may all be one, just as you, Father, are *in* me, and I *in* you, that they also may be *in* us, so that the world may believe that you have sent me. The glory that you have given me I have given to them, that they may be one even as we are one, I *in* them and you *in* me, that they may become perfectly one. (John 17:20–23)

God's dwelling in us is not the *same* as the persons of the Trinity dwelling in one another. But it is analogous. So also, the coinherence among the persons of the Trinity is not the same as the human experience of coinherence among perspectives used by human beings. But it is analogous. Without analogy, we fall back into the error of treating God as unknowable.

Mystery in Perspectives

Coinherence in perspectives helps to explain why it is difficult to make precise the meaning of a perspective. It is difficult because perspectives are not neatly separable from one another. Part of what it means to be a perspective of this kind is that it is coinherent with other perspectives. Now, coinherence among the persons of the Trinity is incomprehensible. This derivative coinherence among perspectives is derivatively incomprehensible. It is incomprehensible because manifestational coinherence in human thinking is indwelt by originary coinherence among the persons of the Trinity: "*in him* we live and move and have our being" (Acts 17:28).

We should praise God both for the mystery of his infinity and for making himself clearly known. Our praise should include the mystery of coinherence. We praise God because his coinherence is mysterious and incomprehensible. It reminds us of his awesome greatness. At the same time, we praise him for making known his coinherence, so that we can understand it enough to see something of his greatness. We praise him for impressing reflections of his coinherence in his interactions with the world he has made.

The Ability of God to Make Himself Known

God makes himself known in theophany as well as in other ways (the Bible and general revelation). A theophany is a reflection of God, mirroring who God is. God can do this in perfect consistency with who he is, because from all eternity God already has within himself an archetypal reflection. The Son is the exact image of the Father (Heb. 1:3). This archetypal reflection is the foundation and source for instances of reflection in theophany. God not only reflects himself in theophany, but reflects in theophany the relation of reflection between the Father and the Son. The production of a reflection is not a "problem" for God because he himself has this capability in his Trinitarian nature. Praise the Lord!

Key Terms

coinherence[3]
connectional perspective
derivative
divine nature
human nature
image
incarnation
manifestational perspective
original
originary perspective
perspectives on reflections
reflection
shadow
theophany

Study Questions

1. What is the relation between Adam's being in the image of God and Adam's fatherhood?
2. What is an archetype, and how is it related to a corresponding ectype?
3. What is the original (the archetype) for Adam's being made in the image of God?
4. What verses indicate that Christ is the image of God?
5. What are the three perspectives on reflections? How are they related to one another?
6. What is the origin for the three perspectives on reflections?
7. What is coinherence? What is the original coinherence, and are there derivative forms of coinherence?
8. What dangers do we confront with respect to the Creator-creature distinction when we talk about coinherence?

3. Key terms in **bold** are defined in the glossary at the end of this volume.

For Further Reading

Poythress, Vern S. *Theophany: A Biblical Theology of God's Appearing.* Wheaton, IL: Crossway, 2018. Chaps. 14–24. A study of reflections that occur when God manifests himself (especially in theophany).

12

Perspectives from Trinitarian Analogies

IN CHAPTER 8, we discussed three main biblical analogies for personal relations in the Trinity. Each of these analogies can serve as the origin of perspectives. In the previous chapter, we considered the analogy with reflections. Let us now consider the analogy with communication and the analogy with a family.

The Analogy with Communication

According to the analogy with communication, God the Father is the speaker; God the Son is the Word; and God the Holy Spirit is the breath of God carrying the Word out. The Holy Spirit also functions in some instances as the *recipient* or hearer of the Word (John 16:13). From this analogy, we can produce three perspectives on communication, based on the three persons of the Trinity.[1]

Communication at both the divine and the human levels involves a speaker, a speech (the word), and an audience. Each of these can be a starting point for a perspective on communication. The perspective from the standpoint of the speaker may be called the *expressive* perspective. The speaker expresses himself through speaking. The perspective from the standpoint of the speech may be called the *informational* perspective. The speaker communicates *content*. This content (information) proceeds from speaker to audience, so the content can be the starting point for considering the entire communication. Finally, the perspective from

1. See further Vern S. Poythress, *In the Beginning Was the Word: Language—A God-Centered Approach* (Wheaton, IL: Crossway, 2009), chaps. 2–4.

the standpoint of the audience may be called the *productive* perspective, because the speech is intended to produce something—to produce an effect.[2] (See table 12.1; fig. 12.1.)

Person of the Trinity	Function in Communication	Perspective
The Father	speaker	expressive perspective
The Son	speech	informational perspective
The Holy Spirit	breath and recipient	productive perspective

Table 12.1. Perspectives on Communication

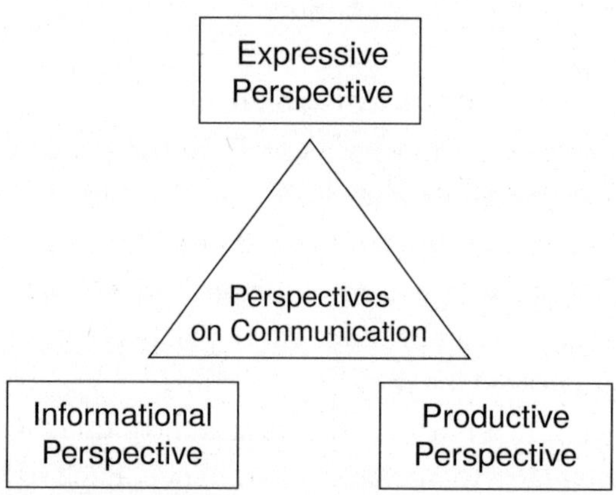

Fig. 12.1. Perspectives on Communication

We should say that the label *informational perspective* is not very satisfactory. The word *information* can in our day be a cold, colorless, bloodless word that denotes data isolated from persons and human purposes. That is not what we have in mind. The informational perspective

2. See Vern S. Poythress, *God-Centered Biblical Interpretation* (Phillipsburg, NJ: P&R Publishing, 1999), 101–7.

leads to and in the end includes reckoning with the person of the speaker and the purposes for the hearer. Maybe the word *content* or *discourse* would be better, but those two labels also have their own potential for misunderstanding. We will stick with the term *informational,* with the understanding that it designates a perspective that starts with the speech or writing and uses it as a perspective on the whole communication.[3]

Each of these three perspectives implicitly encompasses the others. To be expressive implies expressing something by way of content. That is, for someone to be a speaker implies a speech. The expressive perspective encompasses the informational perspective.

For a speaker to be expressive also implies that he intends some effect. That is, for someone to be a speaker implies the existence of someone to whom words are spoken with intentionality. (In the unusual case of soliloquy, the recipient or hearer is the same as the speaker—but there is still an intended hearer.) The expressive perspective encompasses the productive perspective.

To have a speech with information implies the existence of a speaker of the speech. That is, the informational perspective encompasses the expressive perspective.

To have a speech with information implies a destination for the speech. That is, the informational perspective encompasses the productive perspective.

To be the recipient of a speech implies the existence of a speaker and a speech. Thus, the productive perspective encompasses the expressive perspective and the informational perspective. To put it another way, in the process of hearing, the hearer is instinctively drawn in to considering the speech and the speaker. The hearer from his productive perspective naturally considers what the speaker is doing, and thus constructs within his productive perspective an expressive perspective for the speaker to whom he is listening. He also constructs an informational perspective as he considers the meaning of the speech's content. The speaker naturally considers whom he is addressing and what he wants to accomplish. So he begins to have within himself a sense of a productive perspective.

3. Since I used the expression *informational* in an earlier book, I am trying to avoid confusion by not needlessly multiplying terminology (ibid., 102).

Relation of the Trinity to Perspectives on Communication

With human beings, understanding of communication is never exhaustive. Speakers may misapprehend what will be effective for their listeners, and listeners may misapprehend what a speaker intends. Each person involved may be subject to sluggishness or dullness or duplicity. A human speaker may have a view of his audience that does not fully correspond to the audience. For instance, he may use English without realizing that the audience does not understand English. In such a case with human beings, the expressive perspective, from the standpoint of the limited and faulty knowledge of the speaker, does not fully encompass the productive perspective (though the speaker intends that it should). With God, on the other hand, there are no such limitations. So with God, each of the three perspectives is a perspective on the whole of communication.

The three perspectives on communication clearly have a relation to the persons of the Trinity, because the persons of the Trinity offer us the *archetype* or original for communication. All human communication consists in *ectypes* imitating the archetypal communication among the persons of the Trinity. We can therefore summarize the derivation of the perspectives on communication in a diagram that relates the perspectives to the Trinity (fig. 12.2).

The Trinity is the archetype for perspectives on communication, while the perspectives on human communication are ectypes. Even when we use the three perspectives to think about divine communication, our use remains subordinated to or derivative from the Trinitarian character of God, who is one God in three persons. So the perspectives we use are still ectypal.

The relation between the Trinity and the perspectives is a relation of an original (the Trinity) to a derivative manifestation (the three perspectives). This relation offers an instance involving reflection. The perspectives on communication are a reflection of the persons of the Trinity in their relations. The reflection encompasses at least three aspects:

1. Only one communication is being examined, and this communication reflects the unity of God.

2. There are three perspectives on communication, reflecting the three persons in God.

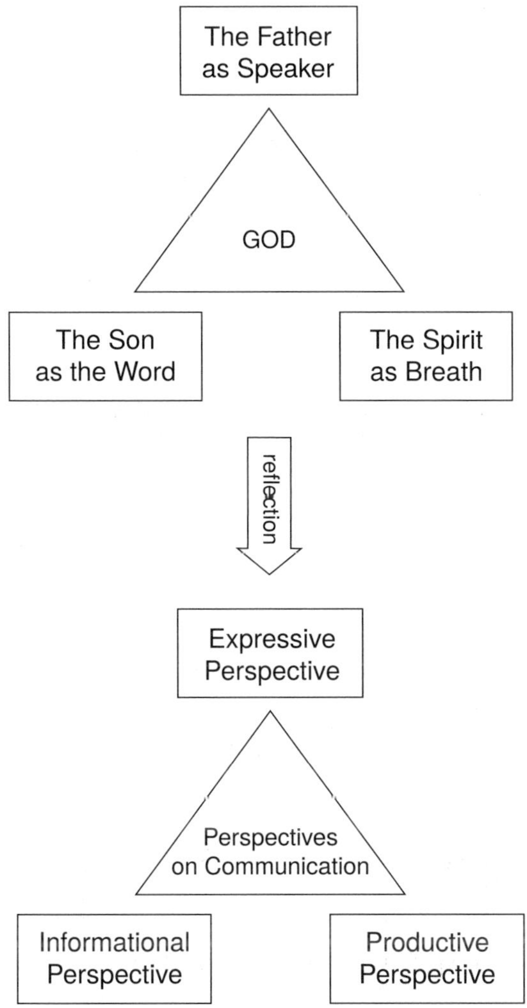

Fig. 12.2. From the Trinity to Communication

3. The three perspectives coinhere (they encompass one another), reflecting the coinherence among the persons in God.

Since the knowledge of the Trinity is mediated to us by divine speech to us, we can represent the mediating status of divine speech to us as a third triad, reflecting the Trinitarian character of God and reflected in turn in human perspectives. The eternal speech of God in his Word is reflected in his speech to us in time (God's covenantal speech). And the pattern shown in his speech is reflected in our human communication. (See fig. 12.3.)

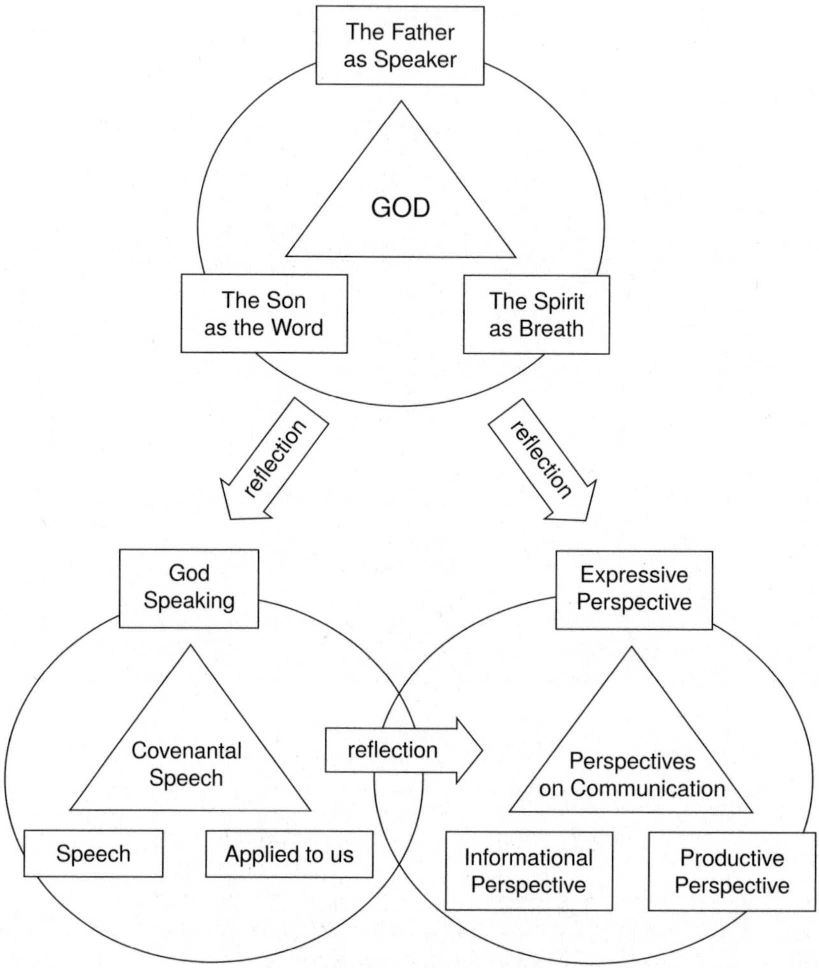

Fig. 12.3. From God through Covenantal Speech to Us

This reflection of God's character in his communication to us has practical bearing. Whenever we listen to God speaking to us in the Bible, we receive communication that has an inner structure reflecting the Trinity. We are supported by God's Trinitarian character, whether we are aware of it or not.

Family Perspectives

Next we consider the analogy that compares the Trinity to a family. It is an analogy using love. The Father loves the Son and gives him the Holy Spirit (John 3:34–35). The action of love can be viewed from the perspective of any of the three persons. The Father is the initiator of love. The Son is the recipient. And the Holy Spirit is the gift who expresses love. (See table 12.2; fig. 12.4.)

Person of the Trinity	Function in Love	Perspective
The Father	initiator	initiation perspective
The Son	recipient	reception perspective
The Holy Spirit	gift expressing love	gift perspective

Table 12.2. Perspectives on Love

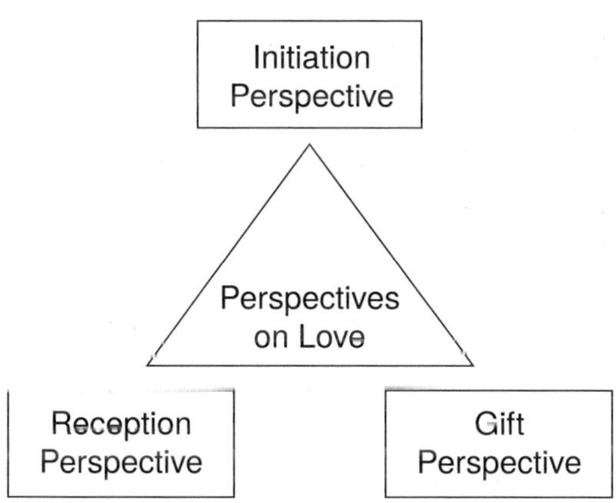

Fig. 12.4. Perspectives on Love

Love is an activity within the Trinity. But it is also an activity in which God engages in relation to human beings. God loves his people.

He is the initiator; the people are recipients and the gift is love, expressed preeminently in the gift of the Holy Spirit: "God's love has been poured into our hearts through the Holy Spirit who has been given to us" (Rom. 5:5). Love is also an activity in which human beings can engage in their relations to one another: "Beloved, if God so loved us, we also ought to *love* one another" (1 John 4:11).

We can see a common pattern with all three of the main analogies from chapter 8. In all three cases, God acts within himself, in relations between persons of the Trinity. God also acts toward us, and we act toward one another. God speaks to us, and we speak to one another. God makes a human being in his image, and fathers produce sons in their image. (See table 12.3.)

Analogy with Communication	Analogy with Reflections	Analogy with a Family
God speaks the Word	The Father begets his Image	The Father loves the Son
God speaks to us (covenantal)	God makes man in his image	God loves us
We speak to one another	Adam fathers Seth in his image	We love one another

Table 12.3. Reflections of Three Main Analogies

The Action Analogy

We are now in a better position to consider the action analogy (introduced in chapter 9). In table 12.2, we have three perspectives: the initiation perspective, the reception perspective, and the gift perspective. These three perspectives are quite general in character and can apply in situations other than the original one, in which we are focusing on God's love. For example, let us focus on the language in the New Testament about the Father's *sending* the Son. The Father is the initiator; the Son is the recipient of the Father's initiative. The Father gives the Holy Spirit to the Son so that the Son carries out the Father's initiative in the power of the Holy Spirit. And in addition, the Son sends the Holy Spirit as a gift to his disciples. The language of sending is still closely connected to the analogy with a family, since the Father is called the *Father* and the Son called the *Son* in connection with the sending.

In fact, since all of God's actions involve his love, we can expand to consider all of God's actions. The analogy with a family then leads naturally to what we have called the *action* analogy, with the Father as planner, the Son as executor, and the Holy Spirit as one who makes application. The Father as planner is the initiator. The Son is the recipient of the Father's plan and his commission, which the Son then executes. The Holy Spirit is the gift from the Father and the Son, and the Spirit is central in the application of the Son's work of redemption.

The action analogy for the Trinity can become the starting point for three perspectives. We can view an action from the standpoint of its planning, or from the standpoint of its execution and accomplishment, or from the standpoint of its completion in application. This triad of perspectives applies to human action. I plan to get bananas from the store. I go to the store and get them—I execute the plan. This act of obtaining the bananas is the stage of accomplishment. And when I get home, my family and I eat them—they become a gift to enjoy. Each stage in the action makes sense only because it goes together with the other two. Let us call these three viewpoints the *planning perspective*, the *accomplishment perspective*, and the *application perspective*. (See fig. 12.5.)

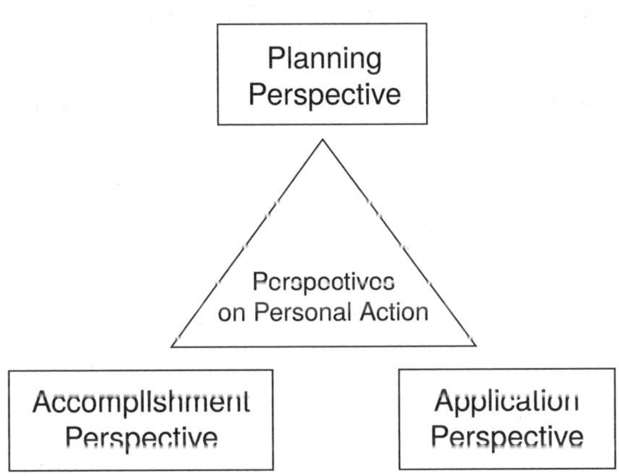

Fig. 12.5. Perspectives on Personal Action

Each of these three perspectives encompasses the other two. Planning is planning for accomplishment and application. So the planning perspective implicitly includes planning an accomplishment and planning an application, and includes within it a picture of both.

Accomplishment is accomplishment of a plan, leading to a conclusion (application). So the accomplishment perspective encompasses the planning perspective and the application perspective.

Application is application of what has been planned and accomplished. So the application perspective encompasses the planning perspective and the accomplishment perspective.

Human actions are not always *fully* planned out beforehand. And they do not always have clear goals in application. So when applied to human intentions, the three perspectives may not fully encompass one another. But God's exhaustive knowledge implies that the perspectives are all-encompassing when we consider divine action. And divine action always undergirds human action, since God sustains us all.

The three perspectives on personal action have their origin in the distinction among the persons of the Trinity. The perspectives in this way are a reflection of the persons of the Trinity. (See fig. 12.6.)

The Trinitarian character of God is the archetype or original. The perspectives are a derivative manifestation in human thought. They are an ectype, a reflection of the original.

The reflection includes several aspects:

1. Only one action is being examined, and this action reflects the unity of God.
2. There are three perspectives on the personal action, reflecting the three persons in God.
3. The three perspectives coinhere (they encompass one another), reflecting the coinherence among the persons in God.

Let us praise God for reflecting his Trinitarian character in his redemptive works and in perspectives that we may use in considering his works. This reflection of God's character has practical bearing. We experience salvation as a work of God. It is God who saves us, not we ourselves. And the way he saves us reflects his Trinitarian character, in planning, accomplishment, and application.

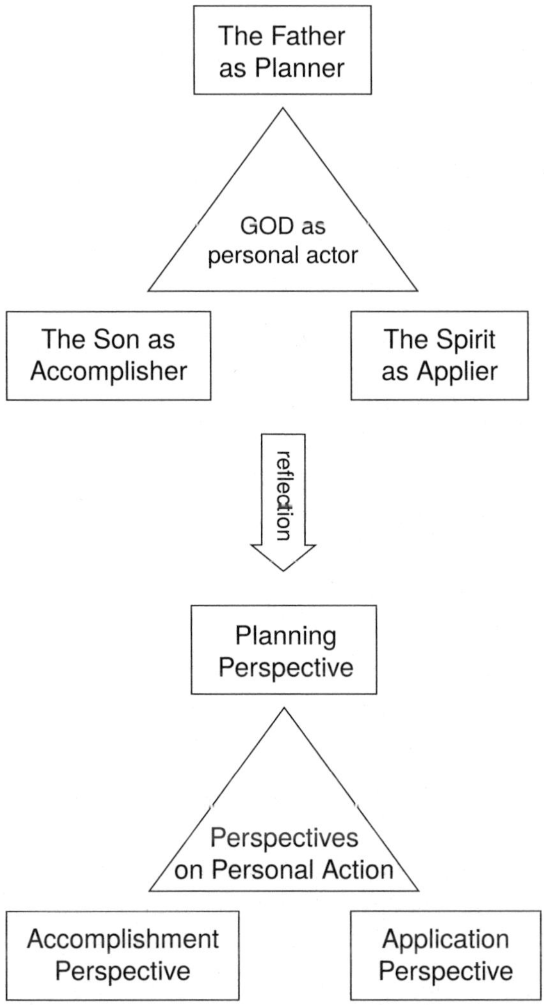

Fig. 12.6. From the Trinity to Personal Action

Key Terms

accomplishment perspective[4]
action analogy
analogy with a family
analogy with communication
analogy with reflections

4. Key terms in **bold** are defined in the glossary at the end of this volume.

application perspective
archetype
covenantal speech
derivative
expressive perspective
gift perspective
informational perspective
initiation perspective
manifestational
originary
perspectives on communication
perspectives on love
perspectives on personal action
planning perspective
productive perspective
reception perspective
reflection

Study Questions

1. In what way can perspectives be derived from the analogy with communication? from the analogy with a family or action analogy?
2. What are the three perspectives on communication? How do these relate to the persons of the Trinity?
3. In what way do the three perspectives on communication cohere with one another?
4. What are the three perspectives on love?
5. In what way do the three perspectives on love cohere with one another?
6. What are the three perspectives on personal action? How do these relate to the persons of the Trinity?
7. In what way do the three perspectives on personal action cohere with one another?
8. By thinking about the perspectives on communication and the perspectives on personal action, what can we learn about human nature and human abilities in relation to God?

For Further Reading

Poythress, Vern S. *God-Centered Biblical Interpretation*. Phillipsburg, NJ: P&R Publishing, 1999. Pp. 101–7. An explanation of the three perspectives on communication.

———. *In the Beginning Was the Word: Language—A God-Centered Approach*. Wheaton, IL: Crossway, 2009. Chaps. 2–4. On the origin of language in God.

13

Perspectives on Ethics

WE NOW CONSIDER some other perspectives that come into view when we consider some of the means by which God reveals himself within the world and interacts with the world. The first set of these perspectives has to do with ethics. Ethical requirements come from God. We know about ethics because God reveals himself within the world that he has made.

The Triad for Ethics

We consider a triad of perspectives on ethics, used by John M. Frame.[1] The three perspectives are the *normative* perspective, the *situational* perspective, and the *existential* perspective. These three perspectives offer three ways of approaching issues in ethics and Christian living.

When we use the normative perspective, we focus on the *norms* for living. These norms are found in commandments in Scripture, such as the Ten Commandments. The commandments need to be interpreted in the light of the larger context of scriptural instruction. In a broad sense, the whole Bible is in focus when we use the normative perspective, because the whole Bible, as the Word of God, has authority for us. It requires that we believe what it says, and that in itself is a normative requirement.

The second perspective, the situational perspective, focuses on the *situation* in which an ethical decision needs to be made. The situation is relevant because we should seek to give glory to God in every situation: "do all to the glory of God" (1 Cor. 10:31). The Bible commands us to "love your neighbor as yourself" (Gal. 5:14). Genuine love involves

1. John M. Frame, *Perspectives on the Word of God: An Introduction to Christian Ethics* (Eugene, OR: Wipf and Stock, 1999); John M. Frame, *The Doctrine of the Christian Life* (Phillipsburg, NJ: P&R Publishing, 2008).

paying attention to your neighbor, who is part of your situation. And it involves paying attention to the situation in which the neighbor is living, because changing things in the situation might be one way of helping your neighbor. The normative perspective leads to the situational perspective, because the normative command to love your neighbor leads to focus on the situation. We might say that the normative perspective encompasses the situational perspective, since we can develop the whole of the situational perspective on the basis of the normative principle of loving your neighbor. (Note that the situational perspective must be radically distinguished from "situation ethics," which is relativistic. God's norms in Scripture inform the situation and inform us about what is ethically proper in all situations.)

The third perspective, the existential perspective, focuses on the attitudes and motivations of the persons involved in an ethical decision. This perspective is also called the *personal* perspective, in order to emphasize the focus on persons and in order to distinguish it from the approach of atheistic existentialism. (See fig. 13.1.)

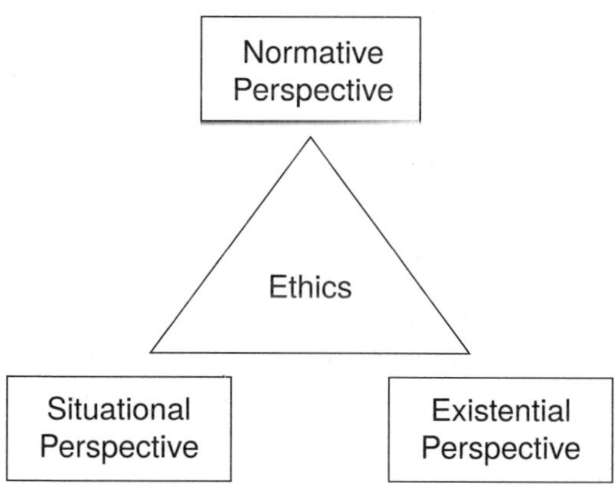

Fig. 13.1. Three Perspectives on Ethics

Personal attitudes are relevant because God's normative commandments include attitudes. The tenth commandment in the Ten Commandments says, "You shall not covet" (Ex. 20:17; Rom. 13:9). Coveting is an attitude. Love includes an attitude as well as actions based on the attitude. Our motive must be love. It should be clear that the normative perspective encompasses the existential perspective. The commandments about love and about coveting tell us that we must use the existential perspective.

The situational perspective, by focusing on the situation, also focuses on God as the most important person in the situation. When we focus on God and what he desires, we must pay attention to his normative instruction. Thus, the situational perspective leads to using the normative perspective. We might say that the situational perspective encompasses the normative perspective, since when we use the situational perspective rightly we find ourselves developing a normative attention within our initial framework.

Similarly, the situational perspective encompasses the existential perspective, since in a broad sense we and our attitudes are part of the situation. The existential perspective encompasses the normative perspective, since an attitude of love includes loving God and therefore paying attention to his desires (his norms). The existential perspective encompasses the situational perspective, since an attitude of love leads to paying attention to our neighbor and inquiring as to what is best within his situation.

Each perspective encompasses the other two. Or at least they *should* function in this way. In human ethics, rebellion against God produces distortions in all three perspectives. Human beings may replace God's norms with substitute norms of their own devising. They may interpret their situation as though it were independent of God. They may have false notions of love and other virtues. Salvation from God must take place to cleanse and transform us, in order that we may do our ethical reasoning rightly and make wise decisions.

Within a Christian approach, the three perspectives show the pattern of coinherence that we have seen before. So is there a relation between the three perspectives on ethics and the Trinitarian character of God? We have seen how a triad of perspectives on communication and a triad for personal action can be related to the Trinity (chap. 12). Is the same true for this triad for ethics?

Deriving the Triad for Ethics from the Trinity

Let us start with the triad of perspectives on personal action. It consists in the planning perspective, the accomplishment perspective, and the application perspective. We saw from the previous chapter that these three perspectives reflect the Trinitarian character of God. What happens when we apply these perspectives to ethics?

The planning perspective, when applied to the sphere of ethics, focuses on God's plan for ethics. His plan is expressed in his norms. Moreover, his plan offers the norms guiding what will happen in the world. So when we use the planning perspective to focus on ethics, we come to focus on norms. The planning perspective leads to the normative perspective on ethics. Thus, the planning perspective on personal action is reflected in the normative perspective on ethics.

The accomplishment perspective, when applied to the sphere of ethics, focuses on the world in which God accomplishes his purposes—that is, it focuses on the situation. God's accomplishments in history arrange our situations. The accomplishment perspective on personal action is reflected in the situational perspective on ethics.

The application perspective, when applied to the sphere of ethics, focuses on the application of ethics to persons, who are responsible to serve God in their situations. That is, the application perspective is reflected in the existential perspective on ethics.

So it makes sense to move from the triad of perspectives on personal action to the triad for ethics. This movement is a movement of *reflection*. Each of the three perspectives on personal action has a distinct reflection in ethics. In each case, this reflection has the form of a perspective on ethics. The planning perspective is reflected in the normative perspective on ethics, and in a similar way the accomplishment perspective and the application perspective are reflected, respectively, in the situational perspective and the existential perspective on ethics. As a whole, the triad for ethics reflects within ethics the triad for personal action. We can summarize the relation of reflection in a table (table 13.1) and in a corresponding diagram (fig. 13.2).

The relation of reflection between the triad for personal action and the triad for ethics includes three aspects:

1. Each triad has a unity, representing unified knowledge of the subject matter.

2. There are three perspectives in the first triad, each one corresponding to one perspective in the second triad.

Perspectives on Personal Action	reflection	**Perspectives on Ethics**
planning perspective	→	normative perspective
accomplishment perspective	→	situational perspective
application perspective	→	existential perspective

Table 13.1. From Perspectives on Personal Action to Perspectives on Ethics

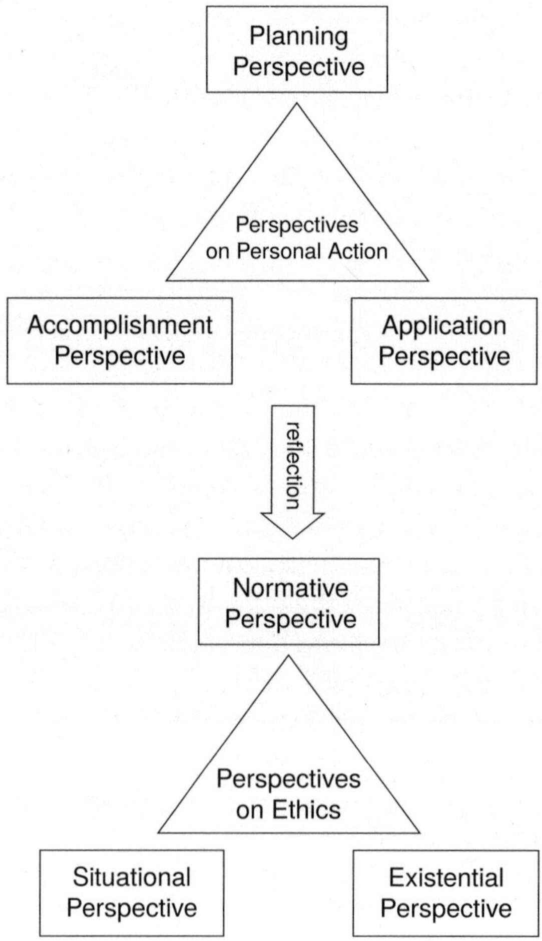

Fig. 13.2. Reflecting Personal Action in Ethics

3. The three perspectives within a triad coinhere (they encompass one another).

We saw in the previous chapter that the triad for personal action reflects the triune character of God. By implication, so does the triad for ethics. (See fig. 13.3.)

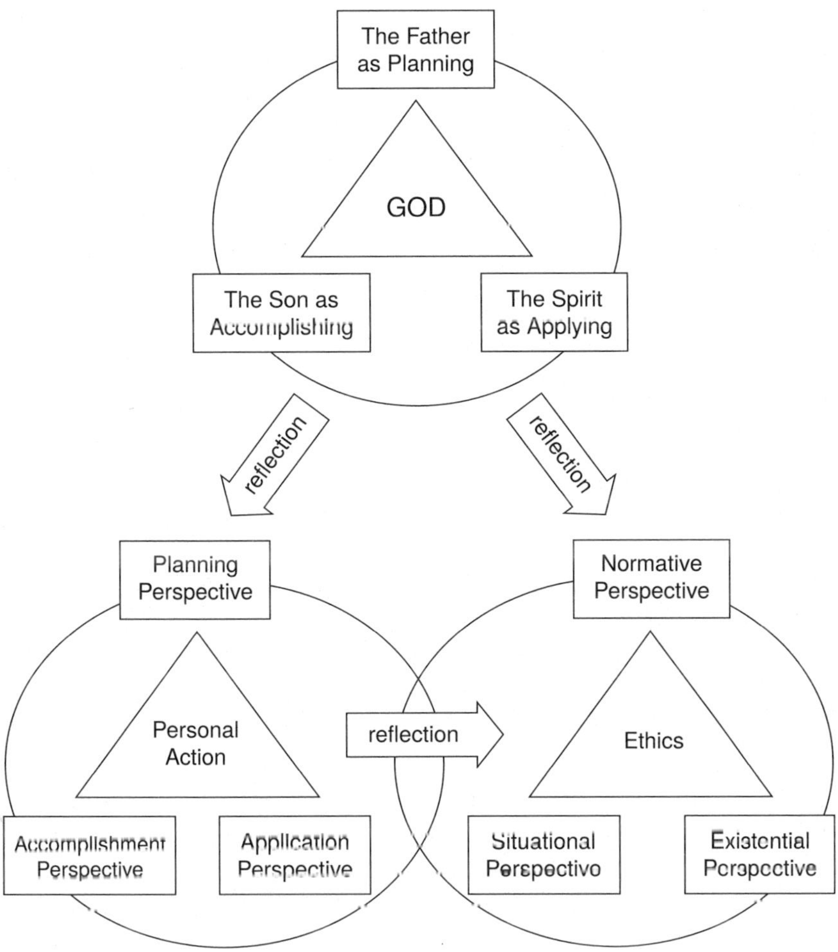

Fig. 13.3. From the Trinity through Action to Ethics

Thus, the coinherence among the perspectives on ethics reflects the coinherence among the persons of the Trinity.

Deriving the Triad for Ethics Another Way

We can also use the triad of perspectives on communication to reach the same conclusion. The triad for communication consists in three perspectives: the expressive perspective (starting with the speaker), the informational perspective (starting with the speech), and the productive perspective (starting with the hearer) (chap. 12). We may ask how this triad can be applied to ethics.

The speaker is the normative source for what he says. It is the speaker who determines what he says (content) and what claims he wants to make on the hearers (results). The expressive perspective, the perspective focusing on the speaker, leads to the normative perspective on ethics.

Next, observe that the speech puts out into the world the expression of the speaker. It puts ideas into a situation. Moreover, typically the speech is *about* the situation or some aspect of it. So the informational perspective leads to the situational perspective on ethics.

Finally, the hearer absorbs and reacts to what is said. The speech has a *personal* focus in its effects. The hearer may be transformed. The focus on the person and on his transformation leads to the existential perspective on ethics.[2] Thus, the triad for communication leads to the triad for ethics.

2. Could we construe the relation between the two triads in another way? Someone might argue that the expressive perspective on communication is reflected most effectively in the existential perspective on ethics, because the expressive perspective focuses on the speaker, who expresses his attitudes. This connection makes some sense. In fact, both the speaker and the hearer are *persons*. In a broad way, both persons might be in focus when we use the existential perspective. Likewise, when we consider the response to a speech by the hearers, the hearers are expected to act within the larger situation. So could the situational perspective be connected with the productive perspective on communication? And could the informational perspective be correlated with the normative perspective on ethics because the speech's contents make demands on the hearers?

We should remember that even within a single triad, each perspective is implicit in the others because of coinherence. Each perspective functions as a perspective on the *whole*. So each of the three perspectives on communication leads in the end to each of the three perspectives on ethics. Yet we can still say that some correlations are more direct and stronger than others. We can see the strongest correlations clearly if we recall that the triad for communication has its archetype in God. In God, God the speaker gives normative authority to his speech. So the expressive perspective on the speaker leads to the normative perspective on ethics. In addition, God's speech may be about the created world, and so addresses the situation directly. The situational perspective on ethics thus derives from the informational perspective, focusing on the speech content. By contrast, the relation of the *hearer* to the situation is more indirect. The

We may consider an ordinary illustration. Suppose that my wife tells me that we are out of bananas and would I please pick some up at the grocery store. My wife as a speaker and my relation to my wife provide normative direction for me to act in a particular way. The speaker leads to the normative perspective. The content of her speech refers to elements in the situation. We are out of bananas and there are bananas at the store. So the information in her speech leads to the situational perspective. Finally, the speech comes to me as a hearer. I have to absorb it and use it as a source for personal motivation. So the impact on the hearer (in focus in the productive perspectives) leads naturally to the existential perspective. Each perspective within the triad for communication leads to a distinct perspective within the triad for ethics. As a whole, the triad for communication has a reflection in the triad for ethics. Since the triad for communication is coinherent, the triad for ethics will be derivatively coinherent. Since the triad for communication reflects the Trinitarian character of God, so does the triad for ethics. (See fig. 13.4.)

We should not be surprised at this result. The analogy with personal action and the analogy with communication are both used in the Bible in describing the Trinity. Both are involved in each other and can be derived from each other (chap. 9).

In conclusion, using either the analogy with personal action or the analogy with communication, we can conclude that the triad of perspectives on ethics is a reflection of Trinitarian coinherence.

We praise God for expressing his character in the way that he interacts with us in the world, including the way in which he gives us ethical guidance and responsibility. God's ways with ethics have a practical bearing. Whether we are consciously aware of it or not, ethical considerations are always present in the background as we live and make our decisions. And these ethical considerations include normative, situational, and existential aspects all the time. These three are in coherent

hearer must first hear, and then decide how to act on his situation. Finally, in the case of God's speech, the speech comes to *us*, those who are persons. Before we begin to act, we must absorb the meaning of the speech. This inward absorption is closely related to the focus on attitudes that takes place in the existential perspective. It seems, then, that it makes more sense to line up the main, salient correlations between perspectives in the way that we have done: the expressive perspective leads to the normative perspective, the informational perspective to the situational perspective, and the productive perspective to the existential perspective. Yet the structure of coinherence means that each perspective at a deep level involves the others.

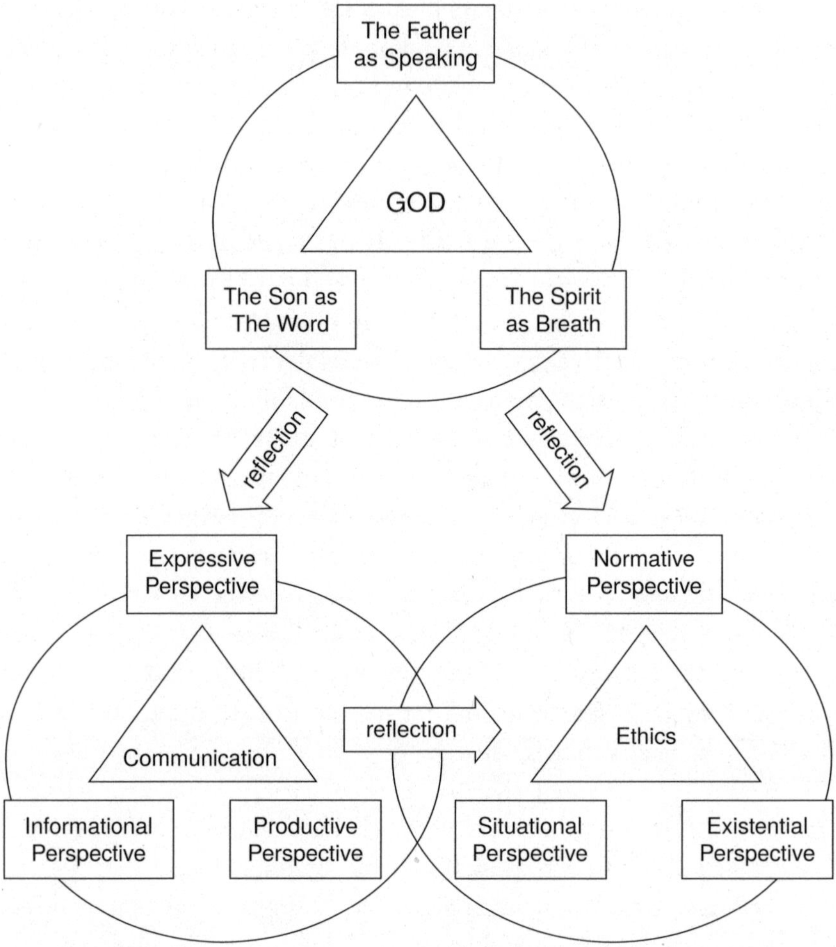

Fig. 13.4. From the Trinity through Communication to Ethics

harmony. God gives us support in our lives through the reflection of his character in the sphere of ethics.

Key Terms

derivation
existential perspective[3]
normative perspective

3. Key terms in **bold** are defined in the glossary at the end of this volume.

personal perspective
perspectives on communication
perspectives on ethics
perspectives on personal action
reflection
situational perspective

Study Questions

1. What are the three perspectives in Frame's triad for ethics, and how do they work?
2. Explain the coinherence of the perspectives on ethics.
3. How can the triad of perspectives on ethics be derived from the triad of perspectives on personal action? How is this derivation an instance of reflection?
4. Does the triad for ethics reflect the Trinitarian character of God? If so, how?
5. How does the derivation of the triad for ethics support the claim that this triad has a biblical foundation?
6. How can the triad of perspectives on ethics be derived from the triad of perspectives on communication? How is this derivation an instance of reflection?

For Further Reading

Frame, John M. *The Doctrine of the Christian Life*. Phillipsburg, NJ: P&R Publishing, 2008. Extensive applications of the triad for ethics, in relation to the Ten Commandments and many ethical questions.

———. *Perspectives on the Word of God: An Introduction to Christian Ethics*. Eugene, OR: Wipf and Stock, 1999. An introduction to the triad of perspectives on ethics.

14

Perspectives on Lordship

IN THE PREVIOUS chapter, we began to consider various perspectives that come to light as we look at the ways in which God reveals himself in the world. The perspectives on ethics are one such means. Now we consider the perspectives on *lordship*.

The Triad for Lordship

The triad of perspectives on lordship is used repeatedly by John M. Frame.[1] There are three perspectives on lordship: *authority, control,* and *presence*. Frame developed these themes as perspectives by examining the biblical theology of lordship throughout the Scriptures.

According to the perspective of *authority,* God exercises his lordship by having authority over what he rules. He has the legal and moral *right,* as the universal Sovereign, to govern and judge the people and things that are under his lordship. And everything is under his lordship. The Ten Commandments vividly express God's moral authority. Human beings such as governors and parents have authority that God has delegated to them. They may or may not use their authority rightly. But God is perfectly holy, and his authority goes together with his moral rectitude.

According to the perspective of *control,* God actually controls the things over which he is Lord. God brought the people of Israel out of Egypt and across the Red Sea. Within the Ten Commandments, he indicates that he will issue rewards for obedience (Ex. 20:6, 12) and punishments for disobedience to his commandments (20:5, 7).

1. See esp. John M. Frame, *The Doctrine of the Knowledge of God* (Phillipsburg, NJ: Presbyterian and Reformed, 1987); John M. Frame, *The Doctrine of God* (Phillipsburg, NJ: P&R Publishing, 2002).

According to the perspective of *presence*, God is personally present as he exercises lordship and rules over his subjects. (See fig. 14.1.)

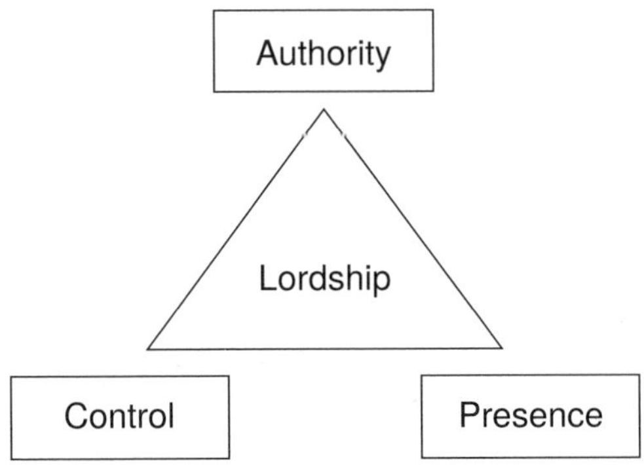

Fig. 14.1. Three Perspectives on Lordship

Each of these three themes (authority, control, and presence) serves as a *perspective* on God's lordship because all the expressions of God's lordship in all circumstances display his authority, control, and presence. God is authoritative and controlling and present in the miracles in Egypt and the crossing of the Red Sea and the issuing of the Ten Commandments and the instructions for the tabernacle. God is the same God when he accomplishes climactic salvation in Christ. Christ shows us God's authority, control, and presence. Every interaction with human beings or the created world shows God's lordship, and in every interaction he exhibits authority, control, and presence. This universal exhibition of lordship is natural because it is in accord with his character. His authority expresses his moral goodness, his holiness, and his absoluteness, as well as his position as Sovereign Creator. His control expresses his omnipotence. His presence expresses his attribute of omnipresence.

The three themes—authority, control, and presence—cannot be isolated from one another because all of them are exhibitions of the one God, who is simultaneously Sovereign Creator and omnipotent and omnipresent.

We can see all three themes in incidents in the Old Testament. Consider Korah's rebellion, as recorded in Numbers 16. God shows his authority especially when he pronounces judgment on Korah (16:21).

He shows his control when he causes the earth to swallow up the rebels 16:30–33). He shows his presence when he appears to the congregation (16:19). But in the light of these key moments in the episode, we can see that God's authority, control, and presence are involved all through the narrative. For example, his authority is displayed when he uses his control to carry out the judgment on Korah that he has earlier pronounced. The actual effects on Korah remind us of the authoritative claims that he has made earlier (in 16:21). And God is present in the act of consigning Korah and his companions to judgment.

Perspectives on Lordship Implying One Another

Because each of the three characteristics of lordship functions as a perspective on the whole, we would expect each to lead to the others and encompass the others. Let us begin with the perspective of authority. God's authority is ultimate. Whatever limited authority human beings exercise, they have it because it has been granted by God: "For there is no authority except from God, and those that exist have been instituted by God" (Rom. 13:1).

The ultimacy and universality of God's authority imply that he has authority over processes and events, not just over the moral *evaluation* of events after they have taken place. To have authority over an event is to control it. So authority implies control.

The universality of God's authority implies that his authority is everywhere. And so God through his exercise of authority expresses his presence everywhere. Authority implies presence.

Now consider God's control. God's control includes control over the evaluation of all events and over the standards for such evaluation. To control the standards is to have authority as a right because authority is manifest in the standards. So control implies authority. By controlling events, God is present to exert his control. So control implies presence.

Finally, consider God's presence. God is present in his absolute sovereignty to each human being all the time. His presence includes his moral presence. Presence implies authority because presence is the presence of the Sovereign God, who has the right to judge and to command. His presence is also the presence of his omnipotence. So presence implies and includes the exercise of control. Presence implies control.

Coinherence in Lordship

The three perspectives on lordship appear to be coinherent, in a manner similar to the other instances of coinherence. As usual, this coinherence leads us to ask for a deeper explanation. Is the coinherence in perspectives derived from the coinherence among the persons of the Trinity, or is the relationship merely accidental?

Since God is the absolute origin and archetype, we naturally suspect that the coinherence in perspectives on lordship is an ectype or reflection deriving from the coinherence in the archetype in the persons of the Godhead. But can we confirm this idea more specifically by finding a relation between the archetypal coinherence among the persons of the Trinity and the ectypal coinherence in the perspectives on lordship?

Deriving the Triad for Lordship

Let us begin with the triad for personal action. It consists in three perspectives: the planning perspective, the accomplishment perspective, and the application perspective (see chap. 12). Now let us use this triad to consider the meaning of God's actions in the world as an exercise of lordship. First, the planning perspective leads to a focus on authority. The planner is the person who has authority to specify the course of action. Second, the accomplishment perspective leads to a focus on control. The person who accomplishes the plan accomplishes it by exerting control in the world. His control leads to the working out of the plan. Third, the application perspective leads to a focus on presence. The person who applies the plan brings it to bear on people, and this bringing to bear of the plan makes it effectively present to those whom it affects.

In fact, the triad for personal action and the triad for lordship are closely connected. The triad for personal action shows how lordship is made manifest in action over time. So we could also start with the triad for lordship and move to derive the triad for personal action.

In sum, the triad of perspectives on lordship reexpresses the triad of perspectives on personal action, and vice versa. Each can be seen as reflecting the other. (See table 14.1; fig. 14.2.) Since the triad for personal action is coinherent, the triad for lordship is naturally coinherent. The correspondence between the two triads includes three principles:

Perspectives on Personal Action	reflection	Perspectives on Lordship
planning perspective	→	perspective of authority
accomplishment perspective	→	perspective of control
application perspective	→	perspective of presence

Table 14.1. From Personal Action to Lordship

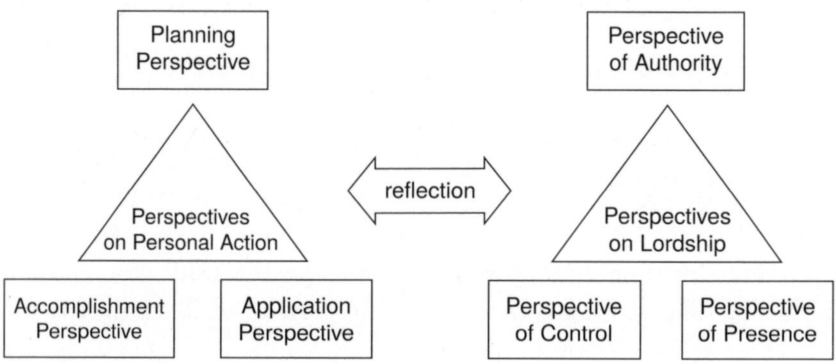

Fig. 14.2. From Personal Action to Lordship

1. Each triad has a unity, representing unified knowledge of the subject matter.
2. There are three perspectives in each triad, and each perspective in the first triad corresponds to one perspective in the second triad.
3. The three perspectives in one triad coinhere (they encompass one another).

Derivation of Lordship from the Trinity

We saw in chapter 12 that the triad for personal action reflects the triune character of God. By implication, so does the triad for lordship. (See fig. 14.3.)

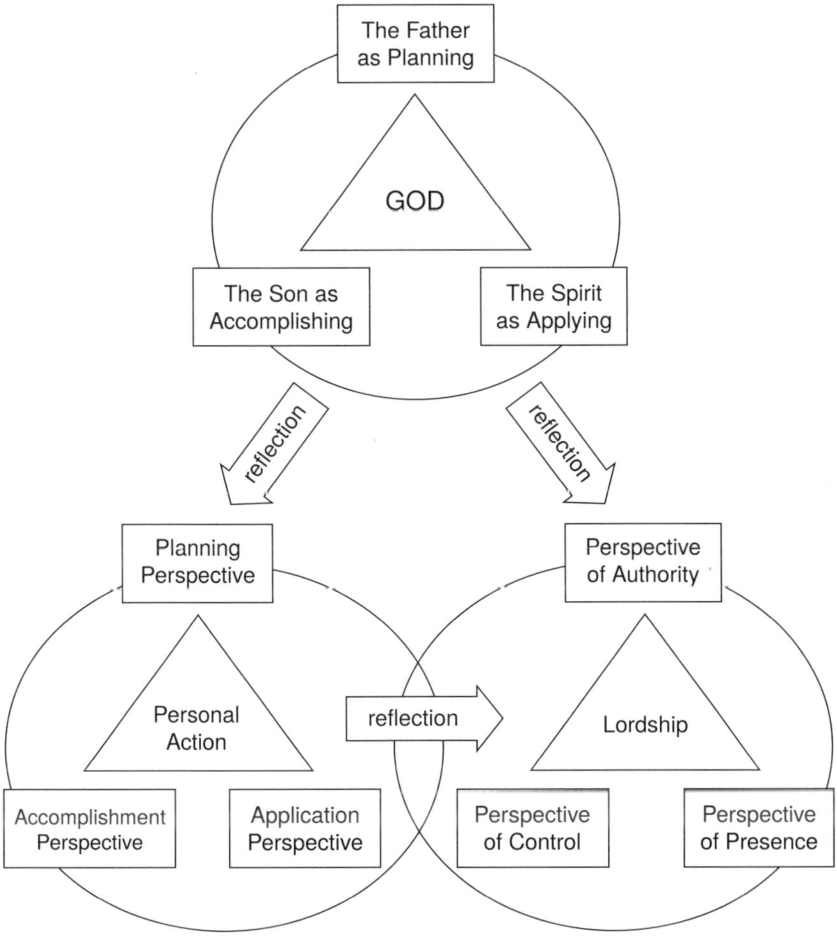

Fig. 14.3. From the Trinity through Action to Lordship

Derivation of Lordship through the Triad for Communication

We can arrive at the same conclusion by starting with the triad of perspectives on communication: the expressive, informational, and productive perspectives (see chap. 12). Since God exercises his lordship by speaking, we can apply the three perspectives on communication to the examination of lordship. The expressive perspective starts with the intention of the speaker—his intention gives authority to the speech. So the expressive perspective leads to the theme of *authority*. The informational perspective focuses on the speech and its contents. These contents control the nature of the speech, and shape the response of those who receive the message. Thus, the informational perspective leads to the theme of *control* (through speech). The productive perspective focuses on the destination of the speech in impacting the hearer. The speech is carried to its destination by breath. The breath or the arrival of the speech in the hearer by some other means makes the speech *present* to the hearer. Thus, the productive perspective leads to the theme of *presence.*

The triad for lordship can thus be derived from the triad for communication. Since the triad for communication reflects the Trinitarian character of God (chap. 12), so does the triad for lordship. (See fig. 14.4.)

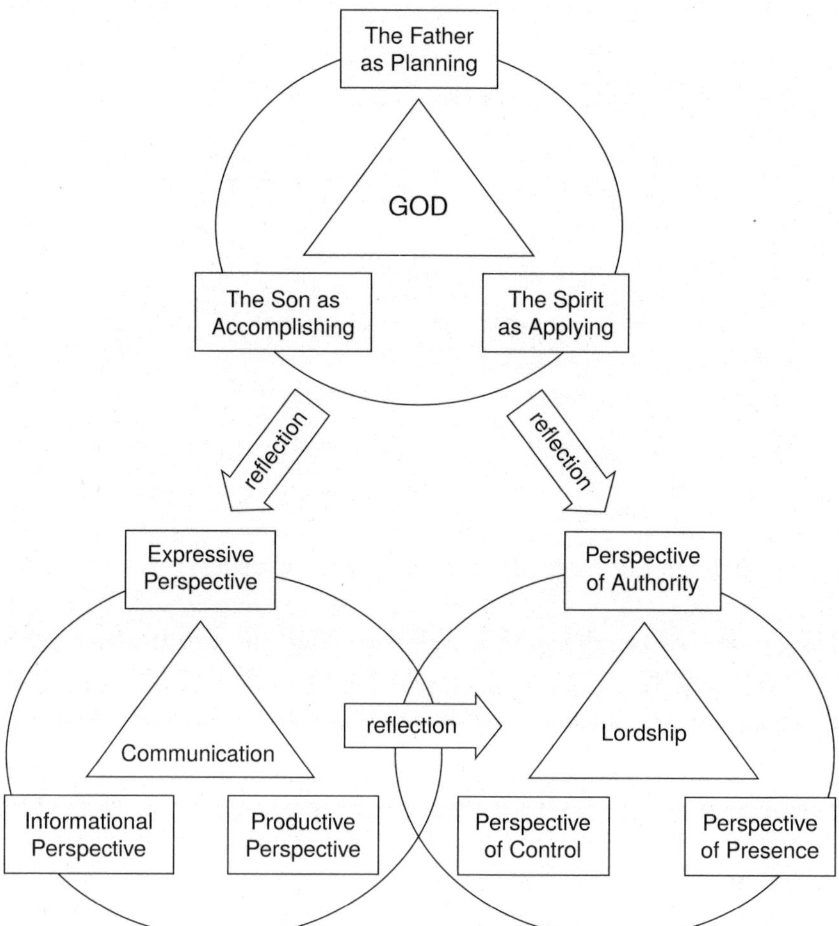

Fig. 14.4. From the Trinity through Communication to Lordship

Derivation of Lordship through the Triad for Ethics

Finally, the perspectives on lordship can be derived starting with the perspectives on ethics. Recall from the previous chapter that there are three perspectives on ethics: the normative, situational, and existential perspectives.

The normative perspective focuses on the source of authority for ethics. Thus, the normative perspective leads to the theme of *authority*.

The situational perspective focuses on the situation in which ethical decisions are made. These decisions rely on the ability of human beings to exercise at least limited control over the situation. And this limited control has its foundation in the exhaustive control exercised by God, a control that actually brings into existence the situation and everything in it. The situational perspective leads to the theme of *control*.

Finally, the existential perspective focuses on the persons and their attitudes and motives. The existential perspective matters because God is the Judge of attitudes and motives as well as external actions. He is the rightful Judge of these things because he is present. He searches the depths of the heart: "And no creature is hidden from his sight, but all are naked and exposed to the eyes of him to whom we must give account" (Heb. 4:13). Thus, the existential perspective leads to the theme of *presence*.

Since the triad for ethics is coinherent, the triad for lordship is coinherent. (See fig. 14.5.)

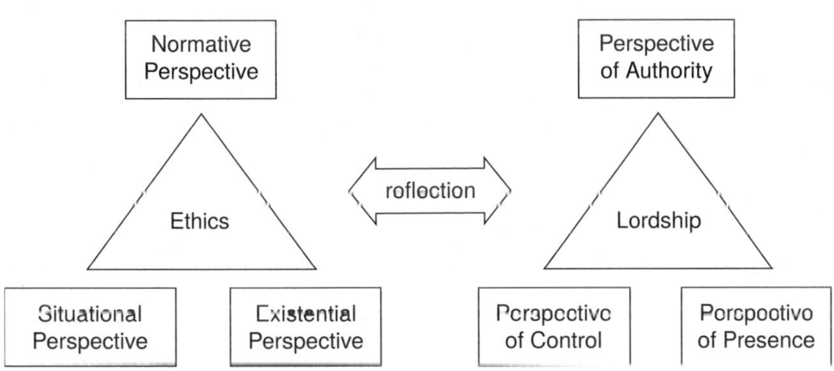

Fig. 14.5. From Ethics to Lordship

Derivation of Ethics from the Triad for Lordship

We may also reason in the reverse direction: we may derive the triad for ethics from the triad for lordship. The triad for lordship consists in authority, control, and presence. Authority implies the right to specify the standard for ethics. Thus, it specifies the norms. The perspective of authority leads to the theme of norms. Control takes the form of control over the entire situation. Control leads to the theme of the situation. Presence means presence to the person involved in ethics, including the hidden attitudes and motives of the person. Thus, presence leads to the theme of attitudes. From this brief sketch, we can see that when the biblical teaching on lordship is rightly understood, it leads naturally to considering ethics in terms of the three perspectives on ethics that we have already examined in the previous chapter—the normative, situational, and existential perspectives.

By earlier reasoning in this chapter, we have seen that the triad for lordship reflects the coinherent relations among the persons of the Trinity. Likewise, according to the previous chapter, the triad for ethics reflects the coinherent relations among the persons of the Trinity. Our final step in reasoning shows that the triad for ethics and the triad for lordship each reflect the other. This mutual reflection confirms the earlier reasoning that both reflect the archetypal coinherence in the Trinity.

These observations about lordship have a practical bearing. Those who belong to Christ by faith confess his lordship: "if you confess with your mouth that Jesus is *Lord* and believe in your heart that God raised him from the dead, you will be saved" (Rom. 10:9). Confessing Christ as Lord implies that we receive his lordship in all three aspects: he has divine *authority* over us; he exercises *control* over us; he is *present* with us (Matt. 28:20) and in us (Rom. 8:10). These are aspects of Christ's lordship, even when we are not consciously aware of all of them. They have their ultimate foundation in the Trinitarian character of God, who rules over us in Christ.

The fact that God meets us in all three ways means that he is caring for us comprehensively. The fact that the three ways coinhere means that God's care brings unity rather than disharmony to our lives.

Key Terms

absoluteness[2]
accomplishment perspective
application perspective
archetype
authority
coinherence
control
derivation
ectype
existential perspective
expressive perspective
holiness
informational perspective
lordship
normative perspective
omnipotence
omnipresence
perspective of authority
perspective of control
perspective of presence
planning perspective
presence
productive perspective
reflection
situational perspective

Study Questions

1. What is the triad of perspectives on lordship? Why is it important?
2. How do the perspectives on lordship coinhere?
3. How can you derive the triad of perspectives on lordship from the triad for personal action?
4. How can you derive the triad for lordship from the triad for communication?

2. Key terms in **bold** are defined in the glossary at the end of this volume.

5. What do the derivations of the triad for lordship show about its Trinitarian roots?
6. How can you derive the triad for lordship from the triad for ethics?
7. How can you derive the triad for ethics from the triad for lordship?
8. What do the derivations and coinherence show about the unity of salvation and the unity in being a disciple of Christ?

For Further Reading

Frame, John M. *The Doctrine of God.* Phillipsburg, NJ: P&R Publishing, 2002. Extensive use of the triad for lordship, in relation to the doctrine of God. Direct discussion of the triad on pp. 36–102.

———. *The Doctrine of the Knowledge of God.* Phillipsburg, NJ: Presbyterian and Reformed, 1987. Introduction to the triad of perspectives on lordship, and extensive discussion of the triad and its use, in relation to the knowledge of God. See esp. pp. 15–18.

15

Perspectives on Office

IN THIS CHAPTER, we consider a third aspect of the way in which God interacts with the world that he has made. This third aspect appears in the Old Testament in the form of human officers or intermediaries. God appoints these intermediaries to represent God to the people or represent the people to God or both. These are the well-known three offices of the Old Testament—the offices of prophet, king, and priest.

The Triad for Offices

We discussed the three offices in chapter 4. In that chapter, we expanded the themes of prophet, king, and priest into perspectives: the prophetic perspective, the kingly perspective, and the priestly perspective. These three perspectives have as their starting themes speaking, ruling, and giving communion, respectively.

Each perspective encompasses the other two. All of Christ's work is simultaneously a way of God's speaking, a way of God's ruling, and a way of God's granting communion. This involvement of the perspectives in one another looks like a form of coinherence. So as usual, we may ask whether the triad for offices can be seen as deriving from the Trinity.

From the Triad for Personal Action to the Triad for Offices

Let us start with the perspectives on personal action. These are the planning perspective, the accomplishment perspective, and the application perspective. The planning perspective is closely related to speaking because planning involves thought, which is expressed in speech. We might say that thought is a kind of internal analogue to speech and that speech is an external analogue to thought. So the planning perspective, when applied to offices, leads to speech, which is characteristic of the prophet. In other words, the planning perspective leads to the prophetic perspective.

The accomplishment perspective involves influential action in the world. It involves the exertion of power. So it leads naturally to the theme of *ruling*, which is characteristic of kings. The accomplishment perspective leads to the kingly perspective.

Finally, the application perspective involves the delivery of the fruit of action to recipients. The delivery makes the action *present* to recipients, and they come into communion with the accomplishment. Communion is the characteristic concern of the priestly office. So the application perspective leads to the priestly perspective.

All together, each of the three perspectives in the triad for personal action is correlated naturally with one of the three perspectives in the triad for offices. (See table 15.1; fig. 15.1.)

Perspectives on Personal Action	reflection	**Perspectives on Office**
planning perspective	→	prophetic perspective
accomplishment perspective	→	kingly perspective
application perspective	→	priestly perspective

Table 15.1. From Personal Action to Perspectives on Office

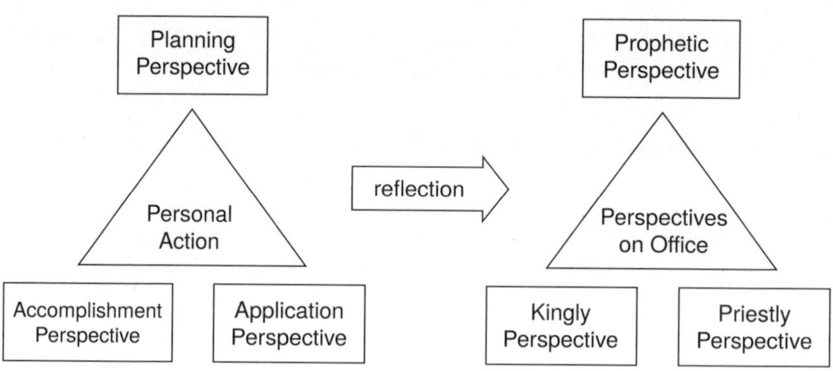

Fig. 15.1. From the Triad for Personal Action to the Triad for Offices

In chapter 12, we saw that the triad for personal action reflects Trinitarian coinherence. The triad for offices reflects in turn the coinherence in the triad for personal action. So the triad for offices is a reflection of the coinherence in the Trinity.[1] (See fig. 15.2.)

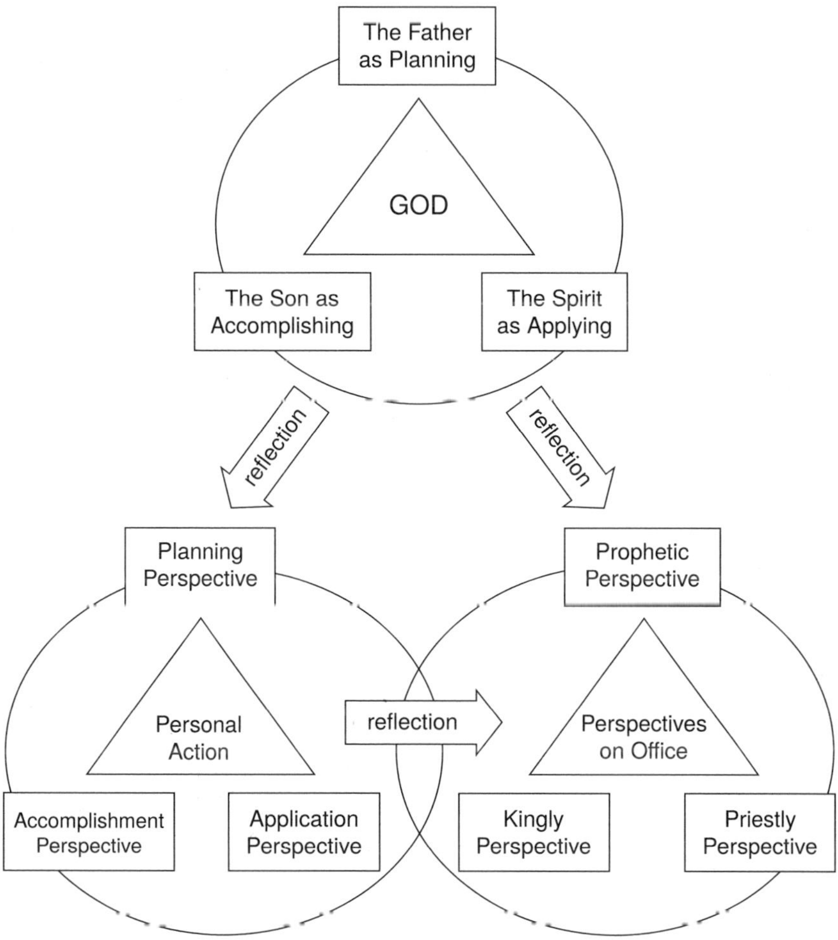

Fig. 15.2. From the Trinity through Action to Offices

1. Why do we list the three offices in the order that we do, as prophet, king, and priest? The correlations between the triad for offices and the triad for personal action provide an answer. The triad for personal action has a natural order, consisting in planning, then accomplishment, then application, in that order. We can also see how the three offices have correlations directly with the three persons of the Trinity. God the Father is preeminently the planner, who then speaks to commission the Son to execute his plan with kingly power. The Holy Spirit expresses

Praise the Lord for his reflections of his Trinitarian character in human capacities for perspectives! This reality has a practical bearing. The Lord is continually interacting with us as Prophet, King, and Priest. We rely on God's Trinitarian nature as the foundation for this interaction.

Key Terms

accomplishment perspective[2]
application perspective
coinherence
communion
intermediary
king
kingly perspective
perspectives on office
perspectives on personal action
planning perspective
priest
priestly perspective
prophet
prophetic perspective
reflection

---

the presence of God, and this presence is correlated with the priesthood, whose task is largely to mediate the presence of God to the people.

But confessional documents such as the Heidelberg Catechism (answer 31) have usually adopted another order: prophet, priest, and king. It is not clear what has led to this preferred order. One suggestion might be that Jesus acts preeminently as Prophet during his teaching ministry on earth. Then he acts as High Priest in his sacrificial death. And finally, he reigns as King now that he has ascended. But this separation of the offices in time is too simple. The Heidelberg Catechism in answer 31 points out that Jesus in heaven "makes continual intercession with the Father," so that his high-priestly work is simultaneous with his kingly reign. And as the Messiah, he was already the King during his earthly life. The Heidelberg Catechism (answer 31) also describes his teaching ministry as being "*our* chief Prophet" (italics mine), which includes an ongoing prophetic ministry to us.

It might also make sense to use the order king, prophet, and priest. God the Father is the ultimate King, and the Son as the Word of God brings us the prophetic word of this King. But the three persons of the Trinity indwell one another, so that we cannot strictly separate these functions. The Father, the Son, and the Spirit are each Prophet and King and Priest. It is true that the Son is called "the Word" (John 1:1), but in this description the Father is the speaker and so has a prophetic function.

2. Key terms in **bold** are defined in the glossary at the end of this volume.

Study Questions

1. What are the three main offices in the Old Testament?
2. How do these three main offices function in mediating God's relation to man?
3. How are the three offices related to three distinct perspectives?
4. How are the perspectives on office coinherent?
5. How can you derive the perspectives on office from the perspectives on personal action?
6. What does this derivation show about the Trinitarian origin of the perspectives on office?
7. How can you derive the perspectives on office from the perspectives on lordship?
8. How can you derive the perspectives on lordship from the perspectives on office?

For Further Reading

Heidelberg Catechism, question 31. http://reformed.org/documents/index.html?mainframe=http://reformed.org/documents/heidelberg.html. Expounding the meaning of Christ as Prophet, Priest, and King.

Westminster Confession of Faith 8.1. http://reformed.org/documents/wcf_with_proofs/index.html. Expounding the meaning of Christ as Prophet, Priest, and King.

Westminster Larger Catechism, questions 42–45. http://reformed.org/documents/wlc_w_proofs/index.html. Expounding the meaning of Christ as Prophet, Priest, and King.

PART 4

CLASSIFYING PERSPECTIVES

WE CONSIDER HOW we may classify the various triads that we have surveyed in the previous chapters.

16

A Triad for Revelation

WE HAVE SURVEYED a multitude of perspectives. We have grouped them into triads. Now let us stand back and ask how we may grasp the multitude of triads. Why *these particular* triads? In a way, it is not too hard to see why. Each triad has some connection with biblical teaching.

In some cases, the connection is fairly obvious. For example, the triad for communication (chap. 12) is based on the biblical analogy describing the relation of the persons of the Trinity to communication. The triad for love (which can also be called the triad for the family, chap. 12) is based on the biblical analogy describing the love between persons of the Trinity (esp. John 3:35; 5:20). The triad for personal action (chap. 12) is based on the biblical analogy describing the distinct manner in which the persons of the Trinity participate in divine action in history. The triad for reflections (chap. 11) is based on the biblical analogy describing the relations of the persons of the Trinity in theophany and in the fact that the Son is the image of the Father.

But can we further classify the different triads?

God's Revealing Himself

To begin a further step in classification, we may recall the distinction that we introduced earlier (chap. 10) between the *ontological Trinity* and the *economic Trinity*. The term *ontological Trinity* designates God apart from interaction with the world. The term *economic Trinity* designates God in his interactions with the world.

If we ponder it, these two ways of thinking about God function like perspectives. In both cases, we are viewing the same object, namely, God. But we view him *through* the window or perspective in which we contemplate his works in interacting with the created world. In that case, we are focusing on the economic Trinity. Or we view him through the window or perspective offered by biblical descriptions of eternal attributes and eternal relations among the persons of the Trinity. God was always holy and omniscient and infinite, even before the world began. God's character and his eternal attributes are always the same, both before and after the creation of the world. The Son is always the Word in relation to God the Father (John 1:1). These descriptions focus on the ontological Trinity. So with respect to God, we may speak of an *ontological* perspective or an *economic* perspective. The ontological perspective focuses on God as he always exists, even apart from creation. The economic perspective focuses on God as he is involved in acting in the world. These two perspectives can be used not only in considering the Trinity but in considering any topic having to do with God.

The two perspectives imply one another. The economic perspective implies the ontological perspective because in considering God through the window of his works, we are implying the existence of God, who is the absolute God even apart from his works in creation. This implication follows from the principle of Christian immanence, according to which we actually know God, the true God, not merely a substitute or a finite replica (chap. 10).

Conversely, the ontological perspective implies the economic perspective because we have come to know God only through God's work of *revealing* himself. He reveals himself to us and in the world, and these acts of revelation are acts of the *economic* Trinity. They are acts in relation to the world. As we have said, God exists even before there was a world. But for us as creatures to have an ontological perspective, we must also implicitly have an economic perspective. In fact, in terms of our experience of growing human knowledge, the economic perspective is the more natural starting point. But it immediately leads to the beginning of the ontological perspective because in knowing God, we come to know that he transcends the world (the Christian principle of transcendence).

In sum, the two perspectives (ontological and economic) are distinct because God is distinct from the world and transcends the world (the Christian principle of transcendence). The two perspectives are involved in each other and imply each other, because through revelation in the world we access knowledge of God (the Christian principle of immanence).

It appears that the two perspectives coinhere. Is this an accident? We may suspect not. So what is the source of this coinherence? Does it reflect the original coinherence among the persons of the Trinity?

We might suspect that it does, not merely because of the common features of coinherence, but because of the nature of revelation. Revelation from God to us is always Trinitarian in character. In redemption, God reveals himself in the Son through the Holy Spirit's work in us. We needed *mediated* revelation because of sin. Otherwise, we would die because of the holiness of God (cf. Isa. 6:5). Jesus is the one *Mediator*:

> For there is one God, and there is one *mediator* between God and men, the man Christ Jesus, who gave himself as a ransom for all. (1 Tim. 2:5–6)

Before Adam's fall into sin, there was no sin to create an obstacle or barrier between God and man. But Christ functioned as *Mediator* of creation in a broad sense:

> Yet for us there is one God, the Father, from whom are all things and for whom we exist, and one Lord, Jesus Christ, *through whom are all things* and through whom we exist. (1 Cor. 8:6)

> For *by him* all things were created, in heaven and on earth, visible and invisible, whether thrones or dominions or rulers or authorities—all things were created *through him* and for him. (Col. 1:16)

God spoke to mankind even before the fall (Gen. 1:28–30; 2:16–17). We may infer that this speaking was a manifestation not only of the will of God, but of the Word of God, who is the Son. And the speaking took place through the "breath" of God, who is the Spirit.

The speech of God to man is Trinitarian because it reflects God, who is Trinitarian. The speech of God reveals God because it is in harmony with who God is.

A Reflection in Speaking

The triad for reflections is relevant for understanding not only the creation of Adam but also God's speech to Adam. Adam is an ectype in relation to God the archetype. We can analyze this relation using the triad for reflections: the originary, manifestational, and connectional perspectives. God's speech to Adam presupposes God's original speech in the form of the eternal Word. In the originary perspective, we focus on God's original speech within the Trinity. In the manifestational perspective, we focus on the specific speeches that God speaks to Adam in Genesis 1:28–30 and 2:16–17. In the connectional perspective, we focus on the relation of harmony between the two.

The originary perspective and the manifestational perspective are indeed in harmony, because God is in harmony with himself and in full command of his own speech. The harmony is fittingly related to the Holy Spirit.

Now, when we focus on God's original speech in the eternal Word, we focus on the ontological Trinity. When we focus on the derivative speech to Adam, we focus on an act of the economic Trinity. We can state the situation more generally. The originary perspective, when applied to God in his distinction from the world, results in the ontological perspective. The manifestational perspective, when applied to God's relation to the world, results in the economic perspective. We conclude, then, that the ontological and economic perspectives on the Trinity agree. The one is a reflection of the other. The two perspectives on the Trinity can be derived from the originary and manifestational perspectives on reflections. They are in harmony, as guaranteed by the connectional perspective. We may even introduce a third perspective in addition to the ontological and economic perspectives, namely, a *harmonistic* perspective, which explicitly focuses on the harmonious character of economic revelation in relation to the ontological reality of God as the original. The connectional perspective, when applied to God's revelation, results in the harmonistic perspective. (See table 16.1; fig. 16.1.)Together, the ontological perspective, the economic perspective, and the harmonistic perspective form a triad of *perspectives on revelation*. This triad is coinherent.

We saw earlier (chap. 11) that the connectional perspective can focus on the connection between the original and its reflection, that

Perspectives on Reflections	reflection	Perspectives on Revelation
originary perspective	→	ontological perspective
manifestational perspective	→	economic perspective
connectional perspective	→	harmonistic perspective

Table 16.1. From Perspectives on Reflections to Perspectives on Revelation

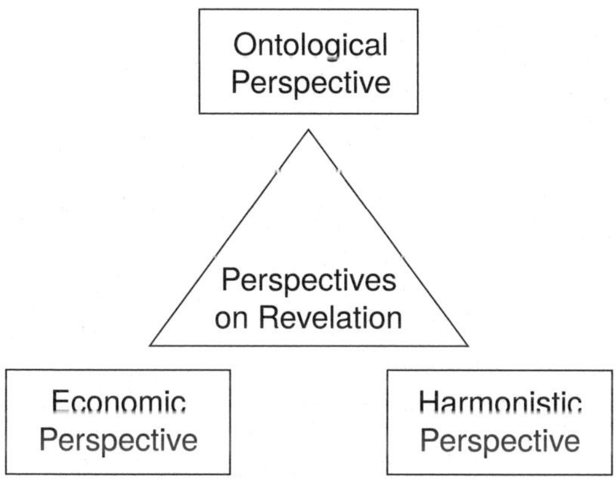

Fig. 16.1. A Triad of Perspectives on Revelation

is, its manifestation. But in the case of theophany, the connectional perspective can also focus on the connection between the reflection (the theophanic appearance) and human *reception*. The same is true of the harmonistic perspective. We can appreciate harmony between the ontological Trinity and the economic Trinity. We can also appreciate harmony between the economic Trinity and human reception of God's acts when the reception is illuminated by the Holy Spirit.

It should be noted that the work of the Holy Spirit in us, in illuminating our minds and hearts, guarantees harmony between our knowledge of the Trinity and the Trinity. We truly *know* the ontological Trinity, not by escaping our creatureliness, but by the work of God actually reaching us and applying to us and being *present* in us, so that our knowledge harmonizes by connection with God, who is original, manifesting himself in his speech and work in interacting with creation.[1]

All in all, we can see that the ontological perspective and the economic perspective on the Trinity are two perspectives that are coinherent. Their coinherence reflects the originary coinherence among the persons of the Trinity. They do so because their coinherence reflects the coinherence in the triad for reflections, and the triad for reflections reflects in turn the triad of three persons in their coinherence. (See fig. 16.2.)

We praise God that he has resources in his own character by which he is able to reveal himself truly and effectively to us.

Key Terms

coinherence[2]
connectional perspective
economic perspective
economic Trinity
harmonistic perspective
manifestational perspective
ontological perspective
ontological Trinity
originary perspective

1. B. A. Bosserman in personal correspondence pointed out to me that each of the three perspectives—ontological, economic, and harmonistic—can be further analyzed into a triad. The ontological perspective is a perspective useful not only for thinking about God in his unity, but for thinking about each person of the Godhead. So we can have an ontological perspective on God the Father, discussing who he always is. And we have an ontological perspective on God the Son, discussing who he always is as the Son. And so for the Holy Spirit.

Similarly, we can have three distinct foci for an economic perspective. We have an economic perspective on God the Father, focusing on the Father's works with respect to creation, providence, redemption, and consummation. And so also we have an economic perspective on the Son, focusing on the works of the Son, and an economic perspective on the Spirit, focusing on the works of the Spirit.

Finally, we can have a harmonistic perspective on the Father, focusing on the Father's work in bringing harmony, especially harmony between God and our knowledge of God. Bosserman quotes Matthew 16:17, "Blessed are you, Simon Bar-Jonah! For flesh and blood has not revealed this to you, but *my Father* who is in heaven." In a harmonistic perspective on the Son, we see that the Son reveals the Father to us (Matt. 11:27). And the Holy Spirit through illumination reveals the Father and the Son.

2. Key terms in **bold** are defined in the glossary at the end of this volume.

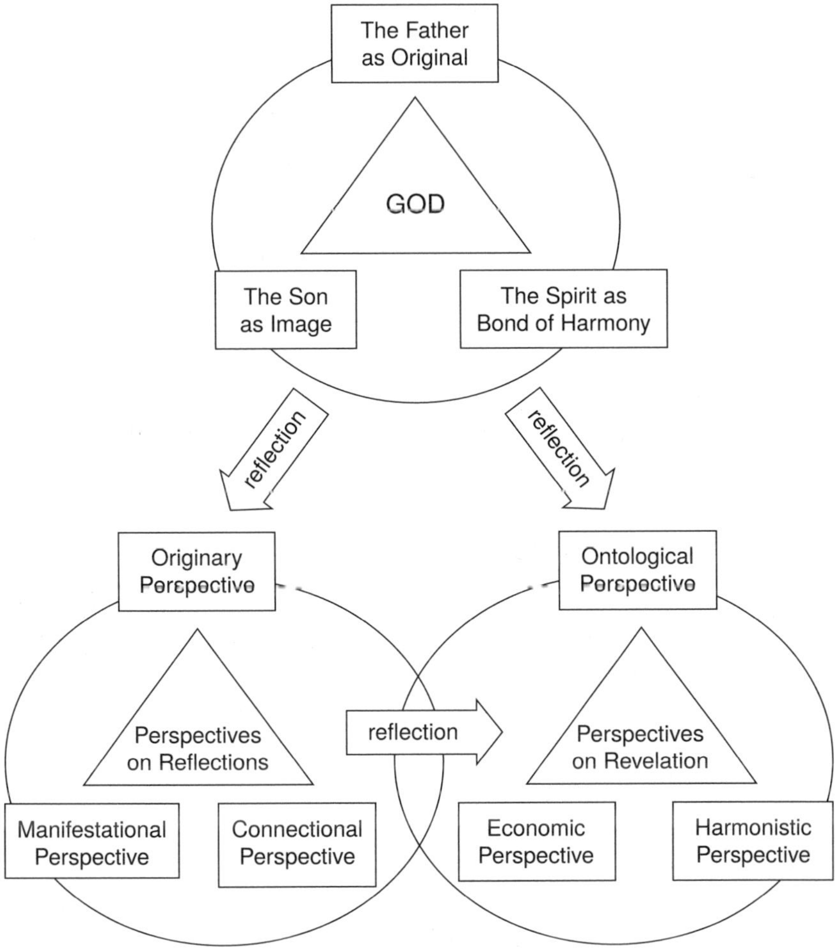

Fig. 16.2. From the Trinity through Reflections to Revelation

perspectives on reflections
perspectives on revelation
revelation
triad
triad for communication
triad for personal action
triad for reflections
triad for revelation

Study Questions

1. What is the triad for revelation?
2. How is the triad for revelation related to the distinction between the ontological Trinity and the economic Trinity? to the distinction between the Creator and the creature?
3. How is the triad for revelation coinherent?
4. How can you derive the triad for revelation from the triad for reflections?
5. What does this derivation show about the Trinitarian source for the triad for revelation?
6. How is the triad for revelation pertinent to our understanding of how we know God?

For Further Reading

Van Til, Cornelius. *Introduction to Systematic Theology: Prolegomena and the Doctrines of Revelation, Scripture, and God.* Edited by William Edgar. 2nd ed. Phillipsburg, NJ: P&R Publishing, 2007. Chaps. 6–11. On revelation.

17

Trinitarian Classification of Perspectives

WE MAY NOW proceed to further classify the triads of perspectives that we have described earlier in the book.

Three Triads for Biblical Revelation Pertaining to the Harmonistic Perspective

Let us consider the three triads deriving from biblical analogies for the Trinity, namely, the triad for reflections (chap. 11), the triad for communication (chap. 12), and the triad for love (chap. 12). (See table 17.1.)

Triad for Communication	Triad for Love	Triad for Reflections
expressive perspective	initiation perspective	originary perspective
informational perspective	reception perspective	manifestational perspective
productive perspective	gift perspective	connectional perspective

Table 17.1. Triads Based on Biblical Analogies for the Trinity

These three triads are triads that we use as creatures. But they derive from analogies in the Bible that speak about eternal *ontological* relations among the persons of the Trinity. The triad for communication comes from the biblical teaching about the Son's being the *Word* of God (John 1:1). He was the Word "in the beginning," that is, even apart from his involvement in creation. The triad for love comes from the biblical teaching about the Father-Son relation, as expressed in love (3:35; 5:20). And the triad for reflections comes from the biblical teaching about Christ's being the image of God (Col. 1:15; Heb. 1:3). The Son is the image of God even before the creation of the world.

In all three cases, these truths about God get illustrated through economic manifestations. For instance, God's speech to create the world illustrates and reflects the fact that the Son is the eternal Word. The analogy with communication uses God's speech addressing the world as the starting point for an analogy. God's eternal speech is analogically represented by his speech addressing the world. The analogy provides us with understanding of who God is, even before he created the world. The analogy thus functions in some ways to provide a cognitive bridge between God's economic activity and God's ontological activity. This bridge function is related to the harmonistic perspective, in which we focus specifically on the harmony between the ontological perspective and the economic perspective. We may accordingly classify the three triads deriving from analogies for the Trinity by grouping all three under the general heading of the harmonistic perspective. (See table 17.2.)

Harmony in revelation (under the harmonistic perspective)	Triad for Communication	Triad for Love	Triad for Reflections

Table 17.2. Summary of Triads under the Harmonistic Perspective

Three Triads for Biblical Revelation Pertaining to the Economic Trinity

We also have some triads whose focus is more on matters pertaining to the *economic* Trinity. That is, the triads deal with the work of God in the world. The triad for ethics explores how God exercises his moral authority over us. The triad for lordship explores how God exercises his lordship over us and over the world. The triad for offices explores how

God exercises mediation of his various kinds of action, often through human representatives (prophets, kings, and priests). Accordingly, we may group all three of the triads under the general headling of the economic perspective. We can summarize our classification in a diagram. (See table 17.3.)

Economic Trinity in revelation (under the economic perspective)	Triad for Ethics	Triad for Lordship	Triad for Offices

Table 17.3. Summary of Sorted Triads

We can combine the two tables 17.2 and 17.3 into a two-row table, and add the fact that the harmonistic perspective derives from the connectional perspective, while the economic perspective derives from the manifestational perspective. (See table 17.4.)

Connectional Perspective →	under the **harmonistic** perspective	Triad for Communication	Triad for Love	Triad for Reflections
Manifestational Perspective →	under the **economic** perspective	Triad for Ethics	Triad for Lordship	Triad for Offices

Table 17.4. Combined Summary of Sorted Triads

Perspectives within Perspectives

In table 17.4, we have actually used the triad for reflections at two distinct points. It is mentioned explicitly in the table (in the upper right corner), and the table also includes the connectional perspective and the manifestational perspective on the left-hand side. Should we be worried about this duplication? No, it is in accord with the nature of God. How?

According to the principle of coinherence in knowledge, the Son knows the Father completely. Also, the Father knows the Son completely (Matt. 11:27). Since the Father knows the Son completely, he also knows the Son's *knowledge* of the Father. Since the Son knows the Father completely, the Father knows this complete knowledge that the Son has of the Father. The Father knows himself completely within the act of knowing the Son completely. And by knowing himself completely, the Father also knows everything about his own knowledge of the Son, which includes knowledge concerning the Son's knowledge of the Father, which includes knowledge concerning the Son's knowledge of the Father's knowledge of the Son. And so on. The same things are true concerning the Spirit's knowledge, and the Son's knowledge of the Spirit. However far we reason, we have the mystery of the Trinity. There is no "bottom" or end point at which our analysis could stop, because the Trinity is infinite and incomprehensible.

The same is derivatively true of perspectives derived from the Trinity. "Inside" the originary perspective is the manifestational perspective, and "inside" the manifestational perspective is the originary perspective. So the originary perspective is in a sense inside itself. And it is inside itself an indefinite number of times.[1] We can see a full triad of perspectives through each one.

So in table 17.4 above, it is actually not surprising that the triad for reflections occurs *within* (indwelling) the connectional perspective, which itself is one perspective within the triad for reflections. The embedding of a triad within itself is an effect of coinherence.

Triples of Triads

Now let us return to the overall organization of table 17.4. The first row contains three triads falling under the general heading of the harmonistic perspective. The second row contains three triads that fall under the general heading of the economic perspective, which focuses on the economic Trinity. Why are there exactly *three* triads in each row? There are three because we picked out the three in each case. But they are related to one another. There is only one Trinitarian God. The three triads belonging under the general heading of the harmonistic perspective all explicate the same reality of the relation of persons within the Trinity, as reflected in revelation. Similarly, for the triads under the general heading of the economic perspective, the three triads

1. We can see a dim analogy to this pattern in fractal patterns in geometry.

all explicate the same reality of God's interacting with the world and with his people. So is each triad of perspectives, when taken together, itself like a perspective? Let us consider it.

Triads under the General Heading of the Economic Perspective

The three triads under the general heading of the economic perspective are the triad for ethics, the triad for lordship, and the triad for offices. (See table 17.5.)

	Triad for Ethics	Triad for Lordship	Triad for Offices
Under the Economic Perspective:	normative	authority	prophet
	situational	control	king
	existential	presence	priest

Table 17.5. Triads under the General Heading of the Economic Perspective

The triad for ethics begins with a focus on the question of ethics, which involves God's normative claim on us. The triad for lordship begins with a focus on God's interaction in power with us and our entire situation. It has a *situational* focus. The triad for offices begins with a focus on the persons whom God raises up to mediate his interaction with us. It has an *existential* focus. Thus, the triad for ethics, consisting of normative, situational, and existential perspectives, can be used at a higher level to explicate the relations among the three triads. The three triads derive, respectively, from normative, situational, and existential focus on God's economic work. (See table 17.6.)

This derivation suggests that the three triads are perspectivally related and coinherent with one another. And such coinherence follows from the fact that we are examining the same reality of God's economic activity, from three perspectives, and that each perspective is a perspective on all of God's economic activity. At an earlier point, we have also seen that there is a detailed correlation between the triad for ethics and the triad for lordship. (See fig. 14.5.) Each of the three triads—for ethics, for lordship, and for offices—can be derived by starting with the triad for personal action (chaps. 13–15).

The three triads are coinherent with one another. This coinherence is a reflection of the coinherence in the triad for ethics, which we used to understand the relation among the three triads. The coinherence in the triad for ethics is in turn a reflection of the coinherence in the Trinity (see chap. 13). (See fig. 17.1.)

	Triad for Ethics		
	↓ Normative ↓	↓ Situational ↓	↓ Existential ↓
Under the Heading of the Economic Perspective:	**Triad for Ethics**	**Triad for Lordship**	**Triad for Offices**
	normative	authority	prophet
	situational	control	king
	existential	presence	priest

Table 17.6. From Ethics to the Triple of Triads under the Economic Perspective

The Nature of the Triad for Personal Action

What about the triad for personal action? We introduced this triad in chapter 12, in close association with the triad for love. But we noted at the time that it did not seem to be "on the same level" as the triad for love, or the other triads based on the main analogies for the Trinity, namely, the triad for communication and the triad for reflections. We are now in a position to give a more thorough account of where this triad fits. The triad does not focus on God's activity within himself, activity that includes communication, love, and reflection. Rather, it focuses on God's actions in the world. So it belongs under the larger grouping made up of triads under the economic perspective.

The triad for personal action can be viewed as the form taken by the triad for lordship when we ask how the expression of God's lordship

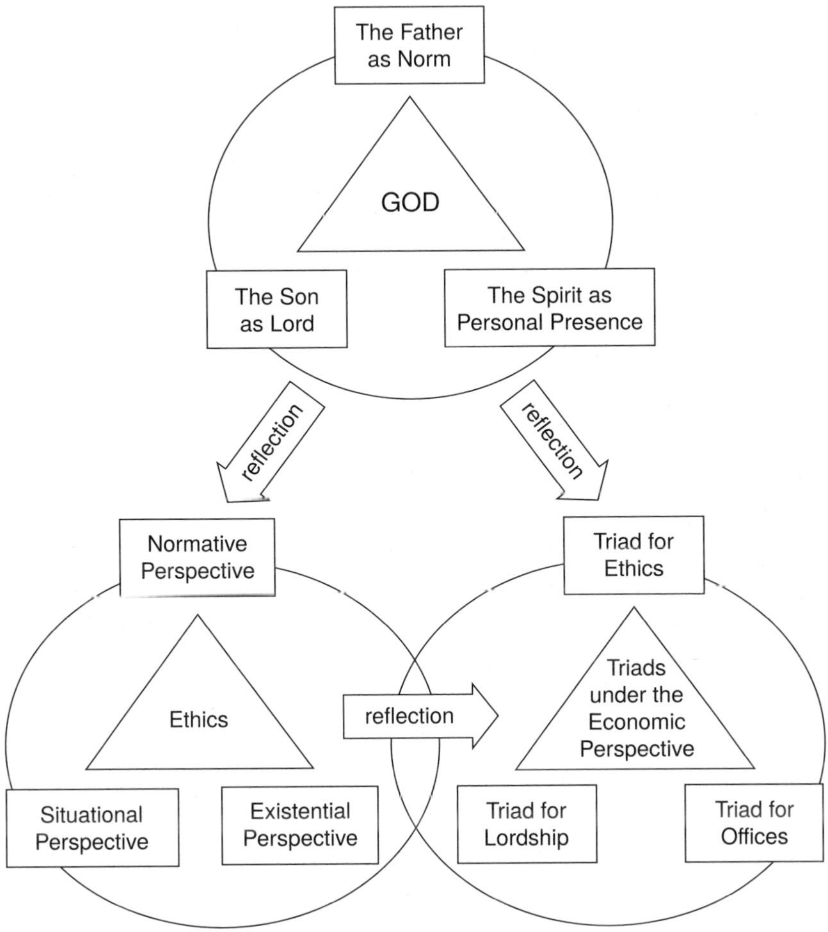

Fig. 17.1. From the Trinity to Ethics to the Triple of Triads under the Economic Perspective

is worked out in time (see chap. 14). The triad for lordship has three perspectives that we can treat as simultaneous: the perspectives of authority, control, and presence. But when we see God's action spread out in time, authority shows itself preeminently in planning, which has to do with laying out the authoritative guide of the accomplishment. Control shows itself preeminently in accomplishment, which must involve exerting control in the world. The presence of God shows itself preeminently in application, in which God comes to bring the fruits of the accomplishment to work personally and intimately on the human recipient. Thus, the triad for personal action may be considered as another way of articulating the triad for lordship.

Triads Belonging under the Heading of the Harmonistic Perspective

Now let us consider more closely the three triads belonging under the general heading of the harmonistic perspective: the triad for communication, the triad for love, and the triad for reflections (from table 17.2).

The triad for ethics can serve as a possible starting point for understanding the distinctions among triples of triads. In the triad for ethics, the normative perspective correlates with the triad for communication, in that communication is a prime source for receiving norms. The situational perspective correlates with the triad for love (also called the triad for family), since love expresses a person's relation to the situation.[2] With a human family, the family is a basic part of the situation. The existential perspective correlates with the triad for reflections, because a process of reflection is the way of bringing about the personal presence of God. Because we are made in the image of God, our own motives should reflect God. (See table 17.7.) Since the triad for ethics is a coinherent reflection of the Trinity, so is the triple of triads under the harmonistic perspective. (See fig. 17.2.)

Now we can combine our insights for this entire chapter. The triads under the general heading of the economic perspective can also be correlated with the triad for ethics, as we saw from table 17.6, in a way that is similar to what we just worked out for the triads under the general heading of the harmonistic perspective (table 17.7). We can therefore summarize the distinctions and relations among many of the triads by using the triad for ethics. (See fig. 17.3.)

2. When we introduced the triad for ethics in chapter 13, love was closely associated with the motivations for ethical action, and therefore was linked with the existential perspective. But the key verses for the expression of love between God the Father and God the Son (John 3:35; 5:20) occur in the immediate context of divine action. The focus is not narrowly on the internal motive of one person, but more broadly on the action, and therefore touches on the "situation" in which one person acts. The situation is composed of the other persons of the Trinity and their relations.

	Triad for Ethics		
	↓ Normative ↓	↓ Situational ↓	↓ Existential ↓
	Triad for Communication	**Triad for Love**	**Triad for Reflections**
Under the Heading of the Harmonistic Perspective	expressive perspective	initiation perspective	originary perspective
	informational perspective	reception perspective	manifestational perspective
	productive perspective	gift perspective	connectional perspective

Table 17.7. From Ethics to the Triads under the Heading of the Harmonistic Perspective

Alternative Organization

We have offered this summary as a useful way for organizing triads of perspectives into a larger whole. And it helps to show that the triads are coinherently related to one another. They are also related to general patterns concerning God and how God interacts with mankind. But is this summary the one right way of doing it? Probably not. All the perspectives that we have considered are understood to be perspectives *on a larger whole*. They can be used in thinking about all of God's works within the created order. The triads under the general heading of the harmonistic perspective—the triad for communication, the triad for love, and the triad for reflections—have pertinence both to the ontological Trinity and to God's works. The triads under the general heading of the economic perspective—the triad for ethics, the triad for lordship, and the triad for offices—focus on God's relations to human beings, but they reflect the nature of who God is, and so they, too, can be expanded to reflect the ontological Trinity.

If all the perspectives are perspectives on the *same* whole, and if all perspectives implicitly include or imply all the other perspectives, it can

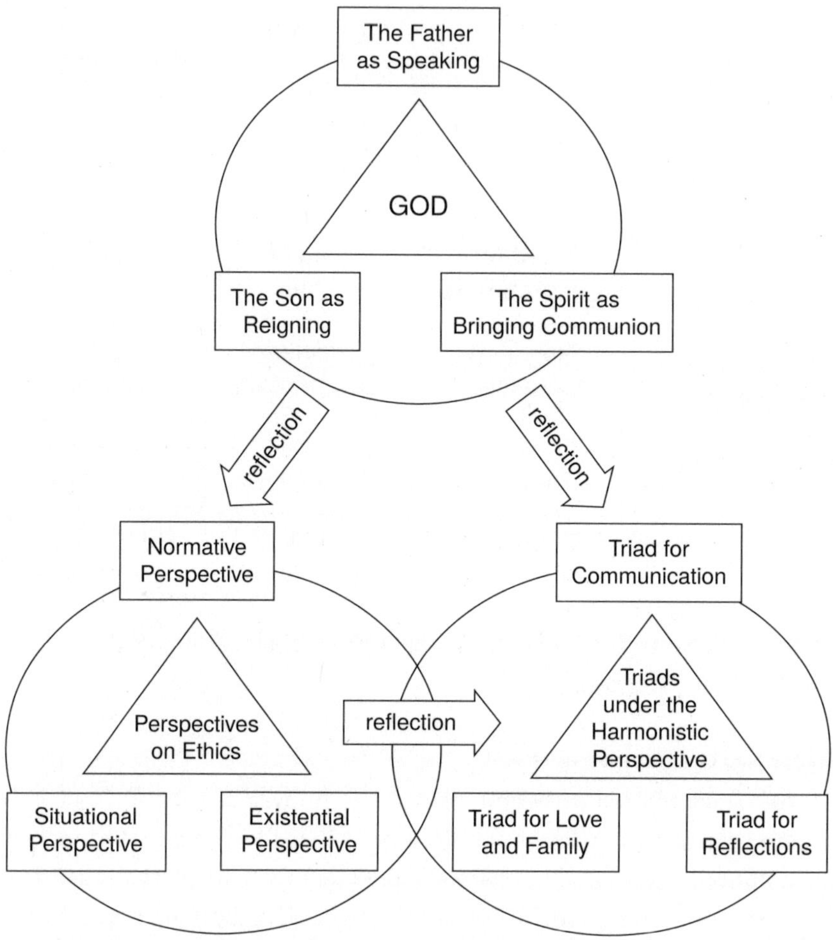

Fig. 17.2. From the Trinity through Ethics to Triads under the Harmonistic Perspective

get difficult to distinguish them at points. So it can also be difficult to classify them. Perspectives tend not to have the "neat," organized boundaries that belong, say, to a biological species such as domestic sheep.

Though perspectives are not so neatly classifiable, the difficulty reminds us of the mystery of God himself. We should be in awe of the many ways that he provides for us to understand him. And we should thank him for giving us the capability of using perspectives.

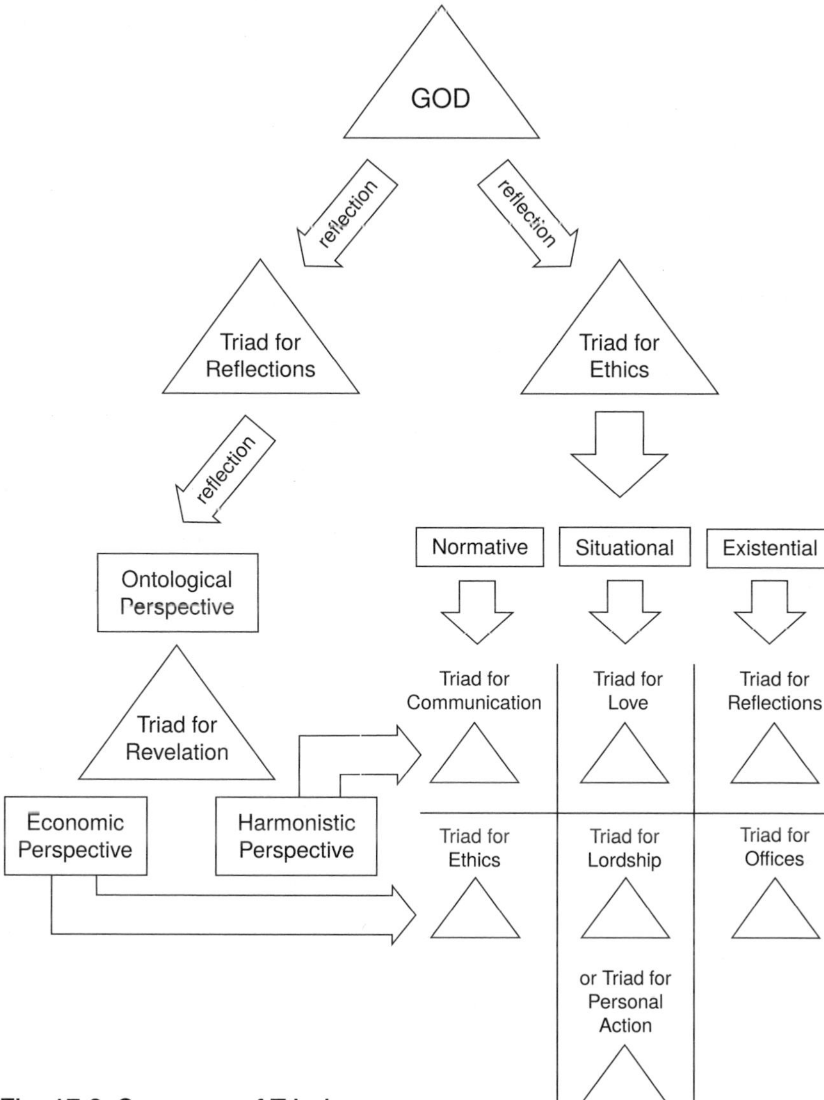

Fig. 17.3. Summary of Triads

Key Terms

classification
economic perspective[3]
harmonistic perspective
ontological perspective

3. Key terms in **bold** are defined in the glossary at the end of this volume.

perspectives on revelation
triad
triad for communication
triad for ethics
triad for lordship
triad for love
triad for offices
triad for personal action
triad for reflections
triads under the general heading of the economic perspective
triads under the general heading of the harmonistic perspective

Study Questions

1. Which coinherent triads from the previous chapters are more closely linked to the harmonistic perspective? Why?
2. Which coinherent triads are more closely linked to the economic Trinity and the economic perspective?
3. In what sense can a perspective be inside itself? Is there an analogy with the coinherent relation between persons of the Trinity?
4. What differentiates the distinctive focus of these three triads: the triad for ethics, the triad for lordship, and the triad for offices?
5. How can you derive the differentiation of triads from the triad for ethics?
6. What differentiates the distinctive focus of these three triads: the triad for communication, the triad for love, and the triad for reflections?
7. How can the triad for lordship be used to differentiate other triads?
8. Why is it difficult to settle on a single way to classify triads, and to claim that it is the only right way?

For Further Reading

Frame, John M. "A Primer on Perspectivalism." 2008. http://www.frame-poythress.org/a-primer-on-perspectivalism/. Republished in *John Frame's Selected Shorter Writings, Volume 1*. Phillipsburg, NJ: P&R Publishing, 2014. A general introduction to perspectives.

PART 5

APPLYING PERSPECTIVES TO THEOLOGICAL QUESTIONS

EXAMPLES ILLUSTRATE HOW the use of perspectives can illumine questions relating to theology.

18

Transcendence and Immanence

WE NOW SHOW some ways in which the use of perspectives can help us in thinking about questions concerning doctrine. We begin with the doctrine of God. Since God is infinite and mysterious, we cannot expect to dissolve the mysteries. But we may explore how perspectives can help us in seeing that the mysteries make sense.

The Mystery of Transcendence and Immanence

The first mystery we consider is that of the relation of divine transcendence to divine immanence. Theologians have sometimes thought that transcendence and immanence are in deep tension with each other. It can be posed this way: transcendence says that God is far off; immanence says that God is close by. How can both be true? We seem to be saying contradictory things.

A Triad instead of a Dyad

John Frame has already addressed this question in his discussion of transcendence and immanence.[1] The terms *transcendence* and *immanence* have a range of meanings, depending on who is using them. We can distinguish a Christian and a non-Christian view of transcendence and immanence (chap. 10).[2] So we must be careful about the meanings of the terms. Frame places the two terms *transcendence* and *immanence*

1. John M. Frame, *The Doctrine of the Knowledge of God* (Phillipsburg, NJ: Presbyterian and Reformed, 1987), 13–18; John M. Frame, *The Doctrine of God* (Phillipsburg, NJ: P&R Publishing, 2002), 103–15.

2. Frame, *Doctrine of the Knowledge of God*, 14–15.

in the context of his triad of terms used for perspectives on lordship: *authority, control,* and *presence.*[3]

We may summarize Frame's treatment in a simple way. The word *immanence* is replaced by *presence,* and *transcendence* by *authority* and *control* together. More precisely, since Frame and others still continue to use the terms *immanence* and *transcendence,* we can say that *immanence* is explained to mean *presence,* while *transcendence* is explained to include *authority* and *control.* (See fig. 18.1.)

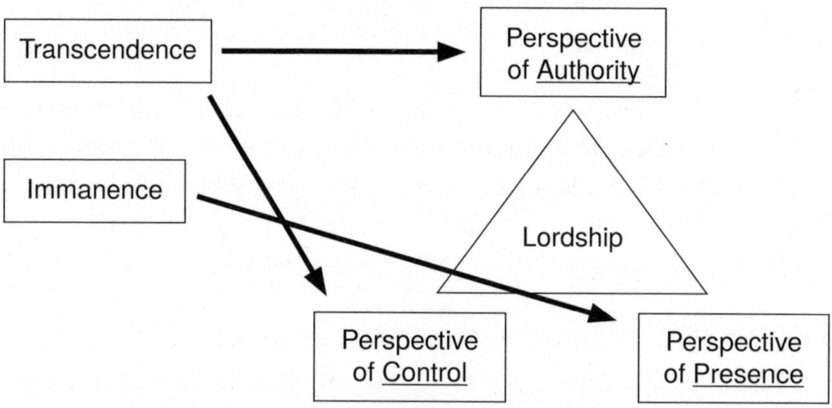

Fig. 18.1. Explaining Transcendence and Immanence

Authority and control are two aspects of transcendence or two expressions of transcendence or two perspectives on transcendence. Frame's terms *authority, control,* and *presence* are still potentially ambiguous if we treat them in a vacuum. Frame intends us to understand them as summary labels for rich biblical teaching on the three themes.

Perspectives instead of Polarity

When we consider the three terms for lordship as summaries of biblical teaching, they are not in tension with one another. As we saw in our earlier discussion of the triad for lordship (chap. 14), they imply one another. Each offers a perspective on the other two. Precisely because God is the ultimate authority, his authority is *present* to hold us accountable. Precisely because God is in control, his control manifests

3. Frame, *Doctrine of God,* 103.

his *presence* in the events and persons that he controls. Because God is present, he is present in his authority and control.

Thus, the three perspectives imply one another and in fact include one another. They are coinherent, which means that each "indwells" the others. Each is already present and implicit in the others. There is deep harmony rather than deep tension. If we return to the original vocabulary of *transcendence* and *immanence*, we say that transcendence and immanence are in harmony when they are understood in a biblically informed way.

Derivation from Harmony in the Trinity

We can further confirm the claim of harmony by reminding ourselves of the root of the triad for lordship. Its root is in the Trinity. The differentiation and harmony and coinherence in the triad for lordship reflect the original differentiation and harmony and coinherence among the persons of the Trinity (chap. 14).

More precisely, the relation among authority, control, and presence reflects the relation among persons of the Trinity. The persons of the Trinity are coinherent. The triad for lordship is derivatively coinherent. Thus, the three perspectives in the triad for lordship are in harmony. Once we accept that the Trinitarian character of God forms the background for the perspectives, and that God as the Trinitarian God is present in his lordship, we can also accept that the three perspectives on lordship are in harmony with one another. Therefore, transcendence and immanence are in harmony. This harmony remains mysterious to us, just as the Trinity is mysterious to us. But it makes sense, because it is a reflection of the harmony in the Trinity.

In explanations such as these, we never dissolve the mystery about who God is. We never obtain infinite and exhaustive knowledge of God. Nevertheless, thinking about the three perspectives may help us, if it enables us to move beyond a false perception that transcendence and immanence are at odds with each other.

Key Terms

authority[4]
coinherence
control
harmony
immanence
lordship
perspectives on lordship
perspectives on transcendence
presence
tension
transcendence

Study Questions

1. Why do some people think that transcendence and immanence are in tension with each other?
2. What two distinct perspectives on lordship does John Frame use as a further explanation of transcendence?
3. What other label does Frame supply for *immanence*, using his theme of lordship?
4. How can we effectively see the harmony between transcendence and immanence?
5. How might it help to introduce a third term, to obtain a triad, rather than having only the original two, *transcendence* and *immanence*?
6. In considering transcendence and immanence, how does it help to be biblically informed? Why do you think that the concepts of transcendence and immanence have proved to be a problem?

For Further Reading

Frame, John M. *The Doctrine of God*. Phillipsburg, NJ: P&R Publishing, 2002. Pp. 103–15. Expounding transcendence and immanence.

———. *The Doctrine of the Knowledge of God*. Phillipsburg, NJ: Presbyterian and Reformed, 1987. Pp. 13–18. Expounding transcendence and immanence.

4. Key terms in **bold** are defined in the glossary at the end of this volume.

19

Attributes of God as Perspectives

FRAME'S TRIAD FOR lordship also suggests a fruitful path to explore in treating the *attributes* of God. Rather than assuming that the attributes are perfectly distinguishable, we consider them as offering *perspectives* on God.

The Triad for Lordship as Providing Attributes

The triad for lordship is closely related to three attributes in classical discussions of God. Control corresponds to the attribute of *omnipotence,* God's comprehensive power. Presence corresponds to the attribute of *omnipresence,* God's comprehensive presence. The third perspective within the triad for lordship, the perspective of authority, is a little more difficult, since *authority* or *having authority* is less often discussed as a distinct attribute of God. But it is closely related to God's sovereignty. God's sovereign *right* to rule is also connected to his rectitude in character—God's moral absoluteness and holiness. So authority summarizes several attributes at once: sovereignty, moral absoluteness, and holiness.

The relation of the triad for lordship to attributes of God suggests that the attributes can be understood as perspectivally related. (See fig. 19.1.)

Each attribute, when properly understood in the context of the full revelation of God, implies the others and in a sense includes the others. God's omnipotence is an omnipresent, holy omnipotence. God's omnipresence is a holy, omnipotent omnipresence. And God's holiness is an omnipresent, omnipotent holiness.

In other words, the attributes are coinherent.[1] This coinherence reflects the coinherence of the triad for lordship, which in turn reflects the coinherence among the persons of the Trinity.

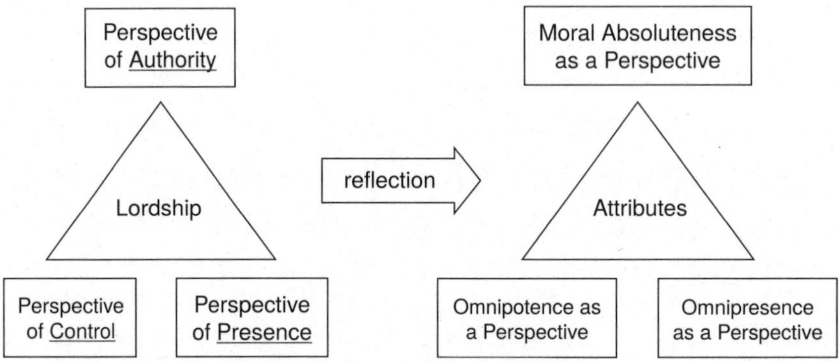

Fig. 19.1. Understanding Attributes Perspectivally

Less Confusing?

This description of attributes might prove helpful for people who have surveyed other discussions of attributes. Some of these discussions wonder whether the attributes are fully included in God or not. Let us consider the first of these alternatives. Suppose that the attributes are included in God. Since God is indivisible, we might be tempted to infer that the attributes are identical with God and so identical with one another. Yet from an ordinary point of view, the terms for God's attributes are not merely synonymous.

So let us consider the other alternative. Suppose that the attributes are not included in God. Then God is apparently dependent on something (namely, abstract attributes) other than God. Such alleged dependence is in tension with his absoluteness.

Treating the attributes as perspectives may help to avoid the perception of a dilemma. The attributes are distinct from one another, and also coinherent. The distinction of attributes refutes the view that the attributes must be identical. The coinherence of attributes refutes the view that they are abstracts outside God. It may also help to encourage

1. See also Timothy E. Miller, *The Triune God of Unity in Diversity: An Analysis of Perspectivalism, the Trinitarian Theological Method of John Frame and Vern Poythress* (Phillipsburg, NJ: P&R Publishing, 2017), chaps. 4–5.

the exploration of ways in which one attribute can be seen "within" another or as implying another.[2]

The relation of attributes to one another reflects the relations of the persons of the Trinity to one another. Since the persons are coinherent, the attributes are coinherent. Since the persons are distinct, the attributes are distinct. Since each person is fully God, each attribute is fully divine. God's holiness is *divine* holiness and describes all of God. God's omnipotence is *divine* omnipotence and describes all of God. Each attribute is a perspective on the *whole* of God. Do the attributes have mystery concerning their relations to one another? Of course they do, but it is a mystery derivative from the mystery of the Trinity. Since the Trinity exists, the attributes do not offer a second, separate mystery. It is the same mystery of the Trinity, reflected in the attributes.

Key Terms

absoluteness[3]
attribute (of God)
authority
control
divine sovereignty
holiness
identity
moral absoluteness
omnipotence
omnipresence
perspective
presence

Study Questions

1. What is meant by *attribute of God*?
2. To what divine attributes are the three perspectives on lordship (authority, control, and presence) related?
3. Discuss the coinherence of three attributes: moral absoluteness, omnipotence, and omnipresence.

2. Ibid.; John M. Frame, *The Doctrine of God* (Phillipsburg, NJ: P&R Publishing, 2002), 228.
3. Key terms in **bold** are defined in the glossary at the end of this volume.

4. What does it mean to treat an attribute as a perspective?
5. Are all of God's attributes related perspectivally?
6. Are all of God's attributes coinherent?
7. How does the coinherence of attributes relate to the coinherence of persons in the Trinity?
8. What is the difficulty in saying that an attribute of God is not included in God? What is the difficulty in saying the opposite?

For Further Reading

Bosserman, B. A. *The Trinity and the Vindication of Christian Paradox: An Interpretation and Refinement of the Theological Apologetic of Cornelius Van Til*. Eugene, OR: Pickwick, 2014. Pp. 189–95. On attributes as one and many. Some people I have talked to have thought that Bosserman's book in its later chapters introduces autonomous reasoning about God. But my personal correspondence with him makes me think that in the whole book he attempts to do all his reasoning inside the framework of biblically revealed truth.

Frame, John M. *The Doctrine of God*. Phillipsburg, NJ: P&R Publishing, 2002. Chap. 19. Discussion of attributes of God.

Miller, Timothy E. *The Triune God of Unity in Diversity: An Analysis of Perspectivalism, the Trinitarian Theological Method of John Frame and Vern Poythress*. Phillipsburg, NJ: P&R Publishing, 2017. Chaps. 4–5. Discussion of using perspectives to explore theological implications.

20

God's Acting in Time and Space

WE CONFRONT MYSTERY when we consider God's acts in time and space. The issue has sometimes been formulated as a puzzle. If even before creation God is "in" time and space in an ordinary way, he is not absolute. He is subject to time and space that he did not create. On the other hand, if God *created* time and space at the point of initial creation of the universe, he is himself beyond time and space. So how can he act in them?

These are among many of the mysteries that we can contemplate with respect to creation. God is the Creator, and everything else has been created by him. Nothing in creation is quite like him. So we should not be amazed that we are unable to fully conceptualize his relation to time and space within creation.

God's Acting in Time

Using perspectives does not dissolve mystery. But in this case, it can suggest analogies. There is in God's eternal existence an absolute archetype from which we can reason about time. God is eternally acting in the relations among the persons of the Trinity. We can see his actions in several aspects. John says that the Father *loves* the Son (John 3:35; 5:20). His love is *expressed* or manifested in time through the work of the Son, which manifests the presence and love of the Father. This manifestation is what we have termed an *economic* manifestation (chap. 16). The economic works of love in time reflect the eternal activity of love from before time.

These two are coinherent, as we have seen (chap. 16). The economic manifestation, in the form of works in time, consists in works that God himself does. It manifests God in harmony with who he is—his ontological character. The ontology of eternal existence harmonizes with the economy of activity in time. It is so because these offer two coinherent perspectives: the ontological perspective and the economic perspective. These two are derivable from the triad for reflections, which is coinherent (fig. 16.2). The triad for reflections derives in turn from the mystery of the Trinity (chap. 11).

The eternal activity of God is mysterious to us. But it makes sense that it would be the model for God's action in time. God acts in accord with who he is. The economic Trinity reflects the ontological Trinity. If we accept the reality of the ontological Trinity, we must derivatively accept the reality of God's acting in time in harmony with who he always is.

At the same time, we recognize a distinction between the ontological and the economic perspectives. Not everything we say of one will necessarily be true of the other. God's acts in time are in harmony with his eternal acts, but the two are not indistinguishable.

The analogy between the Trinity and speaking offers a similar result. God speaks eternally in speaking the eternal Word. This speaking is his archetypal speaking. God speaks at particular times when he creates light and the expanse and the dry land (Gen. 1:3, 6, 9). His speech in time expresses and reflects his eternal speech. Once again the economic Trinity reflects the ontological Trinity. The harmony in God's original speech (the Word, John 1:1) is reflected in the harmony of his speeches in time.

God's Acting in Space

God's actions at particular spatial locations involve a mystery similar to his actions in time. God is not limited or confined to a particular location. But God has in himself an archetype related to space, namely, the relations of indwelling among the persons of the Trinity. The description of these relations uses spatially oriented language, concerning one person's being *in* another. The original dwelling place of God in himself is the archetype for the creation of the universe as the ectypal dwelling place of God (Jer. 23:24). God also selects certain specific places to be the places for specially intense presence in communion with mankind. The garden of Eden was one such place, and then the tabernacle of Moses and the temple of Solomon.[1] These places are reflections of God's archetypal dwelling in himself. God's actions at particular places reflect his eternal action in indwelling. The actions in time reflect the eternal actions because the two are coinherent, as we see by using the ontological and economic perspectives. These perspectives derive from the triad for reflections, which in turn derives from the Trinity. In the Trinity, the Son is the image of the Father. The Son manifests the Father. That is why God can manifest himself at particular times and places. Because the Trinity is real, God's action and presence at particular spaces are real.

The Economic Trinity's Reflecting the Ontological Trinity

Because the Son is the eternal image of the Father, God has "resources," so to speak, in himself—namely, the resources of reflection. The original relation of reflection is the relation of the Father to the Son, who is his image or reflection. The relation of reflection in God serves as the foundation for the actions that reflect God in time and space. The idea of reflections helps to make sense of God as he is independent of time and yet acts in time, and God as he is independent of space and yet acts in space.

Key Terms

action
economic perspective[2]
eternal action
ontological perspective
reflection
space
time

Study Questions

1. What difficulties arise in considering how the eternal God acts in time? What difficulties are there in saying that God is "in" time or "outside" time?

1. G. K. Beale, *The Temple and the Church's Mission: A Biblical Theology of the Dwelling Place of God* (Leicester: Apollos; Downers Grove, IL: InterVarsity Press, 2004).

2. Key terms in **bold** are defined in the glossary at the end of this volume.

2. How are the ontological and economic perspectives pertinent to understanding God's actions in time?
3. What is the archetypal action in God, corresponding to God's actions in time?
4. What difficulties arise in considering how the eternal God acts in space? What difficulties are there in saying that God is "in" space or "outside" space?
5. How are the ontological and economic perspectives pertinent to understanding God's actions in space?
6. What is the archetypal action corresponding to God's actions in created space?
7. How does God's eternal speech relate to his speeches in time, such as his commands in creating light and the expanse (Gen. 1:3, 6)?

For Further Reading

Beale, G. K. *The Temple and the Church's Mission: A Biblical Theology of the Dwelling Place of God*. Leicester: Apollos; Downers Grove, IL: InterVarsity Press, 2004. A study of God's special dwelling places (such as the garden of Eden and the tabernacle).

Bosserman, B. A. *The Trinity and the Vindication of Christian Paradox: An Interpretation and Refinement of the Theological Apologetic of Cornelius Van Til*. Eugene, OR: Pickwick, 2014. Pp. 203–11. On the Christian-theistic foundations for space and time.

21

God's Creating

THE QUESTIONS IN the previous chapter about time and space have affinities to general questions about how it is possible for God to create something outside himself and distinct from himself. We may put the issue another way. God does not change (Mal. 3:6). So how can he undertake a fresh action by creating the world? As usual, these are mysteries that we cannot solve. But as in previous chapters, we can use perspectival analogies to reexpress the mysteries.

God's All-Sufficient Glory

God is sufficient in himself. He is absolute, not dependent on the world. He does not have an inner "need" to create the world in order to enhance or develop himself. He has all glory in himself. He has no need to display his glory more broadly by creating a world that displays it. If so, how can he apparently *add* to his glory by making a world that reflects his glory?

It is useful to start with the activity of reflecting glory within the Trinity. The Son is the perfect manifestation of the glory of God:

> He is the radiance of the *glory* of God and the exact imprint of his nature. (Heb. 1:3)

The Holy Spirit also displays glory (1 Peter 4:14). This all-sufficient glory is the archetype. Precisely *because* of its complete sufficiency, it is the archetype, and can be reflected in creation as an ectype. The glory of God in the created world reflects the original glory of God in the Son and in the Spirit. It also *manifests* that glory, so that it is not a kind of addition alien to the original. God is present in the manifestation.[1]

God's Act of Original Creation

We can also use the analogy with communication for the Trinity as our starting point. God speaks the eternal Word eternally. That is the archetype. God's speaking in a sense *generates* the Word. (But remember that this speaking or "generation" is eternal, not something in time. See chap. 24.) It is an act manifesting God's creativity. The Word is *distinct* from God the Father. At the same time, however, we should note that the Word always exists. So it would be mistaken to say, as the Arian heresy said, that he is created. In discussing the Trinity, the orthodox church fathers were careful to distinguish eternal *generation* (the eternal act of the Father in "begetting" the Son) from creation. We are using the word *creativity* in a broad sense, to indicate an aspect of God's character manifested in eternal generation. We are distinguishing it from the idea of creating the world as something distinct from himself. God is eternally creative, but the creation itself is not eternal. It came into being (Gen. 1:1).

God the Father expresses his character in his speech, that is, in his Son, who is the Word. The constant character of God and the faithfulness of God the Father are manifested in the fact that the Word is in accordance with this character. At the same time, the Son by being distinct represents the *creativity* of God.[2]

This original speech within the Trinity is the archetype for speech that creates the world external to God. The world is distinct from God and is a manifestation of the faithfulness and creativity of God. In this respect, the world reflects the fact that the Son is distinct from the Father and is a manifestation of the faithfulness of God in the creativity of the Son. But the creation of the world also shows something different. The Son, who is the image of God, is himself God. But creation is *not* God. So the creation of the world is unlike the eternal generation

1. See also B. A. Bosserman, *The Trinity and the Vindication of Christian Paradox: An Interpretation and Refinement of the Theological Apologetic of Cornelius Van Til* (Eugene, OR: Pickwick, 2014), 197–212.

2. Vern S. Poythress, *Chance and the Sovereignty of God: A God-Centered Approach to Probability and Random Events* (Wheaton, IL: Crossway, 2014), 58–60.

of the Son. Because the eternal generation of the Son is the *archetype,* it is unique. It is unlike the ectypes that reflect it. At the same time, the creation as an ectypal display of creativity reflects the archetypal creativity of the Son.

Thus, the use of the analogy with communication for the Trinity as a perspective helps in understanding creation. The creation of the world is consistent with who God is.

This use of generation is similar to what Herman Bavinck remarks:

> Without generation [the generation of the Son by the Father] creation would not be possible. If in an absolute sense God could not communicate himself in the Son, he would be even less able, in a relative sense, to communicate himself to his creature. If God were not triune, creation would not be possible.[3]

Coinherence in Creation

The coinherence of perspectives also helps us in thinking about creation. The distinction between the Creator and the creation is closely related to the distinction between archetypal speech and manifestational speech, the speech that creates the world. Archetypal speech and manifestational speech are related in terms of originary and manifestational perspectives. Each perspective is coinherent with the others. So we expect a deep coherence between the doctrine of God and the doctrine of creation. The idea of creation should actually include, as a kind of presupposition, the idea of the Creator. And indeed it does. Creation as an ordered, rational whole testifies to the ordering and rationality of God the Creator's plan. Creation makes sense only if it derives from the Creator. Moreover, God must be Master of the creation, and to be so he must be absolute and not in need of creation. Creation must be free creation. So the very existence of creation implies the absoluteness of God, rather than being in tension with it.

Conversely, for God to be *Creator* (that particular term, not just any designation for God) implies a creation that he creates. To exhibit his

3. Robert Letham, *The Holy Trinity: In Scripture, History, Theology, and Worship* (Phillipsburg, NJ: P&R Publishing, 2004), 22, including the brackets, quoting from Herman Bavinck, *In the Beginning: Foundations of Christian Theology*, ed. John Vriend, trans. John Bolt (Grand Rapids: Baker, 1999), 39.

sovereignty and absoluteness, the created world must be distinct from him, not part of him.[4]

We thus see that the two conceptual sides, the concepts of Creator and creation, are coinherent. (Note: The *concepts* cohere, but God and the created world are distinct.) As usual, this coinherence reflects the original coinherence among the persons of the Trinity. More specifically, it reflects the coinherence between the originary and manifestational perspectives, and these in turn reflect the coinherence between the Father and the Son, joined in the harmony of the fellowship of the Holy Spirit.

Coinherence in Unchangeability

The same kind of reasoning can help us in dealing with God's unchangeability. The unchangeability of God reflects preeminently the unchangeable, stable character of the Father. The Father in generating the Son remains himself the Father, eternally unchanged and unchangeable. At the same time, the Son is begotten and distinct in relation to the Father. The Son represents what we have called the *creativity* of God, or the dynamics of God. This dynamics is actually active among all three persons of the Trinity, though we associated stability first with the Father and creativity first with the Son. The Father is acting and is dynamic in the act of generating. And the Son in being generated is being acted upon. The Father is acting in loving the Son. And the Son is active in receiving the love of the Father and in loving the Father in return. The Holy Spirit is active in love.

Now consider how God manifests himself in creating the world and in interacting with it in providence. His manifestation of himself is in harmony with who he is. In himself he is unchanging in his character and is also eternally active. These two principles, of unchangeability and activity/creativity, are in harmony, because they reflect the original harmony of the Father and the Son in the Spirit. They are in harmony within God himself. And then derivatively they are in harmony in God's manifestation of himself in the world. God's unchangeability harmonizes with God's act of creation because the Father harmonizes with the Son through the Holy Spirit.

4. See also Bosserman, *The Trinity*, 197–203.

Conceptualization

In part, the difficulty has to do with some people's *conception* of unchangeability. Some people have an abstract human conception, which they have tried to produce independent of God. For them, unchangeability means merely the negation of change. They then try to impose this conception as an outside requirement on God. They reason that God must be frozen, without any activity at all. In that case, their original conception of unchangeability bears the marks of would-be autonomous thinking. Using the pattern of non-Christian immanence, they are trying to make God conform to their starting human conception. They project their misconceptions onto God, and then they find themselves in difficulty.

Instead, we should allow God to define himself to us. He defines himself not only as unchanging and eternal, but as Father, Son, and Spirit, in their relations of speaking, generation, love, and reflection. An original conception of unchangeability, which some people may have had in their heads simply by logically negating the idea of change, has to be adjusted according to what God is teaching us. God has in himself, in the person of the Father, the ultimate archetype for stability (unchangeability) and, in the person of the Son, the ultimate archetype of dynamicity and creativity.

The original coinherence in the persons of the Trinity is reflected in the derivative coinherence in stability and dynamicity within the world that God made. We can explore this coinherence further by seeing how stability and dynamicity actually presuppose each other. They always exist in *relation* to each other. (The archetype for this relationality lies in the Holy Spirit, in whom the Father and the Son relate to each other.) To begin with, dynamicity and change within this world have to be observed against the background of other things that remain the same. If, hypothetically, *everything* changed, we could not even identify any one thing at all, so we could not identify anything that changed. It would be like getting a completely new world every moment. And without stability in ourselves and in our memories, we could not compare what things were like before with what they are now. So an understanding of change and an appreciation of change actually presuppose stability as a background.

Conversely, stability presupposes change. Appreciation of stability involves continual interaction with that stability, with the thing that is stable. And the continual interaction is a form of dynamicity. Stability, we might say, is appreciated through a continuous *process* of appropriation.

Both stability and change within this world have roots in God. Some things within this world—things such as mountains—are relatively stable. But over a very long period of time, a mountain gradually erodes. We must have something even more stable, such as a standard of measurement, to compare the height of the mountain at one point in time with its height at another point in time. In comparing cases of greater stability with cases of less, the last and incomparably stable element is God himself. He endures even though the whole world changes (Ps. 102:25–27). So to say that God changes and is not stable involves a self-destructive claim. The alleged change has to be measured, and without God's stability, there is no foundation for the stability of any created thing in terms of which change could be measured.

Likewise, the change in the world has its roots in God—namely, in God's activity, which brings change. To appreciate change, we have to have some means of observing it. Our own eyes are pretty good at observing changes at certain speeds. But if a change is too rapid, in the blink of an eye, it may escape notice. Special instrumentation, such as strobe photography, is needed to observe rapid changes. And incredibly fleeting changes exist at the level of subatomic particles, some of which may "exist" for so short a time that they cannot be directly observed. Their existence is inferred from their decay products. In all this, the point is that change can be observed only if we have an even more rapidly changing process taking place in *observing* the first change.

God is sovereign over all processes of change, including the most rapid. So his action takes place *within* as well as beyond all processes on earth. Thus, change has its roots in divine activity, bringing about change.

Harmony and Mystery

As we have said, once we listen enough to God, we see that the two sides, stability and dynamicity, are in harmony. This harmony is derivative from the original harmony of the persons of the Trinity. Not only are the two sides in harmony, but they imply each other and are coinherent. Each is *in* the other. Stability includes the eternal sameness according to which God the Father *always* loves the Son, and always gives the Spirit to the Son in an eternal act of love. Conversely, the love between the Father and the Son, as a dynamic activity, implies the eternal stability of the persons who love. They are absolutely faithful and constant and dependable in their love. These harmonies exist because the Holy Spirit, as the Spirit of harmony, is the expression of harmony between the Father and the Son.

Is it mysterious? Of course. But it is also wonderful. And it is deeply satisfying. God does not have any logical tensions in himself. He is perfectly self-consistent, because the Father loves the Son, who himself, as the Logos, is the perfect expression of consistency.[5]

Key Terms

communication
creation
creativity
dynamicity
generation
glory
harmony
manifestation
manifestational perspective[6]
originary perspective
stability
sufficiency
unchangeability

Study Questions

1. How do some people see a tension between God's self-sufficiency and the act of creating the world?
2. In what way does God have creativity in himself?
3. How is the generation of the Son unique in comparison to generation in the world?
4. How is the generation of the Son relevant for the creation of the world?

5. See Vern S. Poythress, *Logic: A God-Centered Approach to the Foundation of Western Thought* (Wheaton, IL: Crossway, 2013), chap. 11.

6. Key terms in **bold** are defined in the glossary at the end of this volume.

5. How does God's unchangeability harmonize with his activity?
6. What difficulty could arise from a human would-be autonomous conception of unchangeability? How can such a difficulty be resolved?
7. What does it mean for God to be consistent?

For Further Reading

Bosserman, B. A. *The Trinity and the Vindication of Christian Paradox: An Interpretation and Refinement of the Theological Apologetic of Cornelius Van Til.* Eugene, OR: Pickwick, 2014. Pp. 197–203. On the logic of creation.

Frame, John M. *The Doctrine of God.* Phillipsburg, NJ: P&R Publishing, 2002. Chap. 15. On God's creating the world.

Poythress, Vern S. *Chance and the Sovereignty of God: A God-Centered Approach to Probability and Random Events.* Wheaton, IL: Crossway, 2014. Chap. 11. On Trinitarian foundations for what is new.

———. *Logic: A God-Centered Approach to the Foundation of Western Thought.* Wheaton, IL: Crossway, 2013. Chap. 11. On the Trinitarian foundation for logical consistency.

22

A Mystery of Indwelling

CONSIDER ANOTHER MYSTERY. A mystery occurs in describing the indwelling among the persons of the Trinity because each indwells the others. The Father is in the Son and the Son is in the Father (John 17:21). But in our ordinary thinking about spatially limited objects, such a situation seems impossible.

One-Way Inclusion

How can box *B* be inside box *A* and simultaneously box *A* be inside box *B*? Box *A* would end up being inside itself, and then the second instance of box *A* would be smaller than the first one. The second, smaller version of box *A* would really be a third box, box *C*. (See fig. 22.1.)

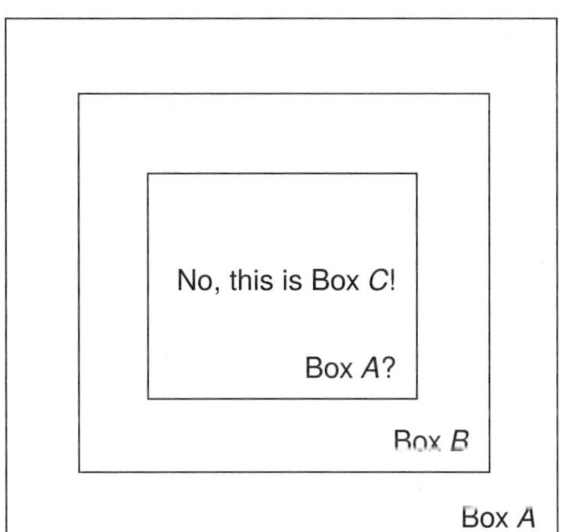

Fig. 22.1. Inclusion of Boxes inside One Another

Coinherence in Knowledge

We can contribute a new perspective to this question by considering coinherence in indwelling as correlated with coinherence in knowledge. The two ways of considering coinherence are perspectives on each other.

Let us begin not with knowledge within the Trinity but with human knowledge. We know that this human knowledge is analogically related to divine knowledge. One human being, Alice, knows another human being, Barbara. Alice knows Barbara, but not exhaustively. In knowing Barbara, she has a kind of store of knowledge about Barbara within her mind. If we want, we can represent this store of knowledge as part of the total knowledge that Alice has about all kinds of subjects. So the "box" of knowledge about Barbara is part of the larger "box" of Alice's knowledge. (See fig. 22.2.)

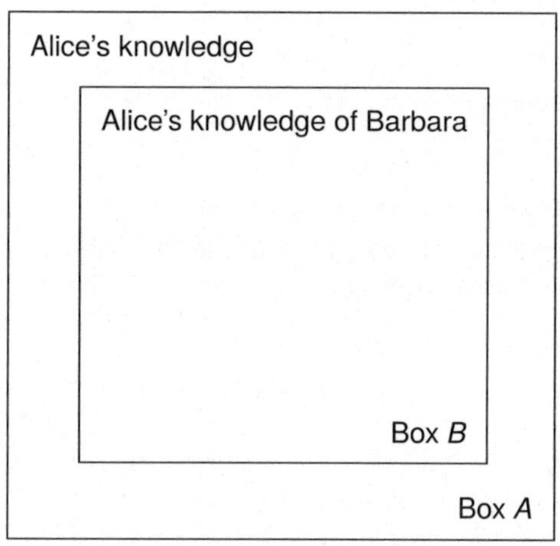

Fig. 22.2. Two Boxes of Knowledge

Loosely speaking, we may say that Barbara is "in" Alice. In her mind, Alice carries Barbara around with her all day. And if she is greatly influenced by Barbara, she may even ask herself from time to time what Barbara would say or think about some decision that Alice is making.

Included in Alice's store of knowledge is some knowledge about what Barbara thinks of Alice. So Alice thinks about Barbara thinking about Alice. (See fig. 22.3.) And if Alice were queried about this situation, Alice would also admit that Barbara probably thinks about what

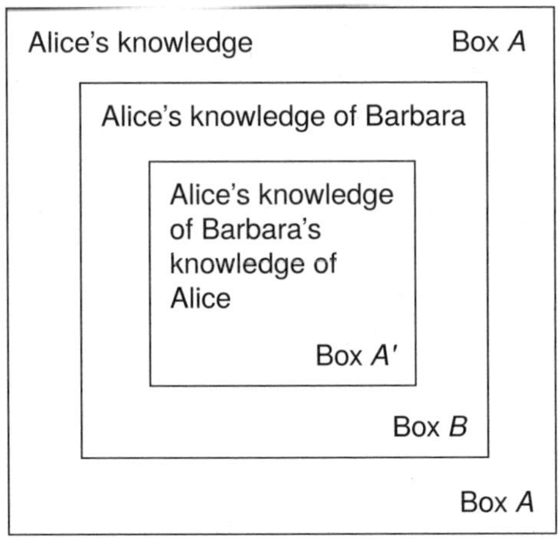

Fig. 22.3. Knowledge Embedded in Knowledge

Alice thinks of Barbara. So now we have Alice thinking about Barbara thinking about Alice thinking about Barbara. The chain can be indefinitely extended, though eventually finite thinkers run out of steam on a practical level.

Alice knows that Barbara is thinking about Alice. The Alice that Barbara is thinking about is basically the real Alice, the same Alice who is doing the thinking about Barbara. But because of limitations in human knowledge, Barbara will know less about Alice than Alice knows about herself. And she may be mistaken about some details.

Coinherence in Knowledge in the Trinity

In divine knowledge, we do not have the same limitations as in human knowledge. Matthew 11:27 says that "no one knows the Son except the Father, and no one knows the Father except the Son." This knowledge is complete and exhaustive. If the Son knows the Father completely, he also knows what the Father knows about the Son—a knowledge that is also complete. So there is no diminution of knowledge in the process of going from one person to his knowledge of the other.

By analogy with coinherence in knowledge, we have coinherence in indwelling. So it makes sense that the Son is in the Father and the Father is in the Son, though we cannot capture this relation in a simple spatial diagram.

In sum, the use of coinherence in knowledge as a perspective helps to make sense of coinherence in indwelling. The one helps with the other because the two approaches, coinherence in knowledge and coinherence in indwelling, coinhere in each other (see chap. 7; Appendix J).

Key Terms

coinherence in indwelling[1]
coinherence in knowledge

Study Questions

1. What is the problem that arises when each of two things is said to be inside the other?
2. In what sense can one person be "in" another in the area of knowledge?
3. How does human knowledge of persons reflect divine knowledge in the Trinity?
4. How does coinherence in knowledge illumine the mystery of indwelling of persons?

For Further Reading

Bosserman, B. A. *The Trinity and the Vindication of Christian Paradox: An Interpretation and Refinement of the Theological Apologetic of Cornelius Van Til.* Eugene, OR: Pickwick, 2014. Pp. 189–95. On depth in God.

1. Key terms in **bold** are defined in the glossary at the end of this volume.

23

The Third-Man Argument

THE *THIRD-MAN ARGUMENT* is the name given to an argument against Plato's theory of forms. The argument first appeared in Plato's dialogue *Parmenides,* and was further developed by Aristotle.[1]

The Gist of the Third-Man Argument

The gist of the argument is that the idea of a generalized form leads to an infinite regress. Suppose that we have human beings, Alice, Barbara, and Charlotte. According to Plato's theory of forms, the fact that they are all human beings is explained by postulating the existence of an abstract *form,* representing the general concept of humanness or humanity. Each human being is an expression of this general form. Now, if the form *humanness* does not partake in humanity, it is not fit to be applied to individual humans. Suppose, then, that it does partake in humanity. Since the form is itself human, people may reason that it looks as though they need another form, a higher form of humanness, to capture what is common to the form *humanity* and the individual human beings Alice, Barbara, and Charlotte. (See fig. 23.1.)

This higher form leads to the label *third man.* It is third in the count if the original human beings are first and the initial form (*humanity*) is second. If people follow Plato and allow this higher form of humanness, they must also by the same reasoning allow for higher and higher levels, leading to an infinite number of forms. This result is unacceptable. So it throws doubt on the initial theory of Plato, the theory that there exist forms such as *humanity* that explain what is common to all human beings.

1. Samuel Rickless, "Plato's *Parmenides,*" in *The Stanford Encyclopedia of Philosophy,* ed. Edward N. Zalta, Winter 2012 ed. (Stanford, CA: Stanford University, 2012), § 4.3, http://plato.stanford.edu/archives/win2012/entries/plato-parmenides/.

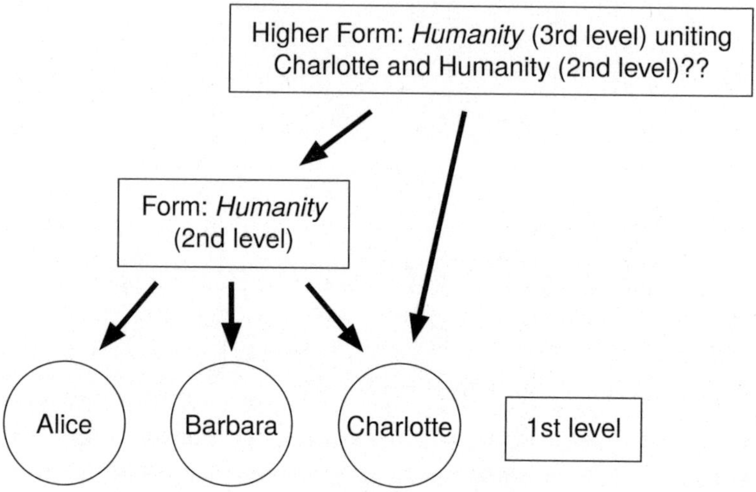

Fig. 23.1. The Idea of the *Third Man*, the Higher Form

An Infinite Number of Relations?

The issue is not tied in every respect to Plato's special theory of forms. Start with Alice (A) and Barbara (B). If the two people are related to each other because both are human, and if relations are real (and not just in our minds), we must postulate a third entity, the *relation* between Alice and Barbara. Call this relation C. (See fig. 23.2.)

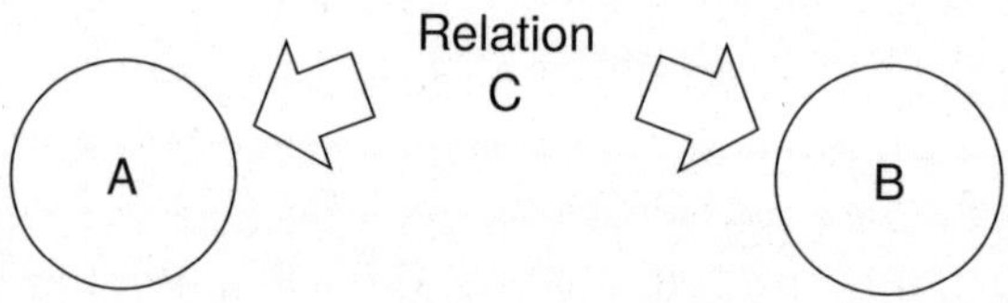

Fig. 23.2. Representing a Relation

Once we have the relation C, we can observe that C is related to both A and B, since A and B are both constituents that together contribute to building the relation C. In particular, C is related to A. So now we must postulate a fourth entity, the *relation* D between C and A. Since C is related to B, we can also put a label E on this *relation* between C and B. (See fig. 23.3.)

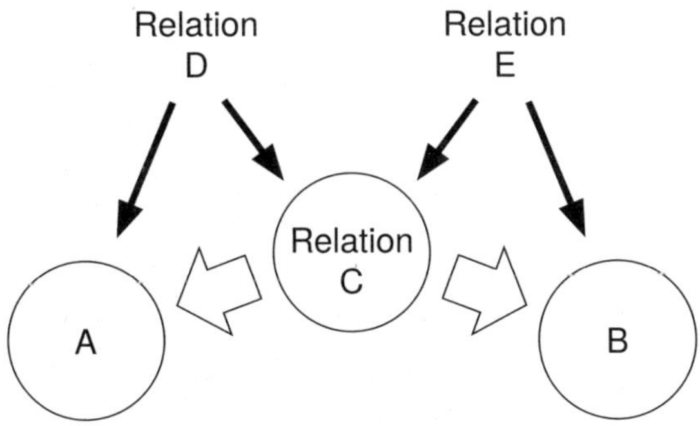

Fig. 23.3 Relations Built on Relations

And then we must postulate further relations: a relation *F* between *D* and *A*; and relation *G* between *D* and *C*. (See fig. 23.4.)

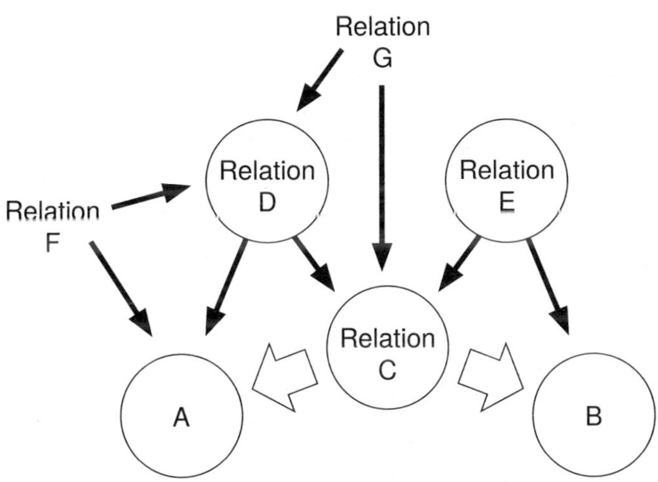

Fig. 23.4. Multiplying Relations

There will be still more relations between *E* and *C*; between *E* and *B*; between *F* and *A*; between *F* and *D*; and so on indefinitely.

Coinherence and Relations

In God, we do not have an infinite regress of persons.[2] As Scripture indicates, there are only three persons. The Father is in the Son and the Son is in the Father. If we ask how they indwell one another, the most reasonable answer is that it is through the Holy Spirit. The Holy Spirit is the Mediator of God indwelling believers. This indwelling as an economic work of the Trinity naturally has its original in God himself.

But now we can ask how the Spirit is related to the Father and the Son. He is related in love, and the love is an expression of the Father and the Son and the Spirit. We do not need to generate an infinite regress. Coinherence always takes us back to the three persons rather than adding a fourth and a fifth person.

We can put it another way. In the context of the triad for reflections, the Father is the original, the Son is the image, and the Holy Spirit expresses the harmony between the Father and the Son. The Holy Spirit functions in this respect as preeminently the *relational* person of the Trinity. But then what do we say about further relations, such as the relation between the Father and the Spirit? The two relate to each other in the context of the Son. But since the Spirit indwells the Son, the Spirit still serves as the foundation for the relation. We do *not* get more persons by contemplating more relations.

Key Terms

indwelling
reflection[3]
relation
third-man argument

Study Questions

1. Starting with individual human beings, why does it seem appropriate to some to postulate a general *form* of humanness?
2. How can the postulation of general forms lead to a regress of more and more forms?

2. See B. A. Bosserman, *The Trinity and the Vindication of Christian Paradox: An Interpretation and Refinement of the Theological Apologetic of Cornelius Van Til* (Eugene, OR: Pickwick, 2014), 192.

3. Key terms in **bold** are defined in the glossary at the end of this volume.

3. How does a similar difficulty arise when we consider *relations* between created things?
4. How is there a kind of final resolution of the regress in the persons of the Trinity?

For Further Reading

Rickless, Samuel. "Plato's *Parmenides*." In *The Stanford Encyclopedia of Philosophy*. Edited by Edward N. Zalta. Winter 2012 ed. Stanford, CA: Stanford University, 2012. § 4.3. http://plato.stanford.edu/archives/win2012/entries/plato-parmenides. Discussion of the third-man argument in philosophy.

24

The Generation of the Son

THE DOCTRINE OF the eternal generation of the Son is a deep doctrine, which we cannot fully discuss here. We intend only to illustrate how the use of perspectives might throw additional light on this issue.

The eternal generation of the Son is a disputed issue in modern times. Some theologians say that the Son is eternally generated by the Father. Others say no. Some of the latter group would observe that the Father and the Son always exist, and according to them the word *generation* would naturally apply only if the generated person were to come newly into existence. (Thus, Seth was *generated* when Adam "fathered" Seth, Gen. 5:3.)

The difficulty lies partly in the question of what we mean by the word *generation* or the related word *begetting*. We know roughly what it means for a human father to beget or generate a son in his image (Gen. 5:3). The generation or begetting from Father to Son in the Trinity would be *analogous*. But any analogy that the Bible supplies to give us knowledge of God includes mystery.

A second difficulty is that the texts describing the "begetting" of the Son have been interpreted in more than one way. Psalm 2:7 says, "The LORD said to me, 'You are my Son; today I have *begotten* you.'" In the context of the Old Testament, the immediate historical background may be the enthronement of the king in the line of David. But since David is a type of the coming Messiah, the text is also pointing forward. Acts 13:33 applies it to the resurrection and enthronement of Christ. Hebrews 5:5 applies it to Christ's being appointed High Priest, which may again have in mind his enthronement at the right hand of God. Hebrews 1:5 quotes the verse from Psalm 2:7 without indicating a specific time of fulfillment. In a sense, the Son is "begotten" in his resurrection and enthronement.

This begetting takes place at a particular time. The *eternal* begetting of the Son would be the original, archetypal background for this work of God in time.

We also have to deal with the expression "the only begotten Son." The KJV uses this English phrase to designate Christ (John 1:18; 3:16; etc.). But lexicographers dispute whether the underlying Greek term *monogenēs* means "only begotten" or simply "only, unique." (Note the use of this Greek term in Hebrews 11:17 in designating Isaac. Abraham also had Ishmael as a son, Gen. 16:15.) Robert Letham presents a judicious case for understanding *monogenēs* in its contexts in John as linked to the new birth of Christians. The eternal begetting of the Son offers the ultimate foundation for the new birth of Christians.[1] But Letham also observes that even if these arguments about *monogenēs* as "only begotten" do not ultimately hold up, there are other reasons for believing in the eternal begetting of the Son.[2]

Trinitarian Analogies

We may consider two Trinitarian analogies: the analogy with a family and the analogy with reflections. The analogy with a family speaks of God the Father as Father, and God the Son as Son. But by itself, it does not say exactly which aspects in human fathering are analogous to the divine Father-Son relation. Does the analogy include or exclude human begetting?

In the incarnation, the Father fathers the Son in the virgin conception through the Holy Spirit. His work as Father in the conception is implied by the language in Luke:

> And the angel answered her, "The Holy Spirit will come upon you, and the power of the Most High will overshadow you; *therefore* the child to be born will be called holy—the *Son* of God." (Luke 1:35)

But this case and the case of Christ's resurrection and ascension involve Christ's human nature. So can we infer an eternal begetting or not? The question is difficult because there are *some* aspects of Christ's incarnation

1. Robert Letham, *The Holy Trinity: In Scripture, History, Theology, and Worship* (Phillipsburg, NJ: P&R Publishing, 2004), 383–88.

2. Ibid., 388.

that have to do with his human nature and that do *not* apply equally to his divine nature.

What would an eternal begetting mean? The Arian heresy said that Christ was merely the first and highest created being. If that were so, there would be a time when he came into existence, and that would be the first "begetting." But John 1:1 indicates that he always existed. He did not come into being.

Ancient church orthodox theologians nevertheless advocated the language of eternal begetting, partly in order to indicate that the Son is fully God, and partly to affirm that the incarnation and the work of God in Christ's resurrection are in appropriate harmony with the distinct character and relations of the distinct persons of the Trinity, as these persons have always existed. In other words, the economic work of incarnation and resurrection corresponds to and reflects the ontological reality of an eternal relation between the Father and the Son.

I think that this argument is correct and faithful to Scripture. It is in harmony with the general principle that God is known through his works. The economic Trinity reflects the ontological Trinity. But we have to be careful, because it is also true that the incarnation of Christ and his resurrection from the dead involve his human nature.

Confirmation from the Analogy with Communication

We can confirm this result by using the perspective offered by the analogy with communication for the Trinity, rather than the analogy with a family. According to the analogy with communication, God the Father is the speaker and God the Son is the Word. The words that God the Father speaks in time are "generated" by him. By analogy, the eternal Word, by being spoken by God the Father, is "generated" by him. The word *generated* is not specifically used in the Bible to describe God's speaking the eternal Word. But the overall representation in the analogy with communication involves an analogy with the idea of generation.

We can also use the analogy with reflections for the Trinity. God the Son is the *image* of the Father. Now, images that appear in time, in the form of theophanies, are "generated" by God. They are particular manifestations that come about through the exercise of his power. So we can expect by analogy that the original image, who is the Son, who is the archetype of the theophanic reflections, is also "generated" by God the Father, who is the archetype. But this generation is eternal, unlike theophanies that appear at particular times within the created world.

Thus, a plurality of perspectives on the relations of the persons of the Trinity fit together, confirming that the manifestations of God in time reflect who he always is. The language concerning the eternal generation of the Son is one of several types of analogical language that we can use to express the fact that, through God's revelation to us, we understand who he is. Generation in time is a reflection of an eternal relation, which we call *eternal generation*. That is appropriate language to underline the principle that the acts of God (economic Trinity) manifest God (ontological Trinity). But we must balance the account by reminding people that the Son always is Son. He had no beginning in time. He is God and exists as God eternally. Moreover, the incarnation consists in the Son's newly taking to himself a full human nature, not a change in his divine nature.

Key Terms

analogy
analogy with a family[3]
analogy with communication
analogy with reflections
Arian **heresy**
begetting
economic Trinity
eternal generation
generation
incarnation
ontological Trinity
reflection
resurrection

Study Questions

1. What is the doctrine of eternal generation?
2. Why is there difficulty in understanding exactly what is being claimed?

3. Key terms in **bold** are defined in the glossary at the end of this volume.

3. What perspectives can be used in further appreciating the biblical basis for eternal generation?
4. What acts in time are analogically related to eternal generation?
5. What is the Arian heresy?

For Further Reading

Letham, Robert. *The Holy Trinity: In Scripture, History, Theology, and Worship*. Phillipsburg, NJ: P&R Publishing, 2004. Pp. 383–88. Discussion of eternal generation.

25

The Procession of the Holy Spirit

WE MAY NEXT ask about the procession of the Holy Spirit. Like the topic of the eternal generation of the Son, this topic is about an eternal relation between the Holy Spirit and the other persons of the Trinity. It is a deep doctrine, which we cannot completely understand. Once again, we intend to illustrate how the use of perspectives might throw additional light on this issue.

The Doctrine of Eternal Procession

One starting point for reflection is a key verse from John:

> But when the Helper comes, whom I will *send* to you from the Father, the Spirit of truth, who *proceeds* from the Father, he will bear witness about me. (John 15:26)

The key word is *proceed*. The verse speaks about the Spirit's proceeding from the Father. What is the meaning?

This verse in John 15 is set in the context of discussion about God's work of redemption. In the technical terminology of chapter 16, it focuses on the *economic* Trinity, rather than wholly on the ontological Trinity. But since the economic Trinity reflects the ontological Trinity, we may infer that the activity of God in time is in harmony with an eternal relation between the Father and the Spirit. The doctrine of eternal procession says just this: with respect to the ontological Trinity, the Holy Spirit proceeds eternally from the Father.

Does the Spirit proceed from the Son as well as from the Father? This question divided the Eastern from the Western church. Both branches accept the Nicene-Constantinopolitan Creed, which says that the Holy Spirit proceeds from the Father. The Western church added to the creed an affirmation that the Spirit proceeded from the Son as well. The Eastern church has not accepted this addition.

John 15:26 indicates that the Son *sends* the Holy Spirit to the disciples "from the Father." John 14:26 says that the Holy Spirit is the one "whom the Father will *send* in my name." So both the Father and the Son "send" the Spirit. There does not seem to be a great deal of difference between the words *send* (Greek *pempō*) and *proceed* ("go out," Greek *ekporeuomai*), except that the former word includes the additional idea of a commission from the sender.

(Some theologians, however, may prefer to use the word *send* to designate the work of the Father and the Son with respect to the redemptive mission *in time,* while the word *proceed* designates the eternal action within the ontological Trinity. In a discussion in which technical precision is desired, some kind of distinction in vocabulary is useful in reminding us that we can distinguish the ontological Trinity from the economic work of the Trinity. But exactly *which* words will be used to express the distinction is a matter of wisdom in choice. No choice of words *automatically* clarifies all mysteries.)

The general principle that the economic Trinity reflects the ontological Trinity would lead us to conclude that the sending of the Spirit in the work of redemption reflects an eternal procession. Since the sending in time is from both the Father and the Son, so would be the eternal procession.

Perspectives on Sending

Do perspectives throw light on the question? The language of sending is most closely related to the analogy of love for the Trinity. Consider the analogy with communication for the Trinity, which is perspectivally related to the love analogy (chap. 17). God the Father speaks the Word by the breath of the Holy Spirit. It makes sense to picture the Word as going out from the Father. And the breath of the Holy Spirit goes out as well.

In human speech, both word and breath go out simultaneously. The word presupposes breath as a medium. At the same time, it is for the sake of the word that the breath is sent out. So does the breath "derive" in some sense from the word? In the purposes of a speaker, words in a sense come first and lead to the speaker's sending the words out with his breath. So there is an order in which, in terms of purpose, the words come before the breath. But the picture we get does not definitively clarify whether this order amounts to the breath "going out" from the word. In practice, word and breath work together in communicating from the speaker to an audience. If we use our analogy to look at divine speech, it confirms that the Spirit proceeds eternally from the Father.

What do we conclude? The analogy with communication leads to a kind of logical order in which the Father is first. (It is not a *temporal* order, since the Father, the Son, and the Spirit all exist eternally.) The second and third persons of the Trinity come from the Father—eternally. (See the further discussion in Appendix I.) We can see how this analogy reinforces the doctrine of the procession of the Holy Spirit from the Father. Also, in a subtle way the Word comes before the Spirit in order, if the Spirit represents the breath used by the Word as the Word goes out. Yet the relationships are subtle. So does the analogy with communication reinforce the doctrine of the procession of the Spirit *from the Son*? It is not so clear. That does not mean that the doctrine is not true—only that it is not clearly derivable from the analogy with communication.

Consider now the analogy with reflections. The Father is the original, the Son is the image, and the Spirit corresponds (among other things) to the glory belonging to both the Father and the Son. With the label *connectional* we express the work of the Holy Spirit in expressing the harmony between the Father and the Son. Harmony between two persons presupposes the existence of the persons. So if we have to choose an order, it would begin with the Father, who is the original, then the Son, who is the image, and then the Spirit, who expresses the connection in harmony.

Does harmony "proceed" in some sense from the Father or the Son or both? It is not so clear. The Father, who is the original for the image, in a sense generates both the Son and the harmony. So once again, we receive a vague confirmation that the Holy Spirit proceeds from the Father.

In some cases in the Old Testament, the cloud of glory, which is associated with the Holy Spirit, forms a kind of outer region for a theophany. Inside the cloud a humanlike figure appears in Ezekiel 1:26–27. Likewise, Isaiah sees a figure on the throne inside the "smoke" that fills the house in a cloudlike manner (Isa. 6:1–4). The spatial arrangement, with an outer and an inner region, suggests that the cloud reflects in an outer realm the more intense manifestation of God in the humanlike figure. The humanlike figure prefigures Christ in his incarnation. The cloud symbolizes the Holy Spirit. So the picture as a whole dimly suggests a kind of movement from Christ to the Holy Spirit, who reflects the glory of Christ.

This kind of picture is suggestive, but it does not amount to clear, indisputable evidence for the idea that the Holy Spirit proceeds from the Son.

Personal Action in Time

Finally, let us return to consider the analogy with personal action as this analogy is manifested in the works of God in time. There are several key events in the accomplishment of redemption.

First, there is the work of incarnation. In the work of incarnation, the Father is the "begetter." The Son takes on human nature. The Holy Spirit is present in power to bring about conception in the womb of Mary (Luke 1:35).

Second, there is the baptism of Jesus. At Jesus' baptism, the Holy Spirit comes from heaven, which represents the abode of the Father. He comes to abide on Jesus for the purpose of his subsequent public ministry (Matt. 3:16–17). John the Baptist had already announced the coming of Jesus as the coming of one who would "baptize you with the Holy Spirit and fire" (3:11). So at the later point in time to which John refers, the Spirit goes from Jesus to those who receive his baptism. This later point in time is the time of Pentecost. We can summarize the movement of the Holy Spirit in two stages:

> The Father sends the Spirit to the Son, who sends the Spirit to the disciples.

Third, there is the resurrection of Christ. In the resurrection of Christ, the Father through the power of the Spirit raises Christ from the dead:

> [He] was declared to be the Son of God in power *according to the Spirit* of holiness by his *resurrection* from the dead, Jesus Christ our Lord. (Rom. 1:4)

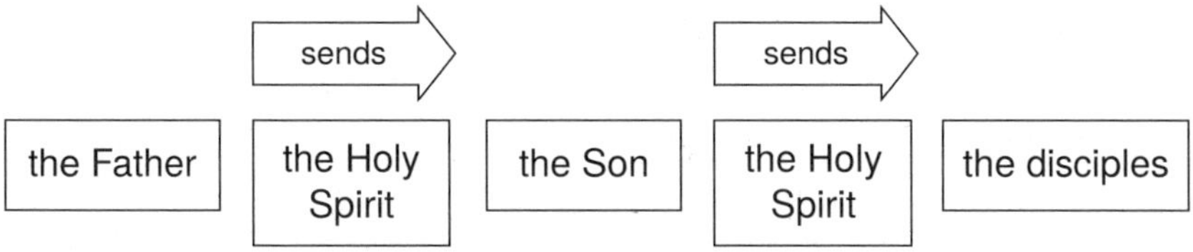

Fig. 25.1. Two Stages in Sending the Spirit

> If the Spirit of him who raised Jesus from the dead dwells in you, he who raised Christ Jesus from the dead will also give life to your mortal bodies through his Spirit who dwells in you. (Rom. 8:11)

In the latter verse, the parallel between resurrection life for Christ and resurrection life for Christian believers indicates that the Spirit is the one through whom resurrection life comes in both cases. The Father is preeminently the one "who raised Jesus from the dead." Thus, a summary of relations might look like this:

> The Father through the Spirit gives life to Christ, who through his Spirit gives life to believers.

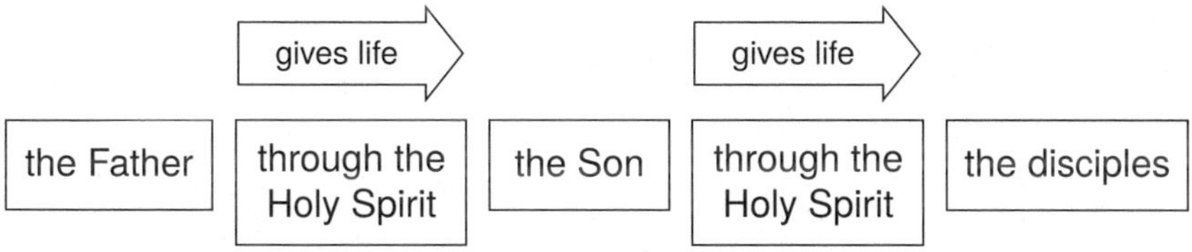

Fig. 25.2. Two Stages in Giving Life through the Spirit

Fourth, there is Pentecost. At Pentecost, the Father gives the Spirit to the enthroned Christ, who pours out the Spirit on the disciples:

> Being therefore exalted at the right hand of God, and having *received* from the Father the promise of the Holy Spirit, he [Jesus Christ] has *poured out* this that you yourselves are seeing and hearing. (Acts 2:33)

If we summarize, we obtain the following sequence:

> The Father gives the Spirit to Christ; Christ gives the Spirit to the disciples.

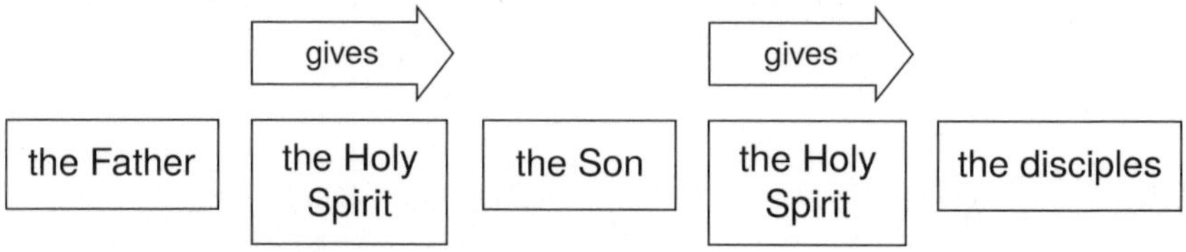

Fig. 25.3. Two Stages in Giving the Spirit

Other Verses with Trinitarian Action

These verses that we have singled out are only the leading edge of a much larger body of verses dealing with activities involving persons of the Trinity. Let us mention a few more that enrich what we have seen.

First, according to John 3:34–35, the Father gives the Spirit to the Son in connection with the Son's ministry on earth:

> For he whom God has sent utters the words of God, for he *gives the Spirit* without measure. The Father loves the Son and has given all things into his hand.

This participation of the Spirit harmonizes with the work of the Spirit that we see in Jesus' baptism.

Second, verses in the Gospel of John speak of the work of *glorifying*. In chapter 8, we saw that the theme of glory has a close relation to the Holy Spirit. So we can consider the language about "glorifying" as indirectly indicating an involvement of the Holy Spirit. The verses in question speak of the Father's glorifying the Son and the Son's glorifying the Father:

> When he had gone out, Jesus said, "Now is the Son of Man *glorified*, and God is *glorified* in him. If God is *glorified* in him, God will also *glorify* him in himself, and *glorify* him at once." (John 13:31–32)

> Whatever you ask in my name, this I will do, that the Father may be *glorified* in the Son. (John 14:13)

> Father, the hour has come; *glorify* your Son that the Son may *glorify* you. (John 17:1)

> I *glorified* you on earth, having accomplished the work that you gave me to do. And now, Father, *glorify* me in your own presence with the *glory* that I had with you before the world existed. (John 17:4–5)

Finally, we have verses about indwelling, such as John 17:23: "I in them and you in me." The language of indwelling is closely associated with the Holy Spirit. So the language in John 17:23 suggests inferences: we might think of "I in them" as implying that Jesus dwells in the disciples through the Holy Spirit, while "you in me" implies that the Father ("you") dwells in Jesus ("me") through the Holy Spirit. This bit of information is in harmony with the pattern that we saw in other cases:

> The Father gives the Spirit to Christ; Christ gives the Spirit to the disciples.

Digesting Biblical Teaching

Assessing the significance of these verses and other verses is challenging, for several reasons. (1) We are dealing with analogical language involving a comparison between divine action and human actions, such as sending, giving, and glorifying. (2) We are involved in analogy when we consider the relation of the economic Trinity to the ontological Trinity. (3) All the verses in question involve the human nature of Christ. Because the human nature is distinct from the divine nature, we must be careful in assessing whether the verses offer a direct basis for reasoning about the divine nature.

For example, in the incarnation, the Holy Spirit is present in power to bring about the conception of the human nature of the Son. With respect to his divine nature, the Son is God, and remains what he always was. In the resurrection of Christ, the Holy Spirit is present to give resurrection life to the dead human body of Christ. Christ's human nature goes from death to life. In his divine nature, he remains what he was. As a foundation for Pentecost, the Father gives the Holy Spirit to Christ as a reward for his obedience (Acts 2:33). The Spirit functions in connection with Christ's rule over the world, as the last Adam. So again his human nature is intimately involved.

We should take into account these challenges, and learn caution. It is still possible to draw some conclusions. (1) We conclude that the Spirit eternally proceeds from the Father, by using John 15:26 and the general principle that the economic Trinity reflects the ontological Trinity. (2) We conclude that the Spirit eternally proceeds from the Father and from the Son, by starting with the language of "sending" in John 14:26 and 15:26, and again using the principle that the economic Trinity reflects the ontological Trinity. Both formulations ("from the Father" and "from the Father and the Son") are theologically sound.

We should also recognize that the Bible itself in the full scope of its teaching has more richness than what is set forth in any simple summary. Granted that major qualification, however, we may still tentatively raise the question whether it would help to explicate the relation of the Holy Spirit to the other persons of the Trinity using language that explicitly expresses greater complexity.

Eastern and Western theologians have expressed reservations and concerns about what might be left out or misunderstood or inadequately expressed using the formulation preferred by the other side. The formulation "The Holy Spirit proceeds from the Father" leaves out a discussion of the Spirit's close relation to the Son, especially in the work of redemption (e.g., John 16:7; Acts 2:33). The formulation "The Holy Spirit proceeds from the Father and the Son" is true, but it does not say everything. It leaves out a discussion of the analogy with communication. And it leaves out a discussion of any difference between the distinct ways in which the Father and the Son participate in the procession of the Spirit. It also leaves out a discussion of the work of the Spirit in resting on Christ and dwelling in him for the accomplishment of his ministry. But as we observed, this last function of the Spirit may wholly have to do with his human nature.

In my opinion, the Western formulation "from the Father and the Son" is true. But the presence of analogy in biblical teaching plus the richness of the teaching means that we can learn more in addition to this basic formulation. We should go back again and again to the full scope of biblical teaching.

We should undertake not to "solve" the mystery of the Holy Spirit, but to use perspectives to enrich our understanding and to encourage us to reexamine the full text of Scripture.

Key Terms

analogy
analogy with communication[1]
analogy with personal action
analogy with reflections
economic Trinity
eternal procession
glory
harmony
mystery
ontological Trinity
procession
sending

Study Questions

1. What is the doctrine of eternal procession?
2. Why is there difficulty in understanding exactly what is being claimed?
3. What perspectives can be used in further appreciating the biblical basis for eternal procession?
4. What biblical verses describe acts in time that are analogically related to eternal procession?

For Further Reading

Letham, Robert. *The Holy Trinity: In Scripture, History, Theology, and Worship*. Phillipsburg, NJ: P&R Publishing, 2004. Pp. 201–20. Discussion of procession and the controversy over whether the Spirit proceeds from the Son (as well as the Father).

1. Key terms in **bold** are defined in the glossary at the end of this volume.

26

Classes, and the Problem of the One and the Many

WE MAY CONSIDER still another problem related to the nature of God, namely, the problem of *the one and the many*. What is this problem?

The Problem of the One and the Many

Philosophers through the centuries have wondered about the one and the many in their relation to each other. There are many horses, but one species of horse. There are many beautiful objects, but one idea of beauty that belongs to them all. How do the many things fit together to display a common single idea?

The philosophical approach known as *realism* says that general categories such as *horse* and *beauty* are *real*. These real ideas are in some sense prior to and more ultimate than the particular instances of horses and of beauty. In the particular instances we see copies or embodiments of the ideas from which they derive. According to this way of thinking, we start with the one, namely, an idea. It might be the idea of beauty. Then we derive the many, that is, the many instances of beauty in beautiful objects.

But this explanation does not provide a satisfying answer for how the many come about. If we start with a monolithic one, how can this one ever become many? In other words, if there really is only one idea, with unity and *no* diversity, how can diversity ever arise? If we say that diversity arises from some outside source, that source is *already* distinct from the one, so there is more than one source even at the beginning. It seems to be the case that we cannot imagine how to create diversity unless we already have it! Moreover, if somehow we get diversity, it might seem to imply a defect. If we have several beautiful paintings distinct from one another, they seem also to be distinct from the beauty that is in the other paintings. So they are distinct from beauty itself. If so, it would seem to imply that none of them is actually beautiful! That cannot be right.

The opposite philosophical approach is known as *nominalism*. Nominalism says that the general categories such as *horse* and *beauty* are simply *names* (*nominal* etymologically means "of a name"). The names are invented by us after the objects already exist. So the many objects are prior to and more ultimate than the one name that unites them.

This approach is also deficient as an explanation, because if the multiplicity of the many is the ultimate reality, why do they have anything at all in common that would justify the unity that we acknowledge by using a single name? We could try to say that the name is simply *imposed* on pure diversity, as a kind of unreal addition. But then we have not really accounted for our intuition that there really is something common to all horses, something that we do not merely invent out of thin air if we invent the name *horse*. It seems that we cannot produce real unity unless it already exists! Even if somehow we get a unity in the concept of *horse*, this concept is not identical to any one horse. So how can we still say that any one horse is a *horse*, using a concept not identical with our one horse?

So neither *realism* nor *nominalism* works as a final explanation of the one and the many.

Cornelius Van Til argued that the Trinitarian character of God provides the only satisfying explanation.[1] God is one God in three persons. So in God, the one and the many (namely, the three persons) are "equally ultimate."[2] The existence of both one and many in God provides the ultimate foundation for the one and the many that we observe in the world that God made. God created horses, and he also ordained the generality, the species of horse. He ordained that the horses should have unifying features that belong to the species. Similarly, God ordains that there should be both beauty (the one) and beautiful objects (the many) in the world. God created a world with one and many because he himself

1. Cornelius Van Til, *The Defense of the Faith*, ed. K. Scott Oliphint, 4th ed. (Phillipsburg, NJ: P&R Publishing, 2008), 47–51.

2. On the three persons, see chapter 37 below.

is one and many. God did not need a pattern outside himself when he undertook to create the world.

We rely on these regular features of the world all the time when we use categories or classifications. On the one hand, we have the general category or class—let us say the class of horses. There is one class composed of all horses. On the other hand, we have all the individual horses that belong to the class. There are many horses.

Two Perspectives on the One and the Many

There are at least two main ways of looking at this situation—two perspectives on the situation. In the first perspective, we begin with the class, and see the instances of horses as fitting into this class that we already have before us. This approach is akin to *realism*. But we admit to ourselves that it is only one perspective on the situation. We may call this approach the *classificational* perspective because its starting focus is on the class (the one). In the second perspective, we begin with the individual instances of horses. We view the class as arising from seeing commonalities among these individuals. This approach is more akin to *nominalism*. We may call this approach the *instantiational* perspective because we begin with the *instances* of horse.

These both function as perspectives because in both cases we are actually dealing with both a class and its instances. We understand the class partly by observing and thinking about the instances, as illustrations of the class. For example, we teach a child what a horse is by exposing the child to actual horses or pictures of horses. We use instances. Conversely, we understand the instances by seeing them as instances embodying a class. We see a particular horse *as a horse*, not as a dog or cat or cow or chicken.

Perspectives for Classification Applied to the Trinity

The ultimate, archetypal example of one and many is the Trinity. Consequently, the Trinity is also the ultimate, archetypal illustration of the interaction of classificational and instantiational perspectives. According to the classificational perspective, we start with the existence of one God. God is a class by himself. Each person of the Trinity is fully God. So each belongs to the class *God*. We understand each person only when we take into account the fact that he is God.

According to the instantiational perspective, we start with the existence of three persons. Each is a person distinct from the other two. There are "many" persons—three, to be exact. At the same time, each "instantiates" the class, that is, God. We cannot have even one person, let alone three, without simultaneously having God. Conversely, we cannot have God without also having the three persons. God *is* three persons. Each of the perspectives, the classificational perspective and the instantiational perspective, includes the other, and each perspective presupposes the other.

As usual, we need to insert a caution about the uniqueness of God. The relation of the three persons to one God is *not* like the relation of three horses to the one class composed of all horses. The three horses are three separable horses. And there are more horses besides. The persons of the Trinity are all one God, not a class consisting of three gods. The persons in the Trinity are distinct from one another, but not *separable*. Each is God. They indwell one another, and so each is found wherever one person of the three is encountered. This unique character of God is highly mysterious.

But precisely because God is one in three, in his uniqueness he is the ultimate source for the created instances of one and many.

The Trinity as Archetype for One and Many

As we have observed, we have an archetypal occurrence of the idea of *many* in the three persons of the Trinity. But here in our analysis we have another occurrence of *many*, namely, the two perspectives classificational and instantiational. These two perspectives are distinct, though they also coinhere, each with the other.

These two perspectives are perspectives in our human thinking. And we know that our human thinking is derivative and dependent. So the perspectives within our thinking are derivative. They are *ectypal*. Where do they have their ultimate foundation? Van Til rightly answers that all instances of one and many within the creation have their ultimate foundation and archetype in God. God is absolute. There is no other ultimate foundation. In particular, the distinction between the two perspectives, which makes them *many*, must go back to the *many* that we know exists in the three persons of the Trinity.

But how is this so? Can we see more specifically how the distinction between the classificational and the instantiational perspectives has roots in the distinction of persons in the Trinity? God the Father is often the chief focus when the Bible uses the general term "God" (2 Cor. 13:14; Gal. 1:3; Eph. 1:3; etc.). In this way, God the Father preeminently represents God in his uniqueness. So God the Father has a natural association with the classificational perspective. God the Father represents the class *God*. God the Father as the representative for the class *God* is the archetype for the classificational perspective as an ectype within our human thinking.

God the Son is the one who becomes incarnate. In his incarnation, he is the prime *instance* of the revelation of God to us. If we use our vocabulary, we might say that he is the *instantiation* of God. God the Son, as the instantiation of God, is the archetype for the instantiational perspective. The language about the Son as the "image" of God (Col. 1:15) and "the exact imprint of his nature" (Heb. 1:3) shows that he functions as the unique manifestation of God even before his incarnation.

What about God the Holy Spirit? In the incarnation, the Holy Spirit participated in bringing about the virgin conception of the Son:

> The *Holy Spirit will come* upon you, and the power of the Most High will overshadow you; therefore the child to be born will be called holy—the Son of God. (Luke 1:35)

In many ways, the Holy Spirit establishes communion. At the time of the incarnation, he mediates the communion between God the Father and the particularity of the incarnation. On this basis, we may suggest the idea of a third perspective on classes: the *associational* perspective. The Holy Spirit represents the communion between the Father and the Son. We can also recall John 3:34–35, where the Holy Spirit is the gift that expresses the communion in love between the Father and the Son: "he gives the Spirit without measure" (John 3:34). This reality of communion is the archetypal communion in the Trinity. It has an ectypal reflection in the associational perspective. The associational perspective begins with the idea of the relation or communion or *association* between class and instances. The instances are instances *of* the class, and *embody* the class. *Association* is this relation of embodiment.

By beginning with the relation of a class to instances, the

associational perspective presupposes the existence of both the class and some instances. Thus, the associational perspective is a perspective on the whole of the mystery of the connection between a class and its instances. It implicitly includes the classificational and the instantiational perspectives. It is a third perspective, coinherent with the other two.[3] (See table 26.1.)

Persons of the Trinity		**Perspectives on Classes**
The Father, representing the unity and uniqueness of God	→	classificational perspective
The Son, who instances God in the incarnation	→	instantiational perspective
The Spirit, who expresses the harmony between the Father and the Son	→	associational perspective

Table 26.1. From the Trinity to Perspectives on Classes

In doing this reasoning, it makes all the difference whether we are operating with a Christian or non-Christian view of knowledge of God. If we are using classes and instances and harmonious associations in creation as a model to which God must conform, we are trying to bring God down to the level of the creature. Such an operation is a form of non-Christian immanence. We are trying to force God into the mold of autonomous human reason. On the other hand, we may say that our experience of classes and instances and associations is an experience that is not self-sufficient, but has its origin and final explanation in God. God himself is the archetype. Subordinately, God reflects who he is in

3. See Vern S. Poythress, "Reforming Ontology and Logic in the Light of the Trinity: An Application of Van Til's Idea of Analogy," *Westminster Theological Journal* 57, 1 (1995): 187–219, http://www.frame-poythress.org/reforming-ontology-and-logic-in-the-light-of-the-trinity-an-application-of-van-tils-idea-of-analogy/. The triad consisting in the classificational, instantiational, and associational perspectives can be seen as a reflection obtained by applying the triad of contrast, variation, and distribution (Appendix F) to the problem of individuals and classes.

the ways in which he relates to the created world (economic Trinity). Classes and instances and associations within the world exist according to the will and purpose of God, who reveals himself. In this way of thinking, we are expressing the Christian view of immanence, which respects the infinity of God and the fact that he has truly revealed himself in accord with who he is.

Deriving Class Perspectives from Reflections

We can arrive at the same conclusion starting with the triad of perspectives on reflections (from chapter 11). In the triad for reflections, we have three coinherent perspectives: the originary perspective, the manifestational perspective, and the connectional perspective. We now use these three to look at the issue of classes. The originary perspective focuses on the one God, who manifests himself in multiple instances of theophany. All theophanies are theophanies of the *same* God. They belong to the class *theophany* because of the unity of the one God that each theophany brings to manifestation. Together, the theophanies are a multitude of instances.

So we can see that the originary perspective on reflections and on theophanies leads to the classificational perspective when applied to classes. The manifestational perspective leads to the instantiational perspective with respect to classes. The connectional perspective leads to the associational perspective on classes.

In sum, the triad of perspectives on classes, which includes the classificational, instantiational, and associational perspectives, reflects the triad of perspectives on reflections, which includes the originary, manifestational, and connectional perspectives. (See fig. 26.1.)

The triad for classes is coinherent in a manner that reflects the original coinherence in the persons of the Trinity. In all these cases, our thinking is derivative, imitative of God's knowledge.

The Trinity as Addressing the Problem

Why is any of this significant? The mystery of the Trinity is significant, and it is what lies behind the classical problem of the one and the many. That is why secular philosophy has not been able to solve the problem adequately. As Christian believers, we do not "solve" the problem either, if that means dissolving mystery. But we can explain

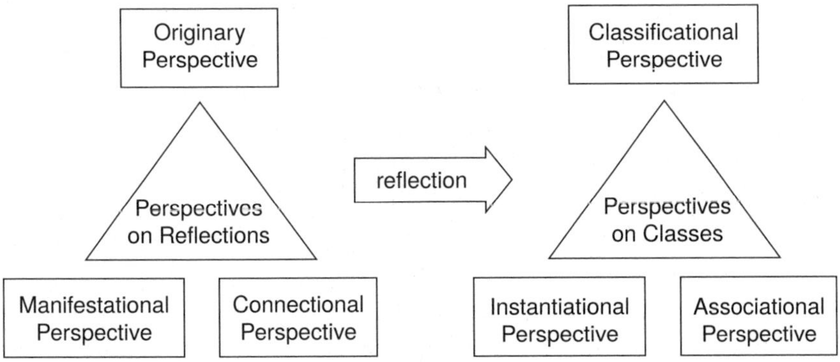

Fig. 26.1. From Reflections to Perspectives on Classes

why there is mystery. And we can see that the plurality of persons in the Trinity lies behind two *different* pluralities that we experience.

The first is the plurality of distinct horses, and the plurality of distinct dogs, and the plurality of human beings, and so forth. (See fig. 26.2.)

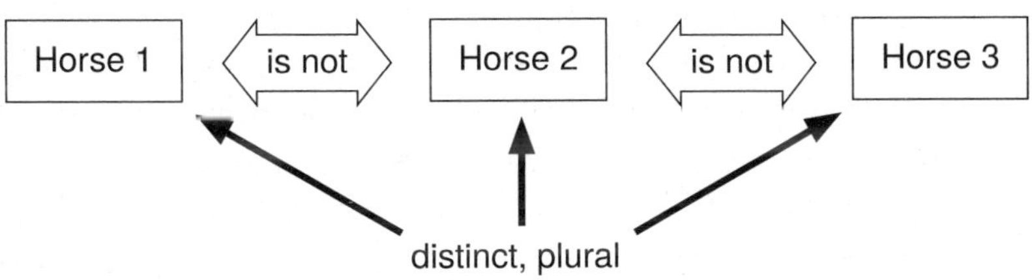

Fig. 26.2. Plurality of Horses

We can include the plurality of distinct persons of the Trinity as well, because this instance is the archetypal instance of plurality.

The second plurality is found in the distinction between classes and their instantiations in particular instances. The class of horses is distinct from each particular horse. That is, we can distinguish a class from a member of the class. (See fig. 26.3.) We distinguish a general category from a particular instance, on the basis of the underlying distinction between the classificational perspective and the instantiational perspective. These two perspectives are distinct because the Father is distinct from the Son.

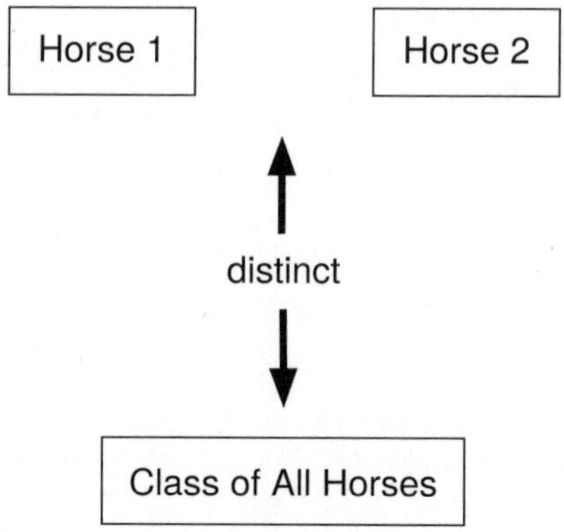

Fig. 26.3. Class as Distinct from Its Members

The coinherence among the persons of the Trinity also has a bearing on the problem of the one and the many. Within a Christian context, the one and the many are coinherent, in a manner that reflects the coinherence of the persons of the Trinity. The class of horses has meaning only in relation to instances of horses that illustrate the class and help to define it. The one includes the many. Conversely, each instance of a horse has meaning only by being included in classes. The many includes the one (the class). Both one and many presuppose a *relation*, the relation that a member has to a class that includes it. A relation is included in the one (the class) and the many (the instances). Conversely, a relation presupposes two things between which the relation exists. So a relation of membership implicitly includes the idea of a member and a class. None of the three—class, instance, and relation—makes sense without the others. All three are coinherent. In this manner, they reflect God.

God manifests himself in the world that he has made. This manifestation includes the display of his wisdom, in that he made the world one and many. He ordained classes and instances and the relations between the two. In this way also, we are continuously dependent on God. And in this way, we have a motive to praise God and exalt the magnificence of his wisdom, glory, and infinite mystery.

Key Terms

archetype[4]
association
associational perspective
category
class
classificational perspective
coinherence
connectional perspective
diversity
instance
instantiational perspective
manifestational perspective
many
name
nominalism
one
originary perspective
perspectives on classes
perspectives on reflections
priority
realism
unity

Study Questions

1. What is the problem of the one and the many?
2. What difficulty arises if reasoning starts with an undifferentiated *one*?
3. What difficulty arises if reasoning starts with the picture of an absolute plurality with no underlying unity?
4. How does the doctrine of the Trinity throw light on the problem in a unique way?
5. How do unity and diversity in the created world have an archetype in the Trinity?

4. Key terms in **bold** are defined in the glossary at the end of this volume.

6. What three perspectives are useful in considering the problem of the one and the many from a perspectival point of view?
7. How are the classificational perspective, the instantiational perspective, and the associational perspective coinherent?
8. How can the triad of perspectives on classes be derived from the triad for reflections?
9. How is the triad of perspectives on classes reflective of the Trinity?

For Further Reading

Poythress, Vern S. "Reforming Ontology and Logic in the Light of the Trinity: An Application of Van Til's Idea of Analogy." *Westminster Theological Journal* 57, 1 (1995): 187–219. http://www.frame-poythress.org/reforming-ontology-and-logic-in-the-light-of-the-trinity-an-application-of-van-tils-idea-of-analogy/. An introduction to the three perspectives on classes.

Van Til, Cornelius. *The Defense of the Faith.* Edited by K. Scott Oliphint. 4th ed. Phillipsburg, NJ: P&R Publishing, 2008. Pp. 47–51. Discussion of the problem of the one and the many.

27

Human Responsibility

HOW CAN GOD be sovereign and man be responsible? If God controls everything in history, including human actions, how can human beings still have free agency?

Many discussions have taken place concerning this important issue. We wish only to illustrate in a sketchy way how the use of perspectives may be illuminating.[1]

Image of God

Understanding human responsibility takes place best when we consider human responsibility in relation to God. It is God who created mankind. And he created them with responsibility to love him and obey him. God created man in his image. So the relation between God and man, in which man reflects God, can be used to try analogically to understand freedom and human responsibility.

Responsibility is an implication of God's lordship. God's will is authoritative. God himself is committed to act in a manner consistent with his own moral character.[2] And of course, he always does so. Since we are made in the image of God, we are responsible to him.

We can further break down the manner in which human responsibility operates. Man made in the image of God has within him a sense

1. A fuller discussion can be found in John M. Frame, *The Doctrine of God* (Phillipsburg, NJ: P&R Publishing, 2002), 119–59; and Vern S. Poythress, *Chance and the Sovereignty of God: A God-Centered Approach to Probability and Random Events* (Wheaton, IL: Crossway, 2014), 53–61. For a similar treatment, see also B. A. Bosserman, *The Trinity and the Vindication of Christian Paradox: An Interpretation and Refinement of the Theological Apologetic of Cornelius Van Til* (Eugene, OR: Pickwick, 2014), 222–29.

2. We can see an articulation of the commitment when God makes covenantal promises (for example, Heb. 6:17–18).

of right and wrong, according to Romans 1:32. That sense of right and wrong goes together, according to the triad for ethics, with three perspectives on ethics. The sense of right and wrong has a close relation to the existential perspective, which focuses on the persons who have ethical responsibility. But that responsibility exists in an environment—a situation. And it is responsibility with respect to norms, which are the focus when we use the normative perspective.

God must be Lord over norms, over the situation, and over the human sense of right and wrong in order to make a transcendent claim on man. He must be Lord over the situation in order to provide a stable environment in which meaningful ethical action is possible. Thus, responsibility presupposes the sovereignty of God and presupposes creation. The involvement of human responsibility with God's sovereignty displays coinherence, in the sense that responsibility actually implies sovereignty. It contains within it the idea of divine sovereignty as a presupposition.

Conversely, sovereignty implies responsibility: because God is sovereign, his authority is ultimate.

Secular theories of ethics have tried to produce alternatives without God in the center, but they fail.[3]

Freedom

Now consider the topic of freedom. Freedom is an implication of God's control. God's control implies his freedom to act. Human freedom reflects divine freedom, just as human power to act reflects divine power to act. And human ethical standards reflect ultimate divine standards.

Freedom presupposes divine sovereignty because God must be free and create man in his image in order for there to be meaningful human freedom. Human freedom is not lawless freedom to do anything, but freedom that reflects the freedom that belongs to God the Son. The Son freely acts in communion with God the Father through the Spirit. By analogy, human action is possible only in communion with God through the Holy Spirit. Peaceful fellowship with God is broken in the fall, but even after the fall, human beings "have [their] being" in God

3. See the extensive critique in John M. Frame, *The Doctrine of the Christian Life* (Phillipsburg, NJ: P&R Publishing, 2008), chaps. 4–8.

(Acts 17:28). Christ the Son always freely acts in accord with the plan of God. And likewise, human beings always act in accord with his plan. Christ always obeys the moral will of God, whereas human beings in their fallen state do not. But even when they do not—when they are in *moral* rebellion against God—they exist by the power of God, and they carry out his plan, sometimes unawares or in spite of themselves (Acts 2:23; 4:25–28).

There is no such thing as truly *independent* moral action by a single person. The character of the Trinity indicates why not. Personal action is always interpersonal as well. It is action in an environment of personal communion, involving joint action of other indwelling persons. Since all human beings dwell in God in the sense of Acts 17:28, their actions are not truly independent. Rather, they reflect actions of divine persons, such as the free actions of God the Son. The Son is free in communion with the Father. Human beings are free as they live in God and have communion with him. Freedom and divine sovereignty harmonize in the persons of the Trinity. So necessarily, they harmonize in reflected form in the world that God made.

Key Terms

divine sovereignty[4]
existential perspective
freedom
harmony
human responsibility
independence
normative perspective
reflection
situational perspective

Study Questions

1. Why do people see a conflict between divine sovereignty and human responsibility?
2. How does human responsibility imply divine sovereignty, and vice versa?

4. Key terms in **bold** are defined in the glossary at the end of this volume.

3. How do secular theories of ethics fail to do full justice to human responsibility?
4. Are there several meanings of the word *freedom*? Discuss the range of meaning.
5. Is human action truly independent action?
6. What do we learn about the idea of independence when we think about the actions of the persons of the Trinity in relation to one another?

For Further Reading

Bosserman, B. A. *The Trinity and the Vindication of Christian Paradox: An Interpretation and Refinement of the Theological Apologetic of Cornelius Van Til.* Eugene, OR: Pickwick, 2014. Pp. 222–29. Discussion of the harmony between divine sovereignty and human responsibility.

Frame, John M. *The Doctrine of God.* Phillipsburg, NJ: P&R Publishing, 2002. Pp. 119–59. Discussion of human responsibility.

———. *The Doctrine of the Christian Life.* Phillipsburg, NJ: P&R Publishing, 2008. Chaps. 4–8. Discussion of the failure of secular theories of ethics.

Poythress, Vern S. *Chance and the Sovereignty of God: A God-Centered Approach to Probability and Random Events.* Wheaton, IL: Crossway, 2014. Pp. 53–61. Discussion of human responsibility in relation to analogies from the Trinity.

28

Conceptual Growth

LET US THINK about the issue of growth in knowledge. Human knowledge of God can grow. We know God already. But because God is infinite, our knowledge can always expand in depth.

Does human knowledge of God grow only by adding new bits, that is, new, specialized facts? And if we think of some addition to knowledge as a distinct bit, is this bit completely separate from what we already know about God?

It is more complex than that, because all knowledge of God fits together into a whole. We know God personally; we do not merely know a list of facts about him. (But knowing someone personally does involve knowing facts.) Rather than merely adding bits, we may grow in our conceptions about God, about the Trinity, and about the attributes of God.

We illustrated this point briefly in chapter 21 when we discussed the unchangeability of God. Our conception of unchangeability grows as we learn about God from Scripture. This growth is only one of a large number of examples. As we illustrated in chapter 18, our concepts of transcendence and immanence can also alter and grow as we interact with the teaching in the Bible. Could we also say that our conception of the Trinity could grow in the process of thinking about the Trinity? Or, if we use a distinct, fresh perspective to look at a garden, might we sometimes expand our conception of the garden? Would the same be true when we use a fresh perspective to look at Old Testament prophets or at the theme of love? If we look at Christ as Prophet, King, and Priest, might we expand our understanding of him? Yes.

Growth in Conception

What would it mean for a concept such as unchangeability to grow or to change?[1] Would it necessarily mean that we change our minds completely and abandon everything we ever thought before about the concept of change? It does not appear to happen that way. We alter the concept subtly, without totally beginning again or without totally altering the very idea of change. And yet the concept *does* grow and change, partly as we see the idea of change or lack of change in a new perspective, in the light of fresh insights, derived from reflecting on God's stability and dynamicity, in the Father and in the Son and in the Spirit.

We can make similar observations about the transcendence and immanence of God, as discussed in chapter 18. At the beginning, we may have thought that transcendence and immanence were in tension with each other. (How can God be far off and close by?) At the end, we still affirm that God is *transcendent* and *immanent*. And the two terms still have some similarity in meaning to what they had at the beginning. But we have enriched our understanding as we have incorporated insights from Scripture. We say that God's transcendence describes his authority and control over us, rather than implying that he is uninvolved and irrelevant.

The same thing happens with the concept of God's presence in spatial locations (chap. 20). It may seem at the beginning that it is paradoxical that God can be present in the world when he is not subject to the limitations of space. And it may seem paradoxical that he can be present in a specially intense way in relation to human beings at some special location, such as the tabernacle of Moses or the temple of Solomon. But after we have thought about the relation of indwelling to the original pattern of indwelling in the Trinity, our concept of indwelling may be subtly changed and we may no longer think that there is a paradox.

Similarly, our concept of human freedom can change as we reflect on the meaning of man's being made in the image of God and the foundation of freedom in God's creativity (chap. 27).

1. See the issue of conceptual change in B. A. Bosserman, *The Trinity and the Vindication of Christian Paradox: An Interpretation and Refinement of the Theological Apologetic of Cornelius Van Til* (Eugene, OR: Pickwick, 2014), 173–78.

Stability and Change

We can see a general pattern in these instances of growth. In all the instances, there is some sense of continuity, and therefore we find a relative stability in meaning. For example, when we are considering the meaning of transcendence, the word *transcendence* does not change to mean "worminess" or "darkness." At the same time, human beings experience a dynamicity in the process of growing in knowledge. The human conception of transcendence subtly shifts or changes or grows.

The human growth takes place, as we might expect, in relation to the archetype, God's knowledge of himself. Human knowledge is relatively stable because God is perfectly stable. And human knowledge can grow, but not because God's knowledge grows. God's knowledge is always complete. But it has infinite depth, and there is always more depth into which we might enter. The dynamicity in human knowledge coheres with the larger dynamicity characterizing history. And history is dynamic because the Father rules history through the power of the Son, who expresses the dynamicity of God (see chapter 21 on the meaning of unchangeability).

Harmony in the Structure of a Concept

In human experience, dynamicity presupposes stability. Change necessitates understanding *what* things change, and those very things must have relative stability in order to be identified. The concept of transcendence, for example, must be identifiable at an earlier and a later stage in human conceptual growth in such a way that we see a measure of continuity. Otherwise, we are just thinking about two different things at two different times, with no relation to each other. In that case, there is no growth.

Conversely, stability presupposes dynamicity. In the case of human beings, the stability involved in being human includes within it the fact that we are active participants. We change, and we make changes. And more specifically, being human includes processes of knowing and coming to know. As we grow, our concept of transcendence cannot actually stay exactly the same, because to some extent we treat it in relation to other things that are happening and other things that we are learning.

The concept of transcendence has a place in our language and in our thought in *relation* to other concepts and various activities of the body, mind, imagination, and will. So here we have also introduced the idea of *relations* in knowledge. A concept with no relations to other ideas and no relations to the world is a complete blank. It actually means nothing. Hence, stable meaning presupposes relations to *other* meanings. Dynamicity of meaning presupposes relations between the earlier and later stages. Relations in meaning presuppose stable meanings to which they relate. A relation between transcendence and immanence presupposes that we have two stable meanings already: the meaning of transcendence and the meaning of immanence.

These thoughts indicate some of the ways in which change and growth in conceptions are not in tension with stability and true knowledge and the stabilities that such knowledge implies. We know the truth, and the truth is stable. Our growth, when it takes place in the right direction, is growth in the truth. God made it so. He did it because this interlocking of stability, dynamicity, and relationality reflects who he is.

These three aspects—stability, dynamicity, and relationality—belong to a coinherent triad. Let us call it the triad of *perspectives on conceptions*. We discuss this triad further in Appendix D.[2] As usual, the coinherence in stability, dynamicity, and relationality reflects the original coinherence in the persons of the Trinity.

Perspectives on Reasoning

The triad of perspectives on conceptions has implications for our understanding of proper reasoning. Reasoning uses conceptions that possess coinherent interlocking of stability, dynamicity, and relationality—all three. Conventional formal deductive logic is a simplification, which virtually ignores dynamicity and relationality. It is a simplification, a reduction.[3] If we think it is not, we will try to put the square peg of formal logic into a round hole formed by human knowledge.

Prominence

Still another idea is available that can help us in understanding how a concept can grow. It is the idea of *prominence*. What do we mean by

2. See also the triad consisting in classificational, instantiational, and associational perspectives (chap. 26), which is coherently related to the triad of stability, dynamicity, and relationality.

3. Vern S. Poythress, *Logic: A God-Centered Approach to the Foundation of Western Thought* (Wheaton, IL: Crossway, 2013), chaps. 19, 22.

prominence? Within a visual scene, there may be a tree in the center that dominates the scene. The tree is *prominent*; it stands out. By analogy, in particular expressions in language, some things stand out. For example, the main theme within a paragraph stands out. Generally speaking, the theme is more prominent than an idea or concept that occurs only once, in some minor role. There is also such a thing as *grammatical prominence* in language. The noun *dog* in the phrase "the small dog" is grammatically the most prominent element.

Prominence is affected by who is doing the observing. A single tree may be visually prominent within a scene, but an observer can always choose to focus on some small piece of the scene, such as an insect on a leaf of the tree. The insect functions prominently in his vision because of the decision that he makes to focus on it.

Not only our language but our thinking and our knowledge rely on prominence. When we consider our idea of a horse, not all the details of every experience that we have had with horses are equally significant. In typical situations, we primarily—that is, prominently—invoke certain features about size and shape when we naively identify a new object as a horse. If we could not single out a few features as prominent, our thinking would be paralyzed. We would be continually overwhelmed with too much information, that is, all the information and all the experiences about horses that we ever had in our entire life.

Prominence plays a role in the growth of concepts. Consider again the idea of transcendence. When our idea of transcendence grows, most of the time the most prominent features that distinguish the idea remain the same. We make adjustments not in a prominent, central feature such as the idea of superiority, but at the periphery. Suppose that Cecelia at the beginning thinks of God's transcendence as including the prominent feature of superiority and the peripheral feature of complete unknowability. As Cecelia grows, transcendence ceases to include for her the feature of being completely unknowable. That feature is altered to become the feature of being partially and truly knowable, but not able to be mastered. In this alteration, one significant aspect—namely, the idea of our having limited knowledge of God in his transcendence—remains. It is somewhat prominent. The idea of God's superiority to us also remains. But the idea that we have *no* knowledge is discarded.

We obviously cannot predict in advance what features may be discarded and what features added or altered. But our sense of continuity is strong if the most prominent features remain in place. In addition, sometimes we have to shift our judgments about what really should be reckoned as prominent. For example, suppose that Donna *does* start out with the idea that the most significant or prominent feature of transcendence is complete unknowability. Somewhere along the line, she may still change. In her own mind, prominence may shift from alleged unknowability to superiority in power and authority. Because of such a shift, Donna is then ready to discard the idea of complete unknowability, but still does not reject the very idea of transcendence as unworkable or false.

If some features are more prominent in transcendence, others are less prominent. We can say that they are *peripheral*. But the aspects that are prominent and those that are peripheral are related. When the two are both present, the prominent aspects invite us to infer the peripheral, or to expect the peripheral. What is prominent effectively influences or involves the related peripheral aspects. And in that relation between the two there lies an innate dynamicity. One aspect leads us to another.

For example, suppose that we see a horse standing on grassy ground. And suppose that we are interested in horses. So for us, the horse stands out as the most prominent thing in view. We are aware of the grassy ground mainly as a background. We expect some kind of field, because horses are typically found in fields. If we begin to focus on the grassy ground, we are likely to think of it in relation to the horse, so we see the grass mainly as potentially supplying food for the horse. The prominent thing, namely, the horse, has influenced our view of the peripheral thing, namely, the grass.

A similar kind of influence can take place in considering transcendence. Suppose that the idea of superiority is a prominent feature in our idea of transcendence. This feature invites us to infer that God is superior in *knowledge* as well as in his being. So we cannot know him completely. We could also mistakenly infer that since God is infinitely transcendent and infinitely superior, we cannot know him at all. That inference is also a form of influence, in which the prominent aspect affects the periphery. But in this case, it is a false inference. Growth takes place by adjusting an inference like this. And the inference itself is peripheral in comparison to the central insight that God is superior. In addition, as we observed, there can be a dynamic shift in what *counts* as prominent.[4]

These dynamic shifts are possible because God ordained a world in harmony with his plan, and therefore also in harmony with his own character. Shifts take place as people are guided by the presence of the Holy Spirit. It should not be surprising that prominence functions as one perspective within a coinherent triad used in the analysis of language (Appendix F). And there is still another pertinent triad that we have not yet discussed: (1) prominence, (2) an influence extending from a prominent center, and (3) a relation of prominence to periphery (Appendix F). Thus, it makes sense that a concept can change and grow, while still remaining in continuity with earlier knowledge.

Key Terms

change
conceptual growth
continuity
dynamicity
periphery
perspectives on conceptions[5]
prominence
relationality
stability

Study Questions

1. Discuss in what sense concepts can grow and yet remain "the same."
2. How can you illustrate the idea of conceptual growth by using the concept of transcendence?
3. What do we mean by *prominence*?

4. In a more thorough exploration, we could also discuss how prominence is affected by context. For example, if we are examining the issue of God's control over the world, God's attribute of *omnipotence* will play a prominent part. If we are examining how God is the source and standard for ethics, God's *holiness* will play a prominent part. For the sake of a special need, we can *choose* to single out some attribute of God or some topic of discussion and temporarily *make* it prominent in a limited context. Our choice of prominence is an aspect of our creativity, reflecting the original, archetypal creativity of God in his Son.

5. Key terms in **bold** are defined in the glossary at the end of this volume.

4. How does the idea of prominence help in understanding how conceptual change is possible?
5. How does God's plan for history form a foundation for conceptual growth?
6. What is the difference between what is prominent and what is peripheral?

For Further Reading

Bosserman, B. A. *The Trinity and the Vindication of Christian Paradox: An Interpretation and Refinement of the Theological Apologetic of Cornelius Van Til.* Eugene, OR: Pickwick, 2014. Pp. 173–78. On conceptual growth.

Pike, Kenneth L. *Linguistic Concepts: An Introduction to Tagmemics.* Lincoln, NE/London: University of Nebraska Press, 1982. Pp. 26–29. An explanation of prominence in the context of linguistics.

Poythress, Vern S. *Logic: A God-Centered Approach to the Foundation of Western Thought.* Wheaton, IL: Crossway, 2013. Chaps. 9, 22. Discussion of the pertinence of stability, dynamicity, and relationality to logic.

PART 6

THE NATURE OF PERSPECTIVES

WE ENDEAVOR TO clarify the nature of perspectives and reasoning that uses perspectives and analogies.

29

Distinctives of Perspectival Reasoning

THE PRECEDING CHAPTERS in part 5 have illustrated how we might use perspectives when we reason about God. Some of the reasoning used in these chapters may seem unusual to theological readers who are not so accustomed to using perspectives and analogies. Having seen the examples in part 5, we can now stand back and ask the broader question, "What is different about reasoning with perspectives?"

First, we should acknowledge the most fundamental distinction between different kinds of human reasoning. It is the difference between unbelievers and believers.[1] In this book, we are trying to reason *as believers* in Christ. Our use of perspectives aspires to follow a Christian form of reasoning, not the kind that might characterize an unbeliever (see chap. 10). But still, we can discern among committed Christians differences in style in how we go about reasoning.

Three Distinctives about Perspectival Reasoning

We can focus on three distinctive aspects that appear in reasoning with perspectives. First, such reasoning uses analogies. Second, it indispensably involves a person who is using a perspective and considering the analogies. Third, it involves a context of other knowledge that colors the person's understanding of his perspective.

These three aspects are closely related to the definition of *perspective* that we gave at the beginning of chapter 2. A perspective is "a view

1. Cornelius Van Til emphasizes this difference, and sometimes uses the terminology *unregenerate* and *regenerate*, rather than *unbeliever* and *believer* (*The Defense of the Faith*, ed. K. Scott Oliphint, 4th ed. [Phillipsburg, NJ: P&R Publishing, 2008]).

from somewhere." More precisely, it is (1) a view of something (2) by someone (3) from somewhere. (See fig. 29.1.)

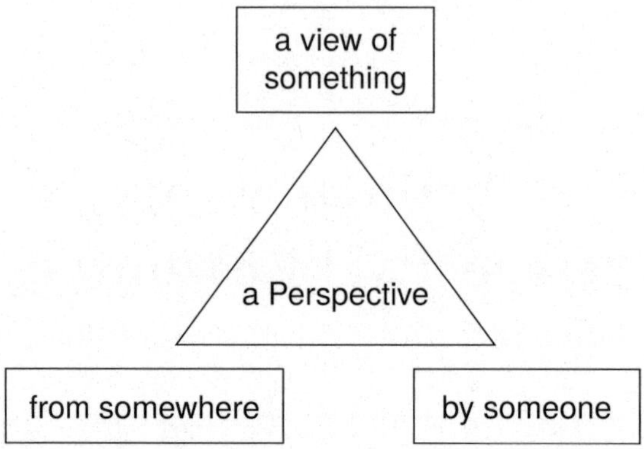

Fig. 29.1. Aspects of a Perspective

The "someone" who is involved is the human viewer. He or she has a perspective or uses a perspective. So there is a person involved.

In addition, the view is a view "from somewhere." Let us consider an example of Irene's viewing a garden through her living room window. Irene has a physical spatial location. But she also has a body of knowledge—things that she thinks she knows. She makes assumptions. Assumptions about the world inform her framework or environment. Her knowledge provides a larger context or mental environment for her observations about the subject matter that she is studying. In a broad sense, it contributes to the idea of her view being "from somewhere."

She has a body of knowledge that includes knowledge of what a garden is, and perhaps knowledge of the history that led to the planting and cultivation of this particular garden. In many cases, she has also chosen an *orientation* toward the garden. A window provides a kind of spatial orientation. She is viewing the garden from a particular angle. But a choice of theme also provides an orientation in a broader sense. She is appreciating the beauty of the garden. Or she is planning on how she can improve it. Or she is wondering whether the vegetables are ripe.

In the case of biblically motivated perspectives on God and on the work of God, human perspectives arise partly through taking a theme and expanding it into a perspective. The theme can be the theme of God's control or the theme of God's presence or the theme of prophetic speech.

The Key Role of Analogy

Analogy is built into this kind of theme. Analogy is typically present for at least two reasons. First, God's character and his actions are analogous to but not identical with human character and human actions. Our thoughts are *analogous* to God's thoughts (Rom. 12:2). God has built into the world not only analogies between himself and human beings, but analogies between himself and other aspects of the created world. For example, Psalm 18:2 says that God is "my rock and my fortress." It uses an analogy between God and a rock and a second analogy between God and a fortress.

Second, in moving from a starting theme to a perspective, the theme is expanded or "stretched," and in the process we use analogy. For example, the prophetic perspective starts with the office of prophet. Moses and Elijah and Isaiah might be typical examples. The prophetic perspective expands this starting point by looking at all speaking activity as analogous to the principal function of someone holding the official status of *prophet*. It observes that any speaker is analogous to a prophet. But we need not confuse things by saying that he *is* a prophet in the narrow sense of the word. The relationship between a broader and a narrower sense involves judgments about whether one action is appropriately analogous to another.

A fine-tuned analysis might say that a thematic perspective involves a subject matter (the garden), a choice of theme (for example, aesthetics of the colors), and an implicit or explicit use of analogy. The analogy would be between stock examples of the theme and its application to the subject matter. If the theme were the aesthetics of colors, stock examples would come from visual arts, such as paintings, and from sample color combinations, which might be represented by several rectangles of color presented side by side. If a person used the prophetic perspective, the stock examples would be the Old Testament official prophets, such as Isaiah and Ezekiel.

Interlocking of the Three Distinctives

So now we have three distinctive aspects to a perspective: (1) an analogical view of something (2) by someone (3) from somewhere. Let us label these aspects as (1) the *analogical aspect,* (2) the *personal aspect,* and (3) the *environmental aspect.* The three distinctives imply one another. To use an analogy fruitfully, we must have a person such as Irene and a body of knowledge. In the nature of the case, an analogy is a relationship that involves both similarities and dissimilarities. We must have a person and a body of knowledge in order to recognize, at least roughly, the relevant similarities and dissimilarities. Use of analogy cannot take place in a vacuum because analogy relies on a richer context. So the use of analogy (aspect 1) implies a person (aspect 2) and an environment or background (aspect 3). (See fig. 29.2.)

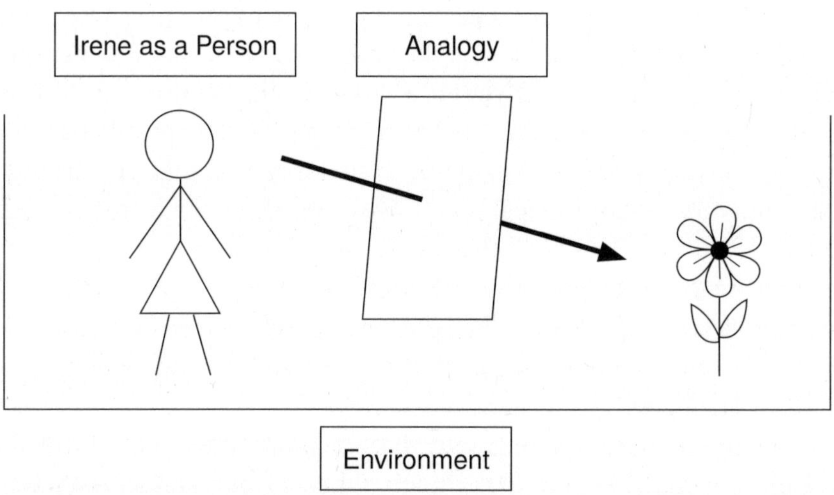

Fig. 29.2. Illustrating a Perspective

Second, Irene in using a perspective uses analogies built into the perspective, and these analogies are appreciated against the background of her knowledge. So if a person uses a perspective, his use implies the presence of analogies and an environment of knowledge. That is, personal use (aspect 2) implies analogy (aspect 1) and a background (aspect 3).

Third, a background of knowledge is applicable only if there is a person to recognize analogies between the background and the object currently being investigated. If Irene confronts something *totally* new, she may be at a loss at first. Fruitful analysis cannot proceed. So actually using an environment of knowledge implies a person and one or more analogies. That is, the environment aspect (3) implies the personal aspect (2) and the analogical aspect (1).

The Bible versus Philosophy

The Bible uses analogies in talking about God—not only the Trinitarian analogies discussed in chapter 8, but other analogies. God is compared to a king, a warrior, a rock, a fortress, a husband, an owner, a father. The list could go on. On the other hand, *philosophical* reasoning about God has often avoided analogies. For this reason, some readers of this book may sense a big difference between perspectives and philosophical reasoning about God. The difference is real, but not absolute. Philosophers of all kinds still live in God's world.

Formal logic tries to avoid overt use of analogy because analogy washes out the univocal meaning of terms, that is, a meaning that remains absolutely the same in each occurrence of the same term. Univocal meaning is needed in order for reasoning to be *purely* formal in nature. For the purpose of formalization, logicians can create a small, logically organized "space" or universe of discourse with specialized meanings. These specialized meanings approximate the purely univocal ideal toward which they strive. But it is the *logicians* as persons who create the space, and it is they who use analogy to judge the relation of their special space to the real world.[2]

Philosophers sometimes wish that reasoning could be purely general and purely formal. They aspire to have reasoning that has no analogy. It would be like a completely isolated view by no one and from nowhere. That is an impossibility, because philosophers are people and they have environmental assumptions. They have presuppositions, including religious commitments.

Formal reasoning constructed within a specially constructed mental "space" or universe of discourse can still be useful. But we have to

2. See the further discussion in Vern S. Poythress, *Logic: A God-Centered Approach to the Foundation of Western Thought* (Wheaton, IL: Crossway, 2013).

realize that in theology we cannot avoid analogy. Perspectival reasoning is just reasoning that consciously exploits the presence of analogies. In this reasoning, we should continually (1) pay close attention to what the analogy reveals, according to the principle of Christian immanence; (2) acknowledge the limited and derivative character of our knowledge and our reasoning, according to the principle of Christian transcendence—we are finite persons; and (3) use the background of knowledge that God has supplied to us about himself. We have knowledge primarily from the whole of Scripture, but then also from general revelation.

Reasoning about God is done not in a vacuum, but in the context of all the fellowship that we have with God through Christ, a fellowship blessed by the work of general and special revelation. We use our background knowledge, not just the statements or concepts immediately in front of us. This background knowledge is part of the meaning of our human existence as finite people with locations in time, space, and situation. The background includes knowledge of God, a knowledge that depends on whether we are believers or unbelievers.

Moreover, human persons are indispensable in reasoning, and their attitudes are indispensable. Our personal involvement includes the commitment of our hearts. Are we for God or against him? Are we in fellowship with God through Christ our Savior or not? These commitments make a difference because reasoning cannot be isolated from the persons or their larger background of knowledge.

Philosophical reasoning about God can be illumining, but should be reframed to recognize that univocal reasoning about God is incoherent, and that analogy, personal involvement, religious commitment of heart, and situational location (including background knowledge) are aspects of human thinking about God. This principle of personal involvement and influence of background applies to modern analytic philosophy of religion.[3]

Coinherence of Three Aspects of a Perspective

We may summarize by saying that the very idea of a thematic perspective includes a perspectival relation between three aspects: a theme

3. For the background of *analytic philosophy*, see *Internet Encyclopedia of Philosophy*, s.v. "Analytic Philosophy," by Aaron Preston, accessed June 27, 2016, http://www.iep.utm.edu/analytic/.

(including analogy), personal involvement, and a context of knowledge (personal "situatedness"). So we have three perspectives on what a thematic perspective is. We may call these three perspectives the *theme-focused perspective,* the *person-focused perspective,* and the *context-focused perspective,* respectively. Together, they are *perspectives on a perspective.* (See fig. 29.3.)

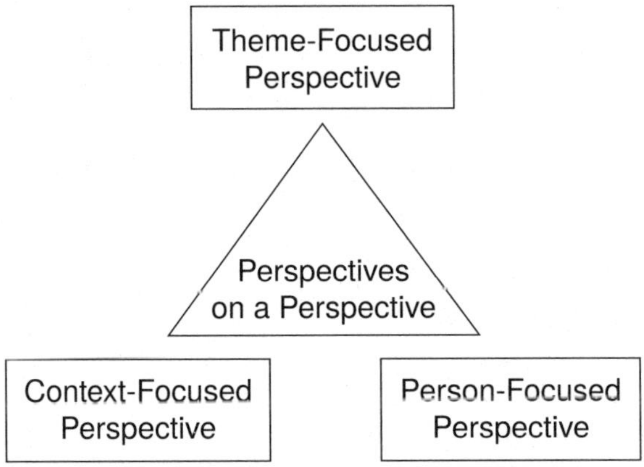

Fig. 29.3. Perspectives on a Perspective

As we observed above, these three imply one another. They are also related to the triad for ethics. The normative perspective corresponds to the theme-focused perspective because the theme in a sense "normatively" guides the perception of the viewers. The situational perspective corresponds to the context-focused perspective. This perspective deals with the situational environment of the person, which includes his spatial situation and the larger "situation" of an accompanying body of knowledge and assumptions. The existential perspective corresponds to the person-focused perspective: we focus on the *person* who uses the perspective. And we pay attention to his heart-level religious commitment. (See fig. 29.4.) The triad for ethics has coinherence that reflects the coinherence in the Trinity (chap. 13). So the triad of perspectives on a perspective also has such coinherence.

We should remember that non-Christians take a different view of ethics, and therefore also a different view of the nature of perspectives. In our discussion, we are considering these things from a Christian point of view.

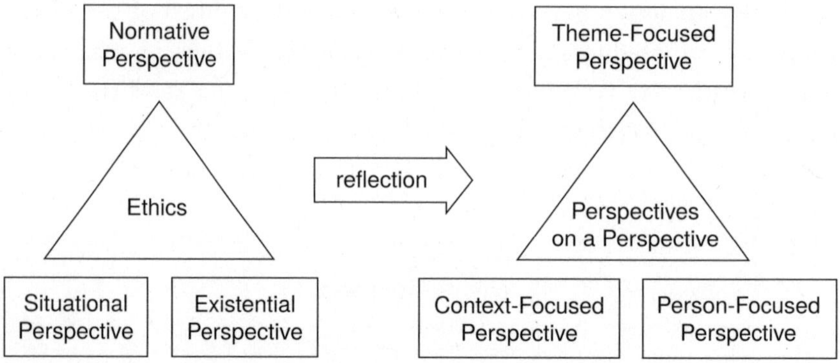

Fig. 29.4. From Ethics to Perspectives on a Perspective

Key Terms

analogical aspect
analogy
analytic philosophy[4]
assumption
context-focused perspective
environmental aspect
framework
personal aspect
person-focused perspective
perspectival reasoning
perspective
prophetic perspective
stock example
theme-focused perspective
univocal meaning
view

Study Questions

1. How do believers and unbelievers differ in their reasoning?
2. What three aspects work together when a person uses a perspective?
3. How do the three aspects cohere?

4. Key terms in **bold** are defined in the glossary at the end of this volume.

4. How does Christian perspectival reasoning differ from reasoning in formal logic?
5. How does formal logic simplify? Why is it still useful?
6. What are the three perspectives on a perspective, and how are they coinherent?
7. How can the triad of perspectives on a perspective be derived from the triad for ethics? What does this derivation show about the foundation for the former triad?
8. What implications does perspectival reasoning have for reasoning in analytic philosophy?

For Further Reading

Poythress, Vern S. *Logic: A God-Centered Approach to the Foundation of Western Thought*. Wheaton, IL: Crossway, 2013. Chaps. 17–23. Discussion of the simplifications in logic for the sake of univocal terms.

30

Perspectival Knowledge in the Trinity

IN CHAPTER 4, WE introduced *thematic perspectives,* and we have been focusing almost exclusively on them. We need to return to look at *personal perspectives* again (from chapter 3). Do personal perspectives have a significant relation to the nature of the Trinity?

Perspectives in the Trinity

We know that there are three distinct persons in the Trinity. Do these persons have distinct "perspectives"? It is wise to begin by putting the word *perspectives* in quotation marks. The quotation marks should remind us that our own thinking, including perspectival thinking, is derivative from and analogous to God's thinking. Our thinking is *not* on the same level. So we should not expect that God would have a "perspective" in quite the same way as we would.

In the context of human knowledge, expressions about having "a perspective" typically include the implication that any one perspective is limited. That perspective may provide truth, but not all truth. Clearly, God does *not* "have a perspective" in this sense; he is not limited in knowledge. Each of the persons of the Trinity is fully God and has unlimited divine knowledge.[1] God understands comprehensively all possible human perspectives. That is precisely because his own understanding is unlimited.

We can still ask ourselves whether there may be some limited

1. Expressions in the Bible indicating limited knowledge on the part of Christ are referring to the limited knowledge that he has *with respect to his human nature* (Matt. 24:36; Luke 2:52). With respect to his divine nature, his knowledge is unlimited and complete. Since he is fully God, he has complete knowledge. Since he is fully man, his knowledge as man is limited. Both realities belong to the one person of Christ.

analogy between human personal perspectives and the knowledge enjoyed by one person of the Trinity. Because there are three distinct persons in the Trinity, are there three distinct personal perspectives on divine knowledge?

Matthew 11:27 is relevant:

> All things have been handed over to me by my Father, and no one knows the Son except the Father, and no one knows the Father except the Son and anyone to whom the Son chooses to reveal him.

This verse is discussing personal knowledge. The Father knows *facts* about the Son. But that is not all. He knows *the Son*. It is a knowledge of intimate personal acquaintance and fellowship, which infinitely exceeds the knowledge that a human father has of his son. The Father knows the Son comprehensively. Since the Son is fully God, the Father knows God comprehensively. He knows all things. Similarly, the Son in knowing the Father knows all things.[2]

So this verse confirms our earlier claim that any one person of the Trinity does not "have a perspective" that *limits* his knowledge. On the other hand, the verse also shows the involvement of the person *in* his knowledge, which is personal knowledge. It is *as the Father* that the Father knows the Son. This knowledge therefore *does* have an analogy with the perspectival personal knowledge that we observe among human persons.

We have said that perspectival knowledge is a view of something by someone from somewhere. The "someone," the viewer, is in this case the Father. The "view of something" is his knowledge of the Son—not, be it noted, merely a generic knowledge of the Godhead that would include within it no focus on a distinct person. The Son is like a distinctive *thematic* focus.

Finally, the Father's knowledge is "from somewhere." Of course, "somewhere" is not a "somewhere" of a spatial location within creation. The Father has his knowledge in the fellowship with the Son and with the Holy Spirit. He has his knowledge in an environment of interpersonal

2. See also Vern S. Poythress, *Symphonic Theology: The Validity of Multiple Perspectives in Theology* (Grand Rapids: Zondervan, 1987; repr., Phillipsburg, NJ: P&R Publishing, 2001), 50–51.

fellowship. This "environment" is not a *created* environment, but the uncreated personal environment of fellowship and coinherence among the persons of the Trinity. That environment is the archetype for the creation of spatial locations (chap. 20).

In sum, the Father has a personal perspective in the sense of including the three aspects that characterize perspectives: (1) a view of something (2) by someone (3) from somewhere. (See fig. 30.1.)

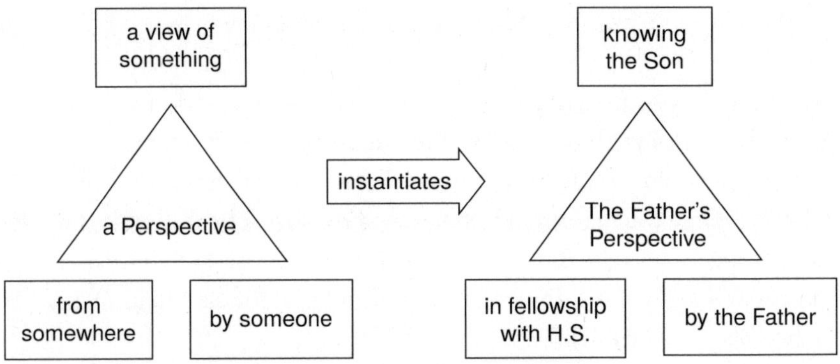

Fig. 30.1. The Father's Personal Perspective

We must be vigilant in maintaining the Creator-creature distinction. God is not man. And the person of God the Father does not "have a perspective" in the same way that a human being has a personal perspective. At the same time, according to the principle of Christian immanence (chap. 10), we maintain that the language about the Father's knowing the Son communicates to us a reality about the Father's personal knowledge. If we break up the language about the Father's knowledge that is found in Matthew 11:27, and we lose the analogy between the Father's knowledge and human knowledge, we evaporate the meaning of Matthew 11:27 and fall into a form of non-Christian transcendence. We would then be acting as though Matthew 11:27 were opaque and told us nothing. And then we would be in darkness.

We conclude, then, that in an analogical sense a personal perspective belongs to each person of the Trinity. There are three personal perspectives in the Trinity: the perspective of the Father, the perspective of the Son, and the perspective of the Holy Spirit. (See fig. 30.2.)

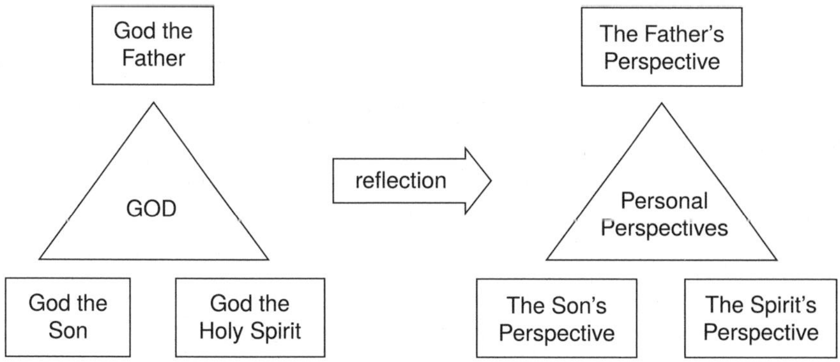

Fig. 30.2. Personal Perspectives in the Trinity

One and Many in Divine Knowledge

The three personal perspectives among the three persons of the Trinity represent a plurality in divine knowledge, an expression of the principle of *the many* (as in chapter 26). At the same time, because there is only one God, there is only one divine knowledge—the knowledge that God has of all things whatsoever. This one divine knowledge is an expression of the principle of *the one.* As usual, the one and the many are "equally ultimate." The two coinhere, in analogy with the coinherence of the persons of the Trinity.

Or we may put it another way. *As the Father,* the Father knows the Son. The Father has a distinct perspective in his knowledge. At the same time, in knowing the Son, he fully knows God and knows all things. So his knowledge in its contents is the *same* as the knowledge of God. This conclusion also follows simply by observing that the Father is God. Therefore, he has the knowledge of God. Is all this mysterious? Of course. What would we expect? In this matter as in others, we should praise God for his greatness.

Perspectives within Human Knowledge

We are made in the image of God (Gen. 1:27). Our experience of personal perspectives is possible because there is one common humanity and there are many individual persons. Barbara can know Carol. In knowing Carol, Barbara experiences the beginning of an understanding of a second person's perspective. There are plural perspectives among human beings. These plural personal perspectives are possible because God created human beings one and many. And this one and many, as we have seen, is derivative from the one and the many in the Trinity (chap. 26).

In sum, human personal perspectives make sense because of divine personal perspectives in the persons of the Trinity. Human personal perspectives between Barbara and Carol partially cohere when Barbara comes to know Carol. This partial coherence is possible because of the infinite prior coinherence in personal knowledge in the three personal perspectives in the Trinity. God has designed human beings in his image. He has planned all along that we should have in ourselves an experience of perspectives. That is why our personal perspectives analogically reflect him.

Key Terms

divine personal perspective[3]
human personal perspective
personal perspective
perspective

Study Questions

1. In what ways is it inappropriate to equate human perspectives with the knowledge possessed by a person of the Trinity?
2. What are the implications of Matthew 11:27 for our understanding of personal knowledge in the persons of the Trinity?
3. In what sense does the Father have a personal perspective on knowledge? Does the same hold for the Son and for the Spirit (cf. 1 Cor. 2:11)?
4. How do the three perspectives on a perspective apply to understanding the Father's personal knowledge?
5. How are the personal perspectives of the three persons of the Trinity coinherent?

For Further Reading

Poythress, Vern S. *Symphonic Theology: The Validity of Multiple Perspectives in Theology*. Grand Rapids: Zondervan, 1987. Reprint, Phillipsburg, NJ: P&R Publishing, 2001. Pp. 50–51. Discussion of knowledge by the persons of the Trinity.

3. Key terms in **bold** are defined in the glossary at the end of this volume.

31

Personal Perspectives and Thematic Perspectives

FOR MOST OF the book, we have concentrated on *thematic* perspectives, as defined in chapter 4. But the previous chapter returned to the topic of *personal* perspectives. Personal perspectives are very deep, since they are rooted in the tripersonal character of the Trinity. This presence of personal perspectives raises the question of the relation between personal perspectives and thematic perspectives. As we saw in part 3, key triads of thematic perspectives have associations with distinct persons of the Trinity. So thematic perspectives are associated with the persons of the Trinity. But this result does not yet include a direct connection with the personal *perspectives* of the persons of the Trinity.

Kinds of Perspectives

So let us consider again the earlier distinctions in chapters 2–4 between *kinds* of ordinary perspectives. There are spatial perspectives (chap. 2), personal perspectives (chap. 3), and thematic perspectives (chap. 4). (See fig. 31.1.) In many ways, these distinct kinds of perspectives may seem very different. Space is not a person, and a person is not a theme. But in fact, these different kinds of perspectives involve one another. Let us see how.

Implications between Kinds of Perspectives

Let us begin with a spatial perspective. A spatial perspective is a visual perspective from some fixed location in space. But it implies the presence of a person who has the visual experience. Yes, for some distant location, we can *imagine* ourselves standing there and what things would

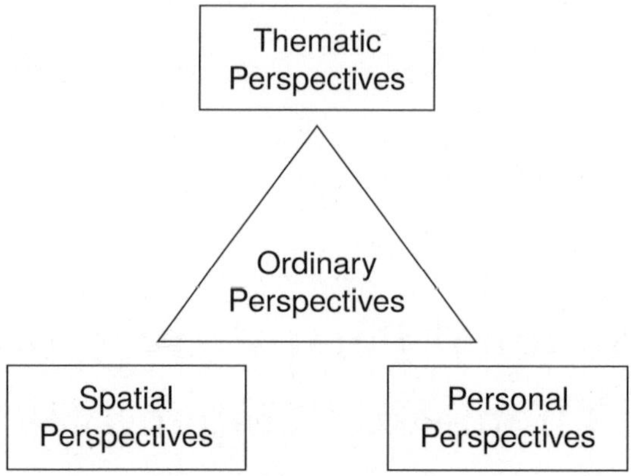

Fig. 31.1. Three Kinds of Ordinary Perspectives

look like from there. But the imagination is still the work of a person. And the imagination is based on the possibility of actually having a person in the location. So the idea of a spatial perspective implicitly involves a person who is looking at the scene from a particular location in space. If so, the spatial perspective is *part of* a larger personal perspective that includes views and attitudes about many things.

Conversely, a human person always has a spatial location. So at any one time, he has a particular location. And he views the visual scene from that location. Thus, at any one time, a human personal perspective always involves a spatial perspective.[1]

Now consider a thematic perspective. A thematic perspective can operate only if there is a person who has chosen a particular theme and who is now looking at a subject with the theme in mind. So a thematic perspective implies a personal perspective in which it participates.

Conversely, a personal perspective at any one time includes focal awareness. If a person is alert, he is focused on some issue or something within his visual field. This focus is one kind of theme, in a broad sense of the word *theme*. So a personal perspective implies a thematic perspective.

One kind of theme is the theme of a fixed spatial location. So a spatial perspective includes a theme, namely, the theme of how things

1. Blind people cannot literally see the scene. But they can feel about, and they can conceptualize where objects are located in a room. So they, too, have a conceptual analogue of vision and a sense of spatial location.

look from the chosen spatial location. Thus, a spatial perspective implies a thematic perspective.

Conversely, a thematic perspective implies a spatial perspective in two ways. First, it implies a spatial perspective by way of the spatial location of the person who is using the thematic perspective. Second, in a metaphorically extended sense of *space*, a thematic perspective organizes the space consisting in the subject matter that is under inspection.

It appears, then, that the three kinds of perspectives, though distinct, also involve one another when we think of actually carrying out the use of a perspective in practice. A person has a theme (a focus of awareness) that he is using in the context of his unique spatial location.

From Ethics to Ordinary Perspectives

May we say that the three kinds of perspectives are coinherent? Maybe. To confirm this idea, let us see whether we can correlate the three kinds of perspectives with one of the coinherent triads that we have already discussed.

We choose the triad for ethics. The normative perspective on ethics correlates with the thematic perspective, because a theme has a kind of "normative" function in guiding the examination of the subject. The situational perspective on ethics correlates with the spatial perspective, because the spatial perspective is part of the total situation of the person using a perspective. Finally, the existential perspective on ethics correlates with the personal perspective of the person who is using a perspective. (See fig. 31.2.) Since the triad for ethics reflects the coinherence in the Trinity (chap. 13), so does the triad for ordinary perspectives.

Metaperspectives

Ordinarily, we classify a perspective as *either* a thematic perspective *or* a spatial perspective *or* a personal perspective (as in chapters 2–4). A particular perspective, such as the prophetic perspective (chap. 4), is only one kind, not all three kinds. The prophetic perspective is a thematic perspective. It is therefore *not* either of the other two kinds—it is not a spatial perspective or a personal perspective.

Yet there is a complementary way of looking at the whole situation. Any one of these classes of perspectives can be "stretched" or

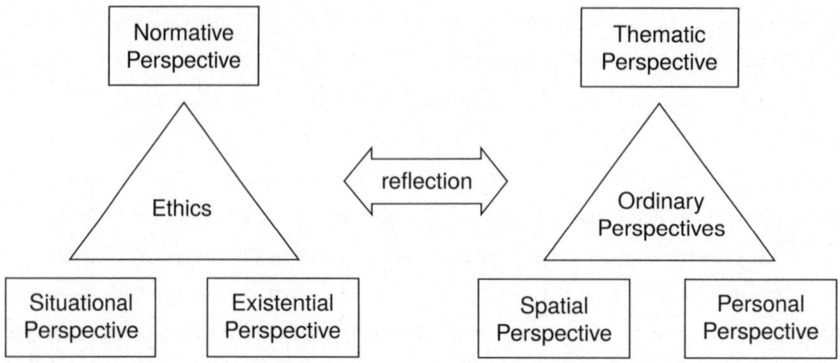

Fig. 31.2. From Ethics to Kinds of Ordinary Perspectives

extended conceptually so that we view all perspectives whatsoever as perspectivally analogous to instances of thematic perspectives, broadly construed. All perspectives have a theme, in a broad sense. For spatial perspectives, the theme is what things look like from a fixed spatial location. For personal perspectives, the theme is what things look like for a particular person. This construal treats the idea of a thematic perspective as a perspective on all perspectives.

It is convenient to introduce a new terminology. Let us employ the term *metaperspective* as a general label for describing any idea that functions as a perspective on a perspective. When the idea of a thematic perspective is extended to become a perspective on all perspectives, it functions as a *metaperspective.* We may call it the *thematic metaperspective.* The thematic metaperspective views all perspectives as analogous to a thematic perspective. Similar observations hold with respect to spatial perspectives. We can metaphorically extend the idea of a space, so that a particular theme becomes the "space" in which we study a subject matter. All perspectives whatsoever can be viewed as metaphorically analogous to spatial perspectives. In this manner, we extend the idea of a spatial perspective to become a perspective on all perspectives. Such a use may be called the *spatial metaperspective.* The same is true with respect to the idea of a personal perspective. The extension may be called the *personal metaperspective.* We then have a triad of metaperspectives: the thematic metaperspective, the spatial metaperspective, and the personal metaperspective. Let us call the triad as a whole the *triad of ordinary metaperspectives* (table 31.1).

Triad of Kinds of Ordinary Perspectives	reflection	Triad of Ordinary Metaperspectives
thematic perspectives	→	thematic metaperspective
spatial perspectives	→	spatial metaperspective
personal perspectives	→	personal metaperspective

Table 31.1. From Ordinary Perspectives to Ordinary Metaperspectives

The Triad of Perspectives on a Perspective and the Triad of New Metaperspectives

We can also see a correlation between the triad of perspectives on a perspective (from chapter 29) and the new metaperspectives. Both show the same three fundamental aspects: (1) a view of something (2) by someone (3) from somewhere. (See table 31.2; fig. 31.3.)

Starting Point	reflection	Perspectives on a Perspective	reflection	Metaperspectives
analogical view	→	theme-focused perspective	→	thematic metaperspective
from somewhere	→	context-focused perspective	→	spatial metaperspective
by someone	→	person-focused perspective	→	personal metaperspective

Table 31.2. Perspectives on a Perspective and Metaperspectives

God has designed the whole range of the way in which we as human beings use perspectives. Here also is a source for praising God.

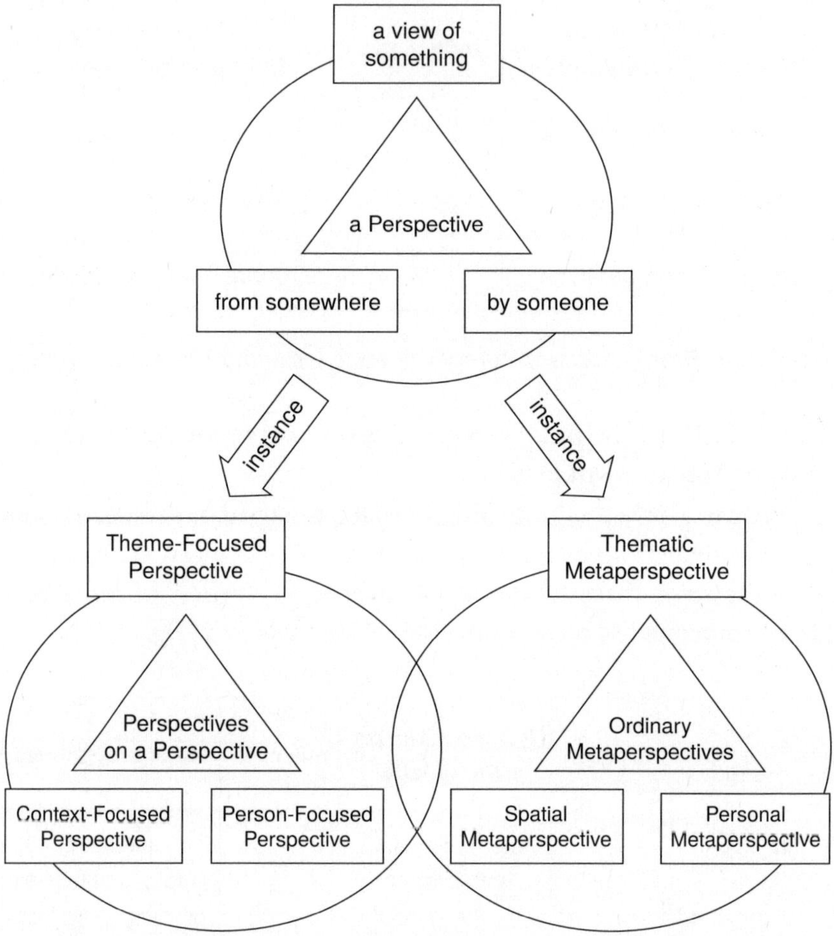

Fig. 31.3. Perspectives on a Perspective Correlated to Ordinary Metaperspectives

Key Terms

context-focused perspective[2]
existential perspective
metaperspective
normative perspective
ordinary metaperspective
ordinary perspective

2. Key terms in **bold** are defined in the glossary at the end of this volume.

personal metaperspective
personal perspective
person-focused perspective
situational perspective
spatial metaperspective
spatial perspective
thematic metaperspective
thematic perspective
theme-focused perspective

Study Questions

1. What are the three general kinds of perspectives (ordinary perspectives)?
2. How do these three kinds of perspectives involve one another in practice?
3. How can the three kinds of perspectives be derived from the triad for ethics? What does this derivation imply about coinherence and the ultimate foundation for the three kinds of perspectives?
4. What is a *metaperspective*? How can the three kinds of ordinary perspectives be converted into metaperspectives?
5. How are the three kinds of perspectives related to the triad of perspectives on a perspective?

32

Attributes of God and Perspectives on God

THE PREVIOUS CHAPTER encouraged us to see a close, coinherent relationship between personal perspectives and thematic perspectives. We may now apply this relationship to a consideration of the personal perspectives of the persons in the Trinity. We will do it in stages.

A Triad of Perspectives on God

We saw in chapter 30 that the persons of the Trinity have personal perspectives. These are the archetype for all human personal perspectives. Might there be in the Trinity some archetype for thematic perspectives? Yes. The attributes of God offer us themes. We saw in chapter 19 that the triad for lordship leads to the lordship attributes of authority, control, and presence—or, in more traditional terminology, moral absoluteness, omnipotence, and omnipresence. Might there also be in the Trinity an archetype for spatial perspectives? The archetype for created space is found in the Trinitarian reality of indwelling (chap. 20).

Let us, then, consider the following triad of perspectives as suitable for thinking about God: a perspective on attributes, focusing on the attributes of God; a perspective on persons, focusing on the persons of the Trinity; and a perspective on coinherence, focusing on coinherence. Let us call this triad the *special triad for God*. All the perspectives in the triad enjoy unity in the unity of one God. (See fig. 32.1.)

Coinherence of Perspectives

Are these three perspectives coinherent? We can begin to answer the question by seeing the correlations between this triad of perspectives

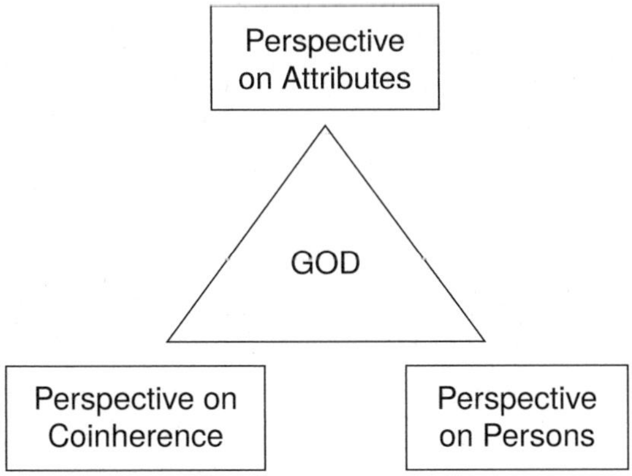

Fig. 32.1. The Special Triad for God

and the triad for ethics. In the triad for ethics, the existential perspective is closely correlated with the perspective on persons. The situational perspective is closely correlated with the perspective on coinherence, because coinherence represents the metaphorical "situation" in which each person of the Trinity exists.

Does the normative perspective on ethics correlate with the perspective on attributes? This correlation is less obvious. But God's attributes are in one sense the "norms" according to which he acts. He always acts in a manner consistent with his attributes. Of course, the attributes are not norms *outside* God, to which he would be subject. They are rather designations of his character. But we can depend on them. And his character also becomes an aspect of the norms to which *we* are subject as human beings, because we are to be like God in righteousness and holiness.

We conclude that the special triad for God is correlated to the triad for ethics. (See table 32.1; fig. 32.2.)

Since the triad for ethics is coinherent, these correlations suggest that the special triad for God is likewise coinherent.

Implications within the Special Triad for God

We can confirm the coinherence of the special triad for God. Let us explore how one perspective of the three can be derived from another. Is one inherent in another? Let us begin with the perspective on attributes. The attributes do not exist in a vacuum, but belong to persons. And the

Perspectives on Ethics	reflection	**Special Triad for God**
normative perspective	→	perspective on attributes
situational perspective	→	perspective on coinherence
existential perspective	→	perspective on persons

Table 32.1. From Perspectives on Ethics to the Special Triad for God

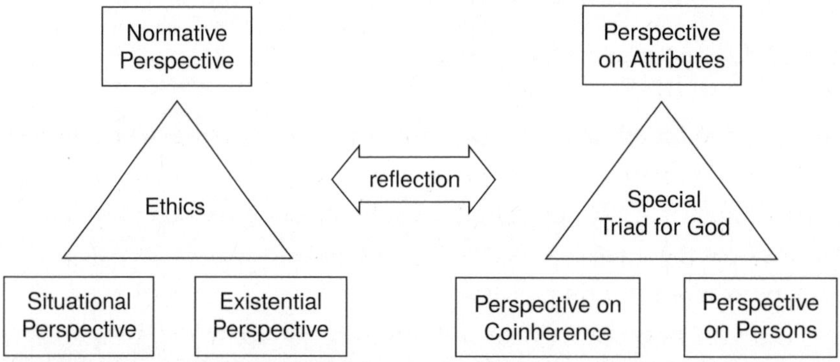

Fig. 32.2. From Perspectives on Ethics to the Special Triad for God

persons exist in an environment, which in this case is the environment represented by coinherence. So the perspective on attributes implies the perspective on coinherence and the perspective on persons.

Or start with coinherence. The coinherence is a coinherence between persons, and the persons have attributes. So the perspective on coinherence implies the perspective on attributes and the perspective on persons.

It is fairly simple to see implications between the three perspectives because attributes belong to persons in an environment, and the presence of one already implicitly involves the presence of all three.

God is in harmony with himself, however we choose to explore who he is. The harmony among attributes, persons, and coinherence reflects the harmony among perspectives on ethics, which in turn reflects the harmony among the persons of the Trinity.

Key Terms

coinherence[1]
existential perspective
harmony
normative perspective
perspective on attributes
perspective on coinherence
perspective on persons
reflection
situational perspective
special triad for God

Study Questions

1. What perspectives are useful in considering the relation of attributes of God to the persons of the Trinity and to coinherence?
2. What is the special triad for God?
3. How can the special triad for God be derived from the triad for ethics? What does this derivation say about the coinherence of the three perspectives within the special triad for God?
4. How can one perspective within the special triad for God be derived from another, or seen to be implicit in another?

For Further Reading

Frame, John M. *The Doctrine of God*. Phillipsburg, NJ: P&R Publishing, 2002. Pp. 387–401. Summary on the attributes of God.

1. Key terms in **bold** are defined in the glossary at the end of this volume.

33

Classical Perspectives concerning God

IF WE LIKE, we can pick out some specific attributes of God and show in more detail how they enjoy coinherence with the persons in God and with the pattern of coinherence. One possible list of attributes comprises the attributes for lordship: authority, control, and presence (chap. 19; see chap. 14). Or we may use the classical labels corresponding to these attributes: moral absoluteness, omnipotence, and omnipresence.

A Triad of Abstract Attributes

Instead of taking this route, we will use more "abstract" categories, in order to show affinities and differences between perspectival reasoning and traditional philosophical reasoning. Philosophical reasoning often starts with highly abstract categories. Within a perspectival framework, we can do something analogous. But when we do it, we explicitly admit that we are using analogies and using a larger context of the knowledge of God. We admit our involvement as persons who use analogies and who discern in what ways such analogies are fitting. And we as persons always stand in the presence of God, who is our Judge. We pray that he may illumine us, through being born again by the Spirit and then being continually guided by him.

The attributes we will consider are absoluteness, simplicity, and personality. God is absolute, simple, and personal. (See fig. 33.1.)

Personal knowledge informs our understanding of any terms that we use. So it is not feasible for us to give a precise definition that eliminates context. All three attributes become *perspectives* on God (see chap. 19).

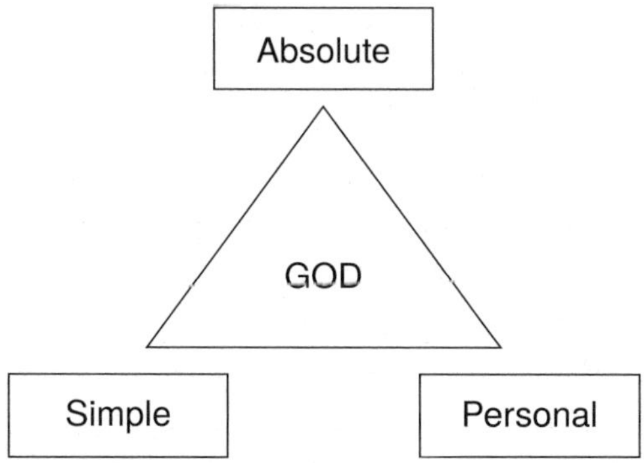

Fig. 33.1. Abstract Attributes of God

The concept of *simplicity* is the most opaque of the three. In theological discourse, it has a special technical meaning. It is not used to deny that God is a rich and wonderful being. Rather, *simplicity* is the opposite of *having parts*. Let us consider an illustration. A machine has parts—rods, gears, belts, axles, and the like. We can contemplate taking it apart and decomposing it into its physical parts. God, by contrast, is not a material being and does not have material parts. He cannot be decomposed into simpler pieces.

Some of the theological definitions of simplicity go beyond this minimal idea of being without parts, and add that God is not dependent on concepts or meanings that have a prior existence outside himself. If he were, he would be conceptually "decomposable," at least in part, into whatever are the outside meanings on which he depends.

In some theological contexts, the word *simplicity* can include still more features that create philosophical puzzles. We will not travel into these areas.[1]

Next, what does it mean for God to be *absolute*? It means that he is ultimate and superior to everything outside him. He is not limited, constrained, or dependent on anything outside him.[2]

We should also say a bit about the attribute of *personality*. We do not mean quite the same thing here as we do when we talk about the

1. John M. Frame, *The Doctrine of God* (Phillipsburg, NJ: P&R Publishing, 2002), 227–30.

2. The dictionary defines *absolute* as "having no restriction, exception, or qualification." *Merriam-Webster*, definition 4, accessed June 20, 2016, http://www.merriam-webster.com/dictionary/absolute.

persons of the Trinity. We mean that God is personal by having abilities analogous to human persons—for example, the ability to know, to speak, to hear, to love, and to be in a personal relationship to human persons (once they exist). Each person of the Trinity is also *personal* in this sense.

Correlations with the Triad for Ethics

Why choose these three attributes—absoluteness, simplicity, and personality? As we indicated, we are choosing them partly because they crop up in philosophical reasoning about God. But we also choose these particular three because they have a correlation with the triad of perspectives on ethics. The normative perspective on ethics leads naturally to God's absoluteness. In a broad sense, God is the "norm" for everything. The situational perspective leads to God's simplicity, because simplicity expresses the idea that God is not dependent on anything separable from him, either inside him (a part) or outside him (a meaning or concept), in an environment or situation. The existential perspective, with its focus on persons, leads to the focus on God's being personal. (See fig. 33.2.)

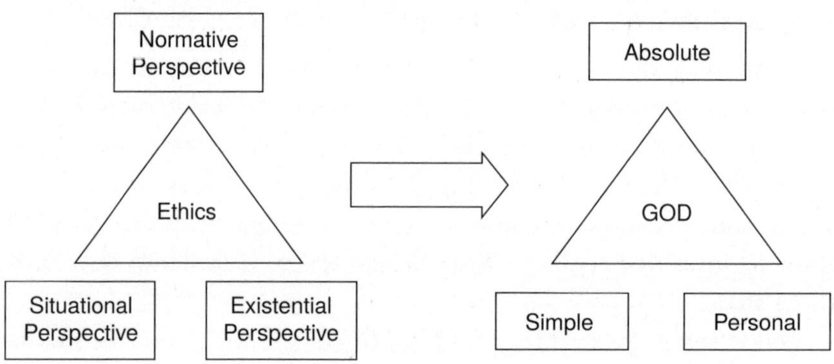

Fig. 33.2. From Ethics to Abstract Attributes

We can also see a correlation between the triad for lordship and the triad of abstract attributes. (See fig. 33.3.) The perspective of authority corresponds to absoluteness. The comprehensive authority of God implies that he is absolute. The perspective of control corresponds to simplicity, because control implies control over all the meanings and

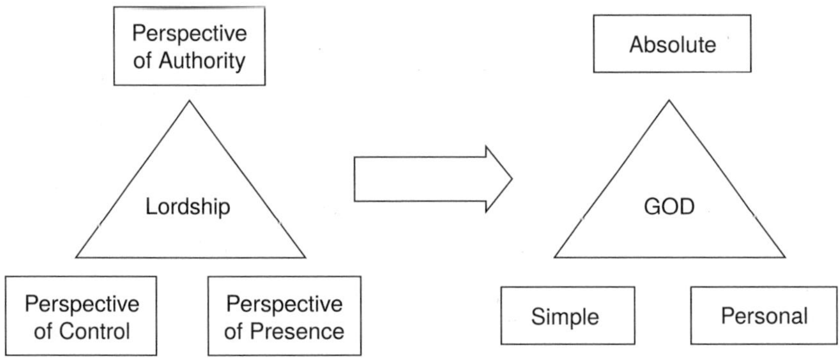

Fig. 33.3. From Lordship to Abstract Attributes

ideas that go into understanding who God is. God is not dependent on an outside concept to determine who he is. The perspective of presence corresponds to God's personal nature. Presence is presence of God in person.

The triad for ethics and the triad for lordship are coinherent. Is the triad of abstract attributes also coinherent? Let us see.

Deriving Simplicity and Personality from Absoluteness

Given our commitment to perspectival reasoning, we will use analogies and background knowledge. So if we "derive" other attributes from absoluteness, we implicitly use a background. Our derivations of other attributes from absoluteness should be understood as not equivalent to abstract philosophical reasoning, which often wants to use human reason alone as norm and to use a reduced, self-contained meaning for each attribute. Rather, we want to be guided by God's Word, found in the Bible. With this clarification in place, we may proceed.

God is absolute. So he is independent. He is not dependent on an internal part or an external meaning or concept that already exists outside him. So God is simple. We have thereby shown that absoluteness implies simplicity.

Next, how might we derive God's personal nature? God is absolute. So he is absolute in knowledge. He knows all the thoughts and feelings and motivations of all persons. Having such knowledge implies that God is personal. It takes a personal being to know persons. Thus, absoluteness implies personality.

Deriving Absoluteness and Personality from Simplicity

Now, let us start with simplicity. *Simplicity* means "lack of dependence on internal parts or external ideas." This lack of dependence is already a negative description of absoluteness. So simplicity implies absoluteness.

Simplicity includes the lack of dependence on outside ideas. So all the ideas are *within* the one that is simple. Ideas are mental in character, and imply a mind that *has* the ideas. The ideas are *known*. And knowledge is innately personal. Simplicity implies the personal nature of God.

Deriving Absoluteness and Simplicity from Personality

Finally, we start with the principle that God is personal. Can we derive absoluteness? We ourselves are finite persons. The idea of a finite person does not include absoluteness, but rather finiteness. Persons are real, and not merely a complex result of moving molecules. Finite persons have meaning only against the background of an ultimate source of meaning, which must include personality. Only personality can produce persons. So the existence of persons implies the existence of God, who is personal and absolute.

(Note here that this reasoning is not like a theistic proof claiming to be independent of Scripture, but one that shows some of the inherent "logic" in biblical revelation.)

The partial coherence between finite personal perspectives, like the perspectives of Barbara and Carol, rests on the infinite coinherence in the absolute knowledge of God. This coinherence implies simplicity because no knowledge or ideas are left out of its comprehensive scope.

In sum, the three attributes of absoluteness, simplicity, and personality imply one another and are implicit in one another. This exploration of mutual implications confirms that the triad of abstract attributes is coinherent in a manner analogous to the coinherence of the triad for ethics, which in turn has its roots in the coinherence among the persons of the Trinity.

Coinherence with the Personal Perspectives of Persons of the Trinity

Now let us recall how, in the previous chapter, we studied the special triad for God. The triad consists in three perspectives: the perspective on attributes of God, the perspective on coinherence, and the perspective on persons in God. This triad is coinherent. So the perspective on attributes coheres with the perspective on persons. The attributes of God implicate the persons, and vice versa. (See fig. 33.4.)

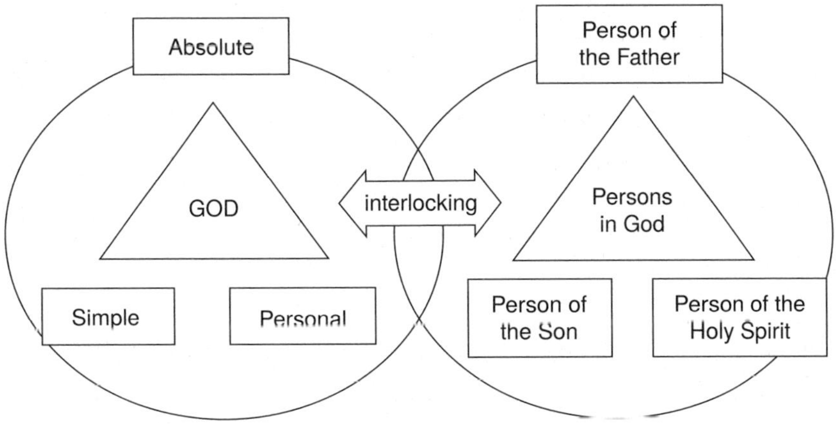

Fig. 33.4. Interlocking of Attributes and Persons

This insight applies to the attributes explored in this chapter: the attributes of absoluteness, simplicity, and personality. These attributes coinhere with the persons of the Trinity. The mystery of the Trinity is always present and implicit in reasoning regarding attributes, including reasoning that takes its start in more "abstract" attributes such as absoluteness and simplicity.

Key Terms

absoluteness[3]
personality
perspective on attributes (of God)
perspective on coinherence
perspective on persons (in God)
simplicity
special triad for God
triad of abstract attributes

3. Key terms in **bold** are defined in the glossary at the end of this volume.

Study Questions

1. What is the meaning of *absoluteness*?
2. What is the meaning of *simplicity* when applied to God?
3. How can we use the term *personal* as a description of God? How is this distinct from the use of the term *person* with respect to the three persons in God?
4. How can the triad of abstract attributes be derived from the special triad for God?

For Further Reading

Frame, John M. *The Doctrine of God*. Phillipsburg, NJ: P&R Publishing, 2002. Pp. 600–608. On absoluteness or aseity.

34

Perspectival Context for Attributes of God

IN THE PREVIOUS chapter, we indicated that reasoning about the attributes of God takes place within a context. We are always reasoning analogically *from* somewhere, and it is *we* as persons who reason. It is useful to remind ourselves in a summary fashion of this context.

Analyses of Perspectives

To what contexts have we appealed? In chapters 29 and 31, we analyzed the nature of perspectives, beginning with a triad of perspectives on a perspective. The triad of perspectives on a perspective is derivable from the triad for ethics (chap. 29). And the same triad also has a close correlation to the triad of kinds of ordinary perspectives (chap. 31). And this triad in turn leads to an application to God in which we use the special triad for God (chap. 32). We can summarize these relationships in a diagram (fig. 34.1).

Expanding the Special Triad for God

We can further differentiate perspectives within the special triad for God. This triad includes three perspectives: a perspective on attributes, a perspective on coinherence, and a perspective on persons. The perspective on attributes can be further differentiated into three attributes—absoluteness, simplicity, and personality—as we saw in chapter 33. The perspective on coinherence can be differentiated into three kinds of coinherence—coinherence in knowledge, coinherence in power, and coinherence in indwelling (from chapter 7). (For a further discussion of this triad for coinherence, see Appendix J.) The perspective on persons

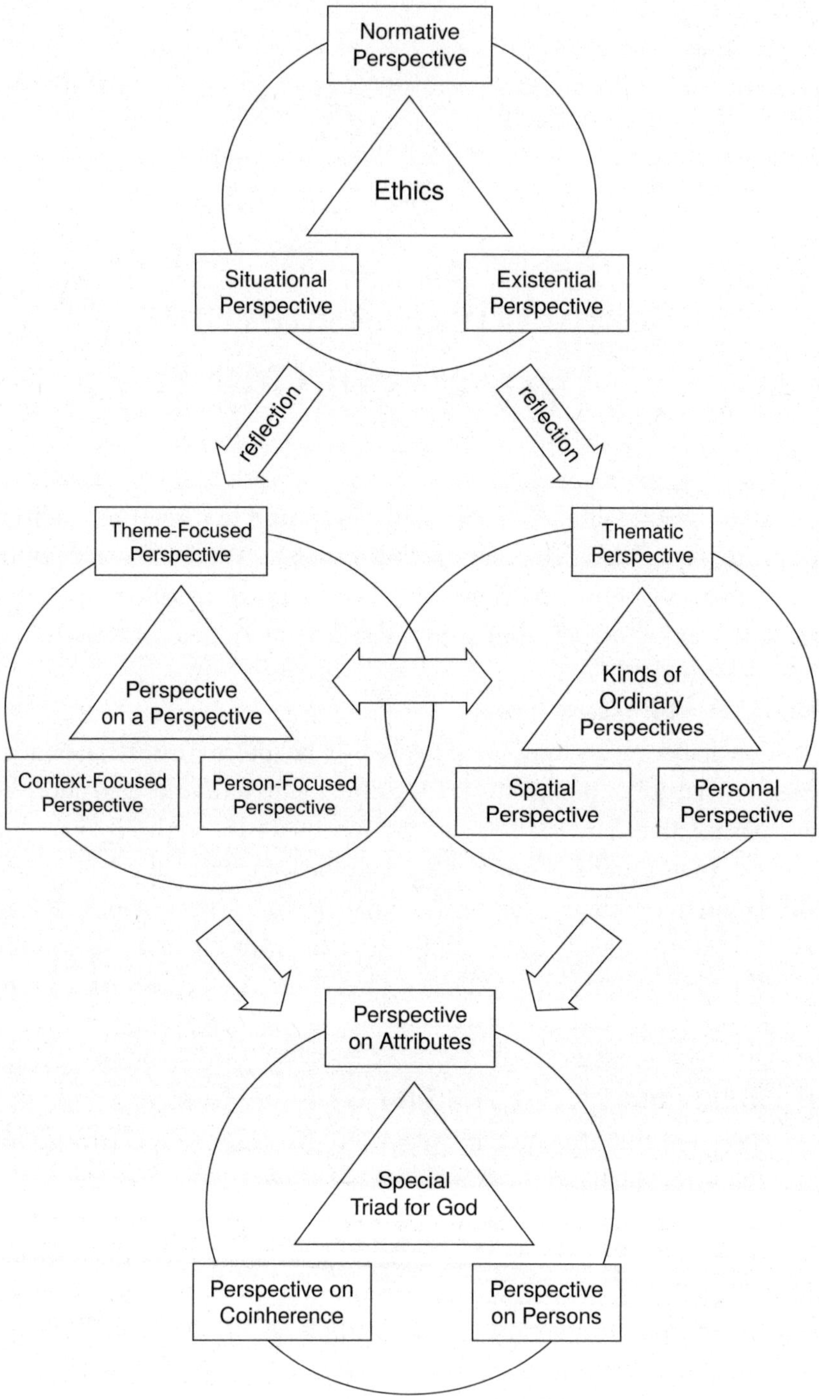

Fig. 34.1. Deriving Perspectives from the Triad for Ethics

can be differentiated into the perspective of the Father, the perspective of the Son, and the perspective of the Holy Spirit. (See fig. 34.2.)

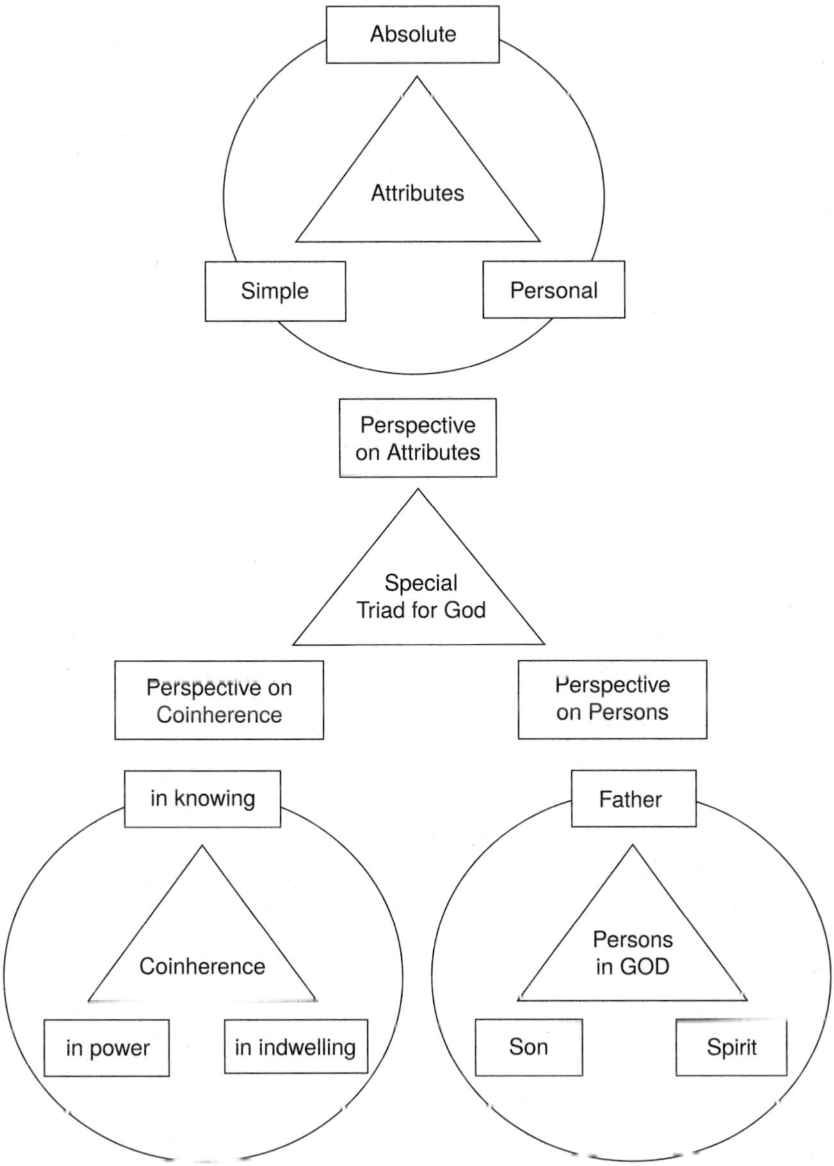

Fig. 34.2. Expanded Special Triad for God

Contextual Influence

When we put together these two diagrams (figs. 34.1, 34.2), they present us with a considerable amount of context for any one of the perspectives we have introduced.[1]

We can say concerning these two diagrams what we said earlier, in chapter 17, about the summary of different kinds of triads. The diagrams are useful ways of organizing triads of perspectives into a larger whole. And they help to show that the triads are coinherently related to one another and to general patterns concerning God and how God interacts with mankind. But are our summaries the one right way of doing it? No. All the perspectives that we have considered are understood to be perspectives *on a larger whole.* If they are perspectives on the *same* whole, and if all perspectives implicitly include all the other perspectives, it can get difficult to distinguish them at points. Hence, it can also be difficult to classify them in some unique, definitive way. (But see chapter 36 and Appendix E for further classifications.)

Limitations in Formal Reasoning

The key summaries in figures 34.1 and 34.2 remind us about the influence of context in understanding perspectives. The summaries thus confirm the limitations of any attempt to idealize reasoning by eliminating context and eliminating the influence of persons who have a background of knowledge (chap. 29).

The summaries in figures 34.1 and 34.2 also serve as an illustration of one of the challenges in dealing with perspectives. In the case of a diamond, we can in principle see every facet of the diamond through the one facet from which we start. And if we look closely at a second facet through the first, we can see within it still other facets. We can go on indefinitely. Likewise, there are perspectives within perspectives. Within a single coinherent triad of perspectives, each perspective has "within" it the other two.

And within any one perspective are still other coinherent triads. For example, consider the perspective of authority. Since God has all authority, he has authority over norms, over situations, and over

1. The diagrams in this chapter are also linked to the principal diagram figure 17.3 in chapter 17, because figure 34.1 comes from the triad for ethics, which is part of figure 17.3. For an integration of figure 34.2 with figure 17.3, see chapter 36, especially figure 36.2.

persons. The perspective of authority thus "includes" within it the triad for ethics, consisting in normative, situational, and existential (personal) perspectives.

Since God controls everything, he controls his speech, his acts of power, and his personal communion. Thus, within the perspective of control, we find the triad for offices: the prophetic perspective focusing on speech, the kingly perspective focusing on power, and the priestly perspective focusing on communion.

As figure 17.3 illustrates, within the triad for ethics are the triad for communication, the triad for love, the triad for reflections, the triad for ethics itself (!), the triad for lordship, and the triad for offices. Figures 34.1 and 34.2 illustrate how, *within* one or more of these earlier triads, we may refocus on aspects of the mystery of the Trinity, and find within this central mystery more instances reflecting coinherent triadic structure. In principle, this process can go on indefinitely because of the depth of God. Each step of increasing depth involves an instance of reflection. And instances of reflection are rooted in the exact image: the Son, who is the image of the Father in the presence of the Spirit. In this process, we never uncover anything other than Trinitarian structure, because God is not dependent on further structures or further themes or further triads outside himself. What would we expect? He is who he is (Ex. 3:14). He has no "needs" that would have to be supplied from outside. He has infinite plenitude in himself. And it is his pleasure that when we are saved through Christ, we should have joy and satisfaction in knowing his plenitude, in reflecting him in ourselves (Ps. 16:11). The culmination of life is in knowing him:

> Father, I desire that they also, whom you have given me, may be with me where I am, to see my glory that you have given me because you loved me before the foundation of the world. O righteous Father, even though the world does not know you, I know you, and these know that you have sent me. I made known to them your name, and I will continue to make it known, that the love with which you have loved me may be in them, and I in them. (John 17:24–26)

Key Terms

absoluteness[2]
coinherence
coinherence in indwelling
coinherence in knowledge
coinherence in power
person
personality
perspective on attributes
perspective on coinherence
perspective on persons
simplicity
triad for coinherence

Study Questions

1. What is the context for reasoning about the attributes of God?
2. What is the triad for coinherence?
3. How do the triad for coinherence and the triad for the persons of the Trinity form contexts for thinking about God's attributes?
4. What do the perspectival contexts for the attributes of God show about the limitations of formal reasoning about God?
5. How does God's self-sufficiency confirm the interlocking of perspectives on God?

For Further Reading

Frame, John M. *The Doctrine of God.* Phillipsburg, NJ: P&R Publishing, 2002. Pp. 387–92. On the larger context for considering God's attributes.

2. Key terms in **bold** are defined in the glossary at the end of this volume.

35

Challenges to Theological Reasoning

IN CONSIDERING LIMITATIONS that belong to decontextualized reasoning, the result from chapter 32 is significant. Attributes of God are coinherent with the persons in God. Coinherence implies the impossibility of strictly *separating* attributes from the persons.

Aristotelian Fundamental Categories: Things and Qualities

This lack of separation is fatal to the Aristotelian system of fundamental categories. The Aristotelian system includes a strict categorical distinction between qualities and substances, that is, the "things" to which qualities apply. For example, *horse* refers to a thing, which is a substance. *White* or *small* or *male* is a quality that may further describe the horse. Suppose that we are determined to conform to Aristotle's system of categories. Then we must suppose that the *substance* of *horse* is cleanly distinguished from the *qualities* that describe the horse.

Now consider what happens when we reason about God. The attributes of God are like qualities, while God himself and the persons in the Godhead are like things, *substances* to which the qualities attach. Coinherence denies that there can be a clean separation between these two kinds of categories—persons and attributes—in the case of God. In effect, the "metaphysics" of God does not match the "metaphysics" presupposed by Aristotle's system of categories.

To try to use an Aristotelian framework for reasoning about God is the equivalent of trying to fit a square peg into a round hole. This limitation has implications for the attempts by Thomas Aquinas and others to apply a basically Aristotelian framework of fundamental categories to rational discussion of God. True rationality among human beings reflects divine rationality; and this rationality conforms to the Trinitarian character of God, not to Aristotle's system.

The Absoluteness of God

We may approach the same issue in another way: by considering the nature of revelation. God's revelation of himself to human beings must necessarily be in harmony with who he is. We come to know him in harmony with who he is. We know God, not a substitute. Since God is Trinitarian, his revelation toward us must also be derivatively Trinitarian. Since the three persons of God are coinherent, God's revelation must be derivatively coinherent. It must be one and many. All three persons are actively involved in all revelation, and this involvement implies coinherence. The one and the many must coinherently interpenetrate, rather than offering us perfectly sharp distinctions that we can master.

Since God is absolute, only God can reveal God. This principle applies to every aspect of revelation. So it should not be surprising that in analyzing how we talk about God and how he acts in the world, we continually meet with coinherent themes. Coinherence implies that each theme tacitly includes the whole. It does so by offering a perspective on the whole. Thus, derivative coinherence in the texture of revelation implies the perspectival structure of revelation. This structure reflects the perspectival character of the personal knowledge enjoyed by the persons of the Trinity.

As we have seen, the coinherence in revelation includes within its embrace the fundamental perspectival coinherence of substances, qualities, and relations in God. (*Substance* corresponds to persons in God, *qualities* to attributes, and *relations* to coinherence.) The Aristotelian framework of fundamental categories is at odds with coinherence. In a word, it is anti-Trinitarian. It requires strict, precise distinctions between the fundamental categories. If reasoning about God depends on a strict categorical separation between things and qualities, it fails to match reality. If modern analytical theological reasoning insists on strict, precise distinctions, and if it feels frustration with perspectival reasoning because of this insistence, it might ask why.

Implications for the Nature of the World

The coinherence between attributes and persons has implications beyond the narrower challenge of analyzing God. It affects how we analyze the world.

God created and governs the world by his word of power (Heb. 1:3). The coinherence in God is reflected in a corresponding coinherence in his word. The word of God in turn structures the whole nature of the world.[1] So the Aristotelian system of categories will not work for the nature of the world.

The Aristotelian system works partway as a *perspective* on the world. But the world is more complex than what the system captures. The system fails if it does not admit its perspectival character and its limitations.

Alternatives to Aristotle's System

Shall we, then, adopt some *other* system, some modern metaphysical or epistemological or logical alternative to Aristotle? Shall we look to some form of Kantianism, or Hegelianism, or process philosophy, or French existentialism, or neoorthodox dialecticism, or ordinary language philosophy, or postmodernist contextual relativism, or critical realism? The list goes on. But practically no one with worldly influence in philosophical circles has broken with the fundamental error of Western philosophy: the error of supposing that we need to affirm and rely on an autonomous conception of human reason as a necessary element in human dignity and human progress. This error has been with us from the time of ancient Greek philosophy and has been magnified since the time of Kant and the Enlightenment.

To be sure, within some approaches, autonomous reason may be reined in and applied to only certain spheres, such as the sphere of science. That is what Kant did. Karl Barth is no different at a fundamental level because he thinks he has to allow space for an effectively autonomous historical-critical approach to the Bible in its own sphere; only after and alongside that, he postulates the mystery of revelation taking place through a Bible that he supposes is strewn with erroneous teachings. Such errors contradict the Bible's own teaching about its

1. Vern S. Poythress, *Redeeming Philosophy: A God-Centered Approach to the Big Questions* (Wheaton, IL: Crossway, 2014), chaps. 10–11.

reliability and the accessibility (clarity) of the Word of God. The result is that Barth's approach denies Christian transcendence and immanence. It is a fundamental error.[2]

Shall we, then, turn to modern reflections on the Trinity? That might seem more promising. Unfortunately, too often the modern Trinitarian speculations of the late twentieth century and early twenty-first century fall victim to the same error. Rather than reforming and transfiguring our ideas about human freedom and science and history and society on the basis of biblical teaching, the nature of the Trinity gets recrafted to serve modern agendas. Theologizing unwittingly or wittingly furthers Kant's program of human autonomy and relativizes the unbreakable character of biblical teaching in its details. We cannot enter into detailed discussion and criticism of the multitude of trends in modern theology, with the many brilliant thinkers and brilliant proposals that inhabit those trends.[3] It must suffice to say that this book does not follow in those trails, nor do we want to suggest that any of the trails is superior to Aristotle *at a fundamental level.* Rather, with few exceptions, the innovative modern trails perpetuate the fundamental error of Aristotle: the error of demanding autonomous reason for the sake of human dignity.

Modern and postmodern ways of thinking as a whole, together with virtually the entire institution of the university system, unite in supposing that the only alternative to human autonomy of the mind, will, imagination, and conscience is obtuse stultification—in the end, the destruction of the mind and will of man, and humanity itself. The reply is at hand: all the time they are relying on the God whom Scripture describes, in whom they live (Acts 17:28), and who speaks Scripture. Sadly, it is they who are stultified with respect to the truth and with respect to imagination.

This calls for repentance. Let us come to Christ, and be captivated in mind and heart and imagination with the glory of God manifest in

2. See John M. Frame, "God and Biblical Language: Transcendence and Immanence," in *God's Inerrant Word: An International Symposium on the Trustworthiness of Scripture*, ed. John W. Montgomery (Minneapolis: Bethany Fellowship, 1974), 159–77, http://www.frame-poythress.org/god-and-biblical-language-transcendence-and-immanence/; John M. Frame, *A History of Western Philosophy and Theology* (Phillipsburg, NJ: P&R Publishing, 2015), 363–86.

3. Frame, *History of Western Philosophy and Theology.*

him through the Spirit. Let us receive with meekness the speech of God in Christ through the Spirit, which the Bible gives us accessibly. Let us "take every thought captive to obey Christ" (2 Cor. 10:5).

Key Terms

Aristotelian category
Aristotle
Barth, Karl
critical realism[4]
derivation
dialecticism
existentialism
Hegelianism
human autonomy
Kantianism
neoorthodoxy
ordinary language philosophy
process philosophy
quality
revelation
substance
word of God

Study Questions

1. Within Aristotle's system of categories, how do qualities and substances relate to each other?
2. What is the difference between Aristotle's sytem with respect to qualities and substances and the structure of God's attributes?
3. What is the major problem with using the Aristotelian system of categories in reasoning about God?
4. Are metaphysical systems other than Aristotle's better? Why or why not?

4. Key terms in **bold** are defined in the glossary at the end of this volume.

For Further Reading

Frame, John M. *A History of Western Philosophy and Theology*. Phillipsburg, NJ: P&R Publishing, 2015. Critical discussion of Western philosophy.

Poythress, Vern S. *Logic: A God-Centered Approach to the Foundation of Western Thought*. Wheaton, IL: Crossway, 2013. Pp. 645–56. A critical discussion of the use of logic in philosophy.

———. *Redeeming Philosophy: A God-Centered Approach to the Big Questions*. Wheaton, IL: Crossway, 2014. Chaps. 10–11. On how God's Word structures the world.

———. *Redeeming Philosophy: A God-Centered Approach to the Big Questions*. Wheaton, IL: Crossway, 2014. Chaps. 12–15. On Christian metaphysics, with perspectives.

PART 7

DERIVING THEOLOGY

WE EXPLORE HOW a few starting principles lead to and reinforce a wider area of theological truths.

36

Expanded Classification of Perspectives

IN THE CHAPTERS in part 6, we introduced a number of new perspectives related to the nature of God, namely, the perspectives summarized in figure 34.2. How do these perspectives relate to the earlier perspectives of part 4, summarized in figure 17.3?

Perspectives Focused on God

The perspectives summarized in figure 34.2 are all closely related to the special triad for God, which consists in the perspective on attributes, the perspective on coinherence, and the perspective on persons (fig. 32.1). Each perspective among these three leads to a triad: the triad of abstract attributes, the triad for coinherence, and the triad for persons, as in figure 34.2. We can resummarize the result in figure 36.1.

All the perspectives in figure 36.1 are perspectives that we as human beings can think about. But they describe realities about the true God. And these realities concern God as he always exists, not merely God's relations to the created world. They concern the ontological Trinity. Let us call them *ontologically focused perspectives*. (This label should not be confused with the ontological perspective, which is one of three perspectives on revelation, introduced in chapter 16. The two labels are related, but distinct.) Now compare these ontologically focused perspectives to the three perspectives on communication or the three perspectives on love or the three perspectives on reflections. Though these latter perspectives have their roots in the eternal character of God, in typical uses we apply them to God's actions with respect to the created world. Accordingly, in chapter 17 we grouped the triad for

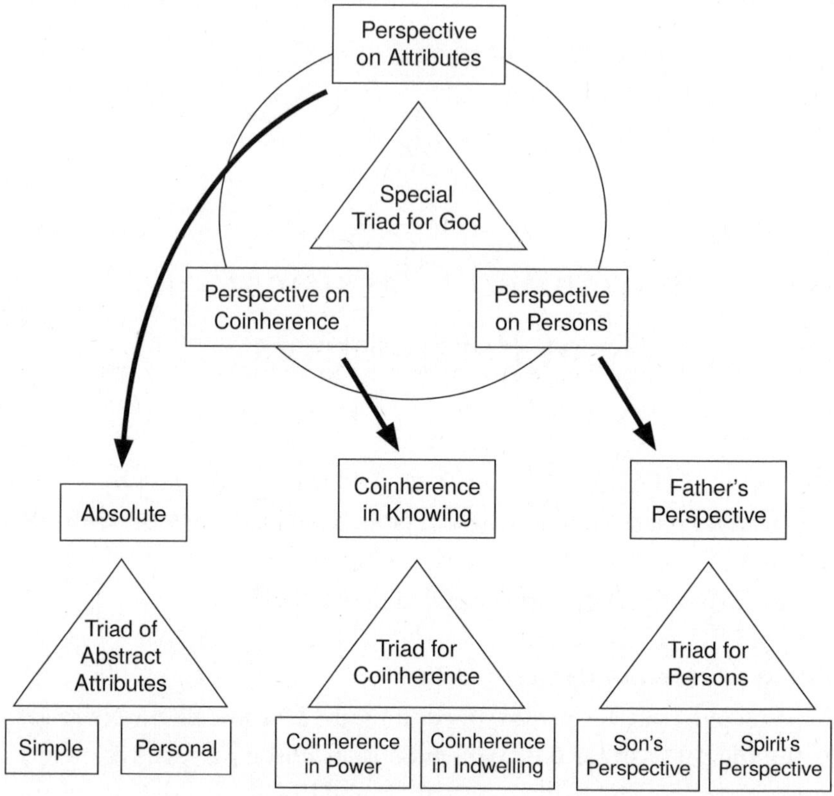

Fig. 36.1. Organization of Triads Focused on God

communication, the triad for love, and the triad for reflections under the general heading of the harmonistic perspective. (See fig. 17.3.)

When we compare the ontologically focused perspectives of figure 36.1 with the triads grouped under the general heading of the harmonistic perspective, we can see that the two groups have different starting points. But these starting points are matters of relative emphasis. Every eternal attribute of God is relevant for how he acts in the world. Conversely, how he acts in the world reflects his eternal attributes. Thus, the two kinds of perspectives do not have a clear separation from each other. They are perspectivally related—as we might expect.

Since the two kinds of perspectives are perspectivally related, can we articulate more specifically *how* they are related to each other? The ontologically focused perspectives (fig. 36.1) can be viewed as falling under the general heading of the ontological perspective. By contrast, the triads grouped under the general heading of the harmonistic perspective obviously fall under the harmonistic perspective. So the ontologically focused perspectives can be included as additional triads within a distinct row (the "ontological" row) within the classification given in figure 17.3. The result is represented in figure 36.2. (The newly added perspectives are the ones included within the oval.)

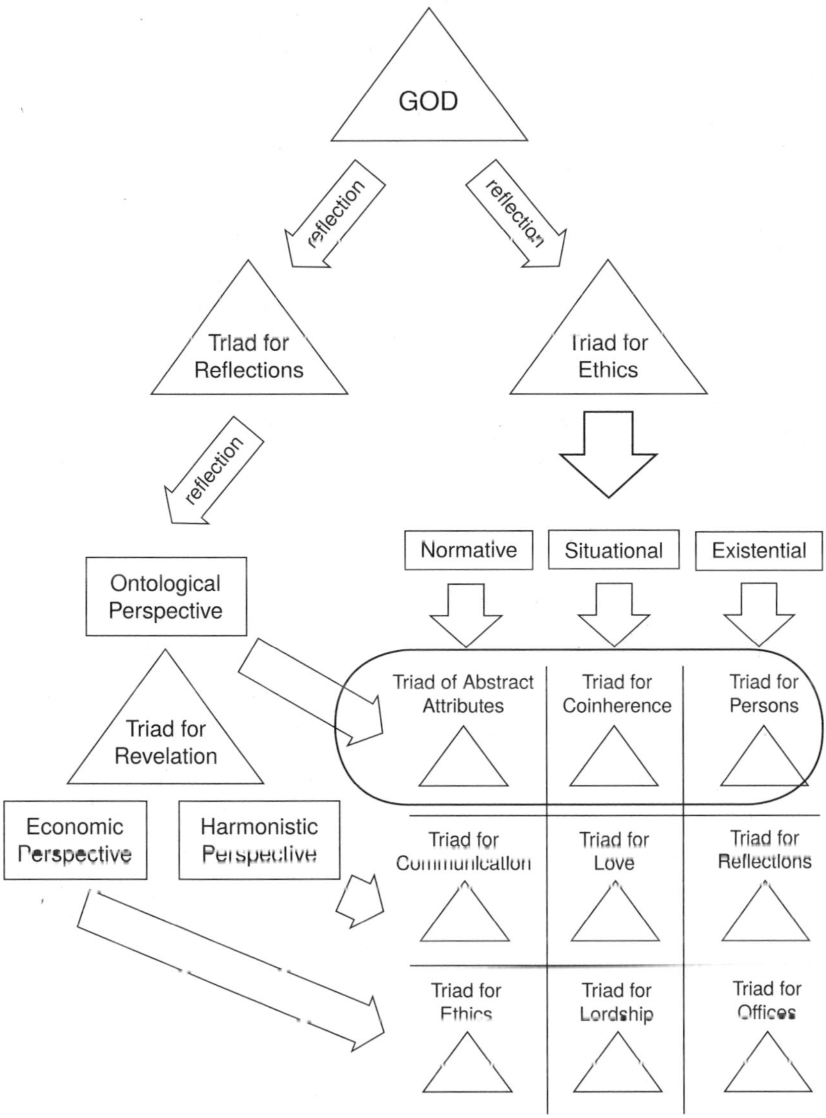

Fig. 36.2. Including Ontologically Focused Perspectives

From Ethics to the Special Triad for God

The three triads containing ontologically focused perspectives lie within a single row, grouped under the ontological perspective (the label provided to the left of the row). Together, these three triads form the first of a total of three rows within a 3 × 3 grid. But do these three triads actually line up in a coherent way with the three *columns* of the 3 × 3 grid? For example, does the first triad, the triad of abstract attributes, line up in an appropriate way under the column headed by *Normative*, that is, the normative perspective on ethics? And does the second triad, the triad for coinherence, line up under the column headed by *Situational*?

To see whether this organization into columns makes sense, let us return to the special triad for God, which consists in the perspective on attributes, the perspective on coinherence, and the perspective on persons. This triad sums up in itself all the ontologically focused perspectives. Let us see whether the triad for ethics, which supplies the headings for the three columns, has suitable correlations with the special triad for God.

The normative perspective on ethics leads to the perspective on attributes, because attributes are like norms according to which God acts. For example, God acts in a manner consistent with his goodness. The situational perspective on ethics focuses on the environment within which personal action takes place. Within God, the "environment" for the action of the persons in God is the environment of coinherence. So the situational perspective on ethics, when applied to ontology, leads to the perspective on coinherence. Finally, let us start with the existential perspective on ethics. The existential perspective focuses on persons, which are the focus of the perspective on persons within the special triad for God. Thus, the three perspectives on ethics have natural correlations with the three perspectives within the special triad for God. (See table 36.1.) Accordingly, the three *triads* under the ontological perspective derive naturally from the three perspectives on ethics. (See table 36.2.)

From the Special Triad for God to the Triad for Ethics

We can also go in the reverse direction, and derive the triad for ethics from the special triad for God. First, consider the perspective on attributes within the special triad for God. Attributes function as

Triad for Ethics	reflection	**Special Triad for God**
normative perspective	→	perspective on attributes
situational perspective	→	perspective on coinherence
existential perspective	→	perspective on persons

Table 36.1. From Ethics to the Special Triad for God

Triad for Ethics	reflection	**Triads of Ontologically Focused Perspectives**
normative perspective	→	triad of abstract attributes
situational perspective	→	triad for coinherence
existential perspective	→	triad for persons

Table 36.2. From Ethics to Triads of Ontologically Focused Perspectives

the norms according to which God acts. So when applied to ethics, the perspective on attributes leads to the normative perspective on ethics. Second, consider the perspective on coinherence. Coinherence is the "situation" or "environment" in which the persons of the Trinity act. So when applied to ethics, the perspective on coinherence leads to the situational perspective. Finally, consider the perspective on persons. When applied to ethics, this perspective focuses on persons, which are in focus in the existential perspective. Thus, each of the three perspectives in the special triad for God leads to a distinct perspective on ethics (table 36.3).

Since the triad for ethics and the special triad for God can each be derived from the other, the special triad for God can replace the role of the triad for ethics in organizing the three main columns in our picture of classification (fig. 36.2). The replacement leads to figure 36.3.

Within the central 3 × 3 grid of triads, the organization of triads has

Special Triad for God	reflection	Triad for Ethics
perspective on attributes	→	normative perspective
perspective on coinherence	→	situational perspective
perspective on persons	→	existential perspective

Table 36.3. From the Special Triad for God to the Triad for Ethics

a logical and symmetrical structure. Each of the triads of perspectives contains within it three perspectives that are coinherent, reflecting the coinherence in the Trinity. In addition, the triads in any one column or any one row are coinherent with the others in the same column or row. The coinherence suggests that various triads are derivable from one another.

Key Terms

existential perspective[1]
harmonistic perspective
normative perspective
ontologically focused perspective
ontological perspective
perspective on attributes
perspective on coinherence
perspective on persons
perspectives on communication
perspectives on reflections
situational perspective
special triad for God
triad for coinherence
triad for persons
triad of abstract attributes

1. Key terms in **bold** are defined in the glossary at the end of this volume.

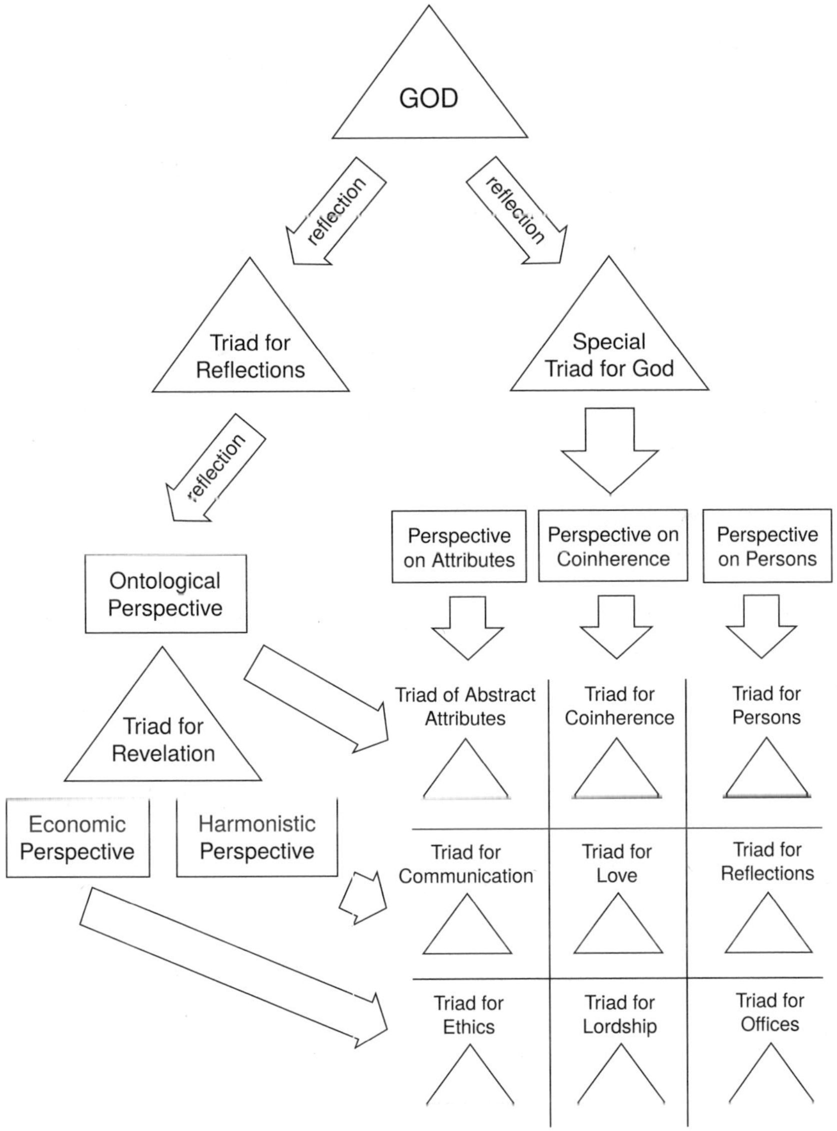

Fig. 36.3. Classification of Triads, Using the Special Triad for God

Study Questions

1. What are ontologically focused perspectives, and how do they differ from most of the perspectives discussed in earlier chapters (fig. 17.3)?
2. How do the triad of abstract attributes, the triad for coinherence, and the triad for persons derive from the triad for ethics?
3. How do ontologically focused perspectives fit into a larger overall classification?
4. What significance can be found in the overall classification of triads in figure 36.3?
5. What does figure 36.3 suggest about the varieties of manifestations of coinherence?

For Further Reading

Frame, John M. *The Doctrine of God*. Phillipsburg, NJ: P&R Publishing, 2002. Pp. 394–99. On classifying God's attributes.

37

Three Persons and Triads

PEOPLE WHO HAVE encountered triads of perspectives sometimes wonder why there are three, instead of two or four or more.

Many Perspectives

Are there cases in which we could use only two perspectives instead of three? For example, could we describe the lordship of God by using *transcendence* and *immanence*? We would be using two fundamental categories, namely, *transcendence* and *immanence*. Superficially, this approach would be distinct from using the three categories employed by John Frame, namely, the categories of *authority, control,* and *presence* (chaps. 18–19). But does it make any real difference whether we use two categories or three? Frame himself realizes that no fundamental doctrinal issue is at stake. In fact, in addition to using the three perspectives on lordship (authority, control, and presence), Frame continues to use the two categories of transcendence and immanence. He simply wants it understood that transcendence includes authority and control. Moreover, in the history of theology, the twofold division into transcendence and immanence has been the more customary way of talking about God's relation to the world.

Instead of using two categories or three, we can use more than three perspectives at a time. John Frame in his book on the Christian life[1] shows that each of the Ten Commandments has a specific focus on a specific kind of moral rectitude and obedience to God, and yet also that each commandment can be used as a *perspective* on the entire Christian life and its moral commitments. So here we have ten perspectives rather than three.

1. John M. Frame, *The Doctrine of the Christian Life* (Phillipsburg, NJ: P&R Publishing, 2008).

The use of perspectives means flexibility. And one kind of flexibility is to use perspectives on perspectives, and find more themes that can be turned into perspectives.

But as the previous chapters in this book have argued, there are also particular triads of perspectives that have mysterious correlations with God's revelation of his Trinitarian character. In these cases, there are three perspectives because these three reflect the three persons in the Trinity.

Three Persons in the Trinity

And why are there three persons in the Trinity, not two or four? Because there are. God is God. God is absolute. He is who he is. There is no principle or thing "above" him to constrain who he is. That is, there is no principle or thing or idea more ultimate than the nature of God to which we could appeal to show that God must be three persons rather than two or four or more. If there were such a principle, that principle or thing or idea would be more ultimate than God. It would itself be a god-like (ultimate) thing in addition to God, and we would have two gods, or more. No. The Bible forbids it. God forbids it, since he is speaking to us in the Bible.

Could God change the number of persons? No, because God is unchangeable. God cannot contradict himself. Or, to use biblical phraseology, "he cannot deny himself" (2 Tim. 2:13). We might say that God is "constrained" in a sense by the very character of who he is. But he is not constrained by anything *outside* him. The "inside constraint," if that is what we want to call it, is a very good thing, because it is necessary if God is reliable. We could not rely on God if we never knew whether he would change into the opposite of what he now is.

So God is always consistent with himself. He is "constrained" by his own character. But we must beware of trying to constrain God from *outside*. That would be a form of non-Christian immanence, according to which human thinking constrains God and dictates what God has to be.

With this caution in view, we may ask again the question about why there are three persons.[2] There is no answer, if we expect that an

2. I am grateful to B. A. Bosserman for encouraging the exploration of analogical reasoning confirming the tripersonal character of God (Bosserman, *The Trinity and the Vindication of Christian Paradox: An Interpretation and Refinement of the Theological Apologetic of Cornelius Van Til*

answer will give a reason that is itself more ultimate than the thing that it explains. Often, "why?" questions want more ultimate explanations. In a scientific context, people may explain why we see a rainbow by giving an account of light refracting in drops of rainwater, and people see the explanation as giving us a deeper or more ultimate ground for what we see. But this explanation still leaves us with the more ultimate question: "Why do light and refraction in raindrops work the way they do?" If scientists provide a further explanation based on a theory of light, we can still continue to ask "why?" We can go deeper and deeper. But in the case of the Trinitarian God, we cannot provide a deeper explanation, because God himself is the final "explanation" for himself. There is nothing deeper than God. There is nothing back of God (such as abstract ultimate principles). That is part of what it *means* for him to be God.

Having rejected that *kind* of explanation, we may still search for a very different kind of explanation. By analogical reasoning, could we see how it makes sense that God is Trinitarian from *inside* the knowledge that we have? Our human knowledge is all derivative knowledge. But it is also true knowledge. So we can see harmonies and "derivations" belonging to our knowledge. We can see how one principle about God leads to or reinforces another.

Triadic Love

Here is one kind of reasoning. God is personal. Is he tripersonal? One aspect of being personal is that God is loving. In loving, there is a lover, a beloved, and the exercise of love between the two. When these three are taken together, they are complete. We do not need a fourth term, but we do need three. According to this analogy, God the Father is the lover, God the Son is the beloved, and God the Holy Spirit dynamically expresses the love binding them. (This summary is similar to John 3:34–35.) (See fig. 37.1.) Saint Augustine and Jonathan Edwards, each in his own way, used something similar to this analogy to confirm the tripersonal nature of God.[3]

[Eugene, OR: Pickwick, 2014], 87, 151–61, 176–82). Bosserman himself offers some arguments of this type.

3. Augustine, "On the Holy Trinity," in *Nicene and Post-Nicene Fathers*, 1st ser., ed. Philip Schaff (London: T&T Clark, 1980), 3:124 (8.10), 215–17 (15.17); Jonathan Edwards, "Discourse

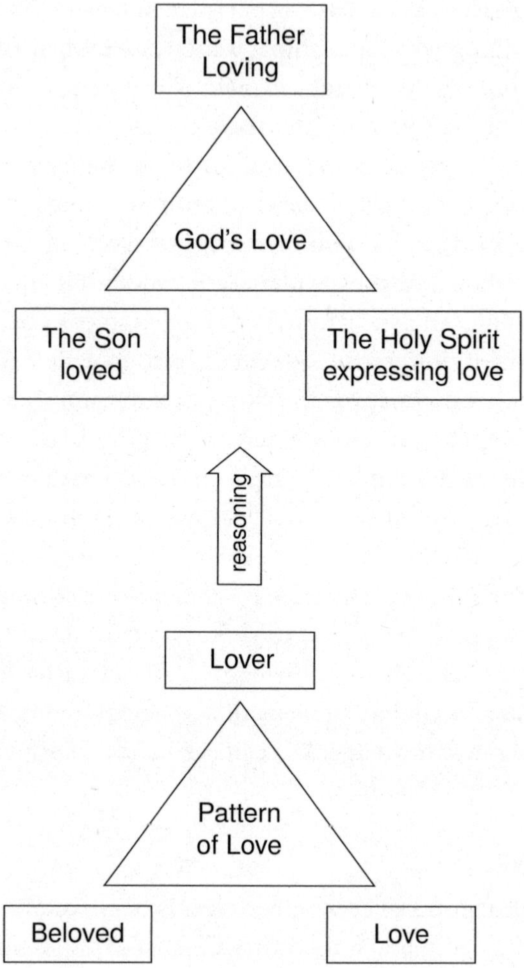

Fig. 37.1. Reasoning from Love to the Trinity

on the Trinity," in *The Works of Jonathan Edwards*, vol. 21, *Writings on the Trinity, Grace, and Faith*, ed. Sang Hyun Lee (New Haven, CT: Yale University Press, 2003), 109–44 [113–14, 121, 131–32]; Jonathan Edwards, "The Mind," in *The Works of Jonathan Edwards*, vol. 6, *Scientific and Philosophical Writings*, ed. Wallace E. Anderson (New Haven, CT: Yale University Press, 1980), 332–93 [364]; Ralph Cunnington, "A Critical Examination of Jonathan Edwards's Doctrine of the Trinity," *Themelios* 39, 2 (July 2014): 224–40, http://themelios.thegospelcoalition.org/article/a-critical-examination-of-jonathan-edwardss-doctrine-of-the-trinity. See also Herman Bavinck, *Reformed Dogmatics* (Grand Rapids: Baker, 2004), 2:327; Timothy E. Miller, *The Triune God of Unity in Diversity: An Analysis of Perspectivalism, the Trinitarian Theological Method of John Frame and Vern Poythress* (Phillipsburg, NJ: P&R Publishing, 2017), 53.

Using Background Knowledge

We must still say that the analogy with love is an analogy. Like all other analogies, it involves similarities and dissimilarities between God's original love and human derivative love. So no one analogy is the definitive one. In invoking the analogy, we are guided by the background of knowledge of God mediated by the entirety of biblical revelation.

The analogy with loving is insufficient if we try to isolate it from the full texture of background knowledge about God. As some analysts have pointed out, at a human level *love* is an action or an abstraction, not a full *person* distinct from the lover and the beloved. But human love is *personal*; it involves personal richness. And it is empowered by the common grace or special grace of the Holy Spirit, who is present in his power. So if we *already* know about the Holy Spirit, human love is no "bare" abstraction, but is already a testimony to the Holy Spirit. So we *do* arrive at the Holy Spirit as a full person. We arrive there because the Holy Spirit is a person and is already present. In every act of human love, the Spirit testifies to who he is. We can also arrive at the same result by observing that God is fully personal. No *impersonal* principle, such as a purely abstract principle of love, is needed to characterize him. That would be an outside principle that would compromise his absoluteness. So in God, the love between the Father and the Son is constituted by the full *person* of the Holy Spirit, as the Father's gift.

We must consider our background knowledge of God whenever we reason about why there cannot be a fourth person in the Trinity. In the end, it is safest to appeal to special revelation, and especially the climactic revelation that comes in Christ (Heb. 1:1–3). The climactic revelation reveals three persons and the coinherent relations among them. There is no fourth person. Could a fourth person appear later on? No, because the economic Trinity truly reveals the ontological Trinity. God is genuinely in harmony with what he has already revealed.

But we can also consider again the analogy with love. Human beings find it possible to love several neighbors at the same time. But in each case, the love has triadic structure: a lover, a beloved, and the relation and activity of loving. An extra person, if brought into the middle of the activity of love, either is outside this particular form of love or is inside. If he is outside, it leaves the love firmly triadic. If he is inside, he is disruptive. Because of coinherence in the Trinity, there can be no outside for an alleged fourth person, and no disharmony or disruption. There are necessarily three persons, not more, not fewer.

Triadic Communication

We can make similar observations when we consider the analogy with communication. God is absolute and personal. As an aspect of his absoluteness and his personal character, he has the ability to speak. If, hypothetically, it were the case that he had the ability to speak but never *did* speak, he would have unrealized potential, which would mean that he would not be all that he could be. In that case, he would not be absolute. It follows that God not only has the ability to speak, but does speak. He does so eternally in his Word (John 1:1).

Now let us consider the analogy with human speech. We have speaker, speech, and hearer. There are three. These three together give us a conceptually complete act of communication. There can be neither more nor fewer aspects belonging to the nature of communication. So by analogy with human speech, God as speaker has speech distinct from him, and a recipient distinct from both. The three aspects in human speech reflect the archetype in God: the three persons of the Trinity—the Father, the Son (the Word), and the Holy Spirit. (See fig. 37.2.)

But again it is necessary to have further background knowledge of God, in order to see the nature of the analogy with human speech. A human speech is not a person. But it is personal. Personal speech among human beings is possible in imitation of the original speech of God, in whose image we are made. Human speech reflects the Word, without being identical with him. The Word is a person, and he is personally present in providential sustaining power even within human speech (Heb. 1:3). So if we *already* know about the Word as a person, we see that human speech testifies to him as being fully a person.

Can there be an extra person in an act of communication? For human communication, there is a sense in which it is possible and a sense in which it is not. God or a single human being can address a group through a single speech. He may do it by directly addressing only the representative head (as when God addresses Moses, and Moses afterward carries the message to the people, Ex. 20:19–20). Or he may directly address everyone in the group (as God does with the initial speech from Mount Sinai, Ex. 20:1, 19; Deut. 5:22). In either case, the

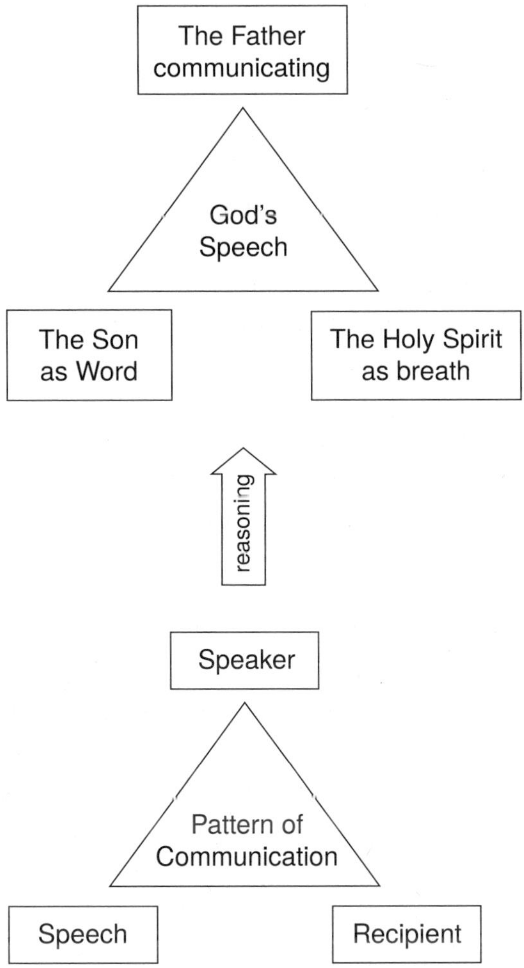

Fig. 37.2. Reasoning from Communication to the Trinity

recipient is not merely an ultimately *impersonal* group, but a person. Even if a group is involved in the context, each person who is a genuine recipient is indeed a recipient. The group in which he belongs is part of his environment, but it is still *he* who receives it individually. This communication to the individual is still triadic. Moreover, the original, archetypal communication in God is unique in its archetypal character. It cannot be a case in which God addresses the Word to a fourth person along with the Holy Spirit as recipient, because then there would be a group of two (or more?) recipients whose relation within their subgroup was not itself coinherent with the Word. In the case of the unique, archetypal communication in God, communication must be triadic, involving three persons, not more, not fewer.

Triadic Reflections

We can develop a similar kind of reasoning using the analogy with reflections. God as the Creator must be able to produce a creation distinct from himself. His own sufficiency implies that he must have resources in himself for the design and the coming into being of creation. The creation must reflect his design. This reflection itself needs an origin. The origin can only be God (because God is absolute). So among the resources in God must be resources for producing reflections.

On the level of the created order, consider Adam's fathering Seth in his image (Gen. 5:3) or a painter's painting an image of a landscape scene. The structure of reflections includes three aspects: an original (Adam), a copy (Seth), and a relation of reflection (Seth in the image of Adam). Mere binary differentiation, the bare fact of Seth's being a creature distinct from Adam, is not enough. Seth must also *reflect* Adam. There is a distinct relation of *likeness* between them. These three aspects together are conceptually complete. (As we have seen from our earlier discussion of reflection in chapter 11, the three are coinherent.)

By analogy with the structure of reflection within creation, God must have in himself the archetypal structure of reflection. Now, within creation, reflection takes place even with subpersonal creatures. The baby lamb is a kind of reflection of its father and its mother. But this reflection is rational, and its rationality testifies to the original rationality of the Creator. So God must be personal. He is also differentiated by the structure that consists in three aspects: (1) the original, (2) the reflection of the original, and (3) a relation of reflection between the two. The original is the planner of the reflection, whom we call Father. His archetypal image must be exactly like him (Heb. 1:3), and so must also be a person. He is the Son. The relation of reflection must be fully personal, and this relation is the work of the Holy Spirit. (See fig. 37.3.)

But we may also observe that the Spirit as "another Helper" (John 14:16) reflects the work of the Son. How can the Spirit be the reflection in one relationship and provide the *relation* of reflection in another? Coinherence in indwelling means that each person is fully present in the

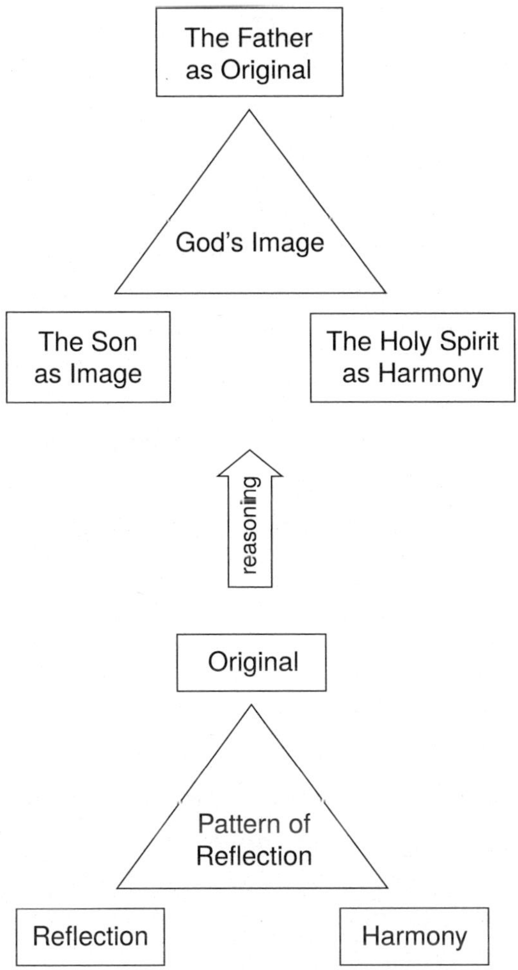

Fig. 37.3. Reasoning from Reflections to the Trinity

others. The Spirit reflects the Son through the presence of the Father, who sends the Spirit. The Father functions in that way as Mediator of reflection because the Spirit indwells him.

In a manner similar to the case with love and with communication, a hypothetical fourth person does not match the structure of reflections. If the alleged fourth person is outside the relation of reflection, he is not God. Or if he is inside, his presence within the original Father-Son relation duplicates the function of the Spirit. He is either identical to the Spirit or disruptive of the completeness of the Spirit's function.

The Necessity of Fully Personal Relations

B. A. Bosserman has offered still another defense of the tripersonal nature of God. He offers an extended explanation,[4] but it could be summarized as a derivation on the basis of the idea of exhaustive (fully complete) personal relations. For God to be self-sufficient and personal, he must have within himself personal relations. Thus, there must be more than one person. And for the relation between them to be fully personal, it must be constituted by a third person, who offers the context for the other two. The Father and the Son relate to each other exhaustively through the Spirit, who is fully personal. And so it is with each of the three relations among two persons of the Trinity. Introducing a fourth person involves introducing an impersonal environment for the relations of the fourth person to the third—and then also for the first and the second. Or if the first person mediates the relation of the third and fourth, the second person has no function in this mediation, and coinherence is broken. Or if both the first and the second mediate for the third and fourth, the relation between the two mediations is undefined. So it is impossible for God to be other than three persons.

A short summary such as this one runs the risk of sounding like a merely abstract argument. It might suggest that there is some ultimate abstract principle of personhood or of relationality that stands above God. But that is not what Bosserman means. Moreover, he is aware of the danger of making human reasoning the *standard* to which God must conform. His argument, like the ones based on love, communication, and reflections, desires to confirm and vindicate Trinitarian revelation by being based on that revelation and not on autonomous reason.

Bosserman's argument may be seen as a generalization of the ones given earlier in this chapter, based on love, communication, and reflections. Bosserman considers the issue of personal relations at a general level, rather than in terms of the specifics of love or communication or reflections. His argument thereby shows a common structure belonging to three more specific arguments. It is in harmony with them.

4. Bosserman, *The Trinity*, 176–82.

Pervasive Testimony to the Trinity

The triad for love, the triad for communication, and the triad for reflections all reflect the Trinitarian character of God. Instances of love, communication, and reflections *within* the world testify to instances of love, communication, and reflections that God expresses in relation to the world (economic Trinity). And these instances in turn reflect the Trinitarian character of God (ontological Trinity). Earlier in this chapter, we have provided specific reasoning, tracing out ways in which the Trinitarian character of God is confirmed by love, communication, and reflections. But the testimony to the Trinity is in fact pervasive. Each of the triads of perspectives reflects the Trinity, and each of the triads manifests itself in the structure of the world that God made. There cannot be a world without the Trinity. And the Trinity is specifically one God in three persons. The very structure of our human minds, as well as the structure of the world, is what it is only because of structure under the authority, control, and presence of the Trinitarian God. We cannot think or even imagine outside this environment. Existence and meaning occur within this environment.

We should still affirm the reality of progressive revelation. Only gradually, in the course of time and history, does God reveal himself to human beings. The full doctrine of the Trinity becomes clear only in the New Testament. But God reveals himself in accord with who he is, so we are confident in seeing anticipations of the fullness of revelation in the earlier stages of history.

Threeness Derived from the Triad for Ethics

We may further illustrate the testimony to the Trinity by using the triad for ethics, consisting in the normative, situational, and existential perspectives (chap. 13). The normative perspective presupposes that there are ethical rules. These rules are languagelike, and language comes from persons. So we can infer that God, who is the source of moral authority, is personal. Each rule has a unified formulation and many applications, illustrating the interaction of one and many. As Van Til and his followers have argued, the one and the many in specific areas such as ethics have their foundation in the one and the many in God. And this one and many in God must be personal. This reasoning confirms that God is one personal God and more than one person. The languagelike character of ethical rules also presupposes God's ability to speak, and this observation leads us back to the inference that we drew above from the triad for communication. There is an archetypal triad for communication in God, consisting in three persons.

But now could we make a similar inference starting directly from the triad for ethics? There are three perspectives. The authoritative character of ethics, associated with the normative perspective, derives from the authoritative character of God as the speaker of ethical rules. Ethics is pertinent to the world, which is the focus of the situational perspective. The pertinence of ethics to situations derives from the fact that contents of God's ethical speech refer to the world and situations in the world. Thus, the situational perspective, focusing on situations, derives from the content of God's speaking, which derives from the eternal Word. The existential perspective focuses on the persons who are obligated by ethics and by ethical rules. The hold that ethical rules have on persons derives from the impact of God's speech on them, which derives from the Holy Spirit as breath and recipient of God's speech. So each of the three perspectives on ethics derives from a person in God. (See table 37.1.)

Persons of the Trinity	Speech Providing Ethics	Perspectives on Ethics
the Father	speaker with authority	normative perspective
the Son	speech referring to the world	situational perspective
the Holy Spirit	speech impacting and gripping people	existential perspective

Table 37.1. Ethics from Persons of the Trinity

Now, could ethics exist with two perspectives instead of three? No. Ethics requires norms from God, situations for application, and persons who are responsible. If we leave out the norms, there is no ethical obligation. If we leave out situations, there are no actions within the situations that would flesh out obedience to the norms. If we leave out the persons, there is no one who is obligated. Any one of these moves evaporates ethics, leaving it with no content.

Could we fuse two of the perspectives, so that there would remain a total of only two perspectives instead of three? If someone collapses the norms into the situations, he gets a form of pantheism that amounts to nature worship. The obligations (in norms) are somehow identical with nature. The person is serving nature as if it were a god. But it does not work, because nature does not have the transcendence of God. Why should we serve it?

If someone collapses norms into persons, he gets a form of pantheism that makes human beings divine. He is worshiping himself as the norm. But this, too, does not work, because a human being does not have the true transcendence of an absolute.

If someone collapses the situation into the persons, the persons are absorbed into nature, as simply one more phenomenon of nature. Then ethical obligation disappears, because all behavior is merely natural. There are no *oughts* distinct from what is.

Could we add a fourth perspective to the three? We can use specialized forms of a perspective. For example, we could consider using the normative perspective in studying the book of Genesis. This use would be a specialized use of the normative perspective. But this kind of use would still be a form of the normative perspective. It would not amount to a genuinely distinct approach. Or we could combine the normative and situational perspectives in a single, more complex exploration. But in a sense, this kind of exploration is always taking place, since the perspectives always presuppose one another. We could try to produce a new perspective totally disjoint from the original three. But something disjoint from norms, situations, and persons has no relevance to ethics.

There must be three and only three fundamental perspectives on ethics because there are three and only three fundamental realms: (1) God, who is the source of norms; (2) the world, which provides the situation; and (3) persons, who are under ethical obligation.

By analogy, there must be three and only three persons in the Trinity, whose original coinherence is reflected in the derivative coinherence of the three perspectives on ethics. Thus, ethics is possible only through God, who is Trinitarian. (See fig. 37.4.)

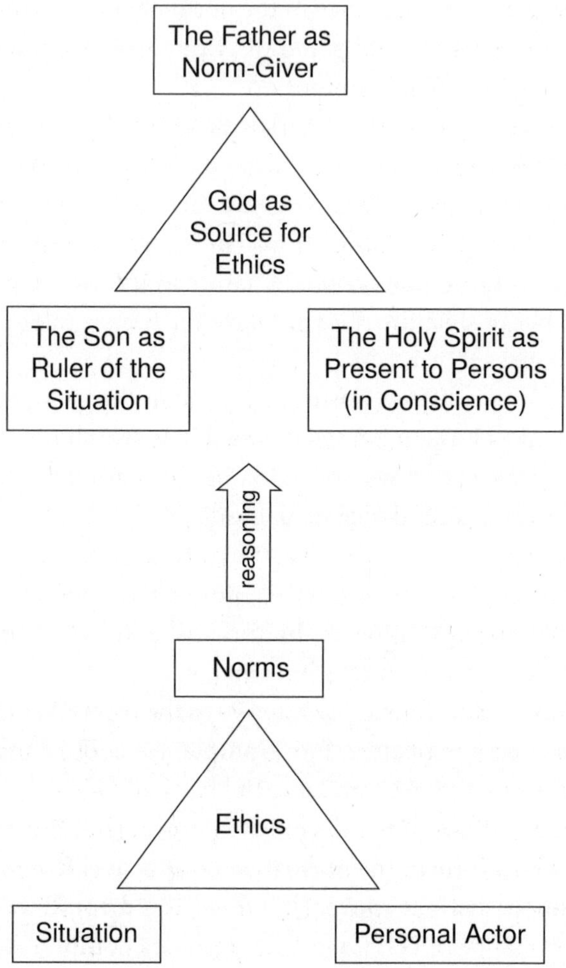

Fig. 37.4. Reasoning from Ethics to the Trinity

Science Testifying to the Trinity

A similar argument can unfold concerning the Trinitarian roots of science. Science necessarily involves three aspects: (1) lawful regularities, (2) a world conforming to these regularities, and (3) observers who have capabilities of interpreting the world and discerning the regularities.[5] These three aspects must work together. Without regularities, the world

5. Compare this triple to John Frame's discussion of the knowledge of God, the knowledge of the world, and the knowledge of persons (John M. Frame, *The Doctrine of the Knowledge of God* [Phillipsburg, NJ: Presbyterian and Reformed, 1987], chap. 2).

is a chaos in which science is impossible. Without a world, the regularities are inaccessible. And without observers with personal capabilities, neither the world nor the regularities get interpreted on earth. The three are interlocking (coinherent). Scientific observers presuppose regularities to understand and a world to observe. The world presupposes regularities in order to be a world rather than pure chaos. And it presupposes scientific observers if there is to be any hope of science analyzing the world. Similarly, if the regularities are to function in science, they presuppose a world and observers.

These three aspects are related, respectively, to the normative, situational, and existential perspectives on ethics. Science always has an ethical background. But here we are not focusing on ethical norms, but the lawful regularities. These are a kind of physically oriented norm governing the world. The world furnishes the situation, and of course, the observers furnish the persons who are the focus within the existential perspective. The argument that derives the Trinity from the three perspectives on ethics carries over to the three perspectives on science. We see science from the perspective of scientific laws, from the perspective of the world that shows the lawful regularities, and from the perspective of the labors of scientists. These perspectives reflect the Trinitarian character of God.

Just as with the three perspectives on ethics, the three perspectives on science can be no more and no fewer than three. A fourth perspective is either irrelevant or already contained within the three.

Thus, science testifies to God, who is Trinitarian. It is possible only because God exists and is Trinitarian. (See fig. 37.5.)

Key Terms

analogy
analogy with communication[6]
change
constraint
derivation
existential perspective
immanence
lawful regularity

6. Key terms in **bold** are defined in the glossary at the end of this volume.

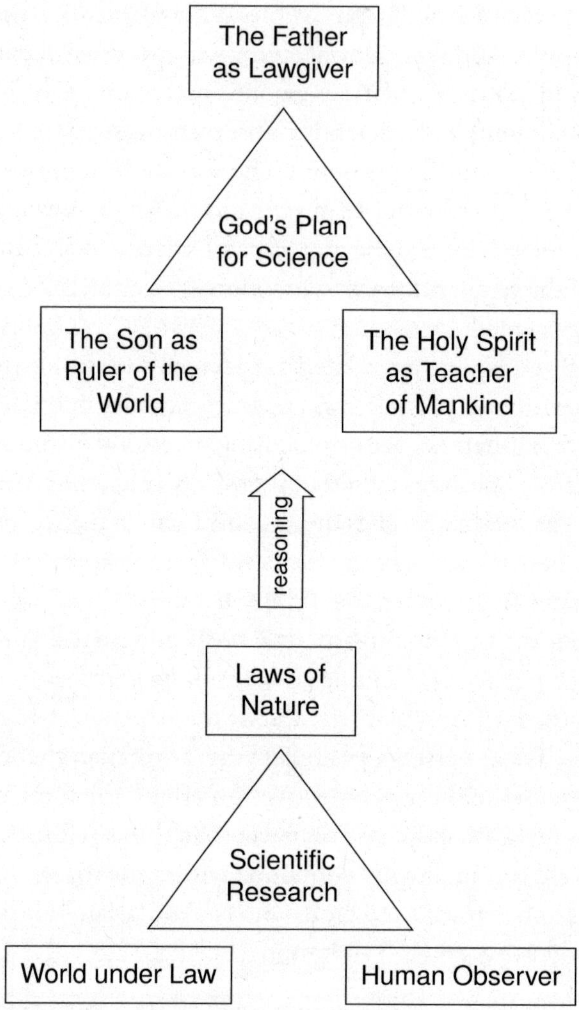

Fig. 37.5. Reasoning from Science to the Trinity

normative perspective
observer
personality
relationality
situational perspective
Ten Commandments
transcendence
world

Study Questions

1. What is an example in which John Frame uses two categories instead of three? In which he uses ten categories? Is anything essential at stake as a result of the number of categories?
2. Can God be anything other than three persons? Why not?
3. What dangers are there in trying to prove that God must be tripersonal? What kind of reasoning is legitimate in support of God's being tripersonal?
4. How does the love analogy support the tripersonal nature of God?
5. How does the analogy with communication support the tripersonal nature of God?
6. How does the structure of ethics confirm the Trinitarian nature of God?
7. How does the structure of science confirm the Trinitarian nature of God?

For Further Reading

Bosserman, B. A. *The Trinity and the Vindication of Christian Paradox: An Interpretation and Refinement of the Theological Apologetic of Cornelius Van Til*. Eugene, OR: Pickwick, 2014. Pp. 176–82. On confirmation of the necessity of three persons in God.

Frame, John M. *The Doctrine of the Christian Life*. Phillipsburg, NJ: P&R Publishing, 2008. Pp. 396–401. Using each of the Ten Commandments as a perspective on the Christian life.

38

Deriving Attributes of God

CAN WE DERIVE all the major aspects of theology from a simple starting point? In the early part of the book (parts 1–2), we devoted most of our energy to moving from specific passages of the Bible to more general formulations. For example, we confirmed the doctrine of the Trinity by appealing to specific texts (chaps. 6–7). As part of this process, we also gradually built up a list of triads of perspectives, indicating how they are based on biblical revelation (part 3).

Two Approaches to Theological Reasoning

This manner of proceeding takes advantage of the key role that the Bible plays in forming doctrine. The Bible's teaching is the infallible source for doctrine. Without the Bible, people go astray in doctrine. Human sin makes people want to distort some doctrines that are distasteful to them. Sin also has effects on the mind, so that people harbor false doctrines and draw erroneous conclusions even when they start from fragments of the truth. They read the Bible itself with a sinful mind. But at least the Bible, because of its clarity and infallibility, offers a check to erroneous doctrine, a rebuke to errors, and a guide to the truth (2 Tim. 3:16). People may also go astray when they add to the Bible other verbal sources to which they attribute divine authority. So we should devote ourselves to studying in detail what God says in the Bible, to use its full contents, and to build doctrine from passages that teach it.

This way of deriving doctrine from the Bible also helps to remind us of our human limitations. We are to submit to what God says about himself, not try to create notions out of our own mind and then insist that God submit to them. That latter course would be a case involving a non-Christian view of immanence, in which a person makes his human mind into the ultimate standard for doctrine (chap. 10).

But in the immediately preceding chapter (chap. 37), we proceeded in a somewhat different way. Rather than deriving the doctrine of the Trinity from biblical passages, we attempted to derive it from some general principles about God. What do we say about these two routes? Deriving doctrine from the Bible is more "inductive" because it starts from particular passages and moves toward general doctrines. Deriving particular doctrines from the nature of God is more "deductive" because it proposes to "deduce" other doctrines from a few starting principles. (See fig. 38.1.)

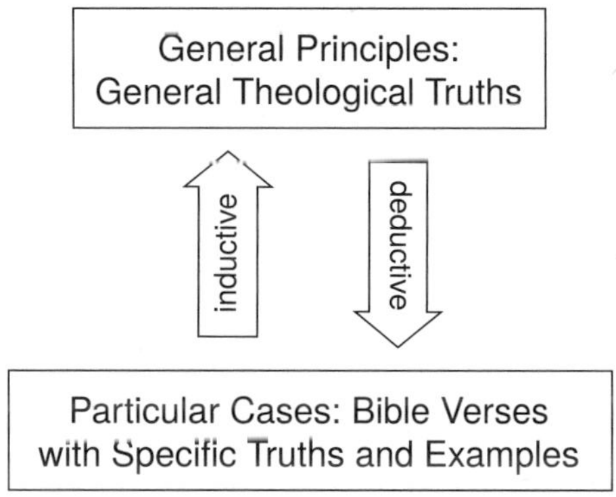

Fig. 38.1. Inductive and Deductive Paths in Theology

Of course, neither of these procedures is *purely* inductive or *purely* deductive. In practice, they both involve interactions between particulars and generalities. And that is the way it will always be, because the particulars and the generalities are always involved in one another. The many (the particulars) coinheres with the one (the generalities).

Now, the second, "deductive" way of proceeding is potentially dangerous because the general principles about God could easily become principles of our own devising. Nevertheless, at its best, such a form of argument has value because it can help to confirm the coherence of doctrine. The different teachings of the Bible make sense when they are all considered in the light of one another. And that includes considering particular doctrines in the light of general principles about God.

We understand more deeply when we see how the various teachings of Scripture fit together.

In addition, it remains true that *any* treatment of doctrine involves dangers. Sin can creep in. It can creep in with the inductive approach, which starts with passages from the Bible. It is possible for someone to grab onto a passage that he likes and make it fit in with his sinfully distorted ideas. And then he may refuse to give up his distorted interpretation even when confronted with other passages and with a larger system of doctrine that show that he has a distorted interpretation. A larger systematic organization of doctrine can have positive value in steering us away from aberrant interpretations of individual passages and aberrant preferences for having our own way.

So let us now consider what it would be like to proceed in a more "deductive" way, and to derive large parts of theology from a few starting principles. But we do not proceed in a vacuum, or by pretending to be autonomous. We need to be born again, and the full range of biblical teaching should continue to inform us at every point.

Even though some of the previous parts of the book have used a more "inductive" approach, they have provided food for thought and have touched on general principles. In a number of cases, the inductive arguments could be run "in reverse," by moving from the more general principles to the more particular cases. According to the principle of the one and the many, the general and the particular are involved in each other and are coinherent. So intuitively it should be the case that we can run many such arguments in reverse.

Using a Deductive Approach

To proceed with a more deductive approach, we first have to find some general starting principles. These starting principles have to be actually true. But they could come from anywhere, because all truth holds together in the mind and plan of God. All truth testifies to him. Thus, in principle there are many kinds of movement from one principle to another that could use a deductive approach. We consider only one such approach.

Because of the Trinity's centrality in our exposition, it is most convenient to start with some principles about God. The most obvious way of obtaining principles would be from biblical passages—which is close to what we have already done. So at this point, let us do something different. Let us begin with a focus on general revelation rather than special revelation. General revelation always needs to be illumined by the light of special revelation. But once we have absorbed the teaching of special revelation in the Bible, we can see more clearly what was always there as general revelation. General revelation does reveal the true God (Rom. 1:18–23). It just takes the light of special revelation (brought home to us by the Holy Spirit's illumining our minds) to see it rightly.

So presupposing that we have a rich and healthy understanding of special revelation, we proceed. We explore one way to try to awaken an unbeliever to what he already knows on the basis of general revelation, but has succeeded in partially suppressing (Rom. 1:18).

Starting with Morality

Let us start with the sense of morality. Are there moral absolutes? Radical relativists would say no. But they show that they know better when they experience injustice from others. Suppose that a thief has just broken in and stolen the valuables from the relativist's home, and in addition trashed the things that were left behind. In his heart, no victim wants to say that the thief has just as much right to his own point of view as the victim does. The thief did what was wrong, and the relativist knows it in his heart, even if he denies it with his lips. There are moral absolutes, even though human sinfulness and selfishness find ways to twist and excuse individual violations of moral standards.

Moral absolutes imply personal responsibility. They also imply that we are persons, not just complex collections of atoms. Persons are ultimately responsible only to persons. Why? Suppose that we come upon an apparently impersonal rule, such as "Stop at a red light." We can always ask why we should see it as having a claim on us. It is just a rule, and who is to say whether it is good or bad? Our moral intuition may say that it is good, but why shouldn't we feel free to violate our intuition? The rule, to make a claim on us, must come from an authority. And authority is always personal. (For stopping at a red light, the authority is the personal authority of people who govern us, and behind them the fact that God has given earthly governors their authority, Rom. 13:1–4.) If we doubt the personal character of authority, we can also observe that a rule must be specific, and this requires languagelike meaning and articulation, which belong only to persons. So moral authority is personal. And to have moral absolutes, the moral authority must be absolute. So we must have a personal absolute. That is already the beginning of a conception of God. In reality, our sense of morality reflects God, who is its source.

Can there be many personal absolutes? The ancient Greeks believed in many gods. But the Greek gods were immoral and fought with one another. A multitude of gods does not offer an absolute. And it disintegrates morality, because there is no guarantee of harmony between different moral demands that allegedly come from different sources.

Hence, there is only one absolute personal God. The human heart testifies to it. That is another way of saying that we know God through general revelation.[1]

The human heart by testifying to God also shows that it was created by God. The absolute personal God is also absolute Creator. That is why we know moral standards (though as sinners we can corrupt the standards, Rom. 1:32). The same conclusion follows just from God's being absolute. If he is absolute, everything that is distinct from him is not absolute, but subject to him. If it is subject absolutely, it is subject in its very being. It owes existence to him. That is to say, he is the Creator of all.

Human responsibility also implies responsibility outside oneself. God must not be identical with the human self. That refutes pantheism. God is distinct from man.

The Trinity

Once we have arrived at a conception of God as Creator, who is distinct from creatures, we can use the derivation from chapter 37. God as Creator specifies the nature of things. To do so, he must speak. The triad for communication leads to the conclusion that God is three persons. So does the triad for love.

There are further derivations. In accord with chapter 33, God's absoluteness implies his personal character and his simplicity (and vice versa). The three persons must be coinherent, as we indicated briefly in

1. A similar argument for God starts with scientific law rather than moral law (see Vern S. Poythress, *Redeeming Science: A God-Centered Approach* [Wheaton, IL: Crossway, 2006], chap. 1).

chapter 34. The perspectives on coinherence are themselves coinherent with the perspectives on persons and the perspectives on attributes. So coinherence can be derived from the nature of God.

We can continue to derive other perspectives and triads of perspectives.

Key Terms

deduction
general revelation[2]
induction
moral absolutes
order
special revelation
triad for communication
triad for love
triad for reflections

Study Questions

1. What is the difference between an inductive and a deductive approach to doctrine?
2. What dangers arise from an inductive approach? from a deductive approach?
3. How can God's Trinitarian nature be derived from his absoluteness?
4. How can the triad for communication be derived from God's absoluteness?

For Further Reading

Bosserman, B. A. *The Trinity and the Vindication of Christian Paradox: An Interpretation and Refinement of the Theological Apologetic of Cornelius Van Til*. Eugene, OR: Pickwick, 2014. Pp. 173–212. On inferences from the nature of God.

2. Key terms in **bold** are defined in the glossary at the end of this volume.

39

Deriving Perspectives

IN CHAPTER 38, WE showed how some attributes of God can be derived from fundamental aspects of general revelation. Let us consider now whether we can do a similar kind of derivation, starting only with God's attribute of absoluteness and including within the derivation the perspectives given in figures 36.2 and 36.3. As in chapters 37 and 38, we must bear in mind that our derivations should take place in submission to God and his revelation to us. We seek to avoid would-be autonomous reasoning.

The Triad of Abstract Attributes

Let us begin by deriving the triad of abstract attributes from absoluteness. In a sense, we have already done this. In chapter 33, we introduced absoluteness as one of a triad of abstract attributes, namely, absoluteness, simplicity, and personality. We saw in chapter 33 that any one of these perspectives is implicit in the other two. Each implies the presence of the other two. In particular, absoluteness implies simplicity and personality. If God is absolute, he cannot be dependent on parts and he cannot be dependent on any attribute that is outside him and logically prior to his existence. So he is simple. If God is absolute, he is absolute in knowledge and absolute in love. Since knowledge and love are personal, God is personal.

As a second derivation, we could observe that if God is absolute, he is absolute over morality. And as we saw in the previous chapter, morality demands a personal absolute. Thus, in a sense simplicity and personality can be derived from absoluteness. Hence, the entire triad of abstract attributes can be derived from absoluteness (fig. 39.1).

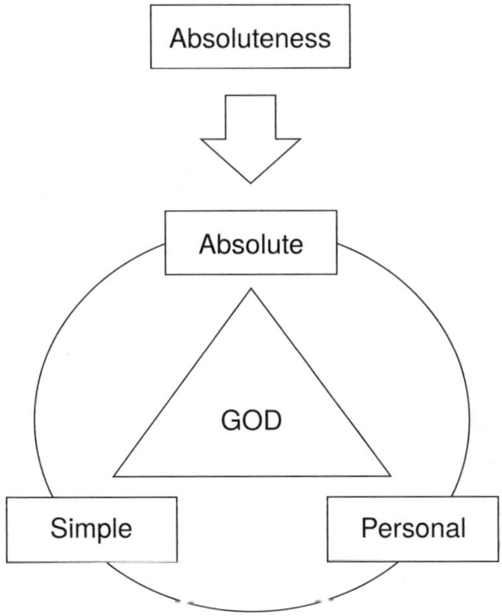

Fig. 39.1. Deriving Abstract Attributes from Absoluteness

The Special Triad for God

Next, let us seek to derive from absoluteness the special triad for God. In chapter 32, we introduced the special triad for God, consisting in the attributes of God, the coinherence in God, and the persons in God. These three together form a triad of perspectives on God. Can we derive this triad from absoluteness?

Absoluteness is an attribute of God and implies the other attributes in the triad of abstract attributes. So it is reflected in the perspective on attributes. In addition, absoluteness belongs only to God. So it indirectly points to everything that makes God who he is. All his attributes belong to who he is. So absoluteness leads to thinking about God through all his attributes. We have thereby gone from absoluteness (within the triad of abstract attributes) to attributes (within the special triad for God).

Next, consider the attribute of personality. Personality implies the ability to have interpersonal relations. Since God is absolute, this ability is not merely potential, but actual. There are interpersonal relations in God. So there is a plurality of persons, and a focus on these persons means a perspective on persons. We have thereby gone in our reasoning from personality (within the triad of abstract attributes) to the perspective on persons (within the special triad for God).

Finally, let us consider the attribute of simplicity. This attribute is the second within the triad of abstract attributes of God. Simplicity concerns God's relation to other things. Simplicity is a denial that God *needs* relations to other things, either to *parts* inside him or to concepts outside him that are prior to him or are needed to characterize him. This attribute thus is closely related to how we think about God's surroundings, his "situation." Now, God needs no "situation" outside himself because he is Trinitarian. Each person of the Trinity has the two other persons as his "situation." And these persons are not outside God, but indwell one another. The coinherence of the Trinity is how we describe God's "situation" at a fundamental level. It is the positive reality corresponding to simplicity. From the attribute of personality, we have already inferred that there is more than one person. But the persons of the Trinity are not and cannot be discrete parts. Rather, each person is fully God and all persons coinhere, so that among the persons there is no "outside," and none of them is a "part" or "piece" of God. By this reasoning, we have gone from simplicity (within the triad of abstract attributes) to coinherence (within the special triad for God).

So we have confirmed that we can derive the special triad for God from the triad of abstract attributes (table 39.1).

Triad of Abstract Attributes	reflection	**Special Triad for God**
absoluteness	→	perspective on attributes
simplicity	→	perspective on coinherence
personality	→	perspective on persons

Table 39.1. From Abstract Attributes to Perspectives within the Special Triad for God

Since the triad of abstract attributes is coinherent, so is the special triad for God. (See fig. 39.2.)

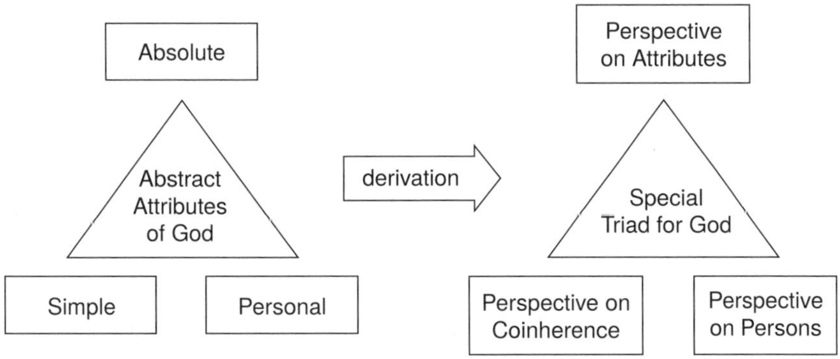

Fig. 39.2. From Abstract Attributes to the Special Triad for God

Deriving the Triad for Coinherence

We can also ask whether we can derive the triad for coinherence from absoluteness. We can do it indirectly. Since we have already derived the special triad for God from absoluteness, we can start with the special triad for God. Within the special triad for God, first consider the perspective on attributes. Attributes are a prime way of expressing the knowledge of God. So when we apply this perspective to coinherence, it leads to the perspective of coinherence in knowledge.

Next, consider the perspective on coinherence within the special triad for God. This perspective, as we observed, is closely related to the question of how God relates outward to either parts or alleged concepts that are outside him. It involves the question of his *situation,* and therefore whether he has absolute power to determine that situation. So the perspective on coinherence leads to thinking about coinherence in power.

Third, consider the perspective on persons within the special triad for God. Closeness among persons is naturally expressed by indwelling. So the perspective on persons leads to the theme of coinherence in indwelling. (See table 39.2.) Since the special triad for God is coinherent, so is the triad for coinherence.

Deriving the Triad for Persons

We can also ask whether we can derive the triad for persons from absoluteness. The triad for persons consists in the Father's perspective, the Son's perspective, and the Holy Spirit's perspective. We have already

Special Triad for God	reflection	Triad for Coinherence
perspective on attributes	→	coinherence in knowledge
perspective on coinherence	→	coinherence in power
perspective on persons	→	coinherence in indwelling

Table 39.2. From the Special Triad for God to Perspectives on Coinherence

derived the triad for coinherence from absoluteness, by going indirectly through the special triad for God. Now it is fairly straightforward to move from the triad for coinherence to the triad for persons. The Father preeminently represents knowledge, since he plans the unfolding of history. The Son preeminently represents the power of God, since the Son executes the plan of God in history. The Holy Spirit preeminently represents the indwelling of God, since he comes to apply redemption and to dwell within believers. Thus, each perspective on coinherence leads naturally to the perspective of one distinct person of the Trinity. (See table 39.3.)

Triad for Coinherence	reflection	Triad for Persons
coinherence in knowledge	→	the Father's perspective
coinherence in power	→	the Son's perspective
coinherence in indwelling	→	the Spirit's perspective

Table 39.3. From Coinherence to Personal Perspectives

This derivation goes in the reverse direction of many of the derivations in the body of the book. It is well to remind ourselves that the persons of the Trinity are not actually "derived" from anything deeper in God. For example, there is no *impersonal* principle in back of the persons, which offers the deepest foundation for why they exist. The persons of the Trinity are as deep as the Trinity. Yet it is still useful to seek to think about derivations in order to grasp more deeply the coherence of everything that is true about God.

Absoluteness as a Starting Point

Thus, from absoluteness we can derive the entire system of perspectives found in figure 34.2, with its center in the special triad for God. (See fig. 39.3.)

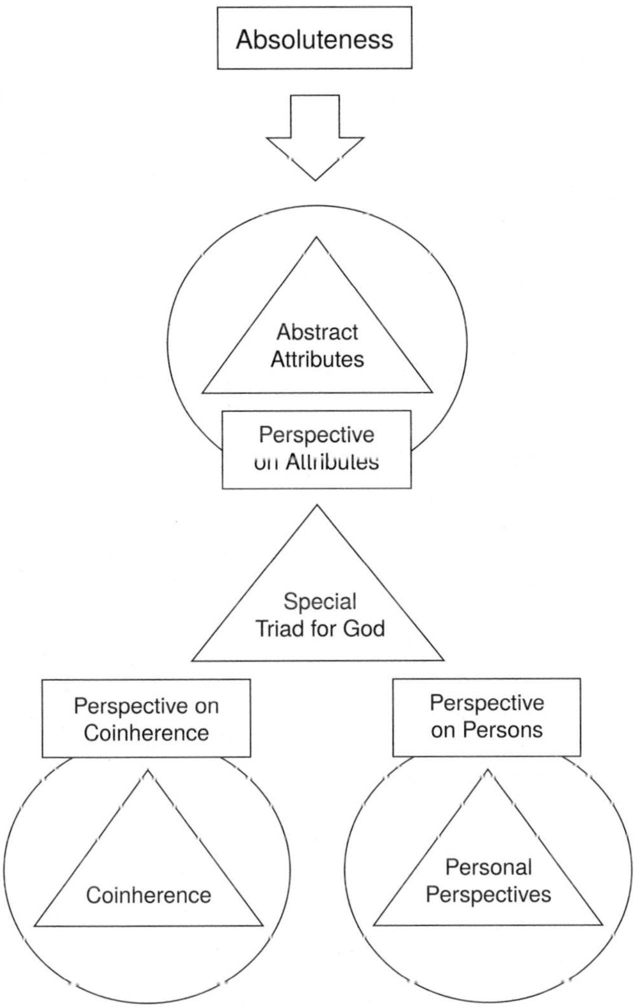

Fig. 39.3. From Absoluteness to Many Perspectives on God Himself

Larger Classification

We have thus begun the process of deriving all the perspectives represented in figure 36.3, beginning with absoluteness. Figure 39.4 shows those perspectives and triads of perspectives that have already been derived.

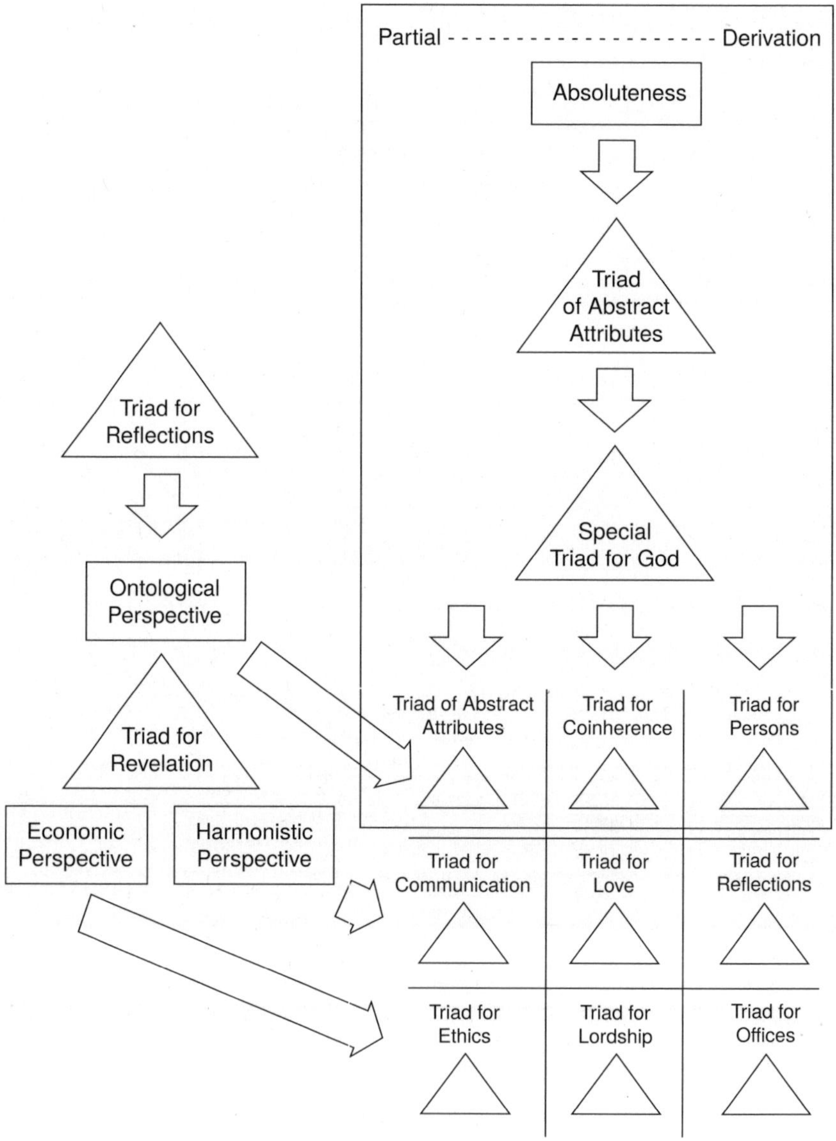

Fig. 39.4. Some Perspectives Derived from Absoluteness

From the Special Triad for God to the Triad for Reflections

We have still not completed the task of deriving all the main triads in figure 39.4 from absoluteness as the fundamental starting point. Can we derive the triad for reflections from absoluteness?

Let us start from the special triad for God, which we have already derived from absoluteness. The special triad for God includes the perspective on persons. Moreover, according to the perspective on coinherence, the persons indwell one another. So each person manifests the presence of the other two. In this manifestation, the person who is manifested functions as the original and the person who is manifesting the other person functions as the manifestation. For God to be self-sufficient (absolute), he must include in himself the divine archetype for the principle of the original and the principle of manifestation. Thus, we derive the originary perspective and the manifestational perspective. Because God is in harmony with himself, the two perspectives are in harmony. If we focus on this harmonious relation, we have obtained a third perspective, the connectional perspective.

Next, as we have seen from chapter 16, the triad for revelation derives from the triad for reflections. Since the triad for reflections, the triad for revelation, and the special triad for God derive from absoluteness, so does the overall structure given in figure 39.4. (See fig. 39.5.)

Deriving Other Perspectival Triads

The triads of perspectives in the 3 × 3 grid in figure 39.5, which we explored in our earlier chapters (chaps. 11–17), can now be derived from absoluteness. Earlier in this chapter, we already derived the triads in the first row, the triads falling under the ontological perspective. So let us go on to the triads in the second row, which fall under the general heading of the harmonistic perspective.

According to the perspective on persons within the special triad for God, God is personal. He is therefore able to communicate. Since he is absolute, he must be in himself the archetype for communication. So we arrive at the triad for communication. He will also be the archetype for loving. So we have in God an archetype for the dynamic of lover, beloved, and loving action. The archetype is the Trinity. So the triad for love is a reflection of the Trinity.

What about the third triad under the general heading of the

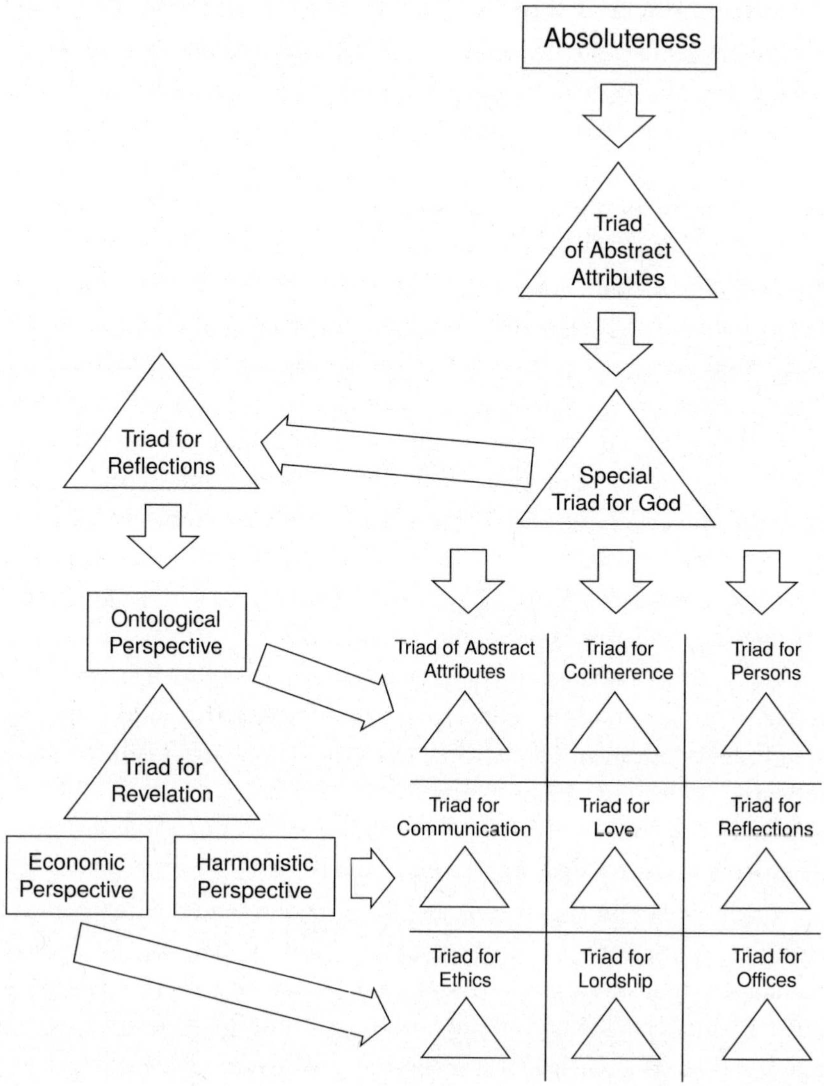

Fig. 39.5. Derivation of Perspectives from Absoluteness

harmonistic perspective, namely, the triad for reflections? We already derived it at an earlier point in this chapter.

Since God is ultimate, he must also be the ultimate source for the differentiation (the threeness) of the three triads: the triad for communication, the triad for love, and the triad for reflections.

Since God is ultimate (absolute), he is ultimate in ethics. His

Trinitarian nature must offer the ultimate foundation for ethical reasoning. God must be the source of norms for ethics, and the source of the situation in which persons act so that they may act responsibly. God must also be the source of the persons, so that they are completely responsible to him. Thus, God is the foundation for the normative, situational, and existential perspectives.

Since God is ultimate, he has ultimate authority and power. He must also be present everywhere to manifest his authority. Thus, God is the source of the three perspectives on lordship, namely, authority, control, and presence.

God as the absolute speaker, ruler, and source of blessing must be able to deliver his speech, his rule, and his blessing to creatures. These three—speech, rule, and blessing—lead to the perspectives on office: the prophetic, kingly, and priestly perspectives.

Order within a Triad

In this discussion, we have temporarily left in the background the issue of *order* among the persons of the Trinity. There is the Father, the Son, and the Spirit, in that order. The order is significant. In Appendix I, we attempt to show that this aspect can also be incorporated into theological reasoning. It helps at some points in trying to discern how a triad of perspectives derives from the Trinity, and does so in a way that takes into account an order within the triad.

Conversely, we can derive an order within the Trinity from the triad for communication. Communication proceeds from speaker to speech to recipient. This natural order has an archetype in God. God the Father speaks the word of the Son with the Holy Spirit as both breath and hearer (John 16:13–14).

Key Terms

absoluteness[1]
connectional perspective
derivation
harmonistic perspective
manifestational perspective

1. Key terms in **bold** are defined in the glossary at the end of this volume.

ontological perspective
order
originary perspective
personality
perspective on attributes
perspective on coinherence
perspective on persons
perspectives on lordship
perspectives on office
simplicity
special triad for God
triad for coinherence
triad for communication
triad for love
triad for persons
triad for reflections
triad of abstract attributes

Study Questions

1. How can we derive the three perspectives in the triad of abstract attributes from absoluteness?
2. How can we derive the special triad for God from absoluteness?
3. How do the triad of abstract attributes, the triad for coinherence, and the triad for persons derive from absoluteness?
4. How can we derive the triad for reflections from absoluteness?
5. What significance can be found in the fact that multiple triads of perspectives can be derived from absoluteness?
6. How does the derivation from absoluteness help us appreciate the unity of doctrine?

For Further Reading

Bosserman, B. A. *The Trinity and the Vindication of Christian Paradox: An Interpretation and Refinement of the Theological Apologetic of Cornelius Van Til*. Eugene, OR: Pickwick, 2014. Pp. 173–249. On derivations.

Conclusion

WE HAVE COMPLETED a survey of the nature of perspectives. It is a survey. There is always room for more thought and for more uses of perspectives in order to grow.[1] God has wonderfully revealed himself in general and special revelation. In special revelation, he has revealed himself progressively. We stand at a point in time when the "last days" mentioned in Hebrews 1:2 have already begun. God "has spoken to us by his Son" (Heb. 1:2). By the Son we have come to know God more fully than in Old Testament times. The Holy Spirit has inspired the Bible. And the Holy Spirit is given from the Father through the Son to dwell in us (Acts 2:33).

The Holy Spirit has come for our sanctification and for our illumination, so that we "might understand the things freely given us by God" (1 Cor. 2:12). We should give thanks to God for the riches of the privileges already given to us in this age, and we should look forward to the fullness of knowledge in the coming consummation:

> For now we see in a mirror dimly, but then face to face. Now I know in part; then I shall *know fully,* even as I have been fully known. (1 Cor. 13:12)

> The throne of God and of the Lamb will be in it, and his servants will worship him. They will *see his face,* and his name will be on their foreheads. (Rev. 22:3–4)

In the meantime, we have endeavored and may continue to endeavor to magnify God for the mystery of the Trinity.

1. For more perspectives, see Appendices.

Having come to know aspects of the mystery of the Trinity, we may also begin to appreciate what the theologians of previous generations sometimes called the *vestigia trinitatis*, "footprints" or marks of the Trinity that come in general revelation. Among other things, perspectival triads alert us to the reflections of God's Trinitarian glory in his revelation. God is present in every square inch of the world he has made, and in every aspect of human interaction with God in the world. God is inescapable, which may well distress unbelievers. But for those of us who have received salvation in Christ, his presence should be a comfort, a joy, and a source of awe and praise. God is present in his Trinitarian nature, and we may continue to grow in appreciation of it.

Key Terms

general revelation[2]
special revelation
vestigia trinitatis

Study Questions

1. What are the privileges in knowledge given to Christian believers in this age? How does this age differ from previous ages in terms of the knowledge of God?
2. What motivations should there be for growing in the knowledge of God?
3. How does our present knowledge of God compare with the knowledge of God to come in the new heaven and the new earth?

For Further Reading

The works of John M. Frame and Vern S. Poythress have many further illustrations of the use of perspectives. See www.frame-poythress.org for bibliographies as well as resources.

2. Key terms in **bold** are defined in the glossary at the end of this volume.

Appendix A:
Further Organization of Perspectives

WE CAN EXPLORE some further features about the organization of the perspectives discussed in the body of the book, in particular the perspectives summarized in figure 39.4. For convenience, the 3 × 3 grid of triads of perspectives given in figure 39.4 is reproduced in a simplified form in figure A.1.

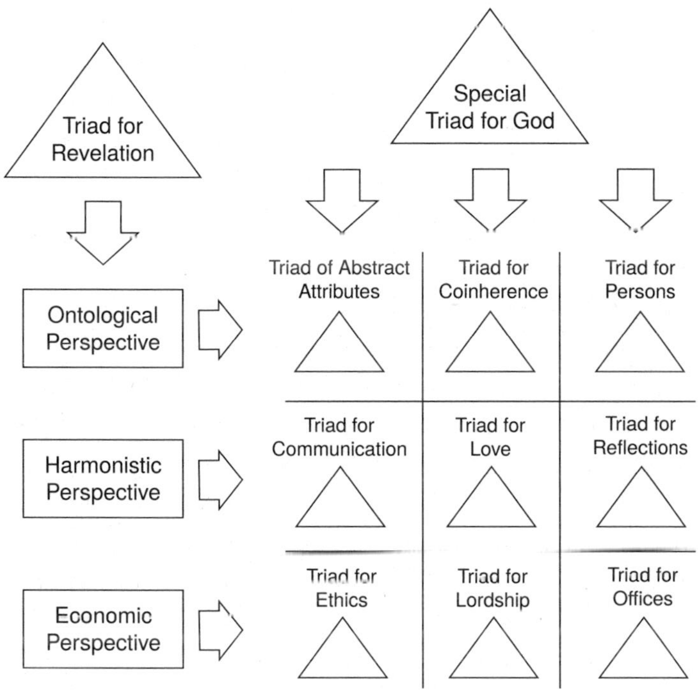

Fig. A.1. The Main Perspectives

What is the relation between the three main rows in figure A.1? Each row falls under a distinctive perspective. The first row across is the one with the label *Ontological Perspective* on the left-hand side. The entries in this row fall under the general heading of the ontological perspective. The entries in the second row fall under the heading of the harmonistic perspective, and the third row under the economic perspective.

Constancy and Activity in God

Now notice a second difference with regard to the rows. The perspectives under the first row focus more closely on constant and stable aspects of God; they focus on God's *constancy,* not on his *activities.* The second and third rows, by contrast, focus on activities, such as communication and love. It is, of course, true that the triad for ethics deals with constant ethical principles. But it is a triad used by human beings in the process of evaluating moral activities. Similar things might be said concerning other triads in the second and third rows. What might be the significance of this difference between constancy and activity?

As indicated in chapter 21, God is eternally active in love and speech among persons of the Trinity. But these activities come into view most easily when we talk about how God acts in relation to the world (actions in view with the harmonistic and economic perspectives). Accordingly, the perspectives found under the general heading of the ontological perspective begin with a closer focus on constancy.

Phases in the Activities of God

In the second row, the three perspectives within a single triad focus on distinct phases of God's activity. For instance, within the triad for communication, the expressive perspective focuses on the speaker. If God is speaking to human beings in time, God as speaker comes first in time. Then comes the speech, which is in focus in the informational perspective. Then comes reception by the hearer, which is in focus in the productive perspective. Thus, the expressive, informational, and productive perspectives focus on three successive phases of communication. Consider next the triad for love. For actions in time, love has three phases that are often temporally successive: first the phase of initiating love, then the phase of acting in love, and then the reception of love by the person being loved. Our previous treatment of the triad for love does not fit seamlessly, because the Son, the second person of the Trinity, is the recipient of love. But we can still see a particular kind of order in which the Holy Spirit comes third: the Holy Spirit functions as the gift given as an expression of the love. The gift presupposes that the love exists. Moreover, the Holy Spirit is the one who preeminently brings God's love to human recipients: "God's love has been poured into our hearts through the Holy Spirit who has been given to us" (Rom. 5:5). This pouring out of love can be viewed as a final phase.

For the triad for reflections, consider what happens when God appears in theophany. God himself precedes his appearance. The originary perspective, focusing on God, is logically first. Then God appears, and the appearance is in focus in the manifestational perspective. The connectional perspective is in a sense simultaneously there with the manifestational perspective. But logically, to speak about connectional features, we must presuppose the existence of the archetype and the image, which share the features. Thus, the connectional perspective logically presupposes the originary perspective and the manifestational perspective. Moreover, if we think about the human perception of theophany, a human being does not *become* the manifestation, but learns from the manifestation some features in the manifestation that reveal God. That is, he learns connectional features. From the point of view of human reception, the connectional perspective is logically the last of the three.

For all three triads under the general heading of the harmonistic perspective, we can describe the three phases as the initiation, the action itself (sending a speech or bringing a benefit, or bringing a curse or judgment), and the reception.

Derivation of Phases

Can we derive these phases from the ontologically focused perspectives in the first row? The absoluteness of God implies that he alone is the ultimate source and foundation for activity as well as constancy. Thus, the activities found in the second and third rows are implicit in God's absoluteness.

In the triad for coinherence, we find a foundation for the three phases in activity. Coinherence in knowledge is the basis for planning an action. Knowledge is needed for action. Coinherence in power is the basis for the power for action. And coinherence in indwelling is the foundation for reception of activity, because the activity comes to "indwell" the recipient when he receives the product of the action. In sum, the triad for coinherence leads to a triad for phases of action. (See table A.1.)

Triad for Coinherence	reflection	**Phases of Action**
coinherence in knowledge	→	initiation
coinherence in power	→	action
coinherence in indwelling	→	reception

Table A.1. From the Triad for Coinherence to a Triad for Phases of Action

Coinherence is reflected in the triad consisting in initiation, action, and reception. It is thus reflected in each of the triads under the general heading of the harmonistic perspective.

The three phases of action are little more than a reformulation of the three perspectives on personal action, namely, the planning perspective, the accomplishment perspective, and the application perspective. (See table A.2.)

Triad for Personal Action	reflection	**Phases of Action**
planning perspective	→	initiation
accomplishment perspective	→	action
application perspective	→	reception

Table A.2. From Personal Action to Phases of Action

They apply not only to the triad for personal action but to the triads in the second row—the triad for communication, the triad for love, and the triad for reflections.

In addition, the three perspectives on coinherence get reflected in the way that the three triads under the general heading of the harmonistic perspective are distinct from one another. Coinherence in knowledge, when expressed outwardly, takes the form of communication, leading to the triad for communication. Coinherence in power, when expressed outwardly, takes the form of personal action in love; it leads to the triad for love. Coinherence in indwelling, when expressed outwardly, takes the form of personal presence in reflections; it leads to the triad for reflections. (See table A.3.)

Coinherence	reflection	**Triads under the Harmonistic Perspective**
coinherence in knowledge	→	Triad for communication
coinherence in power	→	Triad for love
coinherence in indwelling	→	Triad for reflections

Table A.3. From Coinherence to the Triads under the Harmonistic Perspective

Modes of Action under the General Heading of the Economic Perspective

In comparison to the triads under the general heading of the harmonistic perspective, the triads under the general heading of the economic perspective have a different internal organization. Consider, for example, the triad for offices, consisting in the prophetic perspective, the kingly perspective, and the priestly perspective. How do these three perspectives relate to one another? The triad for offices is not organized by successive *phases* involved in personal action. Rather, it is organized by different *ways* in which God confronts human beings, whether by speaking (prophetic), by ruling (kingly), or by personal intimacy in blessing (priestly). But these ways do not exclude one another. When God speaks, he is also ruling and expressing his intimacy. And even when God is not delivering specific verbal utterances, there are meanings in his actions. The prophetic, the kingly, and the priestly aspects are together aspects of all of God's works. They are simultaneous modes of action. Similar observations hold concerning the triad for lordship and the triad for ethics. The latter involves God's interaction with human beings concerning their ethical responsibility. We might say that the divisions within any one triad under the general heading of the economic perspective are divisions not on the basis of *phases* of action, but on the basis of *modes* of action.

These two kinds of division are complementary. In fact, they can be combined. A division on the basis of *phases* of activity can be applied to God's actions that are already described using some of the perspectives under the general heading of the economic perspective. This division is *in addition* to the distinctions that we have already established. For example, consider the prophetic perspective. We consider a particular act of God, such as the communication of God from the top of Mount Sinai. It is a prophetic act of God. It has three phases. The first is the initiative of God, when he speaks; second are the actual words delivered; and third is the reception of the words by the people of Israel. We can consider the same act of God as a kingly act, in which he gives Israel laws that are to regulate them as a kingdom and to ensure justice. Once again, there are three phases. God initiates the relation, acting as a king. The laws are God's permanent gift to Israel. Israel receives them by submitting to the rule of God.

The distinction between *phases* of activity (in row 2) and *modes* of activity (in row 3) helps to make sense of the triad for personal action, first introduced in chapter 12. (See fig. 12.5.) The triad for personal action focuses on three phases of activity, namely, planning, accomplishment, and application. In human action, these three are often spread out in time. We also observed in chapter 12 that the triad for personal action can best be classified as a triad under the general heading of the economic perspective. It focuses on God's acts in history. So the triad for personal action can be seen as the form taken by the triad for lordship if we focus not on *modes* of God's activity as Lord, but on *phases* of his activity as Lord.

Using the Special Triad for God Perspectivally

We can perform a similar kind of combination of perspectives if we start with the triads under the ontological perspective. These triads, as we have observed, focus on what is *constant*. Can we also apply this focus on constancy to the triads under the general heading of the harmonistic perspective and under the economic perspective? In the activities represented by the second and third rows of the 3 × 3 grid in figure A.1, what is constant? The primary constancy belongs to the people and things that participate in the actions. God is the same God, and we describe him by using the triads under the ontological perspective. Human beings are not unchangeable the way God is, but as creatures they still reflect on the creaturely level the stability of God. They are relatively stable in their knowledge, their abilities, their personality, and their abilities, in the midst of constantly changing activities. So human beings can be described using a triad: the person, his attributes, and his derivative *coinherence*, which is expressed by his involvement in his actions and his involvement with other human beings and with God.

Not only human beings, but stable gifts from God, such as the Ten Commandments and the bronze altar in the tabernacle, can be similarly analyzed. They have their own integrity, their attributes, and their relations to people and to things.[1]

Thus, we can contemplate interactions between all the perspectives belonging to the 3 × 3 grid in figure A.1.

Key Terms

action itself
activity
constancy

1. We see a division here between three distinct foci: (1) constancy (row 1 in the 3 × 3 grid), (2) activity in phases (row 2), and (3) modes in relation (row 3). This division is a particular application of the triad for theorizing, which consists in the static perspective, the dynamic perspective, and the relational perspective (see Appendix D).

We may also suggest that the entire organization of perspectives uses a three-dimensional grid. The first dimension is the horizontal dimension represented by a single row. The second dimension is the vertical dimension represented by a single column. The third dimension is represented by the three perspectives within any one triad. These three dimensions may have a distant correlation with the special triad for God. The perspective on abstract attributes is closely related to themes, and distinct thematic focus is the main thing separating the three columns in the 3 × 3 grid of triads. The perspective on coinherence is related to how perspectives have focus within an overall conceptual *space*. This idea of conceptual space or location is the main governing feature that distinguishes the rows. The location consists in the divine location for God's activity or the earthly location of action on earth (for perspectives under the general heading of the economic perspective). Finally, the distinctions within any one triad are distinctions related to the manner of action of a single person, and his choice to exercise his activity in a particular way. So they have a correlation with the perspective on persons within the special triad for God.

economic perspective[2]
harmonistic perspective
initiation
mode of action
ontological perspective
organization
phase of action
reception

Study Questions

1. What are the successive phases in a typical case of divine or human action?
2. How are the phases related to the three perspectives on coinherence? to the three perspectives in the triad for personal action?
3. Discuss ways in which perspectives from the 3 × 3 grid may be combined.

For Further Reading

Yates, Timothy Paul. *Foundations: God's Glory as an Integrating Perspective on Reformed Theology*. Lancaster, PA: Unveiled Faces Reformed Press, 2017. Pp. 19–45. Explaining an approach to counseling that contains further perspectives on God's relation to man.

2. Key terms in **bold** are defined in the glossary at the end of this volume.

Appendix B: Covenantal Reflections

NOW WE LOOK at how perspectives applying to God can be reflected in human beings.

Perspectives Including Both God and God's Actions toward the World

In chapters 17 and 36, we distinguished between the ontological perspective, the economic perspective, and the harmonistic perspective. We classified some triads under the general heading of each of the three perspectives. But all the triads are triads of *perspectives*. They are capable of being applied both in describing God and in describing the works of God. For example, the triad of abstract attributes includes three attributes that apply to God himself, apart from the creation of the world. But the attributes have implications for how God acts in relation to the world. When he acts, he manifests in the world his absoluteness, his simplicity, and his personality. Similar things can be said concerning the triad for coinherence. The three perspectives on coinherence always apply to God himself. But they also apply to God's actions in the world. God's coinherence in knowledge guides his actions; his coinherence in power gives coherence to his acts of power; his coinherence in indwelling implies that all three persons are present when God is present in the world. Finally, the triad for persons applies to God's actions in the world. His actions can always be considered from the perspective of the Father's activity, or the Son's activity, or the Spirit's activity.

The triads under the general heading of the harmonistic perspective also function on both levels, ontologically and economically, in agreement with the fact that they express the harmony between God and his economic activities. For example, the triad for communication applies to the archetypal communication in the Trinity, according to which the Father speaks the Word in the breath of the Holy Spirit. But the same triad also applies to communication in which God speaks to creation ("Let there be light," Gen. 1:3) and to human beings ("Why are you angry, and why has your face fallen?," 4:6). Similarly, the triad for love applies to the archetypal, eternal activity in God, in which the Father loves the Son with the gift of the Holy Spirit. But the triad is also applicable to God's work of salvation, according to which he extends his love to us and gives us the gift of the Holy Spirit (Rom. 5:5). The triad for reflections is similar. It applies to God, in that the Son is the eternal image of the Father. It also applies to God's actions in the world, when God created man in his image.

The triads under the general heading of the economic perspective, namely, the triads for ethics, for lordship, and for offices, can also become perspectives that we use in meditating on God himself. With these three triads, the focus is usually on God's acting in relation to the created world and in relation to us as human beings. But it is *God* who is acting. His actions toward us reveal who he is. For example, the triad for lordship focuses on how God exercises his authority over the world, exerts his control over the world, and is present in the world. All three of these perspectives deal first of all with God's relation to the world. But God's authority over the world reflects the fact that God as the absolute God has *intrinsic* authority within himself, even before he created the world. God's control over the world reflects his *intrinsic* power, his omnipotence, which is his even before he created the world. And God's presence in the world reflects God's presence in and to himself, expressed in the fellowship among the persons of the Trinity and their mutual indwelling (coinherence in indwelling).

Thus, the three triads under the general heading of the economic perspective also apply when we turn to meditating on God. The three triads under the general heading of the ontological perspective are distinct from the three triads under the general heading of the economic perspective, and from the triads under the general heading of the harmonistic perspective, but all nine triads are coinherent. So we should not be surprised that they can be used as perspectives on God himself *and* on God's actions in the world. (See fig. B.1.)

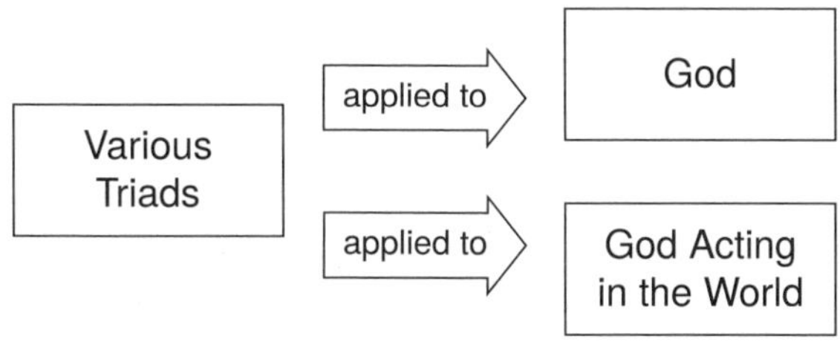

Fig. B.1. Triads Used as Perspectives on God and the World

Reflection in Human Activity

So now, for each of the nine triads in the 3 × 3 grid of figure A.1, we see that the triads apply to two arenas, that is, two areas that we think about. (1) They apply to God himself, as he always exists. And (2) they apply to God's economic activities with respect to the world.

The economic activities concern the whole world that God governs. He governs animals, plants, and nonliving things, as well as human beings. But human beings are made in the image of God and are designed to have fellowship with God. His love comes especially to them, until the fall of Adam disrupts the relationship. But even after the fall, God reestablishes a relationship through covenant. The divine covenants are expressions of personal relationship between God and man. They involve a triad. (1) There is God, the divine initiator of the covenant. (2) There is man, the recipient, whom the covenant binds to God. And (3) there is the covenant itself, which expresses the relationship.

The covenant functions in a kind of mediatorial capacity between God and man, since the covenantal promises and covenantal acts of God allow human beings to be reconciled to God. The Old Testament covenants anticipate Christ, the final Mediator (1 Tim. 2:5; see also Isa. 42:6; 49:8). Since the covenant is mediatorial, standing between God and man, we may appropriately rearrange the order: (1) God the initiator, (2) the covenant, and (3) man the recipient.

The word *covenant* could be narrowly used to designate only those cases in the Bible in which God sets forth a verbal covenant agreement, and in which the agreement is specifically designated to be a "covenant." But here we wish to use the word more broadly, to describe *covenantal relations*. A covenantal relation is any personal relation that includes divine obligations and/or benefits. So we include cases in which God speaks to human beings, but the word *covenant* is not explicitly used. These cases express God's personal communion with mankind, and so they still show features that are associated with cases in which God establishes an official covenant. In fact, *covenantal relations* include all of God's relations with mankind. When God gives "rains from heaven and fruitful seasons," as Paul says in Acts 14:17, this gift of God expresses his faithfulness to the covenant of common grace given to Noah (Gen. 8:22; 9:8–17). All people everywhere have moral responsibility to God and to his moral law. This responsibility is a *covenantal* responsibility and expresses a *covenantal* relation, in the broad sense.

The triads that we studied in Appendix A apply to God himself, as we have seen. They also apply to covenantal relations, because the covenant expresses God's economic activity in relation to mankind. So now each triad can have its focus turned to three arenas of thinking, not just two. The three arenas are (1) God, (2) the covenant as expression of God's economic activity, and (3) man as the recipient. The first of these, God himself, is considered from the ontological perspective. (See fig. B.2.)

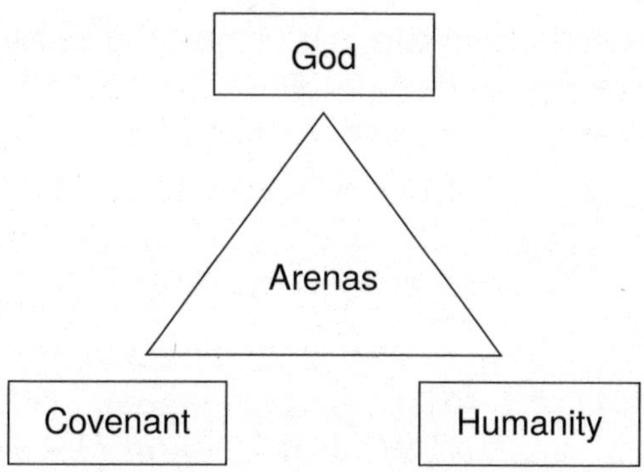

Fig. B.2. Arenas for Focus in Thinking

God's actions in covenant are more closely related to the economic perspective (God's acting in the world). The last of the three, namely, (3) man as recipient, is the one that we have newly added within this appendix. What is the implication of this addition? Human beings can be considered as passive recipients. They receive from God verbal communication, control, and presence. And it would be possible to further elaborate on ways in which our reception of God's gifts takes specific forms.

In addition, we may focus on human activity to which God calls us. We are recipients of the grace of God, but we also become active imitators. For example, we imitate God's speech by speaking. And if we are transformed into the image of Christ, our speaking will be godly in character. We will speak wisdom rather than folly, truth rather than lies. Our speech then reflects God's speech. Similarly, we imitate God's rule by ruling. We rule over whatever things or people for which the Lord has given us authority to rule. We do it with wisdom and with blessing, rather than in selfish manipulation.

We imitate God's presence by being present to others. We imitate God's blessing by being a blessing. All these things we do by analogy. We remain finite and do not become God. But we reflect in our lives the multifaceted wisdom and beauty and glory and truth of God. We are unable to do this by merely human power in isolation. But God has not called us to isolation. He has imparted his Spirit to us (Rom. 5:5; 8:9–17). He gives "life to your mortal bodies through his Spirit who dwells in you" (8:11). The work of God, the presence of God, and the meaning of God in his glory are made manifest in our mortal bodies empowered by the Spirit. In Christ, through the Spirit, God is at work *in* us and *through* us, displaying his glory to others. Praise be to God! And to him be glory forever and ever!

The Three Arenas as Perspectivally Related

It might seem to be the case that these three arenas—God, covenant, and man—are simply three separate areas of knowledge, areas that are unrelated to one another. But in practice, they cannot be separated. We cannot know about one without knowing about all three.[1] We cannot know God himself except in connection with the ways that he reveals himself to us economically, that is, covenantally. Conversely, in covenantal revelation God reveals himself in a way that reflects who he really is. So covenantal revelation presupposes the independent existence of God.

1. In a similar way, John Frame argues that knowledge of God, knowledge of the world, and knowledge of ourselves cannot be separated (*The Doctrine of the Knowledge of God* [Phillipsburg, NJ: Presbyterian and Reformed, 1987], 62–75).

In addition, when God describes himself, he frequently uses analogies with human activities. So we know God through knowing man. Conversely, the significance of human action is properly appreciated only when we understand that man is created for the purpose of imitating the speech, rule, and blessing of God. And it is God who empowers him to carry out these activities. So human action has meaning in the context of divine action.

Are the three arenas coinherent in their relation to one another? The three arenas are derived from the three main aspects that belong to a covenantal relation. And a covenantal relation is constituted by God's speaking to man. Therefore, the triad for communication is relevant. This triad leads to three coinherent perspectives, namely, the expressive, informational, and productive perspectives (chap. 12). When these three are applied to a covenant, the result is a focus on God, on the covenant itself, and on man, whom the covenant binds. The focus on God focuses on God himself and on his actions. The focus on covenant focuses on both the covenant itself and covenantal actions. The focus on man focuses on individual human beings, humanity in groups, and human actions. Thus, the triad for communication is reflected in the triad of arenas. (See fig. B.3.)

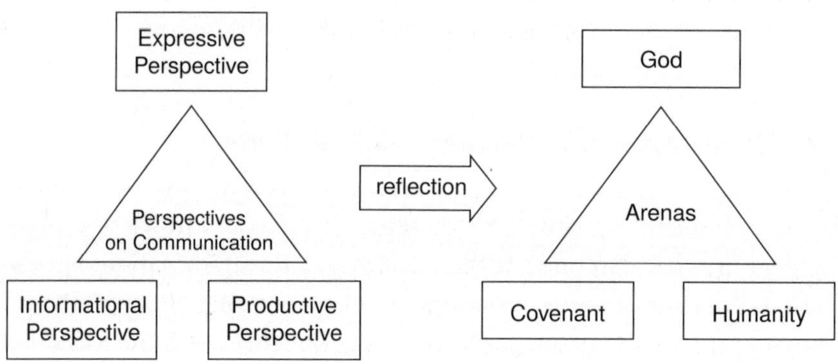

Fig. B.3. From Communication to Arenas

Summing Up the Use of Perspectives

Now we can take each of the triads in Appendix A and apply them to three arenas: the arena of God himself, the arena of God's covenant and his covenantal actions in the world, and the arena of humanity, in which we respond with respect to our covenantal relation to God. In this last arena, if we are Christian believers, we act as we are empowered by the Spirit of Christ, whom God has sent into our hearts. (See fig. B.4.)

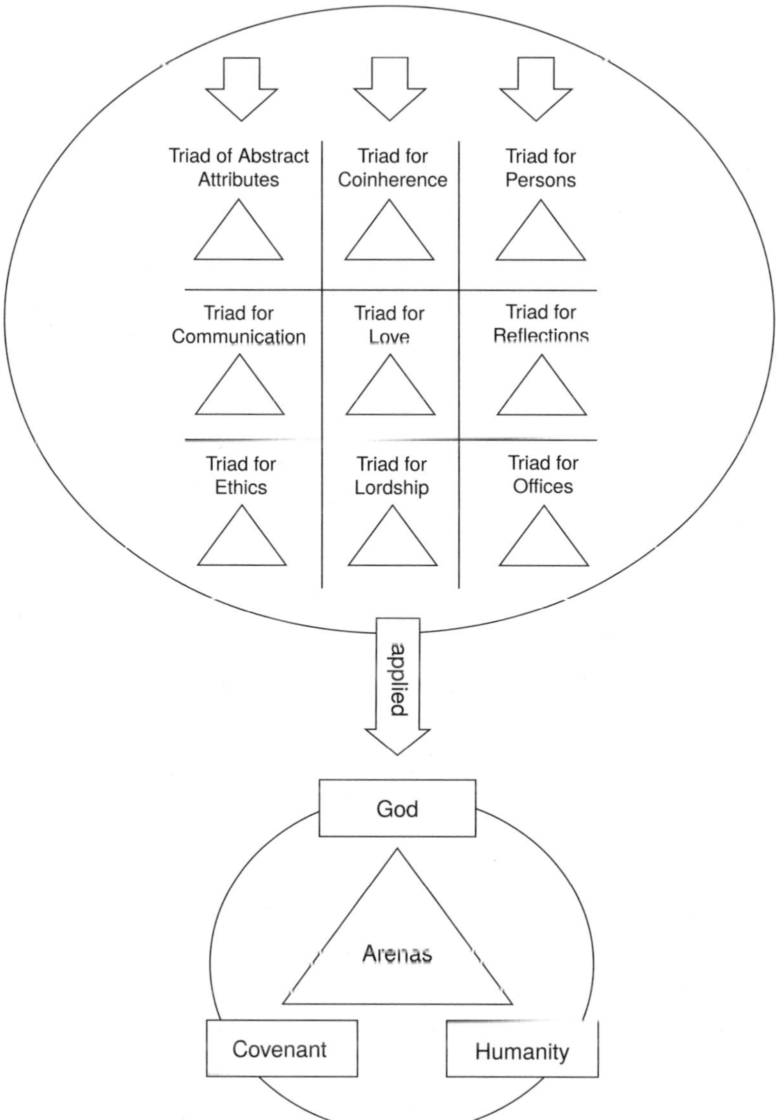

Fig. B.4. Applications of Nine Principal Triads

Should We Add Triads?

Should we multiply the number of triads further? Within the guidelines given by the Bible, we are free to multiply triads indefinitely, since we can have perspectives within perspectives. But the latest expansion represented by figure B.4 does not really produce more triads at a fundamental level. Rather, we have reused the perspectives that already exist in the 3 × 3 grid (from figure A.1). Since the entries in the 3 × 3 grid are *perspectives*, they are innately capable of being applied to a host of different objects that we might want to study. We have simply divided up their use according to what object we are studying—whether God or covenantal relations or human beings.

Key Terms

arena[2]
covenant
covenantal relation
economic perspective
harmonistic perspective
ontological perspective
triad for coinherence
triad for communication
triad for ethics
triad for lordship
triad for offices
triad for personal action
triad for persons
triad for reflections
triad of abstract attributes

Study Questions

1. How do each of the perspectival triads apply both to God and to God's actions in the world?
2. How can each of the perspectival triads apply to the activities of human beings in the image of God?

2. Key terms in **bold** are defined in the glossary at the end of this volume.

3. What is a *covenant,* and how does it function in mediating between God and human beings?
4. How can the covenantal structure be derived from the triad for communication?
5. How does the application of God's work to human beings illumine our humanity and our relation to God?

For Further Reading

Frame, John M. *The Doctrine of the Knowledge of God.* Phillipsburg, NJ: Presbyterian and Reformed, 1987. Pp. 62–75. Discussion of the interlocking of knowledge of God, knowledge of the world, and knowledge of self.

Appendix C: Patterns of Growth

LET US THINK about the implications of Appendices A and B for patterns of human growth.

The Path of Growth

God's goodness is reflected in the fact that he showers us with gifts. What we receive, we may pass on. The typical pattern involves movement. For example, if the gift from God takes the form of a message, the message comes from God, through a covenant, to a human being (see the preceding appendix on covenant). The human being receives the message and possesses it. Then he blesses others as he grows in his possession and becomes capable of passing on what he possesses. A similar pattern occurs when God rules in justice. We receive justice through an act of God toward us; we possess it by experiencing it in our lives; and we pass it on by ministering justice to others. The pattern also occurs when God sends blessings. We receive a blessing, possess it, and pass it on.

When we receive a message, it is an event naturally associated with the prophetic office. When we receive God's rule, it is associated with the kingly office. When we receive a blessing, it is associated with the priestly office. In sum, God meets us through the offices of prophet, king, and priest, all three of which come to fulfillment in Christ (chaps. 4, 15). Through the office of prophet, God speaks to us. Through the office of king, he rules over us in justice. Through the office of priest, God draws near to us in communion that brings blessing. In each case, we receive the gift, we possess it, and we pass it on.

In all these ways, if we are Christians, we are experiencing the centrality of Christ. Christ is God, who together with the Father and the Spirit initiates the message. The message comes as the Word of Christ through covenantal communication: Scripture is the covenant document, in which Christ is at the center of the message. Each of us should receive the message. As we receive it, we receive Christ, through the ministry of the Holy Spirit, who makes our hearts receptive. We are supposed to digest the message. We are vitally united to Christ. If the message is a declaration of our forgiveness and justification, we receive it by being accounted righteous. This righteousness is the righteousness of Christ imputed to us. We are also supposed to absorb into ourselves the joy of being accounted righteous. We pass on the reality to others both when we explain the message of justification and when we forgive others who sin against us. At the center of the message that we pass on is Christ.

Or suppose that we focus on the need for holiness. If the message calls for internal holiness, it leads us to be transformed into the image of Christ in our own inner being (2 Cor. 3:18). As we are transformed into the image of Christ, we are able with our words to bring the light of the glory of Christ to others (4:4–6). Our own words are Spirit-filled words by which Christ reveals himself to someone listening to us. Our words by reflecting holiness call on others to receive the holiness of Christ and to have him live in them, producing holiness in them.

This same pattern can be traced with respect to all the perspectives and triads in figure B.4. The process is more challenging with the ontologically focused perspectives, because these are designed to focus first of all on God and not on us. But the same pattern does still apply to ontologically focused perspectives. For example, consider the absoluteness of God. This absoluteness is originally in God. Then God expresses in covenant the meaning of the fact that he is absolute. His absolute claim and absolute authority and absolute power confront us and descend on us when he comes to us in covenantal words and deeds. We receive his absoluteness not by becoming absolute ourselves, but by acknowledging and submitting to him as the absolute God. We absorb into our being and our living the pattern of submission to him and the molding power of his absoluteness, to which we are responding. We also become content and enjoy a kind of sufficiency when we know God's all-sufficiency.[1] And then in our words and deeds to others, we reflect who God is.

1. Timothy Paul Yates, *Foundations: God's Glory as an Integrating Perspective on Reformed Theology* (Lancaster, PA: Unveiled Faces Reformed Press, 2017), 57–59, 124–28; Tim Yates, "CT 05 Blessing & Cursing Revealed by the Attributes of God Expressed in the Moral Law," course notes for CT 05 in counseling (China Reformed Theological Seminary, 2016), 5.

The same pattern can also be traced with respect to attributes of God other than the ones on which we have concentrated. For example, consider the goodness of God. The goodness of God is reflected in the goodness expressed in God's covenantal words and deeds involving us. We receive God's goodness, we possess the effects of his goodness in ourselves, we become good in our own character, and we pass on good things to others.

Explanation by Prepositions

Dr. Tim Yates has summarized the pattern of God's work in us in a series of prepositions: *from, to, upon, in, by*.[2] The gifts of God come *from* God, *to* us, *upon* us, and *in* us, and then finally are passed on *by* us to others. These key prepositions correspond, respectively, to the stages in the pattern of God's coming. The pattern begins with God, *from* whom the gift comes. The gift comes *to* us in covenantal form. We receive it at the point at which it comes *upon* us. We possess it *in* us. We pass it on so that it comes to others *by* us. (See table C.1.) The stage of having a gift come *from* God focuses on the origin in God, and therefore on God as an actor. The stage of having a gift come *to* us focuses on the covenant as the means for conveying the gift. The stage of having a gift come *upon* us focuses on our *reception* of the gift. The stage of having a gift *in* us focuses on our *possession* of the gift. The stage of having a gift travel *by* us focuses on our *initiation,* in which we take an active part in sending the gift to others.

(Note the three stages within human experience: reception, possession, and initiation. These three reflect in reverse order the three phases of action discussed in Appendix A, namely, initiation, sending a

2. Yates, *Foundations,* 26–30; Tim Yates, "CT 08 Assembling a Counseling Theology for Biblical Counseling Practice," course notes for CT 08 in counseling (China Reformed Theological Seminary, 2016), 1. Yates derives the prepositions from the language of the Westminster Confession of Faith.

I have slightly altered Dr. Yates's conception by suggesting that all of God's blessings to us may have both a receptive and a stable aspect. For example, justification is fundamentally something that we receive. Our new status of being righteous is something "*upon* us"; that is, the clothing of Christ's perfect righteousness comes upon us. But we should also have a stable inward knowledge of our justification and an assurance arising from it. This knowledge is *in* us. In contrast to justification, sanctification is something that God works *in* us. But he works in us by means of the Holy Spirit, who comes *upon* us in order to dwell *in* us. And sanctification is also empowered by the means of grace that act *upon* us in order to transform us within.

Giving Speech	Christ's Presence	Preposition	Types of Involvement
God speaks	in the Word	from	divine initiation
covenantal message	with center in Christ	to	covenantal possession
coming to a human being who:	Christ comes to a human being, so that:	(through):	human response:
receives word	he receives Christ	upon	human reception
possesses word (indwelling: John 15:7)	he possesses Christ	in	human possession
proclaims word	he proclaims Christ	by	human initiation

Table C.1. The Pattern of God's Gift through Prepositions

gift [possession], and reception. The three stages within human experience reflect the phases in divine activity.)

The same pattern concerning God's gifts occurs when we consider how God gives justice. Justice is *from* God. It comes *to* us in covenant form and rests *upon* us in justification (or in condemnation of the wicked). It is found *in* us as we are assured of pardon, and is passed on *by* us when we act in justice toward others, or when we forgive others as we have been forgiven (Matt. 6:12), or when we proclaim the gospel, which includes God's pronouncement of justification. (See table C.2.)

Explanation by Reflections

The pattern for passing on God's word, his justice, and his blessings involves a pattern of *reflections*. The original or archetype consists in God's attributes and his activities, which belong to him at the level of who he is as Creator ("*from* God"). These realities are in focus with

Giving Justice	Christ's Presence	Preposition	Types of Involvement
God brings justice	in the Word	from	divine initiation
covenantal expression of justice (announcing justification and condemnation)	with center in Christ the King	to	covenantal possession
coming to a human being who:	Christ comes to a human being, so that:	(through):	human response:
receives justification	he receives Christ	upon	human reception
possesses pardon	he possesses Christ	in	human possession
shows justice	he shows Christ's justice	by	human initiation

Table C.2. The Pattern of God's Gift of Justice through Prepositions

the ontological perspective. The pattern is reflected in covenantal action, which is the manifestation of God at the level of covenant ("*to* us"). Covenantal action is in focus with the economic perspective. The pattern is then reflected in humanity. Specifically, it is reflected *upon* human beings, *in* them, and *by* them, because they are made in the image of God. Their being and their actions reflect the divine original and manifest the glory of God at the level of the creature.

Each stage in the pattern of reflection offers a perspective on the whole process. The gift reflects the giver, and implicitly points to the whole process, structured by God's plan.

Key Terms

growth
initiation

possession
reception

Study Questions

1. In what ways does human action reflect divine action? Illustrate using the offices of prophet, king, and priest.
2. How can the pattern of the reflection of God's attributes be summarized using five prepositions?
3. What does the organization using prepositions show us about the meaning of actions in relation to God and Christ? In relation to human beings? How should it motivate us?
4. How do the three aspects of human initiation, possession, and reception relate to the triad for personal action?
5. Explain how each of the five prepositions employed by Tim Yates can be used as a perspective on the whole.
6. How does an understanding of the passing on of God's gifts enhance our understanding of human nature and human calling?

For Further Reading

Yates, Timothy Paul. *Foundations: God's Glory as an Integrating Perspective on Reformed Theology*. Lancaster, PA: Unveiled Faces Reformed Press, 2017. Pp. 26–30. Explaining salvation and the human reception of salvation using five key prepositions, which were used in the Westminster Confession of Faith.

Appendix D: Views for Theorizing

LET US CONSIDER another triad that we have not mentioned up to this point: a triad of three "views" that people can take in developing a theory. This triad consists in the *particle* view, the *wave* view, and the *field* view. These are three ways of looking at data in order to construct a theory. Let us call these three views the *perspectives for theorizing*. Kenneth L. Pike first developed this triad.[1] He borrowed the labels from quantum physics, but used them in his own way, to explain three ways of looking at linguistic data. The same three views can also be applied to other areas besides linguistics. In chapter 28, we applied these views to *conceptions*, when we spoke about perspectives on conceptions: stability, dynamicity, and relationality. When we apply the perspectives for theorizing to the analysis of conceptions, it results in the perspectives on conceptions. The second is merely a more specific form of the first.

The Particle View (Static View)

The *particle* view looks at language or some other subject matter and treats it as composed of discrete "particles." In the case of language, the particles are of various sizes. Written words are composed of alphabetical letters. The written words are particles, composed of letters that are also particles. Sentences can be viewed as discrete particles. Sentences are composed of clauses, which are composed of words and phrases.

1. Kenneth L. Pike, "Language as Particle, Wave, and Field," *Texas Quarterly* 2, 2 (1959): 37–54, reprinted in *Kenneth L. Pike: Selected Writings to Commemorate the 60th Birthday of Kenneth Lee Pike*, ed. Ruth M. Brend (The Hague/Paris: Mouton, 1972), 117–28; further explained in Kenneth L. Pike, *Linguistic Concepts: An Introduction to Tagmemics* (Lincoln, NE/London: University of Nebraska Press, 1982), 19–38. See the explanation of the origin of the triad in Vern S. Poythress, "Multiperspectivalism and the Reformed Faith," in *Speaking the Truth in Love: The Theology of John M. Frame*, ed. John J. Hughes (Phillipsburg, NJ: P&R Publishing, 2009), 185–87, http://www.frame-poythress.org/multiperspectivalism-and-the-reformed-faith/.

The clauses, words, and phrases are also particles. Bigger particles, such as sentences, are composed by linking together smaller particles, such as clauses and words.

The particle view can also be called the *static* view because it treats the particles as if they were stable, unchanging objects. Each particle is *static*. The particles can, of course, interact in a dynamic fashion. But even their interaction can be treated in a static fashion, by treating interactions as instances that illustrate the operation of rules. And the rules are stable—they are static. The interactions also take place in ways that involve the composition of larger particles, such as sentences, out of the smaller ones, such as words. So the interaction of words can be treated as part of the composition of larger particles, such as sentences.

The particle view is a *perspective*, as the use of the word *view* already suggests. A researcher who is analyzing language to find particles is adopting a particle *perspective* on the language data. So we may use the expressions *particle view* and *particle perspective* and *static perspective* interchangeably.

The Wave View (Dynamic View)

The second view is the *wave* view. The wave view looks at language as a *dynamic process*. Things develop gradually over time, and one thing flows into another. This flowing character of language is most easily illustrated by considering audible speech. Written language in English uses discrete signs, namely, the letters of the alphabet. But a detailed recording of oral speech shows sounds flowing into each other, with gradual changes in the shape of the mouth and the position of the tongue. There is no sharp boundary between the *oo* sound and the *v* sound in the syllable *moov* (English "move"), because the upper teeth and lower lip *gradually* come together to produce a *v*. The teeth and lip gradually close off the stream of air that is producing the *oo* sound. Even more dramatically, there is typically no sharp boundary between the "eye" sound of the pronoun *I* and the *a* sound of the verb *am* in the sequence *I am* . . . When the sequence is compressed enough, it is really a contraction, *I'm*. Such contractions and other kinds of sound influence are instances of *wave* interaction, or *dynamic* interaction, in a language.

Like the particle view, the wave view is a *perspective*. A researcher who is analyzing language to find waves or gradual transitions is adopting a wave *perspective* on the language data. We may use the expressions *wave view* and *wave perspective* and *dynamic perspective* interchangeably.

The Field View (Relational View)

The third view is the *field* view. The field view looks at language as composed of *relations*. For example, the pronoun *I* can be appreciated for what it is only by taking into account its relations to other personal pronouns: *I, me, my, mine, you/your/yours, he/him/his, she/her/hers, it/its, we/us/our/ours, they/them/their/theirs*. The functions of the pronoun *I* are defined largely in relation to these other pronouns.

Moreover, relations are frequently organized in multiple dimensions. In the case of English pronouns, one dimension is the dimension of first-, second-, and third-person pronouns. Another dimension is the dimension of singular and plural (*I* versus *we*). Still another dimension is the dimension of subject forms (*I, they*, etc.), object forms (*me, them*, etc.), and two kinds of possessive forms (*my, mine; their, theirs*).

Putting together the three dimensions, we can see how the pronouns are arranged in a three-dimensional grid (fig. D.1). This grid is a kind of *field* of relations.

Like the particle view and the wave view, the field view is a *perspective*. A researcher who is analyzing language to find relations or a multidimensional grid is adopting a field *perspective* on the language data. We may use the expressions *field view* and *field perspective* and *relational perspective* interchangeably.

Perspectives Including One Another

Each of the three perspectives presupposes the others. The dynamic perspective presupposes stable end points and stable features, which must be there in order to detect change and flow from one point to another. In other words, it presupposes the static perspective. It also involves *relations* between beginning, middle, and end. It presupposes the relational perspective. The relational perspective presupposes "pieces" or "particles" or identifiable points within a grid that stand in relation to one another. There must be "things" that are somewhat particlelike in order for there to be relations between them. So the relational perspective presupposes the static perspective. The relational perspective presupposes the dynamic perspective, because it must

	first person	second person	third person
subject form	I	you	he/she/it
object form	me	you	him/her/it
possessive form	my	your	his/her/its
perdicative form	mine	yours	his/her/its

PLURAL

we	you	they
us	you	them
our	your	their
ours	yours	theirs

Fig. D.1. A Grid for Personal Pronouns

reckon with the *change* or dynamic alteration that takes place when the observer moves from one point to another in a relation or in a grid.

The static perspective presupposes that the static pieces can be identified and reidentified through time. So it presupposes that we can think about what is the same *in the midst of* change, which involves the dynamic perspective. And the particlelike pieces can be identified by contrast with other pieces that are different. So the static perspective on particles presupposes the meaning given by relations to other pieces, and these relations are in focus in the relational perspective.

Coinherent Perspectives

The mutual relations between the three perspectives for theorizing suggest coinherence. Can we confirm this impression? Are the three perspectives derivable from the relations among the persons of the Trinity?

We can see a relation between the triad for personal action and the triad for theorizing. The plan for a project is a fixed point for action—a fixed point that, in an ideal case of personal action, remains the same from beginning to end. The planning perspective is thus akin to the static perspective.

Next, the accomplishment of the plan takes place in time, and at its heart is the reality of *change*. Accomplishment is inherently *dynamic*. Thus, the accomplishment perspective is akin to the dynamic perspective.

Finally, the application of an accomplishment brings someone or something into *relationship* with the accomplishment. In the application of salvation, *union* with Christ, which is a relationship, is the key means for applying the work of Christ to an individual believer (and to the church). The application perspective is akin to the relational perspective.

In sum, the three perspectives in the triad for personal action correlate well with the three perspectives in the triad for theorizing. (See fig. D.2.)

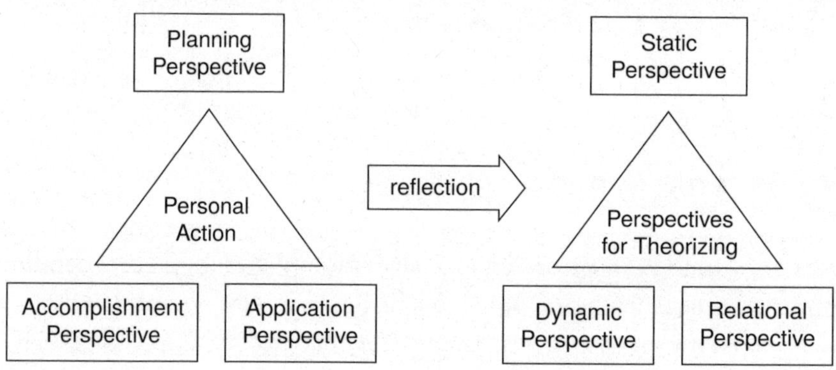

Fig. D.2. From the Triad for Personal Action to the Triad for Theorizing

The perspectives for theorizing derive from the perspectives on personal action, if we apply the latter perspectives to the nature of views about items under analysis.

Since the triad for personal action reflects the coinherence of the Trinity, so does the triad for theorizing.

From Offices to Theorizing

We can confirm this result by using the triad for offices: prophet, king, and priest. The prophet announces the permanently stable word of God. So his work correlates with the static perspective. The king rules and brings about changes through the power of God working in him. So his work correlates with the dynamic perspective. The priest mediates communion with God, and communion is a relationship. So the priest's work correlates with the relational perspective. (See fig. D.3.)

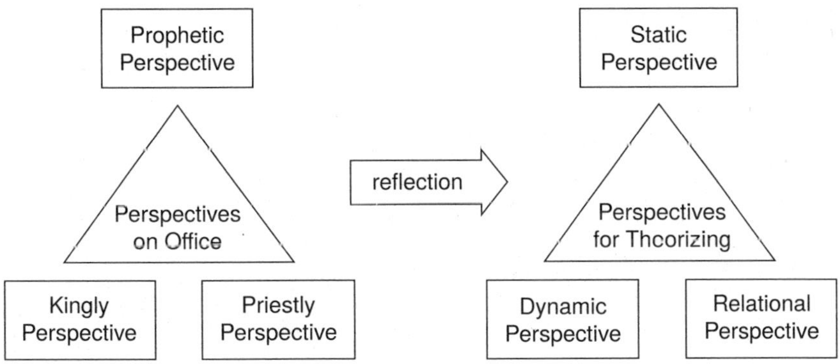

Fig. D.3. From Offices to Theorizing

The correlations with the perspectives on office confirm that the triad of perspectives for theorizing is indeed coinherent.

Key Terms

dynamic perspective[2]
field perspective
field view
particle perspective
particle view
personal pronoun
perspectives for theorizing
perspectives on conceptions
relational perspective
static perspective

2. Key terms in **bold** are defined in the glossary at the end of this volume.

triad for offices
triad for personal action
view
views for theorizing
wave perspective
wave view

Study Questions

1. What three views did Kenneth Pike introduce for analyzing a particular subject?
2. What is the value of having these three views? What does it say about how people form theories?
3. How do the three views interlock?
4. How are the three views coinherent?
5. How can the three views for theorizing be derived from the triad for personal action?
6. What does this derivation imply about the foundation for the three views for theorizing?
7. How can the three views for theorizing be derived from the triad for offices?

For Further Reading

Pike, Kenneth L. "Language as Particle, Wave, and Field." *Texas Quarterly* 2, 2 (1959): 37–54. Reprinted in *Kenneth L. Pike: Selected Writings to Commemorate the 60th Birthday of Kenneth Lee Pike*, edited by Ruth M. Brend, 117–28. The Hague/Paris: Mouton, 1972. The original article introducing the idea of three views used for analysis.

———. *Linguistic Concepts: An Introduction to Tagmemics*. Lincoln, NE/ London: University of Nebraska Press, 1982. Pp. 19–38. Further explanation of particle view, wave view, and field view.

Poythress, Vern S. *In the Beginning Was the Word: Language—A God-Centered Approach*. Wheaton, IL: Crossway, 2009. Chap. 7. Illustrations of particle, wave, and field, in the context of a Trinitarian approach to language.

———. "Multiperspectivalism and the Reformed Faith." In *Speaking the Truth in Love: The Theology of John M. Frame*, edited by John J. Hughes,

173–200. Phillipsburg, NJ: P&R Publishing, 2009. Esp. pp. 185–87. http://www.frame-poythress.org/multiperspectivalism-and-the-reformed-faith/. An explanation of the origin of the particle, wave, and field views.

Appendix E: Triads of Metaperspectives

THE PERSPECTIVES FOR theorizing (in the preceding appendix) have a different function and a different orientation from most of the other perspectives that we considered earlier in this book. Most of the perspectives that we have considered are thematic perspectives. They start with a focus on some particular theme. But the three perspectives for theorizing describe three ways of viewing *any* theme or object whatsoever. We can view any object as particlelike, or wavelike, or fieldlike. These perspectives arose originally because Kenneth Pike noticed that theorists could develop their theories in three kinds of ways. Each theory is like a perspective on the field or subject that it studies. The perspectives for theorizing have been specifically developing not for viewing just any subject matter, but for viewing *theories* or perspectives. In the terminology of chapter 31, they are *metaperspectives.*

Three Triads of Metaperspectives

Two other triads have a similar function: they apply perspectives to perspectives. First, we have the triad of perspectives on a perspective (fig. 29.3). It consists in the theme-focused perspective, the context-focused perspective, and the person-focused perspective, all of which can be used as perspectives that focus on a single object, namely, a perspective that has been singled out for analysis.

Second, we have the triad of ordinary metaperspectives, consisting in the thematic metaperspective, the spatial metaperspective, and the personal metaperspective (table 31.1).

So altogether we have three triads of metaperspectives: (1) the triad of perspectives for theorizing, consisting in the static perspective, the dynamic perspective, and the relational perspective; (2) the triad of perspectives on a perspective, consisting in the theme-focused perspective, the context-focused perspective, and the person-focused perspective; and (3) the triad of ordinary metaperspectives, consisting in the thematic metaperspective, the spatial metaperspective, and the personal metaperspective.

These three triads have a similar structure. In chapter 31, we observed a close correlation between the triad of perspectives on a perspective and the triad of ordinary metaperspectives (fig. 31.3). We can also observe correlations between the triad for theorizing and the triad of perspectives on a perspective. For this purpose, let us use the triad for offices as an intermediate. In the preceding appendix, we already saw correlations between the three offices and the three perspectives for theorizing. It remains to show that the three offices have correlations with the three perspectives on a perspective.

The prophetic office is focused on knowledge, which is embodied in themes. So the prophetic office corresponds to the theme-focused perspective. The kingly office is focused on rule, which results in changes in the *situation* or environment or context. So the kingly office corresponds to the focus on context in the context-focused perspective. The priestly office is focused on communion, which involves personal intimacy. So the priestly office corresponds to the person-focused perspective. (See table E.1.)

Triad for Offices	reflection	**Triad for Theorizing**
prophetic perspective	→	theme-focused perspective
kingly perspective	→	context-focused perspective
priestly perspective	→	person-focused perspective

Table E.1. Correlations between Perspectives for Theorizing and Perspectives on a Perspective

In sum, the three triads of metaperspectives have correlations among them (fig. E.1).

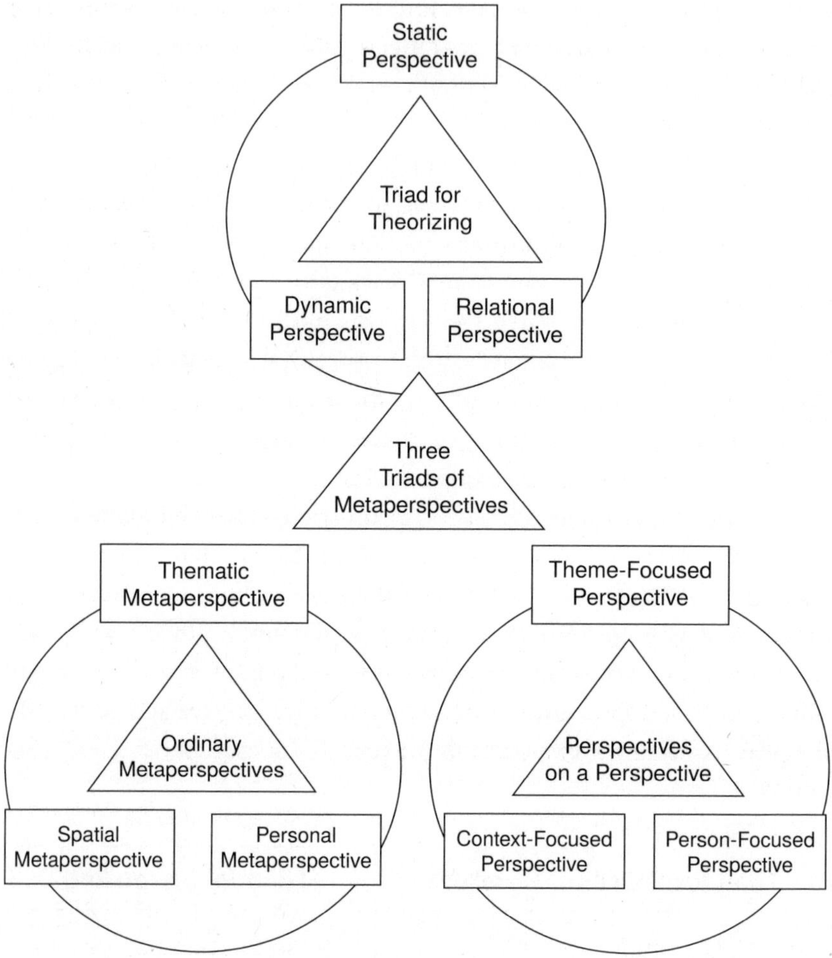

Fig. E.1. Correlations between Triads of Metaperspectives

Organization of the Triads of Metaperspectives

How do the triads of metaperspectives fit into the larger classification given in figure B.4? Perspectives on perspectives arise because our human ability enables us to stand back and analyze human work and human thought. As human beings, we can transcend our immediate situation. This mini-transcendence reflects on a creaturely level the transcendence of God.[1] God knows himself comprehensively. We know

1. Vern S. Poythress, *Logic: A God-Centered Approach to the Foundation of Western Thought*

ourselves and our thoughts, but only partially and derivatively. This derivative self-knowledge is nevertheless knowledge. We are reflecting God at the level of our creatureliness. Perspectives on a perspective arise because transcendence, originating in God, is reflected in man. Our mini-transcendence is then applied in a manner reflecting coinherence in knowledge. We can "indwell" our own previous thoughts, including thoughts using perspectives. Thus, the metaperspectives all derive from coinherence in knowledge. Coinherence in knowledge belongs first of all to God, but it is reflected in a derivative form in our self-knowledge and our ability to use perspectives on a perspective. In this process, human beings function as initiators in exploring knowledge (see Appendix C).

How do we classify the three triads of metaperspectives in relation to one another? The triad for theorizing, as a complete triad, is more focused on theme. Particle, wave, and field are like three themes in metaperspectives, describing the structure of a theoretical perspective. The triad of ordinary metaperspectives, as a complete triad, is more focused on the context, namely, the context of how themes, spaces, and persons give structure to a perspective. The triad of perspectives on a perspective, as a complete triad, is more focused on how persons proceed in using a perspective, by interacting with the theme, context, and personal preferences belonging to a single instance of perspectival thinking. We can summarize by saying that the three triads are organized, respectively, under *theme, context,* and *person*. These three elements correlate with the three perspectives on a perspective. (See table E.2.)

Key Terms

metaperspective[2]
mini-transcendence
ordinary metaperspectives
perspectives for theorizing
perspectives on a perspective

(Wheaton, IL: Crossway, 2013), chap. 45; Vern S. Poythress, "The Quest for Wisdom," in *Resurrection and Eschatology: Theology in Service of the Church: Essays in Honor of Richard B. Gaffin, Jr.*, ed. Lane G. Tipton and Jeffrey C. Waddington (Phillipsburg, NJ: P&R Publishing, 2008), 86–114, http://frame-poythress.org/the-quest-for-wisdom/.

2. Key terms in **bold** are defined in the glossary at the end of this volume.

Triad of Perspectives on a Perspective	reflection	Three Triads of Metaperspectives
theme-focused perspective	→	triad of perspectives for theorizing
context-focused perspective	→	triad of ordinary metaperspectives
person-focused perspective	→	triad of perspectives on a perspective

Table E.2. Perspectives on a Perspective, in Relation to Triads of Metaperspectives

theorizing
transcendence
triad of metaperspectives

Study Questions

1. What distinguishes the triad of perspectives for theorizing (static, dynamic, and relational perspectives) from most of the other perspectives discussed in this book?
2. Besides the triad of perspectives for theorizing, what are two other triads of perspectives that contain metaperspectives?
3. How does the triad of perspectives for theorizing have correlations with the triad of perspectives on a perspective?
4. How do the three triads of metaperspectives fit into a larger overall organization, such as what has been laid out in figure B.4?
5. How do the three triads of metaperspectives display human abilities? How do these human abilities reflect God's archetypal abilities?
6. In what ways do the metaperspectives enjoy a derivative coinherence?
7. What insights are provided into the nature of human theorizing by the metaperspectives?
8. How do these metaperspectives reflect the glory of God and exhibit our dependence on God?

For Further Reading

Poythress, Vern S. *Logic: A God-Centered Approach to the Foundation of Western Thought.* Wheaton, IL: Crossway, 2013. Chap. 45. Explaining human mini-transcendence as creaturely reflection of God's transcendence.

———. "The Quest for Wisdom." In *Resurrection and Eschatology: Theology in Service of the Church: Essays in Honor of Richard B. Gaffin, Jr.,* edited by Lane G. Tipton and Jeffrey C. Waddington, 86–114. Phillipsburg, NJ: P&R Publishing, 2008. http://frame-poythress.org/the-quest-for-wisdom/. Illustrating reflections and transcendence in the context of the quest for wisdom.

Appendix F: Perspectives for Language Theory

USING THE TRIAD for theorizing—the static, dynamic, and relational perspectives (see Appendix D)—we can repeatedly analyze various aspects of language and communication, and find a whole host of triadic perspectives that are useful in a more fine-grained analysis of communication. In this appendix, we provide a sample of some of these triadic perspectives.[1]

Units, Hierarchy, and Contexts

Languages and other systems of communication have (1) units, (2) hierarchy, and (3) contexts. The units are stable pieces, such as words. For example, the word *boy* is a unit in English. Units come into focus in the static perspective. Hierarchy consists in pieces within pieces. In a particular context, the word *boy* may function as part of a larger unit, namely, the phrase "the boy." The phrase may in turn function within a still larger unit, such as the sentence "The boy fed the dog." Each piece, by being embedded in larger pieces, is part of the *flow* of a larger whole. Thus, hierarchy comes naturally into view using the dynamic perspective. Finally, there are contexts—in particular, (1) the context consisting in the subject matter of discourse, (2) the context consisting in the persons and the personal purposes involved in communication, and (3) the context consisting in the symbol system used (natural language or sign language or some other system). These

1. See further Vern S. Poythress, "A Framework for Discourse Analysis: The Components of a Discourse, from a Tagmemic Viewpoint," *Semiotica* 38, 3–4 (1982): 277–98, http://www.frame-poythress.org/a-framework-for-discourse-analysis-the-components-of-a-discourse-from-a-tagmemic-viewpoint/; Vern S. Poythress, "Hierarchy in Discourse Analysis: A Revision of Tagmemics," *Semiotica* 40, 1–2 (1982): 107–37, http://www.frame-poythress.org/hierarchy-in-discourse-analysis-a-revision-of-tagmemics/; Vern S. Poythress, *In the Beginning Was the Word: Language—A God-Centered Approach* (Wheaton, IL: Crossway, 2009).

contexts are *related* to any small piece of language, and the small piece has meaning in relation to the contexts. Contexts come naturally into view when we use the relational perspective.

In sum, units are in focus using the static (particle) perspective. Hierarchy is in focus using the dynamic (wave) perspective. Contexts are in focus using the relational (field) perspective. (See table F.1.)

Static Perspective (P: Particle)	**Dynamic Perspective (W: Wave)**	**Relational Perspective (F: Field)**
Units	Hierarchy	Contexts

Table F.1. Units, Hierarchy, and Contexts

Aspects of Units, Hierarchy, and Contexts

We can look at a unit by using the three perspectives for theorizing. In the static perspective, we focus on the uniqueness of the unit and what distinguishes it from other units (its identity and its contrasts). For example, the word *boy* contrasts with many other words that have other meanings—*girl, man, horse, car,* etc. In the dynamic perspective, we focus on how the unit can change in detail and still remain the same unit. The word *boy* remains identifiable as the same word whether we say it quickly or slowly, loudly or softly, and whether we use it to designate a smaller boy or older boy, an American boy or an Indonesian boy. This potential for change is called *variation.* In the relational perspective, we focus on how the unit exists within a larger environment. The word *boy* functions within an environment where we form sentences using it. This relation to the larger environment is called *distribution.* (See table F.2. *P* stands for *particle*; *W* stands for *wave*; *F* stands for *field*.)

Units
P: Contrast W: Variation F: Distribution

Table F.2. Aspects of a Unit

If we can see three aspects within a unit, using the PWF triad (the triad of perspectives for theorizing), can we use the same PWF triad to look at hierarchy and contexts? Yes, we can. The result is table F.3.

P:	W:	F:
Units	Hierarchy	Contexts
P: Contrast W: Variation F: Distribution	P: Filler W: Prominence F: Function	P: Subject matter W: Locution F: Symbol system

Table F.3. Aspects of Units, Hierarchy, and Contexts

The three aspects of hierarchy and the three aspects of context can be further explored.

There are three aspects in hierarchical relationships, namely, *filler, prominence,* and *function*. These three all have to do with how smaller pieces fit into big pieces. Roughly speaking, the smaller pieces themselves are the *filler*. The role that they play in a larger structure is their *function*. *Prominence* designates the relative importance of a piece within the larger structure in which it is embedded. A particular smaller piece may or may not be *prominent* within the larger structure in which it sits.

It helps to have an example. Consider the phrase "the boy." It has two pieces: the definite article *the* and the noun *boy*. Two words together form a phrase. The words are at a lower level of the hierarchy. The phrase formed out of the words is at a higher level. The words *the* and *boy* are both fillers. They fit together within the phrase by each having a particular function. The function of the word *boy* is to form the head of the noun phrase. In meaning, it functions to indicate what the speaker refers to. The definite article *the* has the function of being a "determiner," which marks the whole phrase as grammatically determinate. In meaning, it usually functions to indicate that the referent has been previously identified. Of the two words, *the* and *boy*, the word *boy* is more prominent. The phrase as a whole is organized around it. (See fig. F.1.)

There are also three aspects of context. One context for communication is the context of the subject matter on which the communication

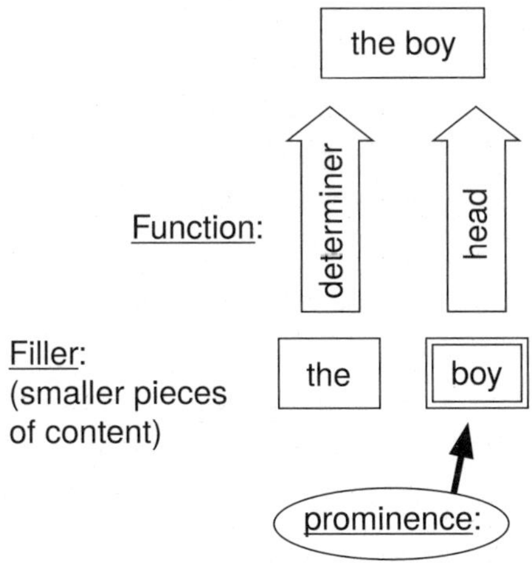

Fig. F.1. Illustrating Aspects of Hierarchy

focuses. The phrase "the boy" obviously has a particular boy as its subject matter. A second context is the personal context of the situation in which persons are communicating with each other. Someone wants to say something about a particular boy to someone else. This context may be labeled the *context of locution*. A third context is the context of the symbol system used in communication. The symbol system can be a natural language or sign language or musical notation or Morse code. For the expression "the boy," the symbol system is the English language.

Aspects of Prominence

We can further analyze what is at work in the case of prominence. We use the same triad for theorizing. We apply it to prominence as a single element, in order to see three aspects within it. The prominent piece within a larger unit is the piece most important for the definition or stability of the larger unit. It has a key role in making the larger unit what it is. For example, within the phrase "the boy," the word *boy* is prominent, and that prominence is in harmony with the fact that the phrase as a whole is a *noun* phrase, which in turn helps to determine how it functions within still larger units, such as clauses and sentences. The idea of prominence is related to stability—the particle view.

In the field view, we look at the *relations* involved in prominence. The meaning of *prominence* always includes the implication that what is prominent has a relation to something else that is less prominent. We can label what is less prominent as the *periphery*. In the case of the phrase "the boy," the periphery is everything else *except* the prominent word *boy*. With the simple phrase "the boy," the periphery is *the*. With a more complex phrase, "the small, freckle-faced boy," the periphery includes all the other words: *the*, *small*, and the hyphenated compound *freckle-faced*. They are spread out in a systematic pattern, with some elements located closer to the prominent piece *boy*.

The relation between prominence and periphery is one-sided. Prominence *determines* the nature of the periphery, more than the reverse. And that leads us to the wave view. The relation between prominence and periphery has a kind of inner dynamics. The prominent element tends to determine a good deal about the periphery, and at the same time the periphery can vary without much disturbing the main thrust of the whole. For example, the word *boy* makes us expect possible modifiers that are appropriate to a person, but not modifiers that are appropriate to an adjective (*very* or *too* or *clearly*) or appropriate to a liquid (*viscous*, *opaque*, *transparent*). (Of course, it is possible to create metaphorical uses.) It is as though the prominent element exerted "force" on the periphery. We expect certain things in the periphery, and we may take it for granted that they are there even if we do not observe them (for example, because noise in the room wipes out part of a speech). Perceptually, a prominent element may "fade off" gradually (dynamically), without a clear boundary to its edge.

In sum, a close look at prominence shows three aspects, namely, the integrity and stability of the prominent center, a one-sided relation to the periphery, and a dynamic influence and fading off from the prominent center. (See fig. F.2.) We can if we wish label these as three perspectives on prominence: a central perspective (focused on the prominent element), an axial perspective (focused on the periphery and the one-sided relation going out from the prominent element as the central "axis"), and a perspective of influence (focused on the influence that the prominent element exerts on its environment). These three perspectives are coinherent. We can call them the *triad for prominence*. (See fig. F.3.) Since the three perspectives for theorizing reflect the coinherence of the Trinity, so do the three perspectives on prominence. Human knowledge and human language are marked by the Trinity.

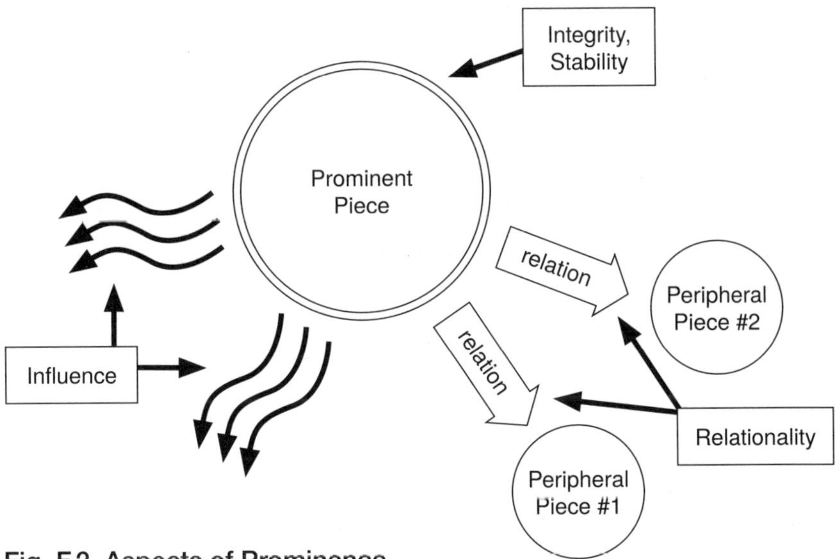

Fig. F.2. Aspects of Prominence

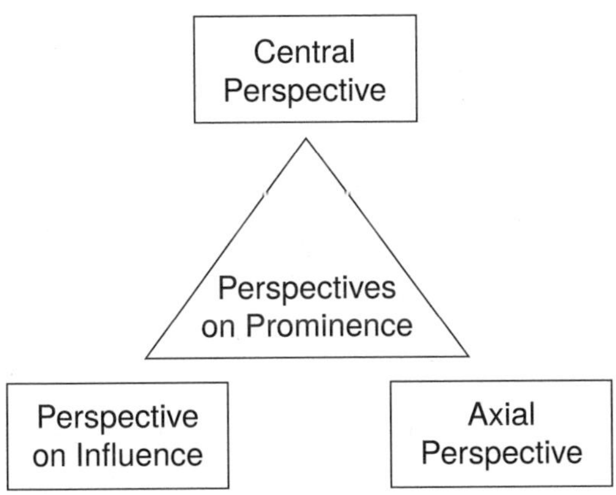

Fig. F.3. Perspectives on Prominence

These perspectives help to illumine how knowledge can grow through interaction over time between prominence and periphery in a concept (chap. 28). Each concept has prominence within it, with regard to the various features associated with the concept. For example, the concept of transcendence has as one prominent feature the idea of superiority. It may also have peripheral features. Change over time can take place in the periphery. In addition, each concept belongs to a larger field of knowledge. The concept of transcendence, for example, belongs to the larger field of knowledge that we have concerning God. Within this larger field, prominent aspects can exert influence, including influence on the concept of transcendence.

It may sound as though conceptual growth were a purely rational process. But it is not, because knowledge can be real and at the same time suppressed (Rom. 1:18). So the dynamics of interaction in knowledge is mysterious and corrupted by human sin. Even without the influence of sin, there is mystery because we are not consciously aware of all the processes involved in the growth of knowledge. Moreover, the Holy Spirit participates indispensably in giving knowledge, and this participation is mysterious (Job 32:8).

Aspects of the Symbol System (Language System)

The system of symbols used in communication can be further analyzed by using the triad for theorizing. In language, we have a referential subsystem for designating things about which we are speaking; we have a phonological subsystem for conveying the message through sound; and we have a grammatical subsystem for internal organization of language structure.[2] (See table F.4.)

Symbol System
P: Referential subsystem W: Phonological subsystem F: Grammatical subsystem

Table F.4. Subsystems of Language

The referential subsystem consists in the resources that a particular language has for talking about the world. These resources include a vocabulary stock (seen in a dictionary) and ways for communicating that make assertions, ask questions, and indicate complex logical, causal, topical, and temporal relations between different thoughts. This subsystem

2. Vern S. Poythress, *In the Beginning Was the Word: Language—A God-Centered Approach* (Wheaton, IL: Crossway, 2009), chap. 32.

is naturally in focus when we use the static perspective on the system for a particular language, because truth expressed in language is stable.

The phonological subsystem consists in the resources that a particular language has for conveying messages through sounds. Different languages avail themselves of different sounds. For instance, French has no "th" sound, while American English has no sound corresponding to *u* in the French word *tu*. The phonological subsystem is naturally in focus when we use the dynamic perspective, because in actual speech sounds go out dynamically in time. (When language takes a written form, it has a *graphological subsystem,* which may or may not correspond closely to the phonological subsystem.)

The grammatical subsystem consists in the resources that a particular language has for putting together morphemes, words, phrases, and clauses to compose larger units that have their own distinctive structure. For example, American English tends to utilize fixed word order in clauses, with the subject first, the predicate next, and objects and predicate nominatives last: "His own people [subject] did not receive [predicate] him [object]" (John 1:11). Koine Greek has free word order in clauses, so that subject, predicate, and object can be in more than one order: οἱ ἴδιοι ("his own people") αὐτὸν ("him") οὐ παρέλαβον ("did not receive"). The grammatical subsystem is naturally in focus when we use the relational perspective, because grammar consists largely in structural *relations.* Smaller grammatical pieces function in relation to other smaller pieces, and fit into a larger grammatical structure.

The three subsystems of language interlock. They do not occur alone, but in combination. So we can have three perspectives, each focusing on the occurrence and use of *one* of the subsystems in a particular discourse. So we may speak of a referential perspective, a phonological perspective, and a grammatical perspective. Together these three perspectives offer a triad of *perspectives on language systems.*

These are only a sampling of the possibilities for more technical analysis of language and other symbol systems. They suggest that reflections of Trinitarian coinherence occur throughout language and penetrate into areas of more technical analysis. God is present, and he shows his glory in the textures of language and symbol.[3]

3. See Poythress, *In the Beginning Was the Word.*

Implications for Reasoning

Our brief survey of language and communication confirms the pervasive presence of God and the presence of reflections of the Trinitarian character of God. This presence of God has implications for how we think about reasoning. Whether we reason in philosophy or in theology or in some other specialized academic sphere, we depend on God, and on language that God has given us. Language and reasoning are closely related. Public reasoning uses language. And even when we reason only within our minds, we are assisted by conceptualizations shaped by language. Reasoning depends at every point on God and his presence.[4] And our God is Trinitarian.

The presence of the Trinity means that we cannot rightly reduce reasoning to pure abstraction (see chap. 29). We are always reasoning in ways that rely on who we are as persons, how we understand key analogies, and how we are guided by a context of background knowledge. Reasoning involves a view of something by someone from somewhere. We are better off if we know God in Christ and admit our dependence on the Trinity.

Key Terms

axial perspective[5]
central perspective
context
context for communication
context of locution
context of the subject matter
context of the symbol system
contrast
distribution
dynamic perspective
filler
function
grammatical perspective

4. Vern S. Poythress, *Logic: A God-Centered Approach to the Foundation of Western Thought* (Wheaton, IL: Crossway, 2013).

5. Key terms in **bold** are defined in the glossary at the end of this volume.

grammatical subsystem
graphological subsystem
hierarchy
periphery
perspective of influence
perspectives on language systems
perspectives on prominence
phonological perspective
phonological subsystem
prominence
PWF triad
reasoning
referential perspective
referential subsystem
relational perspective
static perspective
unit
variation

Study Questions

1. How can the triad of perspectives for theorizing be applied to the analysis of language?
2. What triads exist for analyzing language?
3. How do the triads for language have roots in the Trinity?
4. What significance comes from the roots in the Trinity?
5. What significance do the reflections of the Trinity in language have for our view of language, thought, reasoning, and reality described through language?

For Further Reading

Pike, Kenneth L. *Linguistic Concepts: An Introduction to Tagmemics.* Lincoln, NE/London: University of Nebraska Press, 1982. On triads for language.

Poythress, Vern S. "A Framework for Discourse Analysis: The Components of a Discourse, from a Tagmemic Viewpoint." *Semiotica* 38, 3–4 (1982): 277–98. http://www.frame-poythress.org/a-framework-for-discourse-analysis-the-components-of-a

-discourse-from-a-tagmemic-viewpoint/. Using the three perspectives for theorizing to produce other triads applicable to linguistic analysis.

———. "Hierarchy in Discourse Analysis: A Revision of Tagmemics." *Semiotica* 40, 1–2 (1982): 107–37. http://www.frame-poythress.org/hierarchy-in-discourse-analysis-a-revision-of-tagmemics/. A sequel article further developing triads based on the triad of perspectives for theorizing.

———. *In the Beginning Was the Word: Language—A God-Centered Approach*. Wheaton, IL: Crossway, 2009. Chap. 32. An explanation of the three subsystems of language.

Appendix G: Three Dimensions of Space

ARE THE THREE dimensions of space a reflection of the Trinity? At first, that idea might seem fanciful. After all, a person could claim to find a reflection of the Trinity every time he found three things together. But that would be a superficial observation. Yes, every collection of three things is similar to every other collection of three things, because every such collection has the same number of things in it. But such a connection between all collections of three things does not really display in a robust way the *coinherence* of the persons in the Trinity. Normally, three things are just three things—they do not enjoy coinherence.

The triads that we have discussed in the body of this book have some noteworthy features that are not characteristic of just any group of three things. (1) Each perspective belonging to a triad has a discernible presence in biblical revelation, as a theme.[1] (2) The triads are triads of *perspectives,* not just a list of three objects. (3) The distinct perspectives within the same triad are coinherent, in a manner reflecting the original coinherence in the Trinity. (4) Using Scripture, we can trace out some correspondences between the distinct persons of the Trinity and the distinct perspectives within one triad.

So the main perspectival triads have a special status in several respects, including their relation to the Trinity. Their status should not be confused with many other groups of three, such as the three colors of lights in a stoplight or the three prime colors in human color vision (blue, green, and red) or the three states of water (solid ice, liquid water, and water vapor) or the three coins that happen to be in my pocket.

1. But we should make an exception for metaperspectives (as enumerated in Appendix E), since they are not visible in the Bible very explicitly.

Lack of Matching in the Three Dimensions of Space

Now, what about the three dimensions in space? At first glance, the three dimensions in space do not seem to enjoy all the features (1)-(4) characterizing the main triperspectival triads earlier in this book. To begin with, the three dimensions are not really perspectives, nor are they coinherent.

It is true that the three dimensions are closely related to spatial perspectives (chap. 2). We can look at a chair from above, from the front, or from the side. But we can also use intermediate angles of vision. So there are an indefinite number of spatial perspectives, not just three. This line of thinking does not seem to easily lead to three perspectives that are coinherent.

In addition, at the level of current fundamental theories in physics, all three dimensions and any of the innumerable perspectives obtained by rotation are equivalent from the standpoint of physical law. So it does not appear to be possible to discern a correspondence between God the Father and some one direction in space, or between God the Son and some other direction. Feature (4) of perspectival triads does not seem to be present.

A Suggested Correction

We may nevertheless be able to make suggestive observations if we change our point of view. Instead of looking at the three dimensions from the standpoint of fundamental theories of physics, let us look at them from the standpoint of ordinary human observation and experience. We walk on the ground. The sky is above, and the ground beneath. Within ordinary human experience on earth, not all directions are observationally the same. In particular, the direction of *up and down* is very different from the direction of *in front and behind*, the primary direction involved when we walk. And it is different from the directions of *side to side, right,* and *left*.

God has built the world and us and our bodies in such a way that we experience a spatially organized environment. At this practical level, we experience the three directions differently. And they have different potential for metaphorical associations in meaning.

First, God uses up and down to signify transcendence and authority relations. For example, Isaiah "saw the Lord sitting upon a throne, *high and lifted up*" (Isa. 6:1). The physical position of the Lord symbolizes his transcendent greatness. What is physically above us can symbolize whatever has authority over us or is superior to us. In former generations, kings sat on *elevated* thrones. Their position above the commoner signified their authority and their superiority. While on earth, Jesus sometimes addressed God the Father by lifting "up his eyes to heaven" (John 17:1). Up is the appropriate direction to choose in addressing God as the exalted ruler, dwelling in heaven.

Next, God uses in front and behind to have associations with face-to-face fellowship or confrontation. Exodus 33:11 says that "the Lord used to speak to Moses *face to face*."

God uses the spatial relationship of being side by side in connection with our sense of belonging to a larger environment, much of which is not the immediate focus of our attention. People can labor or walk or travel or fight side by side, in cooperation.

So now, the three directions do have loose associations with biblical themes. In fact, the theme of authority corresponds to the upward direction. The theme of presence corresponds to the front-facing direction. The theme of control corresponds to the side-to-side direction, because God controls the whole environment, and side-by-side human relations often involve cooperative action to achieve a common human purpose. Thus, loosely speaking, the three directions in our human experience reflect the triad for lordship. And the triad for lordship reflects the Trinity.

In human experience, the three directions are perspectivally coinherent. We are simultaneously aware of the directions up, in front, and beside. But typically only one is our immediate focus of attention.

So now we know one reason why our world is three-dimensional.

Key Terms

authority[2]
coinherence
control
dimension
in front and behind

2. Key terms in **bold** are defined in the glossary at the end of this volume.

lordship
presence
side by side
space
up and down

Study Questions

1. In what ways do the triads of perspectives differ from ordinary groups of three things, such as three coins in a bag?
2. In what ways are the three dimensions of space unlike three interlocking perspectives?
3. What are the differences between an ordinary human experiential point of view and the typical point of view used to think about space in the context of theories in physics?
4. Why is the human experiential point of view important?
5. What correlations are there between the human experiential connotations of dimensions in space and the triad for lordship?
6. How do the three dimensions form a coinherent triad when considered from a human experiential point of view?

Appendix H: Three Dimensions of Time

TIME IS PAST, present, and future. Is this threefold division of time derivative from the Trinity?

Perspectives on Time

As in the case of the three dimensions of space (Appendix G), the threefold division of time does not at first seem to be a promising field for Trinitarian manifestation. Are there three perspectives?

Fundamental theories in physics treat all points in time as existing along a continuum. All points are "equal." There is no fundamental distinction between the present and the past because the same physics equations are designed to apply to all points in time.

Yet the three divisions in time are perspectivally related within ordinary human experience. We understand the present against the background of remembrances and experiences in the past. We understand the past as what once was present. We understand the future as what will later be present and then past. So human *understanding* of the three involves three perspectives. Each presupposes a background understanding of the other two.

Action in Time

Human action in time also involves purposes. Human action takes place using a background of intentions and plans from the past. Human action is accomplished and carried out in the present. Human action heads toward a goal or goals in the future. The three divisions of time have distinctly different relations to human action.

As we have seen, human action takes place against the background of divine action (chap. 12). Human action *reflects* divine action. Divine action has a threefold perspectival differentiation arising from the differentiated participation of the persons of the Trinity. The Father is preeminently the planner. According to his plan, he sends the Son. The Son is preeminently the accomplisher. The Holy Spirit is preeminently the one who applies and consummates the accomplishment of the Son according to the plan and commission of the Father. Thus, past, present, and future correlate, respectively, with planning, accomplishment, and consummation (*application*) in a goal. These in turn have a foundation in the distinctive participation in divine action of the Father, the Son, and the Spirit, respectively.

The existence of time testifies to the Trinitarian character of God. Time exists only because the Trinity exists first of all as its presupposition and its archetype. The three main human perspectives on time reflect God's Trinitarian nature.

In our thinking at this point, it is important that we maintain the Creator-creature distinction. God is not subject to time. He does not experience time in the same way that we do. He created the whole world with its temporal order, while he is himself eternal. What we are saying is that the temporal order in human experience is not identical with divine experience, but is a created *reflection* of the uncreated, eternal activity of the Father, the Son, and the Holy Spirit in their activities of love and communication. God understands perfectly our human experience of time, not because he himself is a creature on our level, but because he is the Creator, who in his Trinitarian nature has the archetype or original pattern, which is reflected at a created level in human experience.

When the eternal Son took on human nature in the incarnation, he became within his human nature subject to the normal human experience of time. At the same time, he remains eternally God, in fellowship with the Father and the Spirit. His human experience of time in his human nature was then a created reflection of divine personal relations and activities. Christ is one with us in sharing our humanity. He understands our sufferings and our fears and our struggles within time (Heb. 2:10–14; 4:15–16; 5:7–9). At the same time, he is God, who exceeds our created experience of time.

Key Terms

accomplishment
application

consummation[1]
future
human nature
incarnation
past
planning
present
time

Study Questions

1. What are the three dimensions of time in ordinary human experience?
2. What are the three perspectives on personal action, and how do they provide a basis for thinking about time?
3. Explain the correlation between the three perspectives on personal action and the three dimensions of time.
4. How does the incarnation throw light on our understanding of time? How is it a practical comfort to us?

1. Key terms in **bold** are defined in the glossary at the end of this volume.

Appendix I: Order within a Triad

WITHIN A TRIAD such as the triad for lordship, is there a kind of order to the three perspectives? Or could any one perspective among the three be equally regarded as "first"?[1]

The question of order within a perspectival triad is a difficult and subtle one. If there is an order, is it related to and derivative from the order among the persons of the Trinity?

Order among the Persons of the Trinity

Let us begin by considering the question whether there is an order among the persons of the Trinity. Orthodox Trinitarian theology says that there is indeed such an order: the Father is first, the Son is second, and the Holy Spirit is third. Indeed, the persons of the Trinity are sometimes designated using this order. The Son is sometimes called the *second* person of the Trinity. We have already touched on the question of order in discussing the eternal generation of the Son and the eternal procession of the Holy Spirit (chaps. 24–25). The arguments for eternal generation and eternal procession show that the orthodox idea of order is based on biblical teaching.

Among the persons of the Trinity, the question of order is a subtle one. Several errors must be avoided. First, we must avoid the error of thinking that this order is a *chronological* or temporal order. The heretic Arius said, "There was a *time* when the Son was not."[2] According to

1. Note the work by Timothy E. Miller, who in his book raises the question of order within some of the triads. Miller believes that it is possible to detect an order, and that this order derives from the ultimate order among the persons of the Trinity (Timothy E. Miller, *The Triune God of Unity in Diversity: An Analysis of Perspectivalism, the Trinitarian Theological Method of John Frame and Vern Poythress* [Phillipsburg, NJ: P&R Publishing, 2017], chap. 8).

2. Socrates of Constantinople, "The Ecclesiastical History of Socrates Scholasticus," in *A Select Library of Nicene and Post-Nicene Fathers of the Christian Church*, 2nd ser., ed. Philip Schaff

Arius, the existence of the Son was *chronologically* later than the existence of the Father. But Arius's view is wrong. It makes the Son a creature—the highest and greatest creature, to be sure, but still a creature and not God. Arius's view contradicts John 1:1, which indicates that the Son, who is the Word, always existed. He was there "in the beginning."

Second, we must avoid the subtle error of thinking that the order in which the Father is first and the Son is second means that the Son is somehow less God or is God only in an inferior way. All three persons are fully God, and John 1:1 indicates that the Son "was God." For one of the persons to be God means to be *fully* God. A person cannot be God in some halfway or derivative sense.

Third, we must avoid the opposite error: the error of thinking that there is no order in any way. It is clear from the Bible that there is an order when we contemplate the *works* of God and the *economic* Trinity. The triad for personal action pictures the Father as the planner, the Son as the executor, and the Holy Spirit as the one who sanctifies, applies, and consummates. Among human beings, planning, accomplishment, and application are typically spread out in time, with one chronologically following another. We can see analogous relationships in God's acts in time. God announces his plan of redemption in the Old Testament; he accomplishes it in Christ's earthly life; he applies it through the coming of the Holy Spirit at Pentecost (though the Holy Spirit was also active in the Old Testament in anticipation of the work of Christ).

The Ontological Trinity

As usual, the order of events in God's works is in harmony with who God always is. The economic Trinity reflects the ontological Trinity. Hence, there is an order in the ontological Trinity. This order is reflected in the works of God. The order in the ontological Trinity is the same order of persons as what we observe in the economic Trinity: Father, then Son, then Spirit. If we deny that there is such an order, we undermine the fact that the economic Trinity reflects the ontological Trinity. We undermine the knowledge of God and fall into non-Christian transcendence (see chap. 10).

In the ontological Trinity, there is no question of a *chronological*

(Grand Rapids: Eerdmans, 1979), 3 [1.5] (italics mine).

order, because all three persons are always God. They always relate to one another as Father, Son, and Spirit. The Father begets the Son, not as a temporal act, but—mysteriously—as an eternal begetting. Yet an order is still there. We confess that order when we say that the Son is eternally begotten. Or, more subtly, we imply an order when we call the Son "the Son," because we are implying a relation of order in which the Father is first and the Son is second in relation to the Father.

Order Implied by the Analogy with Communication

We can see that an order is implied in the main analogies for the Trinity (chap. 8). First, consider the analogy with communication. According to this analogy, the Father is the speaker, the Son is the speech, and the Holy Spirit is the breath that carries the word to its destination. The Holy Spirit is also pictured as the *hearer* of the word (John 16:13) or the recipient of understanding (1 Cor. 2:10–11). There are other expressions that put the Holy Spirit on the side of the *destination* of the word.

In human speech, there is clearly a chronological order. The speaker decides to speak. Then the speech goes out. Then it reaches its destination. This chronological order reflects within our experience of created time the eternal relation of order among the persons of the Trinity. The Father as speaker is first in order; the Son as speech is second; the Holy Spirit as breath and as hearer is third. (See fig. I.1.)

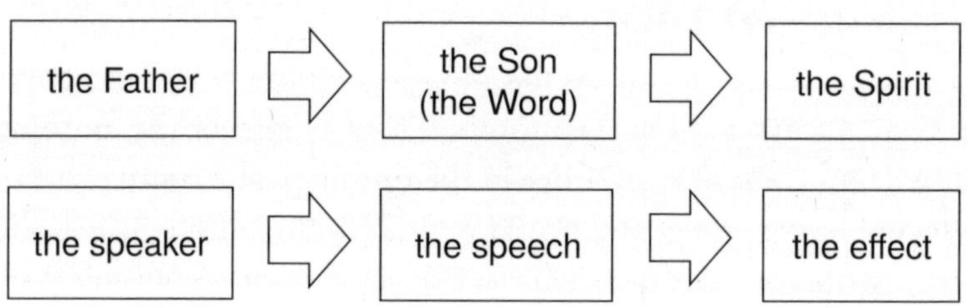

Fig. I.1. Order in the Analogy with Communication

Order Implied by the Analogy of Love

The second main analogy for the Trinity is the analogy of love. The Father is the initiator of love; the Son is the receiver; and the Holy Spirit is the gift given as the expression of love. In the case of human action, there is typically chronological order. This order reflects the original eternal order among the persons of the Trinity.

Order Implied by the Analogy with Reflections

Finally, let us consider the analogy with reflections. The Father is the archetype; the Son is the image; and the Holy Spirit is associated with the glory of theophany. In a theophany within redemptive history, we naturally think of God the Father as first because he is preeminently associated with the origin of theophany. The theophany comes next in time. And in some Old Testament theophanies, the outer circle of theophany is the cloud (Ex. 34:5; Isa. 6:4; Ezek. 1:4). The cloud is the first thing seen by a human recipient, but it is an "outer" manifestation in relation to a humanlike figure, who is the central reflection of God. We can see here an order: the Father as the original, the Son as the image, and the Holy Spirit as the outer manifestation in glory. This order in God's appearing reflects the original order in the ontological Trinity.

Subtlety in Order

Among the persons of the Trinity, the question of order is a subtle one, because the "order" in view is not a chronological order in the works of God, nor is it an order that makes two of the persons a lesser kind of god. Each person is fully God. And therefore we can understand the *whole* of God starting with any one person. Each person gives us a *perspective* on God.

When we think perspectivally with one person as our beginning point, this person is in one sense "first." He is first from the standpoint of the order in our thinking, a kind of epistemic order. Suppose, for example, that we decide to focus at first on the Son, in his incarnation and his public ministry. Within the developing pattern of our thinking, we first think about him. Then, as our thinking progresses, we eventually think about the other persons of the Trinity.

But then suppose that, later on, we embark on a whole new series of thoughts. In this new series, we decide to use the Holy Spirit as our starting point for a perspective. In the order of our thinking, the Holy Spirit is "first" and is chronologically prior. We could also have a similar order in thinking, in which our starting point is God the Father. Clearly, the *chronological* order in our thinking is a product of our choice. Any one of the persons can be "first" in this sense. The *innate* order of the persons in the Trinity does not contradict this practical point. Rather, the coinherence of the persons and the coinherence of the revelation guarantee that we can employ all three perspectives with their different chronological orders.

So what is the innate order among the persons of the Trinity? It is a subtle matter. But we want to confess that such an order exists, because we see it manifested in revelation and divine action in the world.

The Importance of Affirming Order

We may also illustrate the dangers of denying order. If we were to say that there is no innate order, we would imply that it was a matter of indifference whether the Father or the Son or the Spirit became incarnate. And then God's innate character (the ontological Trinity) seems to become unknown, because the original distinctiveness of each person is alleged to be invisible in the works of God toward us. Even the labels *Father* and *Son* and *Spirit* cease to make sense with respect to the persons of the Trinity because they seem to be imposed on persons that lie beyond any meaningful label. What is happening in this reasoning is a disintegration of the knowledge of God as he really is. Such reasoning involves a non-Christian conception of transcendence, according to which God is distant and unknowable and unreachable. The contrast with biblical teaching is sharp because the Bible proclaims clearly that through Christ we can "know you the only true God" (John 17:3).

Order in the Triad for Communication

The subtleties in order are present when we consider some of the triads that we introduced earlier in the book. We have just now considered the three main analogies for the Trinity: the analogy with communication, the analogy of love, and the analogy with reflections. From each of these analogies we derived a triad of perspectives (chaps. 11–12). The triad for communication consists in the expressive, informational, and productive perspectives. These have the same intrinsic order as that of speaker, speech, and hearer. But the order is subtle because any one perspective, not merely the expressive perspective, offers a way of seeing the *whole* of communication.

Let us say that we use the productive perspective. Then we *start* with the issue of the purpose of communication and its effect. We work "back" to the speaker and the speech and the content of the speech. The word *back* still suggests some awareness of order. Yet there is a sense in which, in our conscious reasoning, the focus on the purpose comes first. Then we get to reflect on the speech and the speaker. So it is important that we do not confuse the order of reasoning or the order of several focal points in the *temporal* course of our thought with a kind of "intrinsic" order belonging to the three perspectives as a whole. This intrinsic order belongs to the triad *before* we happen to choose one perspective as our starting point for a train of thought.

But what *is* this intrinsic order? What does it amount to, if in fact we can start anywhere, with any one perspective? It is a subtle kind of order. But we can still see that it is there, if we look in the right "direction," so to speak.

We can look in one of two directions, either at God or at man. First, let us focus on God and divine communication. God's communication expresses the intrinsic order in the Trinity, from Father to Son to Spirit. This order can naturally be expected to be reflected in human communication.

Second, we can focus on human communication itself. In terms of causes, communication starts with a speaker, goes along through a speech, and arrives at an effect in the hearer, an effect caused by the speech, which is caused by the speaker. So there is an order here. Whichever perspective we choose to use on communication, we are tacitly aware of the causal connections. (See fig. I.2.)

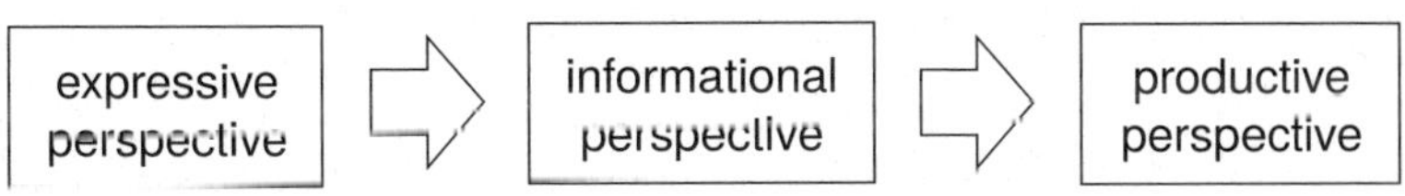

Fig. I.2. Order in the Triad for Communication

Order in the Triad for Love

We can also see an intrinsic order in the triad for love. It consists in the initiation perspective, the reception perspective, and the gift perspective. As we observed earlier, in human events these three typically have a chronological order. Each leads to the next and guides the next. (See fig. I.3.)

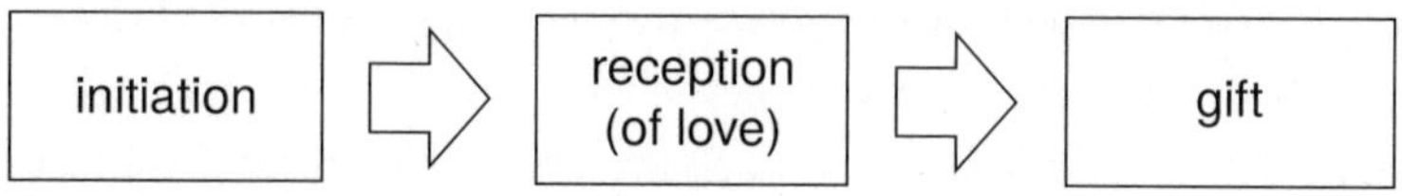

Fig. I.3. Order in the Triad for Love

Order in the Triad for Reflections

We can also see an intrinsic order in the triad for reflections, which consists in the originary perspective, the manifestational perspective, and the connectional perspective. The manifestational perspective has as its starting point a manifestation that is a reflection of an original. The reflected product is derivative from the original. So the manifestational perspective is in a sense derivative from the originary perspective. The connectional perspective presupposes the existence of both an original and a reflection. So it is derivative in relation to the originary perspective and the manifestational perspective. (See fig. I.4.)

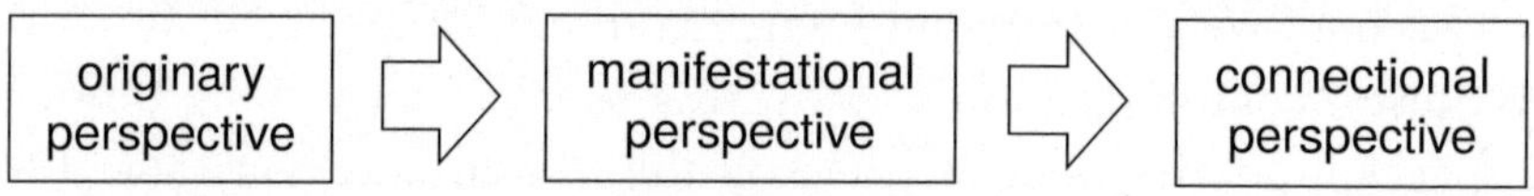

Fig. I.4. Order in the Triad for Reflections

Order in the Triad for Ethics

Consider now the triad for ethics, consisting in the normative, situational, and existential perspectives. Is there an intrinsic order among these perspectives? Ethics makes no sense without first of all having a source of norms. So we can see how in a certain way the normative perspective is "first."

It is more difficult to see an intrinsic order in the situational and existential perspectives. It is possible to move from the order among the persons of the Trinity to the order for the triad for ethics. In order, the Holy Spirit comes after the Son. The application by the Holy Spirit comes after the accomplishment by the Son. The application has as one principal focus the application to individual human hearts, and this is closely connected with the area of attitudes and the existential perspective. We might argue that the internal application to attitudes is a final end point to the broad application of norms to a broader situation. (See fig. I.5.)

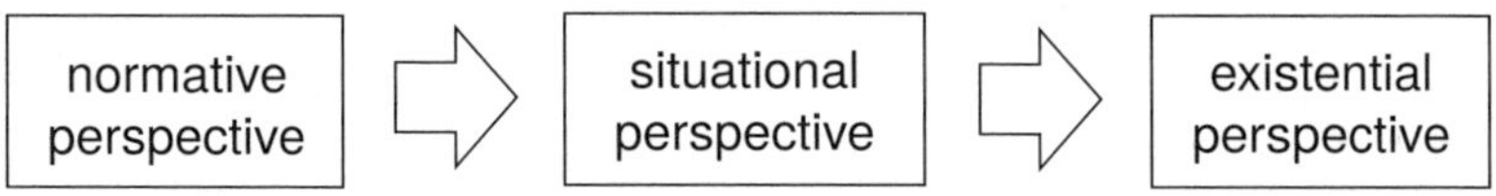

Fig. I.5. Order in the Triad for Ethics

Order in the Triad for Lordship

Consider the triad for lordship, which consists in the perspective of authority, the perspective of control, and the perspective of presence. Authority as normative can be considered "first." Through control God makes himself present, so we can argue that presence is causally derivative from control. So we have an intrinsic order here, but it is subtle. Is it not also true that through his presence God exerts control? (See fig. I.6.)

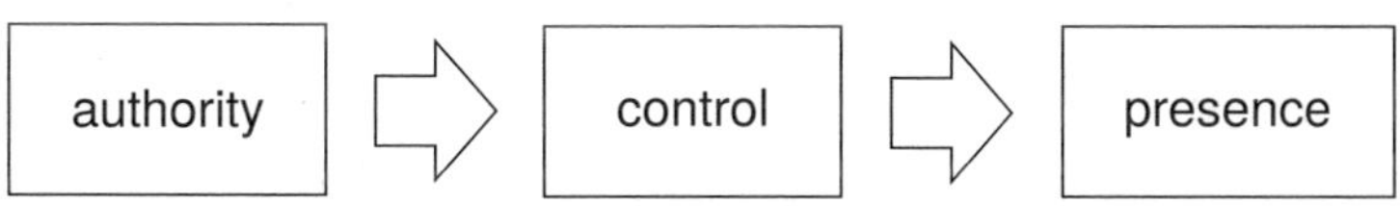

Fig. I.6. Order in the Triad for Lordship

Order in the Triad for Offices

Consider the triad for offices, consisting of the prophetic, kingly, and priestly perspectives. This triad has correlations with the three perspectives on lordship. So the intrinsic order for lordship suggests an analogous intrinsic order for offices: prophet, king, and priest, in that order. It makes some sense. Prophetic speech must announce and define the other two offices, in order for them to exist with proper structure. Kingly power is necessarily at work for the ordination of priests, though the one who ordains is not literally a king. (Think of Moses' role in the ordination of Aaron and his sons in Leviticus 8.) (See fig. I.7.)

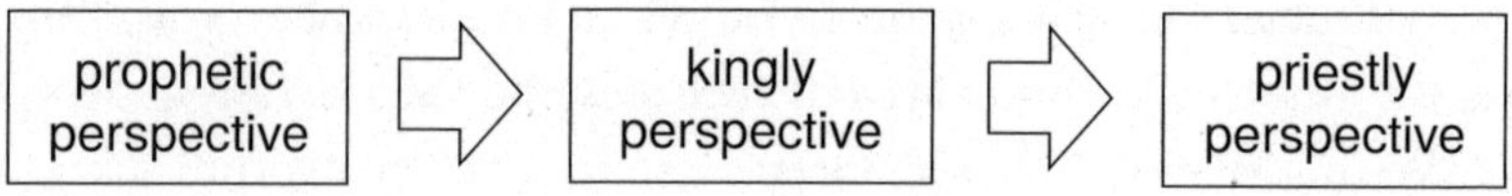

Fig. I.7. Order in the Triad for Offices

We conclude that the main triads include two complementary aspects: (1) through coinherence, any one perspective can be used as the starting point; and (2) there is a certain natural intrinsic order in a triad.

Derivation of Order

What is the origin of the very idea of order, and the idea of one element coming "after" another? The idea originates with God, in the intrinsic order among persons of the Trinity. But within the Trinity, is the idea of order something *extrinsic* to the Trinity—an outside idea, an imposed idea? As we have seen earlier, the absoluteness of God implies that he has all the resources in himself that are needed to fully define himself. So the idea of order is not an abstract, outside idea. Nor is it an impersonal idea, since God is fully personal. So the very idea of order has its archetype in the relation among the persons of the Trinity.[3]

Key Terms

archetype[4]
cause
chronological order
derivation
economic Trinity
intrinsic order

3. The Trinity, as usual, is the final origin. But we may also confirm this conclusion using other triads of perspectives. Consider, for example, the triad for prominence explained in Appendix F. It consists in (1) the central perspective, (2) the perspective of influence, and (3) the axial perspective. These three reexpress and reflect the central truth of the eternal generation of the Son. The central perspective reflects God the Father, who in his person frequently represents God (2 Cor. 13:14). He is intrinsically *prominent* among the three persons. The perspective of influence reflects the Son, who is begotten by the Father. Begetting is the archetype of *influence*. The axial perspective reflects the Spirit, who expresses the generating love passing from the Father to the Son.

4. Key terms in **bold** are defined in the glossary at the end of this volume.

ontological Trinity
order
triad

Study Questions

1. What is the order in the persons of the Trinity? What is the meaning of *order* in this context?
2. What errors should be avoided in thinking about order in the persons of the Trinity?
3. Explain how order among the persons of the Trinity is exhibited in God's works in time.
4. How do we infer order in the ontological Trinity? Why?
5. What is the danger in denying that there is any intrinsic order among the persons of the Trinity?
6. How does the temporal order in our thoughts differ from intrinsic order in the object of thought?

For Further Reading

Letham, Robert. *The Holy Trinity: In Scripture, History, Theology, and Worship*. Phillipsburg, NJ: P&R Publishing, 2004. Pp. 179–80, 479–81. On order in the persons of the Trinity.

Appendix J: A Triad for Coinherence

IN THIS APPENDIX, we undertake to analyze a triad that we introduced earlier (chap. 7, reappearing in chap. 34). In chapter 7, we introduced three ways of looking at coinherence, namely, coinherence in indwelling, coinherence in knowledge, and coinherence in power. These are three perspectives on coinherence. (See fig. J.1.)

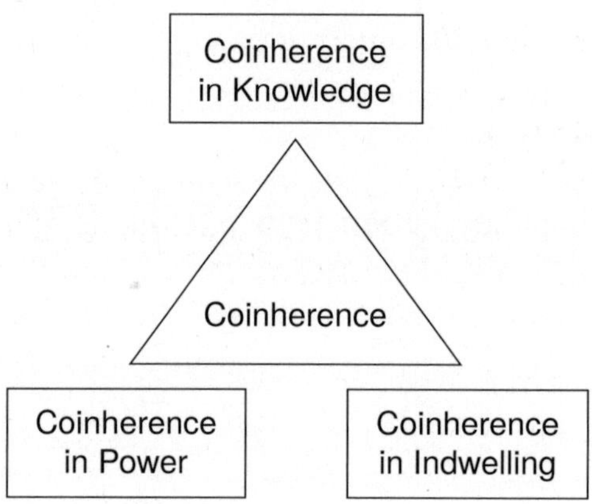

Fig. J.1. Perspectives on Coinherence

In chapter 7, we saw that each led naturally to the others. They mutually imply one another, which means that in one way the idea expressed in one perspective is already implicit in the other two. This means that the three perspectives on coinherence are themselves coinherent with one another.

Correlations with the Triad for Offices

Is this coinherence related to the Trinity? We can explore whether the triad for coinherence is correlated with some other coinherent triads.

Consider, for example, the triad for offices. The kingly perspective focuses on rule and the exertion of power, and correlates with the perspective of coinherence in power. The priestly perspective focuses on communion, which involves the priest's mediating spatial nearness to the presence of God. In fact, the language of indwelling with respect to the Trinity is used in John 17 in analogy with God dwelling in us and us in God:

> That they may all be one, just as you, Father, are in me, and I in you, that they also may *be in us*, so that the world may believe that you have sent me. (John 17:21)

> *I in them* and you in me, that they may become perfectly one, so that the world may know that you sent me and loved them even as you loved me. (John 17:23)

This dwelling of God in us is a form of communion, expressing God's presence. It is correlated in turn with the idea of saints' being a temple of the Holy Spirit (1 Cor. 3:16; 6:19).

The third perspective on coinherence is the perspective of coinherence in knowledge. Knowledge and speech go closely together. Speech is like an external expression of knowledge, and knowledge an internal form of speech. So there is a natural correlation between knowledge and the prophetic office, characterized by God's speaking. Thus, the three offices—prophet, king, and priest—correlate, respectively, with coinherence in knowledge, in power, and in indwelling. (See fig. J.2.)

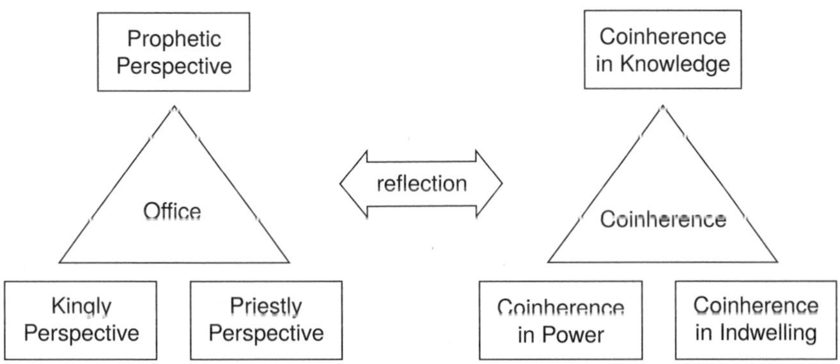

Fig. J.2. From Office to Coinherence

The triad for offices is coinherent in a manner derivative from or reflecting the coinherence of the Trinity (chap. 15). By implication, so is the triad for coinherence. (See fig. J.3.)

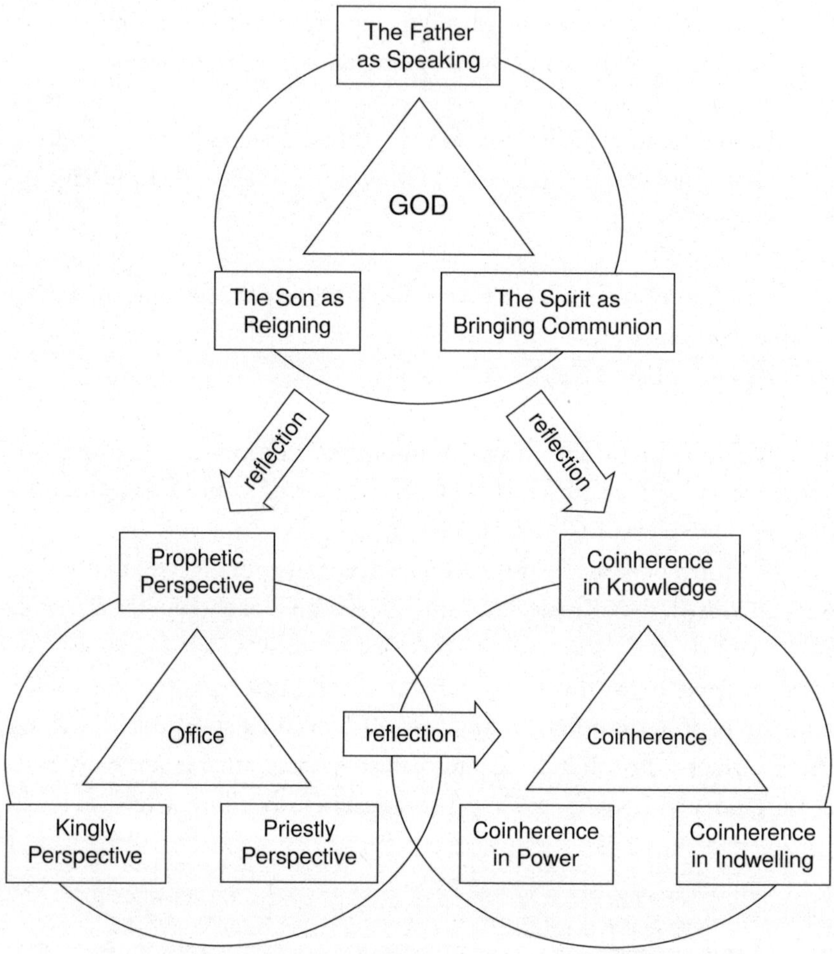

Fig. J.3. From the Trinity through Office to Coinherence

Correlations with the Triad for Ethics

We could also consider correlations between the triad for ethics and the triad for coinherence. The normative perspective correlates with coinherence in knowledge, since knowledge is a kind of norm for action. The situational perspective correlates with coinherence in power, since power is exercised over a situation. And the existential perspective, with its focus on persons, correlates naturally with coinherence in indwelling, which represents the personal communion of the persons of the Trinity. (See fig. J.4.)

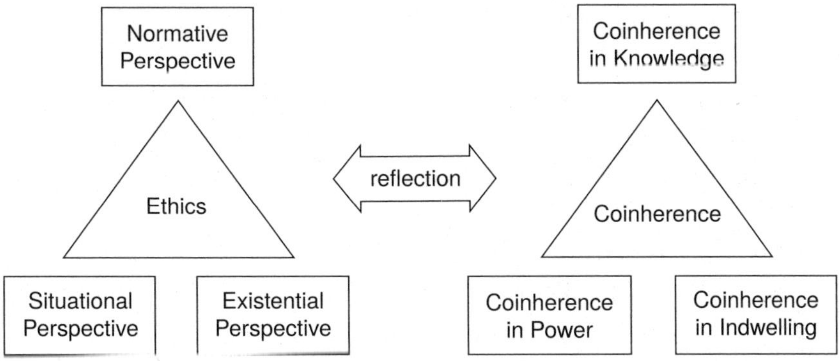

Fig. J.4. From Ethics to Coinherence

This correlation should not be surprising, since the triad for offices and the triad for ethics are themselves correlated with each other (chap. 17).

In sum, the three perspectives on coinherence—namely, coinherence in knowledge, coinherence in power, and coinherence in indwelling—are themselves coinherent. The three together form a coinherent triad, which reflects the archetypal coinherence belonging to the three persons of the Trinity.

Key Terms

coinherence[1]
coinherence in indwelling
coinherence in knowledge
coinherence in power
triad for coinherence
triad for ethics
triad for offices

1. Key terms in **bold** are defined in the glossary at the end of this volume.

Study Questions

1. What are three ways of explaining the coinherence of persons in the Trinity?
2. How do the three aspects of coinherence have correlations with the perspectives on office? with the perspectives on ethics?
3. How do these correlations throw light on coinherence among the three aspects coinherence in knowledge, coinherence in power, and coinherence in indwelling?

For Further Reading

Frame, John M. *The Doctrine of God*. Phillipsburg, NJ: P&R Publishing, 2002. Pp. 693–94. On coinherence.

Glossary

The terms in this glossary usually have special meanings within theology or within this book. Therefore, the definitions usually do not match what would be found in an ordinary dictionary describing general usage.

absoluteness. The property of being unlimited and not dependent on anything. It is an **attribute** of God that says that God is ultimate and superior to everything outside him. He is not limited, constrained, or dependent on anything outside him. This attribute is sometimes described as *aseity* (from Latin *a se*, "from himself," meaning that God has independent existence).

accomplishment perspective. The **perspective on personal action** that starts with a focus on carrying out the action itself. See also **application perspective; planning perspective.**

action analogy. The analogy between human action and divine action, according to which God the Father is the planner, God the Son is the executor, and God the Holy Spirit is the one who applies and consummates.

adoption. A declaration from God that when we are united to Christ, we are his sons, on the basis of Christ, who is the unique Son of God. We then have the privileges of sons, and we are heirs (Rom. 8:17) who inherit eternal life and the new heaven and the new earth.

analogy with a family. The Bible's analogy between a human family and relations among the **persons of the Trinity**. In this analogy, the father in a human family is analogous to God the Father; a son in a human family is analogous to God the Son; and the love and gifts expressing love between father and son are analogous to God the Holy Spirit.

analogy with communication. The Bible's analogy between human communication and communicative relations involving the **persons of the Trinity**. In this analogy, a human speaker is analogous to God the Father; human speech is analogous to God the Son (who is the Word); and human breath is analogous to God the Holy Spirit.

analogy with reflections. The Bible's analogy between **reflections** within the world and relations involving reflection relating to the **persons of the Trinity**. In this analogy, the original for a reflection is analogous to God the Father; the copy or reflection is analogous to God the Son (who is the *image* of God); and the glory of the reflection is analogous to God the Holy Spirit.

analytic philosophy. A tradition of philosophical reasoning that endeavors to clarify the use of concepts and to inspect the use of language in order to address philosophical questions. In some instances, analysis offers arguments crafted to conform to formal logic, in order to achieve rigor. See **ordinary language philosophy.**

application of redemption. All the works of God whereby, through the Holy Spirit, he gives to us all the benefits of the redemption that Christ has accomplished.

application perspective. The **perspective on personal action** that starts with a focus on the goal for the action, consisting in some application to particular persons or things. See also **accomplishment perspective; planning perspective.**

archetype. An original pattern, which may be reflected in a derivative form or image (an **ectype**).

arena. One of three areas to which we may apply **perspectives**. The three arenas are God, **covenant**, and mankind.

associational perspective. The **perspective on classes** that starts with a focus on relation between the one and the many—the one class in relation to the individuals that belong to it. See also **classificational perspective; instantiational perspective.**

attribute. A feature that describes God. Eternality, **omnipotence**, **omnipresence**, and omniscience are attributes of God.

authority. God's moral right to our allegiance. Authority is one of three **perspectives on lordship**. See also **control; presence.**

axial perspective. A **perspective on prominence** that starts with a focus on the relation between the prominent center and the periphery. See also **central perspective; perspective of influence.**

central perspective. A **perspective on prominence** that starts with a focus on the prominent center. See also **axial perspective; perspective of influence.**

classificational perspective. The **perspective on classes** that starts with a focus on the one—the single class to which several individuals belong. See also **associational perspective; instantiational perspective.**

coinherence. The biblical teaching that each **person of the Trinity** dwells in each of the other two persons. Coinherence can be further differentiated using three perspectives on coinherence: coinherence in indwelling, coinherence in knowledge, and coinherence in power. The first of these, coinherence in indwelling, is the more usual starting point in defining coinherence.

coinherence in indwelling. The biblical teaching that each of the **persons of the Trinity** dwells in the other two.

coinherence in knowledge. The biblical teaching that each of the **persons of the Trinity** knows each of the other two comprehensively.

coinherence in power. The biblical teaching that each **person of the Trinity** acts with **omnipotence** in the works of the other two.

connectional perspective. The **perspective on reflections** that starts with a focus on the harmonious relation between an original and its **reflection** (image). See **manifestational perspective; originary perspective.**

consummation. The time when God brings the new heaven and the new earth (Rev. 21:1), and his purposes expressed at earlier times are brought to perfect and climactic fulfillment.

context. A major surrounding environment containing information that informs the interpretation of a single piece of language or a meaningful piece in another area of human analysis. See also **hierarchy; unit.**

context-focused perspective. A **perspective on a perspective** that starts with a focus on the **context** of background knowledge employed by the person using the **perspective.** It matters whether this background knowledge includes spiritually healthy knowledge of God. See also **person-focused perspective; theme-focused perspective.**

context of locution. The **context** of communication consisting in the person originating the communication, the person(s) receiving it, and the immediate environment in which the communication takes place.

context of the subject matter. The **context** of communication consisting in the subject that the communication addresses (in its content).

context of the symbol system. The **context** of communication consisting in the symbol system (language system) used for the communication in question.

contrast. The features of a **unit** that identify it and make it distinct from other units. Contrast goes together with two other aspects that characterize units, namely, **variation** and **distribution**. The features serve not only to produce contrast between one unit and another, but to positively identify the unit. Also called *contrastive-identificational features.*

control. God's governance of all things. All his creatures and all that happens to them are under his governance, so that whatever happens takes place according to his will. Control is one of three **perspectives on lordship**. See also **authority; presence.**

covenant. A solemn commitment between God and man. Sometimes in the Bible the idea of covenant is used analogically for a commitment between two *human* parties (Gen. 31:44). Often a covenant is made by means of an official ceremony of ratification. A covenant may have specific stipulations for the obligations of the two parties, and it may contain blessings or curses that come as a result of obedience or disobedience.

critical realism. A philosophical view that says that things exist before we observe them (the *realism* part), and that our observations of things may lead to true knowledge, but may also sometimes be mistaken (the *critical* part).

deity. Being God.

dialecticism. A form of reasoning that moves back and forth between opposite poles that appear to be contradictory, in the hope of making progress.

distribution. The characteristic **contexts** in which a **unit** is expected to appear. Distribution goes together with two other aspects that characterize units, namely, **contrast** and **variation.**

divine personal perspective. The **perspective** of a **person of the Trinity** (such as the Father) on divine knowledge. Such a perspective is illustrated in the affirmation that "no one knows the Son except the Father" (Matt. 11:27).

divine sovereignty. God's comprehensive rule over all created things and all events.

dynamic perspective. See **perspectives for theorizing; perspectives on conceptions; wave view.**

economic perspective. The **perspective on revelation** that starts with a focus on God's actions (administrative **economy**) in the created world. See also **harmonistic perspective; ontological perspective.**

economic Trinity. The **Trinity** in action in relation to the world. We see and understand the Trinity through the ways in which the Father, the Son, and the Holy Spirit interact with one another and with us and the world as they accomplish the works of creation, redemption, and **consummation**. These ways in which God acts are the Trinity in action, that is, the economic Trinity. See **ontological Trinity.**

ectype. An image deriving from some original pattern (the **archetype**).

equivocism. Claiming that words have completely different meanings (with no real connection) when applied to God and to created things. See **univocism** (the opposite extreme).

eternal generation. The doctrine that the Father eternally generates or "begets" the Son. The doctrine is an expression of the fact that there is an eternal differentiation in the relations in the **persons of the Trinity**, and that this eternal differentiation is the foundation for God's acts in time, in which we see distinct kinds of participation by the distinct persons of the Trinity.

eternal procession. The doctrine that the Holy Spirit eternally proceeds from the Father. The Western church added that the Holy Spirit proceeds from the Son as well. The doctrine is an expression of the fact that there is an eternal differentiation in the ways in which the **persons of the Trinity** act and enjoy relations with one another. This eternal differentiation is the foundation for God's acts in time, in which we see distinct participation by the distinct persons of the Trinity.

existentialism. A stream of philosophical **reflection** associated primarily with the French philosophers Jean-Paul Sartre and Albert Camus, who struggled with the meaning of human existence in the absence of God.

existential perspective. The **perspective on ethics** that starts with a focus on persons and their attitudes and motives. Also called *personal perspective.* See also **normative perspective; situational perspective.**

expressive perspective. The **perspective on communication** that starts with a focus on the speaker and his intent to express himself. See **informational perspective; productive perspective.**

field perspective. See **field view.**

field view. A **perspective** for analyzing a subject that starts with a focus on relations, which often exist within a multidimensional "field" of relations. Also called *field perspective; relational perspective.* See also **particle view; perspectives for theorizing; PWF triad; wave view.**

filler. Material in language that *fills* a place within a larger structure. See also **function; prominence.**

function. The role played by a particular piece or **filler** in a larger structure. See also **prominence.**

general revelation. Those acts of God in which God reveals himself to all people in the things that he has made, so that even those who are not saved know him. See **special revelation.**

gift perspective. The **perspective on love** that starts with a focus on how love expresses itself in giving. See **initiation perspective; reception perspective.**

grammatical perspective. The **perspective on language systems** that starts with a focus on its grammatical structures, as these function with a **grammatical subsystem.** See also **phonological perspective; referential perspective.**

grammatical subsystem. The resources that a particular language has for putting together morphemes, words, phrases, and clauses to compose larger **units** that have their own distinctive structure. See also **phonological subsystem; referential subsystem.**

graphological subsystem. In a language that has a means of writing, the resources for writing—an alphabet, or perhaps a pictographic language in which each word is represented by a distinct pictorial sign.

harmonistic perspective. The **perspective on revelation** that starts with a focus on the harmony between God's action and his eternal nature. See also **economic perspective; ontological perspective.**

Hegelianism. A stream of philosophical thought deriving from Georg Wilhelm Friedrich Hegel's form of idealist philosophy.

heresy. A serious corruption of Christian doctrine that undermines the gospel and thereby prevents people from understanding how to be saved.

hierarchy. A multilevel structure in which smaller pieces (**units**) fit together in regular ways to form larger pieces (units). For example, words form clauses, and clauses fit together to form complex and compound sentences. See also **context.**

holiness. The property of being absolutely pure. God's holiness is his perfect moral purity and superiority to every creature. Accordingly, he is separate from all evil and antagonistic to all evil.

human responsibility. The moral obligation that human beings have to serve God and obey his instructions. Human responsibility also involves the ability of human beings to act in accordance with their plans in such a way that it makes them morally responsible for their acts. (Exceptions are usually made for coerced acts and involuntary acts such as sleepwalking.)

immanence. God's **presence** in all creation. See **transcendence.**

immanent Trinity. See **ontological Trinity.**

incarnation. The event in which God the Son took to himself a full human nature: he became man, by being conceived in the womb of the virgin Mary. He remains fully human and fully divine, one person with two natures, from that time onward, for all future time.

informational perspective. The **perspective on communication** that starts with a focus on the speech or communicative content. See **expressive perspective; productive perspective.**

initiation perspective. The **perspective on love** that starts with a focus on the initiator of love and his initiation. See **gift perspective; reception perspective.**

instantiational perspective. The **perspective on classes** that starts with a focus on the many—the multiple individuals that belong to a class. See also **associational perspective; classificational perspective.**

Kantianism. A stream of philosophical thought deriving from Immanuel Kant.

king. A person appointed by God to express the rule of God, by ruling over human beings under his **authority**. See **office; priest; prophet.**

kingly perspective. The **perspective on office** that starts with a focus on kingly rule. See also **priestly perspective; prophetic perspective.**

lordship. The way in which God has a covenantal relation to us, in which he comprehensively governs the relationship. He is the Lord and we are his servants. Lordship includes **authority, control,** and **presence.** See **covenant.**

manifestational perspective. The **perspective on reflections** that starts with a focus on a **reflection,** which manifests an original from which it derives. See **connectional perspective; originary perspective.**

metaperspective. A **perspective** specifically crafted for use in analyzing perspectives. It is the general label for a **perspective on a perspective.**

mini-transcendence. Human ability to stand back and analyze human thought and work, thus *transcending* the immediate situation. Mini-transcendence is a human ability that reflects on a creaturely level the comprehensive knowledge of God and his transcendent ability to know the whole world in all its dimensions. See **transcendence.**

mode of action. One of several simultaneous ways in which a person acts. For example, the **perspectives on lordship** represent three modes of divine action—with **authority,** with **control,** and with **presence.** See **phase of action.**

neoorthodoxy. A stream of theology associated with Karl Barth, Emil Brunner, and Reinhold Niebuhr.

new birth. The work of the Holy Spirit, described in John 3:1–15, by which we have our hearts renewed and are able to receive the revelation of God with faith and spiritual understanding. The renewal in the new birth also gives our hearts an inclination and desire to serve God, rather than to rebel against him as we were doing before.

nominalism. The philosophical view that only individuals (such as individual horses) are real. Terms for universals are names invented for convenience. Nominalism prioritizes the many (many individuals) over the one (the universal category). (The word *nominalism* is used in more than one way in philosophical discussion, but we are using it in the sense just explained.) See **realism.**

normative perspective. The **perspective on ethics** that starts with a focus on the norms for ethics, particularly God's commandments. But more broadly, the whole Bible as the Word of God functions normatively. See also **existential perspective; situational perspective.**

office. The role of an officially appointed spokesman in the Old Testament. There are three main offices: **king**, **priest**, and **prophet**.

omnipotence. The property of being all-powerful. God's omnipotence is his ability to accomplish whatever he wishes. It is manifested in his complete **control** over every creature and everything that happens.

omnipresence. The property of being present everywhere.

ontologically focused perspective. A **perspective** that starts with a focus on God himself, apart from his relation to creation. Three triads of perspectives, namely, the **triad of abstract attributes**, the **triad for coinherence**, and the **triad for persons**, contain ontologically focused perspectives.

ontological perspective. The **perspective on revelation** that starts with a focus on God in his own existence, apart from the creation of the world. See also **economic perspective; harmonistic perspective.**

ontological Trinity. The **Trinity** as it always is in God himself, independent of his decision to create the world. Also called *immanent Trinity*. See **economic Trinity.**

order. In a technical **context** discussing the **persons of the Trinity**, the Father's being first, the Son second, and the Holy Spirit third. But this is not a chronological or causal order. It is the **archetype** of instances in the created world where God's action or derivative human action involves chronological or causal order. This archetypal order is reflected in intrinsic order within some of the triads of **perspectives.**

ordinary language philosophy. A stream of **analytic philosophy** that tries to clarify or solve philosophical problems by analyzing the meanings of ordinary language. It was influenced by the later thought of Ludwig Wittgenstein.

ordinary metaperspectives. Three interlocking **metaperspectives**, namely, the **personal metaperspective**, the **spatial metaperspective**, and the **thematic metaperspective**. These three together form a coinherent triad.

ordinary perspectives. A triad of three interlocking *kinds* of **perspectives**, namely, **personal perspectives**, **spatial perspectives**, and **thematic perspectives**.

originary perspective. The **perspective on reflections** that starts with a focus on an original, which is reflected in an image or

reflection of itself. See **connectional perspective; manifestational perspective.**

particle perspective. See **particle view.**

particle view. A **perspective** for analyzing a subject that starts with a focus on **units,** particlelike pieces. Also called *particle perspective; static perspective.* See also **field view; perspectives for theorizing; PWF triad; wave view.**

personality. The **attribute** of God that says that he has abilities analogous to those of human persons—for example, the ability to know, to speak, to hear, to love, and to be in a personal relationship to human persons (once they exist).

personal metaperspective. The **perspective** within the triad of **ordinary metaperspectives** that starts with a focus on **personal perspectives.** It views all perspectives as analogous to personal perspectives, in that persons are the ones who use the perspectives. See also **spatial metaperspective; thematic metaperspective.**

personal perspective. (1) Another label for **existential perspective.** (In this book, we consistently use the term *existential perspective.*) (2) The viewpoint that a particular person has concerning the world or whatever topic is being discussed. See also **spatial perspective.**

person-focused perspective. A **perspective on a perspective** that starts with a focus on the person who employs the perspective and its theme. This focus includes attention to the religious orientation of the person's heart. See also **context-focused perspective; theme-focused perspective.**

person of the Trinity. One of the three members of the **Trinity,** each of whom is God and is distinct from the other two persons. The three persons are God the Father, God the Son, and God the Holy Spirit.

perspective. A way of looking at some subject matter.

perspective of authority. The **perspective on lordship** that starts with a focus on God's **authority,** his moral right to our allegiance. See also **perspective of control; perspective of presence.**

perspective of control. The **perspective on lordship** that starts with a focus on God's **control,** his governance of all things. See also **perspective of authority; perspective of presence.**

perspective of influence. A **perspective on prominence** that starts with a focus on the influence that the center has on the periphery. See also **axial perspective; central perspective.**

perspective of presence. The **perspective on lordship** that starts with a focus on God's **presence**. See also **perspective of authority; perspective of control.**

perspective on attributes. The **perspective** within the **special triad for God** that starts with a focus on the **attributes** of God. See also **perspective on coinherence; perspective on persons.**

perspective on coinherence. The **perspective** within the **special triad for God** that starts with a focus on **coinherence** among the **persons of the Trinity**. (Not to be confused with the three **perspectives on coinherence.**) See also **perspective on attributes; perspective on persons.**

perspective on persons. The **perspective** within the **special triad for God** that starts with a focus on the **persons of the Trinity**. See also **perspective on attributes; perspective on coinherence.**

perspectives for theorizing. A triad of interlocking **perspectives** consisting in the static perspective, the dynamic perspective, and the relational perspective. These three perspectives are coinherent. See **field view; particle view; perspectives on conceptions; wave view.**

perspectives on a perspective. A triad of interlocking **perspectives** consisting in the **context-focused perspective**, the **person-focused perspective**, and the **theme-focused perspective**. These three focus on distinct aspects of what happens with a person using a single perspective. Together the three perspectives on a perspective form a coinherent triad.

perspectives on classes. A triad of **perspectives** on the mystery of classes and their members. The three perspectives are the **associational perspective**, the **classificational perspective**, and the **instantiational perspective**. Together these form a coinherent triad.

perspectives on coinherence. A triad of interlocking **perspectives**, consisting in **coinherence in knowledge**, **coinherence in power**, and **coinherence in indwelling**. Together these form a coinherent triad, the **triad for coinherence**. (Not to be confused with the **perspective on coinherence**, within the **special triad for God**.)

perspectives on communication. A triad of interlocking **perspectives** consisting in the **expressive perspective** (focusing on the speaker), the **informational perspective** (focusing on the speech and its content), and the **productive perspective** (focusing on the recipients). These three form a coinherent triad, the **triad for communication.**

perspectives on conceptions. A specialized use of the **perspectives for theorizing** in which the **static perspective**, the **dynamic perspective**, and the **relational perspective** are applied to analyze a concept.

perspectives on ethics. A triad of interlocking **perspectives** consisting in the **normative perspective**, the **situational perspective**, and the **existential perspective.** These three focus on distinct aspects in ethical decision-making. Together they form a coinherent triad, the **triad for ethics.**

perspectives on language systems. Three interlocking perspectives that focus on different subsystems within language: the referential perspective, focusing on the referential subsystem; the grammatical perspective, focusing on the grammatical subsystem; and the phonological perspective, focusing on the phonological subsystem.

perspectives on lordship. A triad of interlocking **perspectives** consisting in the **perspective of authority**, the **perspective of control**, and the **perspective of presence.** These three focus on distinct aspects of God's **lordship**, as exhibited and discussed in the Bible. Together the three perspectives form a coinherent triad, the **triad for lordship.**

perspectives on love. A triad of interlocking **perspectives** consisting in the **gift perspective**, the **initiation perspective**, and the **reception perspective.** These three focus on three distinct aspects of the activity of love, and together form a coinherent triad, the **triad for love.**

perspectives on office. A triad of interlocking **perspectives** consisting in the **kingly perspective**, the **priestly perspective**, and the **prophetic perspective.** These three focus on distinct aspects of the mediation between God and man, as exhibited and discussed in the Bible. Together the three perspectives form a coinherent triad, the **triad for offices.**

perspectives on personal action. A triad of interlocking **perspectives** consisting in the **accomplishment perspective**, the **application**

perspective, and the **planning perspective**. These three focus on three distinct aspects of personal action, and together form a coinherent triad, the **triad for personal action**.

perspectives on prominence. A triad of interlocking **perspectives** consisting in the **axial perspective**, the **central perspective**, and the **perspective of influence**. Together these three perspectives form a coinherent triad.

perspectives on reflections. A triad of interlocking **perspectives** consisting in the **connectional perspective**, the **manifestational perspective**, and the **originary perspective**. These three focus on three distinct aspects belonging to the relation of **reflection** and the process of reflection. Together they form a coinherent triad, the **triad for reflections**.

perspectives on revelation. A triad of interlocking **perspectives** consisting in the **economic perspective**, the **harmonistic perspective**, and the **ontological perspective**. These three focus on distinct aspects of the revelation from God and man, as exhibited and discussed in the Bible. Together the three perspectives form a coinherent triad, the **triad for revelation**.

phase of action. One of three successive phases in intentional action in time, namely, the initiation, the action itself, and the reception. See **mode of action.**

phonological perspective. The **perspective on language systems** that starts with a focus on its sounds, as they function within a **phonological subsystem**. See also **grammatical perspective; referential perspective.**

phonological subsystem. The resources that a particular language has for conveying messages through sounds. See also **grammatical subsystem; referential subsystem.**

planning perspective. The **perspective on personal action** that starts with a focus on the planning for the action. See **accomplishment perspective; application perspective.**

postmodern skepticism. A strand of postmodern thinking, according to which we cannot know real truth, but we have only a **perspective** in which we think that certain things might be true. This skepticism contrasts with the views of John Frame and Vern Poythress, who believe that we can know truth, as God reveals it to us.

presence. God's universal involvement at every point in the world. God is present in all parts of the universe that he has made, and he is intensively present to human beings with whom he has a covenantal relation. Presence is one of three **perspectives on lordship**. See **authority; control.** See also **covenant.**

priest. A person appointed by God to mediate the **presence** and blessing of God. The priest also represents the people in the presence of God. Old Testament priests had a special appointment. Christ is the final High Priest, who brings to an end the need for any other human priesthood (Heb. 7:18–25). And yet each Christian believer can intercede for others. Each Christian is a *priest* in a broader sense because of his union with Christ (1 Peter 2:5, 9). See **king; office; prophet.**

priestly perspective. The **perspective on office** that starts with a focus on priestly blessing, communion, and mediation of presence, especially the **presence** of God. See also **kingly perspective; prophetic perspective.**

process philosophy. A stream of philosophical thought that takes processes rather than things as the fundamental constituents of reality. It is associated with the work of Alfred North Whitehead.

productive perspective. The **perspective on communication** that starts with a focus on the recipients of communication, and how they respond. See **expressive perspective; informational perspective.**

prominence. The greater cognitive or structural weight of some particular **unit** or feature. What is more prominent "stands out." See also **filler; function.**

prophet. A person appointed by God to speak the word of God. Note that this is a broad definition. The Old Testament prophets such as Moses, Elijah, and Isaiah had **authority** from God to speak infallibly. Modern preachers and in fact all believers can speak the word of God, but their words are fallible and dependent on the word of God in the Bible. See **king; office; priest.**

prophetic perspective. The **perspective on office** that starts with a focus on the prophetic **function** of speaking, especially speaking on behalf of God. See also **kingly perspective; priestly perspective.**

PWF triad. The triad of **perspectives for theorizing**, consisting in the **field view** (F), the **particle view** (P), and the **wave view** (W).

realism. The philosophical view that universals (*horse, beauty*) are *real*. Realism prioritizes the one (the unity of the category) over the many (the instances that illustrate or embody the category). (The word *realism* is used in more than one way in philosophical discussion, but we are using it in the sense just explained.) See **nominalism.**

reception perspective. The **perspective on love** that starts with a focus on the person who receives love. See **gift perspective; initiation perspective.**

referential perspective. The **perspective on language systems** that starts with a focus on its meaning-content, as this content functions with a **referential subsystem**. See also **grammatical perspective; phonological perspective.**

referential subsystem. The resources that a particular language has for talking about the world. These resources include a vocabulary stock and ways for constructing sentences that make assertions, ask questions, and indicate complex logical, causal, topical, and temporal relations between different thoughts. See also **grammatical subsystem; phonological subsystem.**

reflection. A thing that is patterned after something else, namely, an original. The relation between the original and its derivative is a relation of reflection.

relational perspective. See **field view; perspectives for theorizing; perspectives on conceptions.**

sanctification. The work of God in Christ through the Holy Spirit, whereby we are made holy and conformed more and more to the image of Christ.

simplicity. The **attribute** of God that says that God is not decomposable into parts.

situational perspective. The **perspective on ethics** that starts with a focus on the situation in which ethical decisions are being made, and asks what will promote the glory of God in this situation. See also **existential perspective; normative perspective.**

spatial metaperspective. The **perspective** within the triad of **ordinary metaperspectives** that starts with a focus on **spatial perspectives.** It views all perspectives as analogous to spatial perspectives. See also **personal metaperspective; thematic metaperspective.**

spatial perspective. A view of a visible scene that a person has from a particular spatial location. See also **personal perspective (2).**

special revelation. Those acts of God in which he reveals himself and his salvation by words or deeds to selected human beings. The Bible is special revelation in permanent form. See **general revelation.**

special triad for God. A triad of three interlocking **perspectives** consisting in the **perspective on attributes**, the **perspective on coinherence**, and the **perspective on persons**. These three perspectives form a coinherent triad.

static perspective. See **particle view; perspectives for theorizing; perspectives on conceptions.**

thematic metaperspective. The **perspective** within the triad of **ordinary metaperspectives** that starts with a focus on **thematic perspectives.** It views all perspectives as analogous to thematic perspectives. See also **personal metaperspective; spatial metaperspective.**

thematic perspective. A temporary thematic starting point for exploring a subject matter, with the hope of discovering more and growing in the truth. See **ordinary perspectives.** See also **personal perspective; spatial perspective.**

theme-focused perspective. A **perspective on a perspective** that starts with a focus on the theme employed by the person using the **perspective**. See also **context-focused perspective; person-focused perspective.**

theophany. An instance of God's appearing visibly, such as the appearance at Mount Sinai.

third-man argument. A particular argument highlighting a paradox. Two human beings belong together because they share the feature of humanness and have the common form (the general concept) *human*. Then the form *human* must also share a common form with the individual humans. This common form would be a third level of humanness (the third man), beyond the individual humans and beyond the form *human*. This production of new, higher forms can continue indefinitely, leading to an infinite number of forms.

tolerance. As used by some people, the concept that one *must* accept other people's views as equally valid with one's own. This kind of "tolerance" actually involves intolerance toward anyone who claims to have universal truth and therefore labels someone else's view as untrue. Within a Christian framework, *tolerance* implies that one should respect and care about people with erroneous views because they are still human beings made in the image of God.

transcendence. God's superiority to and independence from any creature. It includes his **authority** and **control** over every creature. See **immanence; mini-transcendence.**

triad for coinherence. The group of three coinherent **perspectives on coinherence.**

triad for communication. The group of three coinherent **perspectives on communication.**

triad for ethics. The group of three coinherent **perspectives on ethics.**

triad for lordship. The group of three coinherent **perspectives on lordship.**

triad for love. The group of three coinherent **perspectives on love.**

triad for offices. The group of three coinherent **perspectives on office.**

triad for personal action. The group of three coinherent **perspectives on personal action.**

triad for persons. The group of three coinherent **perspectives** consisting in the perspective of God the Father, the perspective of the Son, and the perspective of the Holy Spirit.

triad for reflections. The group of three coinherent **perspectives on reflections.**

triad for revelation. The group of three coinherent **perspectives on revelation.**

triad of abstract attributes. Three interlocking **perspectives**, each of which is an **attribute** of God: the attributes of **absoluteness, simplicity**, and **personality**. Together these three attributes form a triad of coinherent perspectives.

Trinity. God as only one true God, existing in three persons: the Father, the Son, and the Holy Spirit.

unit. A particlelike piece within language or some other area of human analysis. See also **context; hierarchy.**

univocism. Claiming that words mean exactly the same thing when applied to God and to created things. See **equivocism** (the opposite extreme).

variation. The ways in which distinct instances of a **unit** can be different, while it still remains identifiably the same unit. Variation goes together with two other aspects that characterize units, namely, **contrast** and **distribution.**

vestigia trinitatis. Marks or "footprints" of the **Trinity** in the created world, that is, **reflections** of the Trinity.

wave perspective. See **wave view.**

wave view. A **perspective** for analyzing a subject that starts with a focus on dynamic interaction (*waves*). Also called *dynamic perspective*; *wave perspective.* See also **field view; particle view; perspectives for theorizing; PWF triad.**

Bibliography

Augustine. "On the Holy Trinity." In *Nicene and Post-Nicene Fathers,* 1st ser., edited by Philip Schaff, 17–228. London: T&T Clark, 1980.

Bahnsen, Greg L. *Van Til's Apologetic: Readings and Analysis.* Phillipsburg, NJ: P&R Publishing, 1998.

Bavinck, Herman. *In the Beginning: Foundations of Christian Theology.* Edited by John Bolt. Translated by John Vriend. Grand Rapids: Baker, 1999.

———. *Reformed Dogmatics.* 4 vols. Grand Rapids: Baker, 2003–8.

Beale, G. K. *The Temple and the Church's Mission: A Biblical Theology of the Dwelling Place of God.* Leicester: Apollos; Downers Grove, IL: InterVarsity Press, 2004.

Bosserman, B. A. *The Trinity and the Vindication of Christian Paradox: An Interpretation and Refinement of the Theological Apologetic of Cornelius Van Til.* Eugene, OR: Pickwick, 2014.

Bray, Gerald L. *The Doctrine of God.* Downers Grove, IL: InterVarsity Press, 1993.

Carson, D. A. *The Intolerance of Tolerance.* Reprint, Grand Rapids: Eerdmans, 2013.

Cotton Faustina manuscript B. VII, fol. 42v, ca. A.D. 1210. British Library. https://en.wikipedia.org/wiki/File:PetrusPictaviensis_CottonFaustinaBVII-folio42v_ScutumFidei_early13thc.jpg.

Crisp, Oliver D., and Fred Sanders, eds. *Advancing Trinitarian Theology: Explorations in Constructive Dogmatics.* Grand Rapids: Zondervan, 2014.

Cunnington, Ralph. "A Critical Examination of Jonathan Edwards's Doctrine of the Trinity." *Themelios* 39, 2 (July 2014): 224–40.

Edwards, Jonathan. "Discourse on the Trinity." In *The Works of Jonathan Edwards,* vol. 21, *Writings on the Trinity, Grace, and Faith,* edited by Sang Hyun Lee, 109–44. New Haven, CT: Yale University Press, 2003.

———. "The Mind." In *The Works of Jonathan Edwards*, vol. 6, *Scientific and Philosophical Writings*, edited by Wallace E. Anderson, 332–93. New Haven, CT: Yale University Press, 1980.

Frame, John M. *Apologetics: A Justification of Christian Belief*. 2nd ed. Phillipsburg, NJ: P&R Publishing, 2015.

———. "Backgrounds to My Thought." In *Speaking the Truth in Love: The Theology of John M. Frame*, edited by John J. Hughes, 9–30. Phillipsburg, NJ: P&R Publishing, 2009.

———. *Cornelius Van Til: An Analysis of His Thought*. Phillipsburg, NJ: P&R Publishing, 1995.

———. *The Doctrine of God*. Phillipsburg, NJ: P&R Publishing, 2002.

———. *The Doctrine of the Christian Life*. Phillipsburg, NJ: P&R Publishing, 2008.

———. *The Doctrine of the Knowledge of God*. Phillipsburg, NJ: Presbyterian and Reformed, 1987.

———. *The Doctrine of the Word of God*. Phillipsburg, NJ: P&R Publishing, 2010.

———. "God and Biblical Language: Transcendence and Immanence." In *God's Inerrant Word: An International Symposium on the Trustworthiness of Scripture*, edited by John W. Montgomery, 159–77. Minneapolis: Bethany Fellowship, 1974. http://www.frame-poythress.org/god-and-biblical-language-transcendence-and-immanence/.

———. *A History of Western Philosophy and Theology*. Phillipsburg, NJ: P&R Publishing, 2015.

———. *John Frame's Selected Shorter Writings, Volume 1*. Phillipsburg, NJ: P&R Publishing, 2014.

———. *Perspectives on the Word of God: An Introduction to Christian Ethics*. Eugene, OR: Wipf and Stock, 1999.

———. "A Primer on Perspectivalism." 2008. http://frame-poythress.org/a-primer-on-perspectivalism/. Republished in *John Frame's Selected Shorter Writings, Volume 1*. Phillipsburg, NJ: P&R Publishing, 2014.

———. *Theology in Three Dimensions: A Guide to Triperspectivalism and Its Significance*. Phillipsburg, NJ: P&R Publishing, 2017.

George, Timothy, ed. *God the Holy Trinity: Reflections on Christian Faith and Practice*. Grand Rapids: Baker, 2006.

Hughes, John J., ed. *Speaking the Truth in Love: The Theology of John M. Frame*. Phillipsburg, NJ: P&R Publishing, 2009.

Keathley, J. Hampton, III. "The Trinity (Triunity) of God." May 18, 2004. https://bible.org/article/trinity-triunity-god.

Keller, Timothy. *The Reason for God: Belief in an Age of Skepticism*. New York: Dutton, 2008.

Kelly, Douglas. *Systematic Theology: Grounded in Holy Scripture and Understood in the Light of the Church*. Vol. 1, *The God Who Is: The Holy Trinity*. Ross-shire, Scotland: Mentor, 2008.

Kline, Meredith G. *Images of the Spirit*. Grand Rapids: Baker, 1980.

Kline, Meredith M. "The Holy Spirit as Covenant Witness." Th.M. thesis, Westminster Theological Seminary, 1972.

Köstenberger, Andreas J., and Scott R. Swain. *Father, Son, and Spirit: The Trinity and John's Gospel*. Nottingham, England: Apollos; Downers Grove, IL: InterVarsity Press, 2008.

Kuyper, Abraham. *Lectures on Calvinism: Six Lectures Delivered at Princeton University under Auspices of the L. P. Stone Foundation*. Grand Rapids: Eerdmans, 1931.

Letham, Robert. *The Holy Trinity: In Scripture, History, Theology, and Worship*. Phillipsburg, NJ: P&R Publishing, 2004.

Miller, Timothy E. *The Triune God of Unity in Diversity: An Analysis of Perspectivalism, the Trinitarian Theological Method of John Frame and Vern Poythress*. Phillipsburg, NJ: P&R Publishing, 2017.

Owen, John. *A Brief Declaration and Vindication of the Doctrine of the Trinity*. 1669. In *The Works of John Owen*, edited by William H. Goold, 2:365–454. Reprint, Edinburgh/Carlisle, PA: Banner of Truth, 1965.

———. *Communion with the Triune God*. Edited by Kelly M. Kapic and Justin Taylor. Wheaton, IL: Crossway, 2007. [Modernization of John Owen, *Of Communion with God the Father, Son, and Holy Ghost*.]

———. *Of Communion with God the Father, Son, and Holy Ghost*. 1657. In *The Works of John Owen*, edited by William H. Goold, 2:1–274. Reprint, Edinburgh/Carlisle, PA: Banner of Truth, 1965.

Packer, J. I. *Knowing God*. Downers Grove, IL: InterVarsity Press, 1993.

Pike, Kenneth L. "Language as Particle, Wave, and Field." *Texas Quarterly* 2, 2 (1959): 37–54. Reprinted in *Kenneth L. Pike: Selected Writings to Commemorate the 60th Birthday of Kenneth Lee Pike*, edited by Ruth M. Brend, 117–28. The Hague/Paris: Mouton, 1972.

———. *Language in Relation to a Unified Theory of the Structure of Human Behavior*. 2nd ed. The Hague/Paris: Mouton, 1967.

———. *Linguistic Concepts: An Introduction to Tagmemics*. Lincoln, NE/London: University of Nebraska Press, 1982.

Poythress, Vern S. *Chance and the Sovereignty of God: A God-Centered Approach to Probability and Random Events*. Wheaton, IL: Crossway, 2014.

———. "A Framework for Discourse Analysis: The Components of a Discourse, from a Tagmemic Viewpoint." *Semiotica* 38, 3–4 (1982): 277–98. http://www.frame-poythress.org/a-framework-for-discourse-analysis-the-components-of-a-discourse-from-a-tagmemic-viewpoint/.

———. *God-Centered Biblical Interpretation*. Phillipsburg, NJ: P&R Publishing, 1999.

———. "God's Lordship in Interpretation." *Westminster Theological Journal* 50, 1 (1988): 27–64.

———. "Hierarchy in Discourse Analysis: A Revision of Tagmemics." *Semiotica* 40, 1–2 (1982): 107–37. http://www.frame-poythress.org/hierarchy-in-discourse-analysis-a-revision-of-tagmemics/.

———. *Inerrancy and the Gospels: A God-Centered Approach to the Challenges of Harmonization*. Wheaton, IL: Crossway, 2012.

———. *Inerrancy and Worldview: Answering Modern Challenges to the Bible*. Wheaton, IL: Crossway, 2012.

———. "An Information-Based Semiotic Analysis of Theories concerning Theories." *Semiotica* 2013, 193 (February 2013): 83–99. http://frame-poythress.org/an-information-based-semiotic-analysis-of-theories-concerning-theories/.

———. *In the Beginning Was the Word: Language—A God-Centered Approach*. Wheaton, IL: Crossway, 2009.

———. *Logic: A God-Centered Approach to the Foundation of Western Thought*. Wheaton, IL: Crossway, 2013.

———. "Multiperspectivalism and the Reformed Faith." In *Speaking the Truth in Love: The Theology of John M. Frame*, edited by John J. Hughes, 173–200. Phillipsburg, NJ: P&R Publishing, 2009. http://www

.frame-poythress.org/poythress_articles/AMultiperspectivalism.pdf.

———. "The Quest for Wisdom." In *Resurrection and Eschatology: Theology in Service of the Church: Essays in Honor of Richard B. Gaffin, Jr.*, edited by Lane G. Tipton and Jeffrey C. Waddington, 86–114. Phillipsburg, NJ: P&R Publishing, 2008. http://frame-poythress.org/the-quest-for-wisdom/.

———. *Reading the Word of God in the Presence of God: A Handbook for Biblical Interpretation*. Wheaton, IL: Crossway, 2016.

———. *Redeeming Mathematics: A God-Centered Approach*. Wheaton, IL: Crossway, 2015.

———. *Redeeming Philosophy: A God-Centered Approach to the Big Questions*. Wheaton, IL: Crossway, 2014.

———. *Redeeming Science: A God-Centered Approach*. Wheaton, IL: Crossway, 2006.

———. *Redeeming Sociology: A God-Centered Approach*. Wheaton, IL: Crossway, 2011.

———. "Reforming Ontology and Logic in the Light of the Trinity: An Application of Van Til's Idea of Analogy." *Westminster Theological Journal* 57, 1 (1995): 187–219. http://www.frame-poythress.org/reforming-ontology-and-logic-in-the-light-of-the-trinity-an-application-of-van-tils-idea-of-analogy/.

———. *The Returning King: A Guide to the Book of Revelation*. Phillipsburg, NJ: P&R Publishing, 2000.

———. "Semiotic Analysis of the Observer in Relativity, Quantum Mechanics, and a Possible Theory of Everything." *Semiotica* 2015, 205 (2015): 149–67, http://frame-poythress.org/semiotic-analysis-of-the-observer/.

———. *The Shadow of Christ in the Law of Moses*. Reprint, Phillipsburg, NJ: P&R Publishing, 1995.

———. *Symphonic Theology: The Validity of Multiple Perspectives in Theology*. Grand Rapids: Zondervan, 1987. Reprint, Phillipsburg, NJ: P&R Publishing, 2001.

———. *Theophany: A Biblical Theology of God's Appearing*. Wheaton, IL: Crossway, 2018.

Preston, Aaron. "Analytic Philosophy." In *Internet Encyclopedia of*

Philosophy. Accessed June 27, 2016. http://www.iep.utm.edu/analytic/.

Rickless, Samuel. "Plato's *Parmenides*." In *The Stanford Encyclopedia of Philosophy*. Edited by Edward N. Zalta. Winter 2012 ed. Stanford, CA: Stanford University, 2012. http://plato.stanford.edu/archives/win2012/entries/plato-parmenides/.

Sanders, Fred. *The Deep Things of God: How the Trinity Changes Everything*. Wheaton, IL: Crossway, 2010.

Sayers, Dorothy L. *The Mind of the Maker*. New York: Harcourt, Brace and Company, 1941.

Schaff, Philip. *The Creeds of Christendom with a History and Critical Notes*. 3 vols. Reprint, Grand Rapids: Baker, 1966.

Socrates of Constantinople. "The Ecclesiastical History of Socrates Scholasticus." In *A Select Library of Nicene and Post-Nicene Fathers of the Christian Church*, 2nd ser., edited by Philip Schaff, 1–178. Grand Rapids: Eerdmans, 1979.

Taylor, Justin. "Trinity 101." Desiring God. October 12, 2007. http://www.desiringgod.org/articles/trinity-101.

Toon, Peter. *Our Triune God: A Biblical Portrayal of the Trinity*. Wheaton, IL: Victor, 1996.

Van Til, Cornelius. *The Defense of the Faith*. Edited by K. Scott Oliphint. 4th ed. Phillipsburg, NJ: P&R Publishing, 2008.

———. *Introduction to Systematic Theology: Prolegomena and the Doctrines of Revelation, Scripture, and God*. Edited by William Edgar. 2nd ed. Phillipsburg, NJ: P&R Publishing, 2007.

Ware, Bruce A., and John Starke, eds. *One God in Three Persons: Unity of Essence, Distinction of Persons, Implications for Life*. Wheaton, IL: Crossway, 2015.

Yates, Timothy Paul. *Foundations: God's Glory as an Integrating Perspective on Reformed Theology*. Lancaster, PA: Unveiled Faces Reformed Press, 2017.

Index of Scripture

Index of Subjects and Names